Authorities in Early Modern Law Courts

EDINBURGH STUDIES IN LAW

https://edinburghuniversitypress.com/series/esil

EDINBURGH STUDIES IN LAW
VOLUME 16

Authorities in Early Modern Law Courts

Edited by Guido Rossi

EDINBURGH
University Press

Edinburgh University Press is one of the leading university presses in the UK.
We publish academic books and journals in our selected subject areas across the
humanities and social sciences, combining cutting-edge scholarship with high editorial
and production values to produce academic works of lasting importance. For more
information visit our website: edinburghuniversitypress.com

Edinburgh University Press Ltd
The Tun – Holyrood Road
12(2f) Jackson's Entry
Edinburgh EH8 8PJ

First published in hardback by Edinburgh University Press 2021

Typeset in New Caledonia by
Servis Filmsetting Ltd, Stockport, Cheshire,
printed and bound by CPI Group (UK) Ltd
Croydon, CR0 4YY

A CIP record for this book is available from the British Library(hardback)

ISBN 978 1 4744 5100 0 (hardback)
ISBN 978 1 4744 5101 7 (paperback)
ISBN 978 1 4744 5102 4 (webready PDF)
ISBN 978 1 4744 5103 1 (epub)

Contents

Preface

This collection of essays is clustered around an apparently simple question: what role did law courts have in the development of early modern law in different parts of Europe? The question hides a fundamental problem: how did early modern law develop? The importance of the problem is magnified by the relative lack of interest among scholars. The early modern period – especially in works written in English (which nowadays means the vast majority of the literature that circulates internationally) – is considered the age of natural lawyers. Somehow encouraged by the legal humanism and foreshadowed by the Salamanca School, the Age of Natural Law brought order to the chaotic – and, by then, stale – approach of the epigones of Bartolus, paving the way for the first wave of codification (which begins with the so-called "Natural Law Codes"). This narrative, the standard one among legal history textbooks, ultimately builds a bridge between the late *ius commune* (often called *mos italicus*) and the codification movement. It is an elegant bridge, which dispenses with the need to cross the muddy river of reality. Thanks to this scholarly construction we have come to appreciate the civil law as a set of abstract, dogmatic constructions, which could be neatly contrasted with the practice-based common law, and thus encompass most of continental Europe – especially those countries that are members of the European Union. A common legal heritage, made of general principles and abstract rules, was the perfect starting point for legal harmonisation of discrete portions of private law. There was a certain elegance in this model, despite its patent ideological drive. From the viewpoint of continental European *Dogmengeschichte*, the narrative may even have some historical merits.

Despite the recent setbacks and failures of the European integration, the appeal of legal abstractions has not faded away. Partly because the interest of some scholars has shifted towards a broader picture (towards global approaches, postcolonial studies, and so on), and partly because of a renewed interest in local history (where European-wide discussions have no place), few scholars are still working on early modern *European* legal issues. Thus, whether the focus is far broader or much narrower, either way it is best to stay clear of that general narrative. Almost paradoxically, while specific strands of legal-historical scholarship are making very significant progress, that grand narrative lingers on – almost by way of inertia.

A crucial problem of early modern law is that it is difficult to capture into a precise definition. Even the term *usus modernus pandectarum* – which supposedly defines what happens in the German territories – does not explain much. Confining this definition – and everything that it represents – to the *Reich* has contributed to strengthen the impression that its main features did not reach beyond a large but specific European region, thus preserving the broader European-wide narrative. Admittedly, some features of the German *usus modernus* are not to be found in most other territories. So, for one, the *Aktenversendung* (the "dispatching of the records" from the law court that was hearing the case to a law faculty for a – non-binding yet authoritative – opinion) remained typical of (most of) the German territories. This was partially a consequence of the non-professionalisation of most low courts, but also the result of the political situation of the German territories. Political fragmentation fostered legal pluralism. As the jurisdiction of law courts did not stretch beyond the boundaries of specific principalities (with the exception of the Imperial Chamber Court and the Aulic Council, which will be discussed in this volume), transmitting the records to a university also helped to maintain some uniformity in the interpretation of the law.

Beyond the specificities of the *Reich*, however, some of the main features usually ascribed to the *usus modernus* may be found in many other parts of Europe, two of which are especially important to mention. First, the subsidiary nature of the *ius commune* and the precedence of local statutes and customs. Second, and crucially, the progressive re-organisation of the law *ratione materiae* – that is, on the basis of specific, discrete subjects. Both features answered clear practical needs: on the one hand, the growing number of specific legal sources (the great variety of statutes, ordinances and various by-laws, everywhere present in the early modern period) required to clarify the relationship between specific *iura propria* and the general *ius commune*. On the other hand, this combination of *ius proprium* and *ius commune* began to be observed, discussed and interpreted on the basis of its practical application. This practical approach slowly became the main criterion to organise the law itself. Specific branches of the law emerged from the rather chaotic structure of the Justinian compilation; lawyers started to think of private law as a set of discrete subjects, each governed by its own specific rules. The same practical reasons leading to this subject-based approach also favoured a slow but progressive replacement of the kinds of legal authority. Medieval authorities would still be cited, but increasingly less frequently, just as the old commentaries on the *Corpus Iuris* would gradually cease to be printed. Their place would be taken by more modern scholars (who in their turn would write on specific subjects) and, crucially, by decisions of law courts.

This volume focuses on the role of law courts in the development of the law. There are many excellent works looking at early modern high courts from a comparative viewpoint.[1] But few of them have sought to investigate their influence on substantive legal developments, all the more in a comparative context. From time to time, supreme courts would issue decisions where the lack of clear boundaries between judicial and legislative powers is apparent. It is the case, for example, with the *Gemeine Bescheide* of the *Reichskammergericht* in the German territories, the *assentos* of the Portuguese *Casa da Suplicação*, the *arrêts de règlement* of the French parliaments. But these decisions – and, more broadly, the so-called *stylus curiae* – would normally address procedural matters. Did law courts, especially high courts, also contribute to the shaping of substantive law? The question is clearly too modern to find a precise answer in early modern sources. But it could well be adapted to its historical context: were the pronouncements of law courts considered to be authoritative even beyond the specific cases on which they were rendered? If that was (even just partially) the case, was such authority given by the pronouncement of the court itself or by its wide use and circulation among both legal practitioners and judges? Shaped this way, the question acquires relevance for civil law and common law alike (hence Chapter 4 on England in this volume). There is no *stare decisis* in early modern times. But if law courts played no significant role in the eyes of their contemporaries, it would be hard to explain the collection and printing of so many volumes of decisions (not to mention their wide circulation and, often, their great editorial success) throughout the early modern period. A common feature of what might be called *usus modernus europaeus* lies in the combination of forensic practice and learned treatises – and at the heart of that forensic practice lay the high courts. Looking at their role as a legal

---

1 Among the works written in English, it suffices to name a few: A Wijffels (ed), *Case Law in the Making. The Techniques and Methods of Judicial Records and Law Reports*, vol I: *Essays*, Berlin: Duncker & Humblot, 1997; S Dauchy, W H Bryson and (for the second volume) M C Mirow (eds), *Ratio decidendi. Guiding Principles of Judicial Decisions*, 2 vols, Berlin: Duncker & Humblot, 2006–2010; P Brand and J Getzler (eds), *Judges and Judging in the History of the Common Law and the Civil Law*, Cambridge: Cambridge University Press, 2012; C H van Rhee and A Wijffels (eds), *European Supreme Courts. A Portrait throughout History*, London: Third Millenium, 2013; I Czeguhn, J A López Nevot and A Sánchez Aranda (eds), *Control of Supreme Courts in Early Modern Europe*, Berlin: Duncker & Humblot, 2018.

authority is therefore of great importance to appreciate more adequately the complex and multifaced reality of early modern legal practice. It is also important to do this in a comparative dimension, lest we might consider the central role of law courts and the authority of their pronouncements as a peculiarity of specific jurisdictions, not as a feature of the early modern period. It is perhaps not fortuitous that one of the greatest advocates of this line of historical enquiry, Gino Gorla, was a comparative lawyer and not a legal historian.[2]

Speaking of European legal history as something with specific, neat and uniform features requires a rather cavalier attitude towards (social, cultural, economic, institutional and of course legal) history, or towards geography (clipping away country after country until what is left on the map is sufficiently uniform). Just as it makes little sense to speak of *a* European legal history, so it is not possible to describe the role of the high courts in the development of substantive law as a phenomenon spanning across the whole of Europe at the same time and in the same way. This volume takes into account such differences, looking at a complex, multiform and variegated reality, and adding a further layer of complexity: the variegated approach of different scholars. Not everybody would consider early modern high courts as a source of authority and therefore as an important factor in the development of substantive law. Arguments such as the absence of motivation in the decisions of some high courts, the weight of local particularism, and the readiness of many lawyers to cite whatever authority they could find in support of their client are well known. This volume, especially in some contributions, seeks to take such arguments into account so as to present to the reader a picture as multiform in the scholarly debate as it is variegated in the legal geography of the Continent.

The approach to legal authorities remained considerably different across early modern Europe and, with it, the role of the high courts as a source of authority. Claiming uniformity would seek only to replace one broad nar-

2 G Gorla, *I "grandi tribunali" italiani fra i secoli XVI e XIX: un capitolo incompiuto della storia politico-giuridica d'Italia*, Rome: Quaderni del Foro Italiano, 1969. Of the same author see also, for example, "I tribunali supremi degli stati italiani fra i secoli XVI e XIX quali fattori della unificazione del diritto nello stato e della sua uniformazione fra stati", in G Gorla, *Diritto comparato e diritto comune europeo*, Milano: Giuffrè, 1981, 543–617; "La giurisprudenza come fattore del diritto", ibid, 263–301; "L'origine e l'autorità delle raccolte di giurisprudenza" (1970) 44 *Annuario di diritto comparato e di studi legislativi*, 4–23; "Civilian Judicial Decisions: An Historical Account of Italian Style" (1970) 44 *Tulane Law Review*, 740–749; "Die Bedeutung der Präzedententscheidungen der Senate von Piemont und Savoyen im 18 Jahrhundert", in E Von Caemmerer, S Mentschikoff, K Zweigert and M Rheinstein (eds), *Ius Privatum Gentium: Festschrift für Max Rheinstein zum 70 Geburtstag*, Tübingen: Mohr Siebeck, 1969, 103–125.

rative with the next. The point of this volume is something else: the role of law courts in the making of the *usus modernus* across Europe, while hardly uniform, is more consistent than is often thought.

The papers collected in this volume were originally delivered on 25–26 May 2018 at a conference organised by the Centre for Legal History of the University of Edinburgh, School of Law. It was the fourth mini-conference planned by the Centre for Legal History. The previous one, in 2013, led to the publication of John W Cairns and Paul J du Plessis (eds), *Reassessing Legal Humanism and its Claims. Petere Fontes?* (2016) [Edinburgh Studies in Law, vol XV], and it announced the present volume. The next mini-conference will be devoted to Pandectism.

This volume, and the conference that preceded it, would not have been possible without the generous financial support of the Edinburgh Legal Education Trust and the School of Law, University of Edinburgh. On behalf of the whole Centre for Legal History, it is my pleasure to gratefully acknowledge their support. The School of Law, Research Office provided invaluable assistance in the organising of this conference, and Matthew Cleary was hugely helpful in the editorial stages of the publication process. Finally, I wish to thank the Editorial Board of the Edinburgh Studies in Law, together with the previous and current series editors, Professors Elspeth Reid and Alexandra Braun respectively, for accepting this volume.

GR
Old College, Edinburgh
January 2020

A Note on Names and Book Titles

The chapters collected in this volume refer to a large number of jurists from the sixteenth to eighteenth centuries. As was the convention of the early modern period, many of these jurists were known by the Latinised versions of their names and surnames in addition to their names and surnames in the vernacular languages of early modern Europe. To assist the reader in traversing this issue, every effort has been made to verify both the vernacular and Latinised versions of the names of jurists using the library catalogues of the British Library and of the Max-Planck Institute for Legal History. While the most renowned jurists have been largely Latinised, no attempt has been made to standardise names across the volume, as to do so would have interfered too much with the individual chapters. Instead, guidance is provided throughout where names might create confusion.

List of Contributors

GÉRALDINE CAZALS, University of Rouen

JOHN D FORD, University of Aberdeen

JAVIER GARCÍA MARTÍN, University of the Basque Country

DAVID J IBBETSON, University of Cambridge

GUSTAVO CÉSAR MACHADO CABRAL, Federal University of Ceará

SABRINA MICHEL, University of Lille 2, Centre d'Histoire Judiciaire

MACIEJ MIKUŁA, Jagiellonian University in Kraków

ANNAMARIA MONTI, Bocconi University of Milan

PETER OESTMANN, University of Münster

HEIKKI PIHLAJAMÄKI, University of Helsinki

GUIDO ROSSI, University of Edinburgh

ISABELLE STOREZ-BRANCOURT, University of Paris II-Panthéon-Assas, Institut d'Histoire du droit, CNRS

PHILIP THOMAS, University of Pretoria

ALAIN WIJFFELS, Universities of Leiden, Leuven, Louvain-la-Neuve and Lille 2, Centre d'Histoire Judiciaire

1 Law Reports of the Parliament of Flanders and their Authority in the Parliament's Practice

Géraldine Cazals, Sabrina Michel and Alain Wijffels

A. CONTEXT
B. THE PARLIAMENT'S LAW REPORTS
   (1) Typology of sources produced by practitioners on the Parliament's practice
   (2) Handwritten sources
   (3) Printed sources
C. THE USE OF LAW REPORTS IN THE PRACTICE OF THE FLEMISH PARLIAMENT
   (1) Case I: the legal capacity of the separated wife
   (2) Case II: the perfection of *fideicommissa*
D. CONCLUSION

A. CONTEXT

The Parliament of Flanders was a French provincial sovereign court, initially created in order to act as the supreme judicature for the territories of the Habsburg Netherlands conquered by Louis XIV (or perhaps, from the French vantage point, reunited with the French Crown):[1] those territories comprised mainly large tracts of the southern part of the county of Flanders,

---

1 For a more detailed historical survey, see V Demars-Sion, "Le Parlement de Flandre: une institution originale dans le paysage judiciaire français de l'Ancien Régime" (2009) 91/382 *Revue du Nord. Histoire Nord de la France, Belgique, Pays-Bas*, 698–725; for the view of a contemporary witness and participant: Matthieu Pinault, *Histoire du Parlement de Tournay. Contenant l'Etablissement et les Progrès de ce Tribunal avec un detail des Édits, Ordonnances et Reglements concernants la Justice y envoyez*, Valenciennes: Gabriel François Henry, 1701.

but also the territory of Tournai and the Tournaisis, and parts of the county of Hainaut. The territorial jurisdiction of the court at first benefited from the military and diplomatic successes of the French Crown, but it was strongly reduced as a result of the outcome of the Spanish War of Succession. The court was first established as a sovereign court (*conseil souverain*) in 1668, at the end of the War of Devolution. In 1686, the court was elevated to the rank of parliament. Its original seat was in Tournai. In 1709, Louis XIV's military setbacks forced the court to withdraw to Cambrai. In 1714, it was permanently established in Douai. Except for the years 1771–1774, when it was replaced by a council under the reforms attempted by Maupeou, it continued to adjudicate as a parliament until the revolutionary lawmaker abolished the *Ancien Régime* jurisdictions and created a new system of courts in 1790.

The Flemish towns and regions conquered by Louis XIV were granted the right to retain their laws and many of their institutions. The legal landscape in those regions was in many respects similar to that in the Northern French *pays de coutume*, where many different local rural and urban customs prevailed. Statute law, both local and general, remained in force. The latter had been issued since medieval times by local authorities or by the sovereign (nominally always as the sovereign prince for each individual territory of the personal union in the Netherlands since the Burgundian, later Habsburg, rule). When the territories came under French rule, French royal legislation was introduced. To some degree over time this led to fostering French legal and institutional culture: a development today often referred to in French historiography as *"francisation"*. At the same time, these were considered peripheral regions to both the French realm and the Habsburg dominions. The traditional French-Habsburg rivalry on the European scene, which only abated in the second half of the eighteenth century, entailed that the population and local authorities were confronted with changing borders resulting from recurrent warfare in their region and diplomatic negotiations establishing new borderlines in the wake of peace treaties. Such considerations, together with the strong legal particularism which prevailed in the Southern Netherlands until the end of the *Ancien Régime*, may to some extent explain why the local authorities in the jurisdiction of the Flemish Parliament on the whole insisted on retaining their traditional customs and laws. Characteristically, an author such as Georges de Ghewiet (1651–1745),[2] would publish (among several other, mostly

---

2 G Van Dievoet, sv "Ghewiet, Georges de", in *Nationaal biografisch woordenboek*, VI, Brussels: Paleis der Academiën, 1974, col 340–347.

unpublished, practice-oriented works related to French Flanders and sur-rounding territories) a systematic treatise on "Belgian" law, drawing much from the legal tradition in the Habsburg Netherlands, while he pursued an advocate's career first in Tournai, then in Lille and Douai (i.e. in the ter-ritories ruled by the French Crown). De Ghewiet's work, as most writings by other late seventeenth and eighteenth-century lawyers who worked in the parts of Flanders under French rule, continued to refer extensively to statutes, customs and legal literature of the Southern (and occasionally also Northern) Netherlands, especially (although not exclusively) predating the French rule.

As a sovereign court, the *conseil souverain* (and later *Parlement*) replaced for the territories annexed by the French Crown the Council of Flanders, which remained the superior appellate court in Habsburg Flanders with its seat in Ghent. The Council of Flanders, however, was not a sovereign court; its decisions could be challenged by appeal to the Great Council of Mechlin. In that sense, the sovereign French Parliament of Flanders took over the role of both the Council of Flanders and of the Great Council. Similarly, decisions of the superior court of Tournai could also (until 1782) be chal-lenged in appeal before the Great Council. The latter's procedural style and precedents played a significant part in the practice of the French-Flemish *Parlement*. (The provincial court in Mons for the county of Hainaut, in contrast, acted since the early sixteenth century, at the latest, as a sovereign court, not subordinated to the Great Council). Thus, a substantial number of cases which had for centuries been handled (mostly in appeal) by the Great Council, and which were sometimes referred to in legal literature, had origi-nated in the territories of French Flanders (including other areas, such as Tournai), often raising issues of local customary or statute law. In addition, many cases dealing with the implementation and interpretation of general statutes in the Habsburg Netherlands, and the literature discussing such cases, were deemed relevant in the practice of the Parliament of Flanders, in particular for enactments prior to the advent of French rule.

B. THE PARLIAMENT'S LAW REPORTS

(1) Typology of sources produced by practitioners on the Parliament's practice

In the jurisdiction of the *Parlement de Flandre*, the increasing importance of law reports reflects the practical concerns of the *Ancien Régime* lawyers.[3] For most reporters, whether judges or counsel, the aim was to facilitate their daily business, which was significantly hampered by the complex intertwining of legal authorities. In Flanders, the difficulty was exacerbated because the court's territorial jurisdiction depended on the vicissitudes of the French Crown's foreign policy. The majority of law reports remained in manuscript form. They were to be used privately, or at least remain within the circle of the court's practitioners. During the first decades of the court's existence, while the court's business kept growing, and its case law still had to be developed from the very beginning, law reports were relatively plentiful. It was the golden age of the French-Flemish "arrestography" – *"arrestographie"* being the phrase conventionally used for referring to (French) law reporting during the last centuries of the *Ancien Régime*. After the transfer of the court's seat to Cambrai in 1709, the territorial arrangements of the Treaty of Utrecht (1713) resulted in a limitation of the amount of litigation the court had to deal with and of the court's staff. When the seat was finally established in Douai (1714), the staff was once again cut down. In the history of the court and of its reports, an era had ended. In the following years, few new reports were initiated: some of those have not survived and most were never printed. On the other hand, the reports dating from the end of the seventeenth century and from the early years of the eighteenth century continued to circulate, both in the *Parlement* and in the lower courts of its jurisdiction.

---

3 On the Flemish law reports, see especially P Godding, "L'origine et l'autorité des recueils de jurisprudence dans les Pays-Bas méridionaux (XIIIe–XVIIIe siècles)", in *Rapports belges au VIIIe Congrès international de droit comparé (Pescara, 29 août–5 septembre 1970)*, Bruxelles: Centre interuniversitaire de droit comparé, 1970, 1–37; Id, *La jurisprudence*, Turnhout: Brepols, 1973; Id, "Jurisprudence et motivation des sentences", in C Perelman and P Foriers (eds), *Motivation des décisions de justice*, Bruxelles: Bruylant, 1978, 37–67; S Dauchy and V Demars-Sion (eds), *Les recueils d'arrêts et dictionnaires de jurisprudence (XVIe–XVIIIe siècles)*, Paris: La mémoire du droit, 2005; S Dauchy, "L'arrestographie science fort douteuse?" (2010) 23 *Sartoniana*, 87–99; Id, "L'arrestographie genre littéraire" (2011) 31 *Revue d'histoire des facultés de droit*, 41–53; G Cazals, *L'arrestographie flamande. Jurisprudence et littérature juridique à la fin de l'Ancien Régime (1668–1789)*, Genève: Droz, 2018. On the different types of report, see again G Cazals, "Les arrêts notables et la pensée juridique de la Renaissance", in G Cazals and S Geonget (eds), *Des arrests parlans. Les arrêts notables à la Renaissance*, Genève: Droz, 2014.

They were used by judges and advocates alike. Manuscript versions supplemented the printed copies as a matter of course. Those that were published are among the most informative reports, providing the best insight into the legal culture and legal reasoning of the judges at the Flemish Parliament. Pinault's and Pollet's reports were the first to appear in print, those by de Blye, Baralle, Flines and Dubois d'Hermaville were only published at a much later stage, in 1773.[4]

(2) Handwritten sources

Among the first generations of judges at the sovereign council of Tournai (from 1668 onwards) – *Parlement de Flandre* since 1686 – some members of the court were keen law reporters. During the early years of the court, the judges were appointed among the best legal minds in the conquered territories. They were recruited from the provincial court of Artois, the bailiwick of Tournai, the councillors acting as legal counsel in the cities of Douai, Lille and Tournai, and during their earlier career they usually had already acquired some experience in law reporting. In the same vein as their colleagues at the sovereign court in Mons, many of the judges at Tournai appear to have started drafting reports soon after taking up their new office. In doing so, they usually made notes in a private capacity on those decisions that caught their attention.

Jean-Baptiste de Blye, who was appointed First President by the king in June 1668, was the first to write a report of cases decided by the sovereign council in Tournai. From the inception of his office onwards, de Blye[5] started collecting notes on the court's decisions which seemed particularly interesting. His work resulted in two series of reports, which occur both in the printed edition of 1773 and in a manuscript now in the City Library of Lille. The first series includes decisions of the sovereign court in Tournai in cases where the court reached a "final judgment" ("*dans les causes sur lesquelles sont intervenus des arrêts de la Cour*"). The second series consists of decrees ("*arrêtés*") of the court on different sections of the criminal ordinance of August 1670.[6] The whole collection is not particularly extensive:

---

4 For a more detailed survey of all those reports, see Cazals, *L'arrestographie flamande*.
5 On this author see P Arabeyre, J-L Halpérin, J Krynen, *avec la collaboration de* G Cazals (eds), *Dictionnaire historique des juristes français*, Paris: Presses universitaires de France, 2007, 91–92 (S Castelain).
6 City Library Lille, MS 661; Jean-Baptiste de Blye, *Résolutions du conseil souverain de Tournai . . .*, et *Arrêtés du conseil souverain de Tournai sur différents articles de l'ordonnance criminelle*

the first series has fifty-eight decisions, the second only seventeen. The account of the decisions is fairly brief. The author reports the decisions in short and impersonal terms, such as "it has been decided that", "it was adjudicated that", "the Bench found that" (*"on a décidé que"*; *"on a jugé que"*; *"la compagnie a témoigné qu'il y avoit"*). The end result is somewhat vague. Sometimes, the author leaves out the name of the litigants, the date of the judgment, or even the statement of the facts on which the case rests. The reports therefore occasionally seem to express rather abstract maxims of the law without any contextual information. De Blye's collection was obviously intended to be a working tool for private use, and that would explain the author's approach.

Other members of the court also wrote reports. During the early years of the court, cases were reported by Guislain de Mullet, who was appointed a judge on 9 January 1671 and promoted to the rank of *président à mortier* on 2 October 1675. He was the father of Charles-Albert, author of *Préjugés*.[7] Reports were also written by Jean Heindericx, appointed on 11 September 1673.[8] De Mullet's and Heindericx's reports were probably drafted for their own private use. Neither of these reports has survived, which may suggest that in each case, only a single copy was drafted. Their memory has survived only because later reporters occasionally referred to them.[9]

After 1686, more law reports were written. No doubt the elevation of the court to the status of *Parlement* by Louis XIV in 1686 was a strong stimulus. At that time, the prerogatives and the jurisdiction of the court were augmented, and the court's internal organisation was strengthened with the creation of a third division. The staff included three presidents, eighteen judges, a proctor general with a deputy, three registrars and honorary knights. The new generation of judges joining the court was obviously keen to collect its decisions. Among the newly appointed members of the court, several tried their hand at drafting law reports. Not all their works have survived. The collections and reports by Maximilien Hattu de Vehu, Adrien-Nicolas de Burges, Pierre-François Tordeau de Crupilly, and some members from the Odemaer family (maybe Bernard-François) are known only

du mois d'août 1670 . . ., in *Recueil d'arrêts du parlement de Flandres*, Lille: J-B Henry, 1773, T 2, 369–397 and 399–414.

7 On Guislain de Mullet, see P-A Plouvain, *Notes historiques relatives aux offices et aux officiers de la cour de parlement de Flandre*, Douai: Deregnaucourt, 1809, 65.

8 On Jean Heindericx, see ibid, 54.

9 Jacques Pollet and Georges de Ghewiet refer to their works. Cazals, *L'arrestographie flamande*.

through references made to their work by later reporters.[10] Yet, the reports by François Le Couvreur (appointed judge at the *Parlement* on 31 October 1689) show how useful such writings could be within the cenacle of the court. Le Couvreur's work only contains about forty reported cases, dating from 11 August 1690 until 20 January 1708, and the cases are mostly summarily dealt with. The reports were not printed, only two manuscript copies are known. The concept of the reports is markedly didactic. Throughout the work, in the form of a continuous dialogue, the author appeals repeatedly to his reader, in an effort to convey his personal experience of the court's workings and of the discussions in chambers leading to the decision. In some cases, he mentions by name his fellow judges and their particular opinions, or the vote count.[11] Le Couvreur's reports show that the manuscript circulated among the judges, thus contributing to the development of the court's own case law, explained through the direct experience of one of its judges.

Other contemporary reports, by Baralle, Flines and Dubois d'Hermaville show developments along the same lines. Ladislas de Baralle's reports, although written over a short period (from his appointment to the Parliament in 1688, until he was appointed Proctor General in 1691),[12] has been preserved in one manuscript at the City library of Lille, in several volumes at the City Library of Douai, and in the printed edition of Henry from 1773.[13] The author discusses the cases fairly comprehensively. He introduces a case by stating, often in interrogative form, the legal issue at stake. In a few reports, he provides the date of the judgment and the names of the litigants. Although he recurrently notes general rulings devoid of any legal reasoning, especially on procedural matters, he nonetheless usually gives a careful and precise account of the facts, quoting if need be passages from key documents in the case at hand: for example, a term inserted in a contract or an

---

10 The reports by Adrien-Nicolas de Burges and Pierre-François Tordeau de Crupilly are mentioned by Georges de Ghewiet; Pollet refers to the collection by Odemaer; Maximilien Hattu de Vehu's work is mentioned by Henry, who in 1773 announced that he was planning to have it published. Cazals, *L'arrestographie flamande*. On those different authors, see Plouvain, *Notes historiques*.

11 City Library Douai, MSS 1223–1224. On Couvreur, see Plouvain, *Notes historiques*, 29.

12 On Baralle see *Dictionnaire historique des juristes français*, 34 (C Souyris Aboucaya), C Fontaine, *Le ministère public au parlement de Flandre: étude sur l'activité de Ladislas de Baralle au cours de l'année 1691*, unpublished master's thesis in legal history (Master 2), Université de Lille 2, 2013; Id, *Histoire du parquet du parlement de Flandre. Ladislas de Baralle, Procureur général (1691–1714)*, unpublished doctoral dissertation, Université de Lille 2, 2019.

13 City Library Lille, MS God 111; City Library Douai, MS 628 and MS 664; Ladislas de Baralle, *Recueil d'arrêts . . .*, in *Recueil d'arrêts du parlement de Flandres*, Lille: J-B Henry, 1773, vol II, 1–261.

excerpt from a custom. He remains discreet about the personal opinions expressed by his colleagues, but nevertheless readily provides the reasoning followed by the court, to which he sometimes adds references to the authorities that he thought had been decisive.

Séraphin de Flines is another judge who started writing his reports after he had been appointed to the Parliament of Flanders in 1689. It is also a relatively small collection, with only seventy-one reported cases in the version published by Henry. The author continued reporting cases until the last years of his life (he died on 30 December 1703). The work has a more personal ring to it than Baralle's, but nowhere does it appear that its author had publication in mind. That is probably not a coincidence, for de Flines provides more information on his own opinions, and he also discusses at greater length the debates triggered by the cases before the court. Thus, he specifies in which cases the decision was reached *omnium votis*, but also what the individual opinions were of his colleagues, whether the president Hattu, or his fellow-judges Roubaix, Desnaux, Buissy or Le Couvreur, whom he all refers to by name. He gives the opinion which prevailed in the court's decision, but also discloses which arguments were put forward in dissenting opinions, or how the vote was split during the discussion of the case. His reports provide direct information on the court's ways to deal with cases: how judges may argue opposite views, how Bartolus' authority is weighed against that of Alciato,[14] bringing debates within the court to life.

The reports by Antoine-Augustin Dubois d'Hermaville were written between August 1690 and 21 January 1692, starting after the author's appointment as a judge (in October 1689), but ending long before his promotion to *president à mortier* on 7 February 1695.[15] His collection is far more extensive than the previous reports. In the printed version, Dubois d'Hermaville's collection includes 122 judgments, covering a total of 483 pages in-4°. Its length therefore exceeds that of the printed edition which contains the three collections already mentioned, drafted by Jean-Baptiste de Blye, Ladislas de Baralle and Séraphin de Flines: the total volume of those three works is 427 pages, but it also includes a commentary on the custom of the Salle de Lille by de Blye. Dubois d'Hermaville did not produce a work which was significantly different from his predecessors' reports, at least if one considers his approach in discussing cases (which, in any event, may vary

14 City Library Lille, MS 661; Séraphin de Flines, *Recueil d'arrêts . . .*, in *Recueil d'arrêts du parlement de Flandres*, ibid, vol II, 263–368. About the author, *Dictionnaire historique des juristes français*, 335 (S Humbert).

15 *Dictionnaire historique des juristes français*, 262–263 (T Le Marc'hadour).

from one case to another). What stands out in at least some of his reports is the author's efforts for raising the narrative quality of his work. Dubois d'Hermaville expresses a much broader culture than the former reporters, but he definitely also had a special talent and feel for building a narrative, especially when he dealt with striking cases.[16] He also paid more attention to legal literature, and was anxious to ensure that the particular legal traditions within the jurisdiction of the court remained honoured, while at the same time he displayed a vast knowledge of European legal scholarship and civil law. The specific features of the cases and even the judgments themselves were not his main concern, as he preferred to focus on those fundamental "maxims" for which legal literature since the seventeenth century, not least the literature on landmark cases, had shown much interest.[17]

The growing number of law reports makes it clear that by the beginning of the eighteenth century, the time had come to achieve a synthesis. Mathieu Pinault and Jacques Pollet were the judges whose reports went in that sense.[18] Each of their collected reports is even more extensive than the previous collections in manuscript form, and both were published. These two reports achieved success on the eve of a less prosperous era for the Parliament, and appear, with hindsight, to have heralded a period during which the court's judges became less inclined to write reports. The thriving and flourishing years of the court belonged to the past and a page was turned in the history of French-Flemish law reporting. After 1716, when the Parliament had settled in Douai, no judge appears to have continued the law reporting tradition or to have written any other legal work. Only a handful of advocates and less important court officials started more or less effectively a few new collections.

Some of those later works, in particular the collections compiled from the beginning of the eighteen century onwards until the 1720s by members of the Malotau family (viz Henri-Philippe Maloteau de Millevoye, king's counsel at the bailiwick of Tournai, and later Ferdinand-Ignace Malotau, lord of Villerode, admitted in 1722 as honorary judge at the Flemish Parliament), cannot stand the comparison with the earlier reports. These collections may well take monumental proportions (several thousands of pages covering hundreds of judgments), but they are no more than compilations of judgments copied from the Parliament's records. As such, they do not contain

---

16 City Library Lille, MS 767 ; Antoine-Augustin Dubois d'Hermaville, *Recueil d'arrêts* . . ., in *Recueil d'arrêts du parlement de Flandres*, Lille: J-B Henry, 1773, vol I.
17 Cazals, "Les arrêts notables", 203–224.
18 See, (3) Printed sources, this chapter.

any substantial legal annotations. Their purpose was obviously to form a
source of documentation for private use, or alternatively also for use in the
bailiwick. Beyond that limited area, they do not appear to have captured
much attention.[19]

Conversely, the bulky volume written between 1724 and 1730 by the
advocate Georges de Ghewiet (1651–1745) takes, together with the reports
by Pollet and Pinault, a place of pride in French-Flemish law reporting.
Georges de Ghewiet was a nephew-in-law of Jacques Pollet. Throughout his
professional life, he collected an impressive documentation, both in printed
and manuscript form, of which his library bears witness.[20] He was well-
informed about the latest developments in legal literature and was probably
influenced by the law reports of Brillon (of which he had a copy) when he
ventured into his large-scale *Jurisprudence*, one of his practical works which
was intended to guide him in his own legal practice. The *Jurisprudence*
remained at the stage of a manuscript. It made the most of all the previous
reporters' works, whether in printed or manuscript form. In de Ghewiet's
mind, his reports were another contribution to his local jurisprudence. It has
been acknowledged as "the last expression of Flemish law reporting".[21] De
Ghewiet's work is the only collection which deals in-depth with the case law
both from the Flemish Parliament's golden age and from the court's practice
when it was established in Douai, from 1714 onwards. Although de Ghewiet
must have spent a substantial part of his time in writing the monumental
Jurisprudence, in which he displays a broad legal culture, he apparently left
it unfinished and started writing other works, which appeared in print. In
1727, he published in Lille a small *Précis des institutions du droit belgique,
par rapport principalement au ressort du parlement de Flandre* (Lille, C-L
Prévost, 1727). Partly conceived as a primer, this book offers a general
survey of the law applicable in the jurisdiction of the *Parlement* of Douai. It
follows a conventional structure, in order to bring a synthesis according to
the *summa divisio* of the Roman Law Institutes which had become popular
in early modern legal scholarship. The book was well received and was soon
reprinted (Brussels, Simon t'Serstevens, afterwards Fr t'Serstevens, 1732,

---

19 City Library Lille, MS 771–774; MS 775–777. On Ferdinand-Ignace Malotau, lord of Villerode,
    see Plouvain, *Notes historiques*, 61 ff.
20 On Georges de Ghewiet's library, of which G Cazals discovered the catalogue in the course of
    her research, see S Dauchy and V Demars-Sion, "La bibliothèque du juriste flamand Georges de
    Ghewiet", (2007) 48 *BCRALOB*, 277–320.
21 S Dauchy and V Demars-Sion, "Introduction", in G de Ghewiet, *Jurisprudence du parlement
    de Flandre*, Bruxelles: Service public fédéral Justice, Recueil de l'ancienne jurisprudence de la
    Belgique, 2008, XV.

1750). In 1736, de Ghewiet published a work which may be regarded as a synthesis of the *Jurisprudence* and the *Précis*, under the title *Institutions du droit belgique par raport tant aux XVII provinces qu'au pays de Liège* (Lille, C-M Cramé, 1736). Here, the author gave a systematic outline of the law in the Southern Netherlands: section after section, de Ghewiet states a number of rules of law, supported by more explicit and detailed references to statutes and customs, but also to legal literature and to case law which showed how those rules had been applied in practice. He thus overcame the twofold inconvenience of the dense and complex arrangement of topics in the *Jurisprudence*, and the terseness of the *Précis*. The *Institutions* reflected a self-confident author in command of his subject and method, effectively implementing his scholarship and ambitions.

It seems obvious that for the author himself, and probably in the mind of many readers, law reporting as it was still conceived and carried out in the *Jurisprudence* had become obsolete in the light of the growing emphasis on systematisation and codification as a reflection of the "triumph of legal rationalism". The *Précis* and the *Institutions du droit belgique* clearly met the demands of many provincial practitioners much better than the *Jurisprudence* would have done. Georges de Ghewiet must have been aware of those shifts, and that may have persuaded him to abandon the publication of the latter work. However, for legal historians interested in the legal culture and jurisprudence prevailing among eighteenth-century Flemish lawyers, the *Jurisprudence du parlement de Flandre* is of special interest. That explains why, almost three centuries after it was written, it was eventually published and has now joined the select group of printed Flemish law reports.[22]

(3) Printed sources

During the *Ancien Régime*, printed law reports in French Flanders were not common. Those that were published in printed form aimed at meeting two distinct demands. First, at the beginning of the eighteenth century, practitioners felt a need to have a synthesis of the court's case law. Second, by the 1770s, publishers noticed the constant interest for Flemish law reports, at a

---

22 City Library Bergues, MS 65; City Library Douai, MS 662–1 ; G de Ghewiet, *Jurisprudence du parlement de Flandre*; S Dauchy and V Demars-Sion, "A propos d'un 'recueil d'arrêts' inédit: la *Jurisprudence du parlement de Flandre* de Georges de Ghewiet" (2009) 77 *Tijdschrift voor Rechtsgeschiedenis*, 157–189. For information about the author, see *Dictionnaire historique des juristes français*, 235–236 (S Dauchy).

time when provincial customs and the political role of the parliaments were drawing much attention.

The two best-known reports of the Flemish Parliament, by Mathieu Pinault and Jacques Pollet, were printed in 1702 and 1716. Mathieu Pinault († 1734) was born in Château-Gonthier, Anjou. He obtained a doctor of laws degree at the University of Douai, taught mathematics, and became a member of the Flemish *Parlement* in 1693. He published *Coutumes générales de la ville et duché de Cambray*, Douai, M Mairesse, 1691; Valenciennes, Gabriel-François Henry, 1701. Today, his reputation still rests on his substantial *Recueil d'arrêts notables du parlement de Tournay*, published in 1702, and supplemented in 1715 by another volume: *Suite des arrêts notables du parlement de Flandres*.[23]

The two printed volumes comprise almost 500 reported cases. Most of them were familiar to the author. Pinault would often act as *rapporteur* to the court before the discussion of the outcome. He had therefore plenty of opportunity for applying himself "to take in the spirit of the judgments, and to enter into the meaning of the judges who had formed the decision". That appears clearly from the precision of the information Pinault gives about the cases he reports, from the initial facts of the case onwards, up to the final dictum of the judgment. As for previous reporters, the authorities cited by the litigants, the judges or ultimately by Pinault himself were of particular interest to him. More than in earlier Flemish reports, he gives a central role to Roman law. There is hardly a page without a quote – sometimes a fairly lengthy quotation – from the *corpus iuris civilis*, often indirectly through late medieval or early modern legal scholarship that Pinault was acquainted with. Because he had in mind the publication of his work, his reports do not contain revelations on the discussions of the court *in camera* or on the actual reasons of the decisions, in contrast to a common practice among earlier reporters whose collections were not meant to come out in print. However, he regularly adds a personal touch on behalf of his readership by including his personal opinion or by mentioning his role in the judgment, or sometimes the name of the *rapporteur* in a particular case. Otherwise, he simply refers his reader to additional authorities, or to the memoranda or personal collections of the said *rapporteurs*. In general, Pinault only rarely volunteers detailed information, which may sometimes be found in manuscript law

---

23 Mathieu Pinault, *Recueil d'arrêts notables du parlement de Tournay* . . ., Valenciennes: Gabriel-François Henry, 1702; Id, *Suite des arrests notables* . . ., Douai : Michel Mairesse, 1715. For information about the author, see Plouvain, *Notes historiques*, 69; *Dictionnaire historique des juristes français*, 626 (J Lorgnier).

reports, with regard to the splitting of the vote, the lack of unanimous opinions or the referral of the case to a different division of the court. Nor is he prepared to explain the reasons given by the judges for their opinions, even when these reasons are based on general considerations of equity or justice.

Jacques Pollet (1645–1714) started his legal career at the bailiwick of Tournai as a contemporary of Charles-Albert de Mullet and Séraphin de Flines. He was appointed a judge at the *Parlement de Flandre* on 31 October 1689, at the same time as Flines, Le Couvreur and Dubois d'Hermaville. In parallel to his peers, he soon started reporting cases of the Parliament and continued writing reports until his death. His friend Grenet took it upon himself to "collect the various parts of the author's manuscript, which were not in a state easily disentangled". He then prepared the reports' publication, in 1716, under the title *Arrêts du parlement de Flandre sur diverses questions de droit, de coutume et de pratique*.[24] Grenet presented those printed reports in the wider context of a movement towards the unification of French customary law. In the foreword which he included in the published version, he explains that in writing his reports, Pollet was pursuing three goals or at least "three views". First, to report cases on the basis of a selection of important issues. Second, in order to examine the decisions given on any section of his province's custom, so as to establish, so to speak, its interpretation. And third, but least importantly, to state simple rulings on general issues, whether on questions of usage, procedure or practice.[25] Here as well, a vast legal culture was required. On every page of the volume, late medieval commentators of the civil law rub shoulders with early modern legal writers. Pollet appears to have had a profound knowledge of their works and was exceedingly well informed on the manuscript legal literature produced by Flemish lawyers. Beyond the specifics of the reported cases, Pollet also sought above all to trace the reasons of the court's decisions, the foundation of its case law. He therefore does not conceal the internal divisions of opinions among the judges. But for the *rapporteurs*, he does not refer to his colleagues by name, and uses general phrases so as to preserve their anonymity, such as "those in favour of his opinions agreed that" ("*ceux*

---

24 Jacques Pollet, *Arrests du parlement de Flandre sur diverses questions de droit, de coutume, et de pratique* . . ., Lille: Liévin Danel, 1716. For information about the author, see *Dictionnaire historique des juristes français*, 632 (N Derasse).

25 Grenet, "Préface", in Jacques Pollet, *Arrests du parlement de Flandre, fol.* [°°1*v*]: "La I.ere de rapporter les questions choisies et importantes. La 2.e d'observer les arrêts qui interviendroient sur chaque article des coûtumes de cette province, pour en fixer, pour ainsi dire, l'interpretation. Et la 3e. qui est la moins considérable, de donner de simples arrêtez sur des points generaux, soit d'usage, de procédure, ou de pratique."

qui étoient de son avis convenoient que"), or "the contrary opinion prevailed" (*"l'avis contraire a prévalu"*). He also tried to formulate the general
principles based on reason and equity, which he believed had inspired the
court's decisions. This way, he offers a remarkable synthesis of the local law
reporting's jurisprudence, which is brilliantly topped by his own reasoning
and opinions.

After the publication of Pinault's and Pollet's reports, in which
practitioners were able to find answers to some of the essential questions
that they encountered in their day-to-day legal practice, and in spite of the
disaffection of the new generations of judges towards pursuing the practice
of law reporting, the interest for the existing law reports remained very
strong. Throughout the eighteenth century, these law reports continued to
be held in great esteem by local practitioners. The printed copies were easily
available, but they also sought out manuscript copies, which they sometimes
consulted at a registrar's office or in libraries where they were made available. Some were copied and discussed. Flanders may not have played "any
part" in the publication of customs at the height of the trend between 1711
and 1750,[26] but that was clearly because the main works which dealt with
local laws circulated abundantly in manuscript form. In the "ancient world
of jurists"[27] where transmission within a family played an important part,
those legal manuscripts were regarded as an especially valuable heritage.
Manuscript and printed version continued all the more easily to be used on a
daily basis, because the costs of producing a manuscript remained very com-
petitive in comparison to the pricing of printed volumes. The handwritten
form of communication was still "one of the important gateways to building
the public spirit during the century of the Enlightenment".[28]

The continuing interest for the genre of homegrown law reports and
the relative scarcity of manuscript reports may to some extent explain why,
during the 1770s, printers based in Lille took the initiative to publish a collective edition of some of the old manuscript law reports on cases decided
by the Flemish Parliament. The Lille librarian Jean-Baptiste Henry started
that ambitious editorial enterprise "in the public interest", in order to allow

---

26 A Gouron, "Coutumes et commentateurs, essai d'analyse quantitative", in *Droit privé et institu-
    tions régionales: études historiques offertes à Jean Yver*, Paris: Presses universitaires de France,
    1976, 326.

27 The phrase is borrowed from the title of the journal *Droits. Le monde ancien des juristes* (2004)
    40.

28 F Moureau, *La plume et le plomb. Espaces de l'imprimé et du manuscrit au siècle des Lumières*,
    Paris: Presses de l'université Paris-Sorbonne, 2006.

young men keen to embark on a "profound" study of the law, or advocates who were confronted with issues "which encompass all the countries" to find in those newly printed volumes "decisions founded on authorities and all the reasons put forward by the litigants and weighed on the scales of justice". In 1773, under the general title *Recueil d'arrêts du parlement de Flandre*, he published the law reports collected between 1671 and 1702 by Jean-Baptiste de Blye, Séraphin de Flines, Ladislas de Baralle and Antoine-Augustin Dubois d'Hermaville.[29]

It seems that the edition was a success. The publisher may even have sold out of his stock within a short period. In any event, in 1777, another librarian, Charles-François-Joseph Lehoucq, took over the editorial project on an even larger scale. The *Arrêts recueillis par MM. Dubois d'Hermanville, de Baralle, de Blye et de Flines* were only an instalment of the series *Jurisprudence de Flandres*, which now also comprised a *Commentaire sur la coutume de la Salle de Lille* (attributed to Jean-Baptiste de Blye), the *Arrêts* of the Great Council of Mechlin represented by the reports of Claude de Humayn, Nicolas Du Fief, Pierre de Cuvelier and Guillaume de Grysperre, the collection of opinions and advices by the Advocate General Waymel Du Parc (already published by Henry in 1775), and also the *Commentaire sur le titre premier de la coutume "de la jurisdiction des droits & autorités des hauts-justiciers, seigneurs vicomtiers & fonciers"*, a total of six volumes.[30]

On the eve of the French Revolution, the French-Flemish law reports, as many other works written by Flemish lawyers, were at long last more generally available in printed book form.

C. THE USE OF LAW REPORTS IN THE PRACTICE OF THE FLEMISH PARLIAMENT

Two examples of legal proceedings before the *Parlement de Flandre* may illustrate various aspects of how, in practice, legal authorities were used both in the course of arguments adduced in court and in law reporting.

---

29 *Recueil d'arrêts du parlement de Flandres* . . ., 2 vols, Lille: J-B Henry, 1773.
30 *Jurisprudence de Flandres* . . ., 6 vols, Lille: C F Lehoucq, 1777.

(1) Case I: the legal capacity of the separated wife[31]

A couple had agreed to separate by common agreement, officialised by the ecclesiastical judge and ratified by the secular authorities. The sources often refer to their "divorce", but that must be understood as a *divortium a mensa et thoro*. It was common ground that separation could not end marriage as a sacrament. Ten years later, the couple was reunited, and the husband claimed that the conveyances of real property owned by his wife and sold during their separation without his consent had to be invalidated. The case was first brought before the local jurisdiction of Sint-Winoksbergen (Flanders), which dismissed the husband's claim (15 December 1702). In appeal before the court of the bailiwick of Ypres, the decision of the lower court was overruled and the litigants were allowed to produce evidence (29 October 1703). The purchasers of the property (related to the wife) appealed to the Parliament in Tournai, followed by the original claimant who appealed *a minima*. The Parliament, in its decision of 14 March 1704, restored the judgment of Sint-Winoksbergen. The husband then initiated *cassation* proceedings before the Council of State, which in 1717 eventually decided to dismiss the appeal in *cassation*.

The central issue was whether the custom of Sint-Winoksbergen required the authorisation of the husband for acts of conveyance by his wife with respect to her own goods, while husband and wife were formally separated. The written custom, however, did not address specifically the question. It included a general section (Rub XVII, art 21) which stated that a wife could not enter a contract, acknowledge a debt or take up an obligation, or pursue any action in court, without the knowledge and authorisation of her husband (except in the case of a wife acting as a public merchant).[32] In this particular case, the husband relied on the general terms of that article, while the purchasers claimed that the general principle did not apply in the case of formally separated spouses: in such a situation they claimed, the woman,

---

31 In future, the case will be studied more in detail by Mrs S Michel: additional investigation will be needed in the records of Bergues Saint-Winoc, Ypres and Paris.

32 The custom of Sint-Winoksbergen (in Flemish) has been checked in the two editions mentioned by A Gouron and O Terrin, *Bibliographie des coutumes de France. Editions antérieures à la Révolution*, Geneva: Droz, 1975, 54. Also in the editions *Costumen der stede, casselrye ende vassalryen van Berghen S. Winocx*, Ghent: Maximiliaen Graet, 1664; *Costumen der stede, casselrye ende vassalryen van Berghen S. Winocx*, Ghent: Petrus de Goesin, 1777. The Dutch version is printed with a French translation in *Les coustumes et loix des villes et des chastellenies du comté de Flandre traduites en François . . .*, vol II (1719), Cambrai: Nicolas-Joseph Douillez, sv Bergh S. Winox, 59.

although still married, would recover the full capacity to dispose of, or pledge, her own property.[33]

The records of the Parliament of Flanders contain lawyers' memoranda presented during the proceedings preceding the appeal at Tournai.[34] These memoranda show that the counsel had adduced essential authorities to customs and legal literature already at that stage of the proceedings. In addition, both Matthieu Pinault[35] and Jacques Pollet[36] have included a section on the case (as decided by the *Parlement*) in their law reports. The case is also included in Georges de Ghewiet's *Jurisprudence du Parlement de Flandre*.[37] The decision by the State Council (on 2 October 1717) was published in a series of official acts and statutes related to the jurisdiction of the Flemish Parliament.[38] A few years before the French Revolution, the case, and in its wake several of the legal authorities referred to in the earlier law reports (which in turn took their cue from the opinions in the case file), was discussed in J-N Guyot's repertory[39] and repeated in Merlin's continuation of that repertory.[40]

The two printed reports on the case reflect different approaches by the reporters. Pinault's report states the facts and proceedings, and then some of the main arguments put forward by the litigants or their counsel. For the main appellants at the Parliament (the purchasers), Pinault reports the names of some of the legal authors that they referred to, a case from 1666 decided by the local court of Tournai, and a handful of French customs, all adduced in favour of the capacity of the separated wife. None of these

---

33 On the (controversial) status of the separated wife in the Southern Netherlands, see P Godding, *Le droit privé dans les Pays-Bas méridionaux du 12e au 18e siècle*, Brussels: Palais des Académies, 1987, 81 and 290.

34 Lille, Archives Départementales du Nord (hereafter, ADN), 8B1/14873 and PF 27495. The individual documents are not calendared.

35 M Pinault, *Suite des arrests notables du Parlement de Flandres*, vol III, Douai: Michel Mairesse, n LVI, 1715, 177–182.

36 J Pollet, *Arrests du Parlement de Flandre sur diverses questions de droit, de coutume, et de pratique*, Lille: Lievin Daniel, 1716 (note the sub-title of the volume: *Ouvrage utile pour l'intelligence des Coutumes et des Usages du Païs*), n XXVIII, 75–80.

37 That work was only published in the twenty-first century: De Ghewiet, *Jurisprudence du parlement de Flandre*, 91–92. The same author also refers to the case in his Institutes: G de Ghewiet, *Institutions du droit belgique par raport tant aux XVII. provinces qu'au Pays de Liège Avec une Métode pour étudier la Profession d'Avocat*, Lille: Charles-Maurice Cramé, 1736, 364 and 516.

38 *Recueil des édits, déclarations, arrests, et règlemens, Qui sont propres et particuliers aux Provinces du Ressort du Parlement de Flandres*, Douai: Jacq Fr Willerval, 1730, 714–719.

39 *Répertoire universel et raisonné de jurisprudence civile, criminelle, canonique et bénéficiale*, ed [J-N] Guyot, vol XVI, Paris: Visse, 1785, sv "Séparation de biens" , 223–224.

40 P A Merlin, *Répertoire universel et raisonné de jurisprudence*, Cinquième édition (1828), vol XIII, Bruxelles: H Tarlier, sv "Séparation de biens", 401.

authorities is specified by any detailed reference to the author's works or by any specific section of the customs mentioned. On the other hand, the same reporter emphasises the policy considerations proffered by the litigants: on behalf of the husband, moral and religious considerations on the ascendancy of the man in a marital relationship, and the inconvenience for the husband if, during a period of separation, the wife would be allowed to dispose of her patrimony at will, only to fall back on her husband's estate once her profligacy has exceeded her means. On behalf of the purchasers, the emphasis is on the need to protect the wife (and her estate) from the ill treatment by a cruel husband, while they dismissed the risk of a wife squandering her patrimony, as women are (their counsel submitted) notoriously avaricious. Pinault ends by briefly reporting the decision of the court without stating or suggesting any reasons for the decision.

Pollet's presentation differs in that, after stating briefly the facts, he discusses the contrasting legal arguments on the central legal issue. The way of introducing these legal arguments does not tell the reader whether these were arguments and authorities actually put forward by the litigants: the contrasting arguments are discussed as diverging opinions with regard to the legal issue, much in the same way as they might be in a work of legal doctrine, independently from any particular case. Yet, the general *pro et contra* discussion of the arguments tends to establish that the reasoning in favour of the eventual outcome of the case was the better one. On the other hand, most of the authorities referred to are detailed in footnotes, with specific references (according to the prevailing *modus citandi* of the time in legal works).[41] The whole of Pollet's discussion is far more focused on the legal authorities and their reasoning with regard to the legal issues.

Neither Pinault nor Pollet tells the reader explicitly whether the contrasting arguments were put forward or discussed during the proceedings at the Parliament. What remains of the case file in the Parliament's records shows that all the arguments and authorities brought forward – which may well have been included in the arguments before the Parliament – had already been articulated before the lower courts. The archival evidence available so far does not make it possible to assess whether such a use of authorities before lower courts was common or not before these lower courts, or was in this particular case perhaps stimulated by the fact that some of the litigants (certainly on the side of the wife's relatives) held official and legal offices,

---

41 References in the following footnotes are not meant to identify the editions used by the practitioners or law reporters, which in most cases would not be possible.

and were therefore more likely to be acquainted with legal authorities and literature.

Comparing the extant records and the two printed reports on this case, it appears that the litigants were referring to different types of authority and legal literature. It also appears from the records that some controversy arose around a few of the authorities, to which the litigants' counsel attributed different importance. Two categories of authority appear prominently: on the one hand, references to legal literature from the Netherlands, and on the other, references to French customs and French commentaries on customs. The two categories complement each other in the present case: when read in favour of the capacity of the married woman, the Netherlandish literature supports the principle that the separated woman, although her marriage as a religious institution still stands, is no longer subjected to the authorisation of her husband for disposing of her property. Older authors from the Southern Netherlands, and through them references to customary practice and judicial precedents, serve to establish that by common usage and acceptance, confirmed by legal practice, the incapacity of married women no longer applies when they are separated.[42] More recent authors from the Northern

---

42 The authors from the Southern Netherlands are Petrus Peckius, *Tractatus de testamentis conjugum, in quinque libros distinctus*, in Id, *Opera Omnia*, Antverpiae: Apud Hieronymum Verdussen, 1679, IV 12, n 1–2, 606–607: "Quia separatio matrimonii facta . . . adeo ut libere ea obligare, alienare, et divendere possit, nisi statuto impediatur, id quod nuper in hoc Magno Senatu decretum fuit"; Johannes Wamesius, *Responsorum sive consiliorum ad ius forumque civile pertinentium Centuria quinta*, Antverpiae: apud Henricum Aertssens, 1641, Cons 99, 312–313 (Separatio tori inter coniuges), n 5; Id, *Responsorum sive consiliorum de iure pontificio*, vol II, Lovanii: Typis Iacobi Zegers, 1643, Cons 551, 555–556 (very much in the same words as in his civil *consilium*: it is against reason and law to argue that the husband would retain his authority and power, and even in such a case, the judge's authority can replace the husband's); Paulus Christinaeus (1625), *In leges municipales civium Mechliniensium . . . notae seu commentationes*, Antverpiae: Apud Martinum Nutium, IX 4, additamenta, lxxii (the married woman is not able to enter contracts or make gifts, unless she is a merchant or separated as to property); Antonius Perez, *Praelectiones in duodecim libros Codicis Justiniani imp.*, Amstelaedami: Apud Ludovicum & Danielem Elzevirios, 1661, ad C 5 12, 372, sv Hodiernis moribus; Robert de Flines (who was a contemporary author, ob 1703, and whose commentary on the custom of Tournai was not published but circulated in manuscript form). Two manuscripts are mentioned by R Dekkers, *Bibliotheca Belgica Juridica. Een bio-bibliographisch overzicht der rechtsgeleerdheid in de Nederlanden van de vroegste tijden af tot 1800*, Brussels: Koninklijke Vlaamse Academie voor Wetenschappen, Letteren en Schone Kunsten van België, 1951, 57: MS Kortrijk 288 (now at the Archives of the Realm in Kortrijk), which contains only part of the commentary, but not the one here referred to; and Mons 755 (now in the Library of UMons under 315/262 R 2/G). De Flines discusses the controversy with respect to the separated wife, first referring to Louet et al for the opinion against the power of the wife to dispose without the consent of her husband, but then expresses approvingly the opposite opinion ("Contrarium tamen et melius tenant . . ."), referring to several of the works also quoted in the case (viz P Peck, P van Christijnen, Baldus, J Wamèse, R Choppin, Ch Dumoulin and A Tiraqueau). He then goes on referring to the Tournai

Netherlands were also emphatically referred to,[43] partly probably because they offered a systematic survey of the opinions on the issue, partly because even by the end of the seventeenth century, the assumption of a general "Belgian" legal tradition encompassing both the Catholic and the Protestant Netherlands was apparently still widespread. The French customary and judicial tradition seems to have been more restrictive, allowing the separated woman only the mere administration of her property (i.e. without disposing of her goods) or minor forms of disposal when these proved necessary in her interest.[44] However, the same line of argument also highlights that some French customs[45] also explicitly provided that separated wives could enter

judgment indirectly mentioned in Pinault's report: "Et sic iudicatum fuit 13 novembris 1666 inter viduam N. Le Clercq donatariam uxoris Marci Crespeel, et viduam Petri Cuvelier et consortem, quia per separationem tollitur viro dominium, et administratio bonorum uxoris a consuetudine tributa, quorum causa necessaria erat authoritas, nec consistit amplius matrimonium in suo pro-prio et pleno significato, et quoad effectus civiles, quos praesertim attendit consuetudo, sed solum spirituale vinculum, quod enim contrariae opinionis authores dicunt separationem inductam ad evitandam donandi libertatem, satis solvitur ex eo, quod etiamsi separatio fiat ex causa vitandae dilapidationis a marito fiendae, tamen ad consequentiam dictae separationis, mulier eximitur dominio, et fit sui juris, consequiturque libertatem, ut ipsa disponat, quemadmodum cessante mariti potestate, et competit ex consuetudine tit. de ceux qui sont tenus pour agés, idem tenet Pirr. Angleb. ad cons. Aurel. tit. 9 cap. 5 n.7 de societate vide Pap. lib. 7 tit. 1 arr. 10" (fols 170v–171r).

43 Christianus Rodenburgius, *Tractatus de jure conjugum. In quo de viri in uxorem potestate, eorumque obligationibus, judiciis, mutuis gratificationibus, bonorum communionem, pactisque dotalibus, illustriores controversiae, ad usum fori patrii, vicinarumque regionum expenduntur, cum tractatione praeliminari de jure, quod oritur ex statutorum, vel consuetudinum discrep-antium conflictu*, Trajecti ad Rhenum: Apud Gisbertum Zylium, et Theodorum ab Ackerdijck, 1653, Tit III, cap 1, n 14, 327–330, starting with a survey of the controversies among legal schol-ars; Abraham a Wesel, *De connubiali bonorum societate*, in *Opera omnia*, Amstelodami: apud Henricum, & Viduam Theodori Boom, 1701, 218–219, n 35 ff.

44 A key reference, also often referred to by the later authors from the Southern and Northern Netherlands who wrote on the topic, is Georges Louet, *Recueil d'aucuns notables arrests, donnez en la cour de Parlement de Paris . . .*, Nouvelle et dernière edition, *Reveuë, corrigée, et augmentée de plusieurs Arrests intervenus depuis les Impressions precedentes, et d'autres notables Decisions, Par Me Iulien Brodeau, Advocat au Parlement*, Paris: P Rocolet and Iean Guignard, 1650, Letter F, art 30 (Femme séparée de biens, si elle peut aliener sans estre authori-sée de son mary), 439–441.

45 Pollet's references include: *Le coustumier du pays de Bourbonnois. Avec le Proces Verbal. Corrigé et annoté de plusieurs Decisions et Arrests, par M. Charles du Molin . . .*, Lyon: pour Georges Vernoy Libraire de Molins, 1599, 54, art 170 (with in the margin an annotation by Charles Dumoulin: whereas article 170 states that "Femme mariée est en la puissance de son mary", Dumoulin notes: "Indistincte, etiamsi non sint communes in bonis, secus facta separa-tione"); *Les loix municipales, et coustumes generales du balliage de Chaulmont en Bassigny et ancien ressort d'iceluy, corrigées, interpretées et annotées fidellement de plusieurs decisions, sen-tences, arrests, et autres raisons y convenables: et concordées à plusieurs autres coustumes de ce Royaume de France: Par M. Iean Gousset . . .*, Espinal: Pierre Hovion, 1623, 43–47, art 66, at 45, n 7 (Sans l'authorité): the husband's authority and power applies ". . . N'estoit qu'elle fust sepa-ree par sentence de juge competent; et partage fait et executé sans fraude . . . "; *Commentaire sur les coustumes de la prevosté et vicomté de Paris, divisé en trois livres, Composé par M. René Choppin . . .*, vol III, Paris: Louis Billaine, 1662, Liv II, Tit I, n 14, 132–133; *Coustumes de la cite*

into contracts without the authority of their husbands. The argument may also be understood to make the point that, whereas the practice was controversial or divided in French customary law, the more general practice in the "Flemish" customs was in favour of the married wife.

The authorities referred to were therefore drawn from several centuries, although mostly from the sixteenth century and the advent of printed legal literature onwards. The authorities were also drawn from both the customary *iura propria* and from the civil law tradition.[46] It seems clear that the religious divide in the Low Countries does not seem to have inhibited the French practitioners from quoting Protestant authors, even on a religion-sensitive topic such as marriage. Beyond the customary traditions of the Low Countries, a civil author from the North who was a popular authority throughout Europe, such as Vinnius, was also referred to.[47] In this particular case, legal literature from beyond France and the Low Countries was largely ignored[48] with few exceptions – such as a spurious reference to António da Gama (1520–1595): an advocate of the courts below repeated A Wesel's reference to the Portuguese practice, but the case discussed by Gamma deals with a different issue.[49]

---

et ville de Rheims ville et villages regis selon icelles, avec le commentaire . . . Par M. Iean Baptiste de Buridan . . ., Paris: Louis Billaine, 1665, art 13, n 12, 32–33: where the commentator mentions the opinion stating the husband's continuing authority in the case of separation, but that opinion is rejected by de Buridan; *Coustume du bailliage de Troyes, avec les commentaires de Me Louis Le Grand . . .*, Nouvelle Edition, Paris: Jean Guignard, 1681, Tit V, art 80, n 47–48: relying on the custom of Paris and cases decided by the Paris Parliament, the author argues that even the separated wife requires authorisation of her husband in order to dispose of her property. Of these authors, Pinault only mentions Dumoulin on the custom of the Bourbonnois; however, he also mentions (referring to the counsel's arguments) the customs of the Dunois and Montargis (A Gouron and O Terrin, *Bibliographie des coutumes de France*, 124 and 145–147, esp n 1123–1124). The latter was also mentioned in the memoranda submitted at Sint-Winoksbergen.

46 Pinault includes in his report a reference to Antoine Mornac, *Observationes In viginti quatuor priores Libros Digestorum. Ad usum Fori Gallici*. Nova editio locupletior et auctior, vol I, Paris: Franc. Montalant, 1721, ad D 24.2.2.1, col 1426, mentioning restrictive circumstances of necessity when the separated wife may validly dispose of her property: such restrictions may be relevant to explain the purchasers' insistence on the cogent reasons why the wife had conveyed her property at the time of her separation.

47 Arnoldus Vinnius, *In quatuor libros Institutionum imperialium Commentarius Academicus et Forensis*, Lyon: Anisson & Joan. Pasuel, 1700, ad I. 2.8, 309.

48 Pinault reports counsels' arguments debating the relevance of some Roman and canon law authorities (oc, 79), along which Thomas Sanchez' treatise on marriage (Thomas Sanchez, *De Sancto matrimonii sacramento . . .*, Viterbo, Venice: Apud Nicolaum Pezzana, 1754, vol I, 94, 103–106)

49 The quote in the counsel's memorandum (ADN 8B1/27495) is copied from Abramam Wesel, *Opera omnia*, vol II. *De Connubiali Bonorum Societate, & Pactis Dotalibus*, Amstelodami: Apud Henricum, & Viduam Theodori Boom, 1701, Tr II, C IV, n 36, 219, referring to ao Antonius de Gamma, *Decisionum Supremi Senatus Lusitaniae Centuriae IV*, Antwerp: Apud Viduam et filium Joannis Baptistae Verdussen, 1699, Dec 357, 475, n 2 ("Hinc dubitatio orta est, *an matrimonio sic separato requiratur mandatum uxoris in lite mota super immobilibus?* Ut in processu Fernandi Paez & Gasparis Lopez Godinho, ubi judicatum extitit non requiri mandatum, nec

Case law (always through the medium of legal literature) is instrumental in different argumentative strategies. On behalf of the purchasers, the unidentified reference to a (sixteenth-century) case decided by the Great Council and mentioned by Peckius was controversial, but the purchasers' counsel argued that it was relevant because the Great Council had been for centuries the supreme appellate court for the Flemish regions and because Peckius' standing, who had been a judge at the Great Council, vouched for the accuracy of his reference to a judgment by that court. In any case, counsel argued, that precedent was not necessary in order to establish the usage in Flanders.[50] On behalf of the husband, the references to the restrictive decisions of the *Parlement de Paris*[51] forced the opponents to emphasise the particular laws of Flanders, buttressed by policy considerations: the Paris cases had been inspired, counsel submitted, by the concern over a rising tide of divorces (i.e. separations), a tendency which had not affected the Flemish regions. Surprisingly, the reporters did not pick up any references to the Flemish *Parlement*'s own precedents. Yet, De Blye's reports on cases decided by the sovereign council of Tournai included a brief section on precisely the same legal issue, with a summary of the reasoning attributed to the court for having validated disposals of property by a separated wife.[52]

consensum in venditione rerum immobilium facta per maritum, matrimonio separato propter saevitias mariti. Et idem judicatum extitit in hoc senatu in processu Baccalaurii de Celrico contra Georgium Fiz anno 1543. Per Christophorum de Lucena, Mendum de Saa, & Sebastianum de Matos." The main theme of the *decisio* is "Utrum acquisita ab altero conjugum, si matrimonium separatum est judicio Ecclesiae, communia effecta sint". In the advocate's manuscript, the reference is to Dec 357, whereas in the edition of Wesel mentioned *supra*, another Decision is mentioned (also on a different issue), probably due to a typographical error (Dec 257, 329–330: "Utrum maritus nullo interveniente consensus uxoris, possit acceptando emphyteusin se ipsum obligare perpetuo ad annuam pensionem").

50 The argument is worked out in the *quadruplique* on behalf of the purchasers during the original proceedings before the aldermen of Sint-Winoksbergen (AND 8B1/14873), art 31 ss (where counsel confutes the purport of the opinions attributed by his opponent to the authors of the Southern Netherlands Peckius, Wamesius and Christinaeus), and artt 84–86 (". . . Aussi les deffendeurs ne sont pas destitué d'un jugement en cet esgard, puisque le docte Peckius rapporte que la question a esté jugée ainsy de son tems au Grand Conseil de Malines et quoy qu'il ne cite point l'arrest ni ne declare entre quelles personnes il ait esté rendu cela ne doit en rien diminuer la preud'homie de cet autheur qui estoit membre du Grand Conseil. Et ledit conseil qui a esté depuis plusieurs siecles entiers le juge d'appel en dernier ressort de cette ville et chastellenie estoit asse celebre pour confirmer ledit usage et faire en sorte que personne n'en eust plus douté apres ce jugement . . .").

51 In that light, it is not surprising that at the stage of the *cassation* proceedings, the husband had requested that the case should be referred to the Paris Parliament for a new trial (*Recueil des édits* . . ., cit, 715).

52 Jean-Baptiste de Blye, *Résolutions du Conseil Souverain de Tournai, Dans les causes sur lesquelles sont intervenues des Arrêts de la Cour*, Lille: J B Henry, 1773, 373, art I. Art I does not refer to any litigants or give any date; if art II (ibid, 373–374) is to be read as a continuation on the same case, the date of the judgment would be 10 December 1670. On De Blye's reports:

Perhaps less surprisingly, it is noteworthy (in the light of the controversy over Peckius' reference to the Great Council) that Paulus Christinaeus' commentary on the Mechlin municipal laws is quoted, but not his reports.[53]

(2) Case II: the perfection of *fideicommissa*

The available records on the case which serves here as a second illustration of references to case law in the practice of the Flemish Parliament are too fragmentary for a full reconstruction of the factual context.[54] By the end of the seventeenth century, and during the 1720s, litigation before the Parliament opposed the descendants of someone who had established a *fideicommissum* in his will (in 1625), and their creditors. The Parliament eventually delivered a judgment on 8 August 1729 in favour of the heirs, but that judgment was challenged in *cassation* proceedings. The main records available are the address and a memorandum by the Proctor General of the Parliament and, as a result of the *cassation* challenge, a reasoned version of the Parliament's judgment.[55]

    Cazals, *L'arrestographie flamande*, 33–40. De Blye's report on the issue of the separated wife is mentioned by De Ghewiet in his annotations of *Jurisprudence du Parlement de Flandre*, cit, 94, n 5. De Ghewiet also mentions that he learned from a judge who was a member of the court at the time of the case decided in 1704, that the court hesitated over the outcome because the French authorities were against the capacity of the separated wife. He also suggests that the Flemish *Parlement* should issue an *arrêt de règlement* along the lines of that of the Parliament of Rouen in 1600, which would only allow the separated wife to dispose of property under restrictive conditions (ibid, n 8–9).

53 With regard to non-legal authorities, the *quadruplique* of 1702, mentioned above, also includes a refutation of the opponent's argument based on the use of the phrase "jouir" ("to enjoy") in the separation contract, and for which the opponent had apparently relied on the dictionary of the French Academy: "Aussy il semble que le demandeur et son conseil ayent oublié leur principes de la philosophie quand ils insistent tellement sur la prétendue signification dudit mot *jouir* et qu'on en devroit chercher la vraye intelligence et etymologie dans l'accademie francoise a Paris, ils doivent se representer que les voix et mots sont des signes vrayment arbitraires que tel mot peut estre d'une telle signification en telle ville ou province, qui soit d'une signification differente ou contraire dans une autre, l'on pourroit rapporter une infinité d'exemples sur ce sujet, et mesme dans la ville de Paris telle peut estre la signification d'un mot suivant l'esprit et stile des notaires qui soit tout autre suivant l'intelligence de l'accademie. Il n'y a donc rien de plus frivole ni de plus impertinent que de vouloir tant insister sur l'intelligence dudit mot *jouir* et rien ne peut estre de plus ridicule que de vouloir emprunter cette intelligence de l'accademie a Paris, cette accademie n'est pas autorisée a decider souverainement de la fortune d'une famille sur la pretendue signification et etymologie d'un mot."

54 A case study on the litigation and legal issues was published by A Wijffels, "La loi dans le discours judiciaire: l'article 15 de l'Édit Perpétuel de 1611 dans le ressort du Parlement de Flandre", in É Bousmar, P Desmette and N Simon (eds), *Légiférer, gouverner et juger. Mélanges d'histoire du droit et des institutions (IXe–XXIe siècle) offerts à Jean-Marie-Cauchies à l'occasion de ses 65 ans*, Brussels: Presses de l'Université Saint-Louis, 2016, 317–335.

55 ADN 8B1/2383, 8B2/560, 8B2/2019 and 8B2/9.

The main legal issue around which the extant records focus is whether the duty imposed by statutes according to which, in order to assert a *fideicommissum* against creditors, perfection of the *fideicommissum* had to take place, was enforceable or not.[56] In the Netherlands, such a statute had been issued in 1586 (under Philip II) and, because the central government in Brussels had found that the statute had been poorly enforced, again as section 15 of the Archdukes' Perpetual Edict of 1611.[57] On behalf of the descendants whose ancestor had settled the *fideicommissum*, it was argued that those statutes had never been implemented or applied in Douai (in the county of Artois), and therefore had no legal force on the grounds of desuetude. The Proctor General (and, perhaps at his instigation, the creditors) strongly denied such desuetude or contrary usage, or even, as the Proctor General emphatically argued as a matter of principle and policy, the admissibility of such a contrary use in the case of a statutory provision of public interest. The reasons provided *ex post* by the Parliament for justifying their judgment in the *cassation* proceedings assert the opposite view, but not as their main theme: the Parliament's argument focuses on the evidence with regard to the enforcement of the statutes. The non-application of the statutes is inferred mainly from three findings: (a) the admission by the lawmakers themselves that the provisions on registration of *fideicommissa* had not been implemented; (b) a close examination of official records in Douai and Artois, from which the court concluded that they did not reflect any sustained practice of such registration; and (c) a limited number of judicial authorities, which in the court's view did not amount to prove that *fideicommissa* had been registered according to the statutory prescriptions.

As is so often the case when an (unwritten) custom or usage had to be established in litigation, judicial precedents also play a substantial part in the proof of what the practice was. Thus, three cases decided by the Flemish Parliament, and which had probably been cited by counsel during the litigation before the Parliament, were targeted in the Proctor General's address in order to be dismissed, but they also appeared in the court's *ex post* reasoning of the judgment. The three precedents were comparatively recent, more or

---

56 On the legal issue in general, H F W D Fischer, "De publicatie van fideicommissen" (1953) 16 *Tydskrif vir Hedendaagse Romeins-Hollandse Reg*, 159–239 and (1954) 17, 45–81; Godding, *Le droit privé dans les Pays-Bas méridionaux*, 388–389 and 292; G Martyn *Het Eeuwig Edict van 12 juli 1611. Zijn genese en zijn rol in de verschriftelijking van het privaatrecht*, Brussels: Algemeen Rijksarchief, 2000, 261–309.

57 See the text of art 15 (both in Dutch and in French) in the reprint: G Martyn, *Het Eeuwig Edict van 12 juli 1611. Facsimile uitgave van een originele druk . . .*, Antwerp: Berghmans Uitgevers, 1997.

less contemporary to the protracted proceedings in the litigation at hand. The first referred to a case of 1698, about a *fideicommissum* on a house in Douai. The Proctor General objected to the authority of that case on several grounds: (a) the Proctor General's office (*gens du roi*) had not been involved, even though public interests had been at stake; (b) the litigation had opposed heirs and other beneficiaries of the estate, but not creditors as third parties; and (c) conflicting decisions in that litigation had been reached by the courts of Douai and the *gouvernance* of Douai.[58]

The second precedent was very recent: it dated from 1726.[59] The Proctor General again objected that the case had been decided without his office being heard and that a judgment reached by a simple majority of the justices could not prevail over an enactment passed by the sovereign.[60]

The third precedent dated back to 1697. In the course of that litigation, the Proctor General's predecessor was said to have strongly opposed the argument of desuetude, but the court had not followed his objections. In 1729, the Proctor General referred to his predecessor's arguments, but

---

58 ADN 8B1/2383, 3 (reasoned justification by the Parliament), and address of the Proctor General (on the latter's argument against the authority of the precedent: ". . . enfin l'arrest qui dans le sens de ceux qui l'employent auroit preferé le pretendu non usage à l'edit, ne pouvoit pas se soutenir *d'autant plus qu'il a esté rendu sans les conclusions des gens du Roy* puisqu'on ne peut disconvenir que la disposition de l'edit perpetuel a cet egard ne soit une loy qui appartienne au droit public, à la sureté et à la bonne foy dans les contracts de la societé civile, en effet la province de Flandres par sa constitution fondamentale est un pays de namptissement ou l'on ne peut acquerir au prejudice d'un tiers aucunes realisations sans les oeuvres de loy, ainsy cette question n'a pu etre vallablement jugée sans conclusions des gens du Roy, suivant les maximes generalles de tous les parlemens et en particulier suivant la disposition du reglement donné au Conseil d'Estat le 6 may 1681 pour les fonctions du remontrant, qui ordonne la communication des procés dans les matieres qui regardent le publicq et qui requierent des conclusions, même lors qu'il ne s'agit que de concilier un article avec un autre article des ordonnances, a plus forte raison lorsqu'il s'agit d'aneantir pour le tout l'authorité de la loy du Prince, ce defaut de forme emporte la nullité des arrests et donne lieu a se pourvoir contre iceux suivant l'edit du mois de mars 1674, art 26 concernant les requetes civiles.").

59 ADN 8B1/2383, 3 (reasoned justification by the Parliament), and address of the Proctor General. The court's reasons mention that the division among the judges in that case had not been on the issue of the non-usage of art 15 of the Perpetual Edict ("Il est vray qu'il y a eu un arrest de partage en cette affaire mais cela ne doit en rien diminuer les merites de l'arrest. Les juges qui avoient eté du jugement ont assuré la chambre pendant l'examen de ce proces que le partage n'avoit pas regardé le defaut de l'enregistrement, mais deux autres questions, scavoir s'yl y avoit fideicommis et si les trois degrés auxquelles sont bornez les fideicommis par l'edit perpetuel n'etoient pas epuisez.").

60 Ibid, address of the Proctor General: ". . . ces arrests on estez pareillement rendus sans les conclusions du remontrant, et n'ont pu vallablement decider que le pretendu non usage de la ville ou de la Gouvernance de Douay doit l'emporter sur l'edit perpetuel, le Procureur General croit etre en droit de soutenir au contraire qu'une pluralité acquise dans l'une des chambres (peut etre d'une seule voix) n'est pas capable d'aneantir l'authorité souveraine dans une ordonnance si respectable et si interessante, si juste et si necessaire au bien public, et bien moins encore sans l'entendre en ses conclusions".

he also argued that the case of 1697 had differed from the present case on
essential points: the property was situated not in the city, but in the *gouvernance*, the *fideicommissum* had been established in 1601 (i.e. before the 1611
statute), the court's decision had been reached with a majority of a single
vote and the victorious litigant had been dissuaded by a threat of *cassation*
proceedings to have the judgment enforced.[61]

The Proctor General's conclusion went far beyond the pending case, for
he argued that the first two judgments had to be declared void because his
office had not been heard, and the third because it had erred. He called
upon the court, all three chambers united, to state as a point of law that article 15 of the Perpetual Edict had to apply to all *fideicommissa* "for the past"
and that such would also be the rule in future; the present case was to be
referred to the second chamber to be tried according to that rule.[62]

In a separate memorandum, the Proctor General argued that the sovereign courts (referring to the practice of the Flemish Parliament, the Great
Council of Mechlin and the Paris Parliament) only admitted the validity
of *fideicommissa* which had been duly registered.[63] The Proctor General
also objected to a document produced in 1723 by the heirs, tending to
prove the non-usage of the registration. The document was – one may infer
from the Proctor General's counter-argumentation – a manuscript attributed
to Dubois d'Hermaville, who had been advocate, judge and president at
the Tournai *Parlement*.[64] On the issue of the non-usage, the manuscript

61 Ibid, 2 and 6. Additional marginal notes gainsay the assertion that the judgment was not enforced
     and insist that the decision reflected the general practice at the time.
62 The proposal would have been similar to issuing an *arrêt de réglement*. The Proctor General
     avoided the issue of how such an annulment of judgments rendered several decades earlier
     would have affected the family properties. That issue did not escape the attention of the author
     of marginal annotations (probably a judge of the Parliament at the stage of the *cassation*, when
     the reasons of the Parliament's judgment had to be drafted), who dryly remarked opposite that
     passage of the Proctor General's conclusion: "Cela ferait un bel effet dans cent et cent familles".
     The reasoned justification of the Parliament's decision criticised the Proctor General's demand:
     "Il est vray que M le procureur general s'est fort elevé. Il n'a pas moins pretendu que de faire
     annuller tous les fideicommis non enregistrez depuis un siecle entier, tous les arrests rendu
     depuis quarante huit ans en deça et touttes les sentences meme anterieurs qui avoient <eté>
     confirmées. Le parlement qui est assurement aussy zelé que luy pour faire observer les edits et
     les declarations du Roy et des roys ses predecesseurs pour lesquels il aura tousjours infiniment
     de respect, a cru qu'en cette occasion le zele de M. le procureur general alloit trop loin qu'il ne
     le pouvoit pas suivre sans rendre la jurisprudence arbitraire, ce qui est tres pernicieux, et sans
     s'ecarter entierement de l'esprit de ladite declaration et du Grand Roy qui l'avoit donnée."
63 For the Great Council, the Proctor General mentions a decision from 1664. The cases of the
     Parliament of Paris he refers to were appeals from the Council of Artois (ibid and 8B2/2019).
64 On Antoine-Augustin Dubois d'Hermaville and his reports, see Cazals, *L'arrestographie
     flamande*, 58–73.

appeared to confirm that it had been admitted by the Parliament in 1692.[65] The Proctor General cast doubt on the attribution of the manuscript and argued it was not reliable.[66]

In this case, too, French law and legal literature supplement the argumentation primarily based on legal authorities of the Habsburg Netherlands and the practice in Artois and French Flanders. Belgian case law, rulings of the Privy Council in Brussels and legal practice showed that in many parts of the Southern Netherlands the registration of *fideicommissa* had been poorly implemented or neglected. Article 15 of the 1611 Edict, as well as other provisions of that statute, had been inspired by sixteenth-century French royal legislation, and French legal practice and case law could therefore be taken into consideration. In France, too, the implementation of royal legislation requiring the perfection of *fideicommissa* had proved at times an uphill struggle.[67] The most often cited statutes were the Ordinance of Saint-Germain-en Laye of 1553 (art 5), and the Ordinance of Moulins of 1566, supplemented by a Declaration of 10 July 1566.[68] For documenting the practice in other French regions, counsel relied on (printed) law reports and treatises. The few surviving records in this case include references to law reports of the Parliament of Toulouse[69] and Jean Ricard's treatise on gifts and bequests.[70]

---

65 The reference may have been to the reported case 119 in Dubois d'Hermaville's report, which was only printed in 1773 (and again in 1777).

66 The marginal annotator in the manuscript of the Proctor General's address (ADN 8B1/2383, 7), remarked "Le recueil de Mr d'Hermaville est en mains de tout le monde". The annotator also contradicted the Proctor General's doubts about the reporting judge in the same case. However, Cazals, *L'arrestographie flamande*, 272, mentions only one manuscript of Dubois d'Hermaville's report.

67 For a survey of the issue towards the end of the Ancien Régime: *Répertoire universel. . .* (1785), ed J-N Guyot, cit, vol XVI, sv "Substitution fidéicommissaire", 483–490.

68 *Recueil général des anciennes lois françaises, depuis l'an 420, jusqu'à la Révolution de 1789*, A F Isambert, A Decrusy and A J L Jourdan, eds, vol XIII, 1546–1559, Paris: Belin-Leprieur, 1828–1829, 314–321 (art 5 of the Ordinance of 3 May 1553 at 316–317); vol XIV, pt 1, *juillet 1559–mai 1574*, 189–212 (art 57 of the Ordinance of February 1566 at 204); ibid, 213–217 (on art 57 of the Moulins ordinance: 216). See also, 493–499, the Edict of Blois of June 1581.

69 Iean de Cambolas, *Decisions notables sur diverses questions du droit, jugées par plusieurs arrests de la Cour de Parlement de Toulouse. Divisées en six livres*, Toulouse: Guillaume-Louis Colomiez & Ierosme Posvel, 1682, lib V, cap 46, 183 ; Simon d'Olive, Sr du Mesnil, *Questions notables du droit decidées par divers arrests de la Cour de Parlement de Toulouse*. Nouvelle édition, Toulouse: Jean-Dominique Camusat, 1682, cap 4, 556. Both authors quoted as admitting that the registration requirements were not applied in the jurisdiction of the Toulouse Parliament, at least with regard to creditors.

70 Jean-Marie Ricard, *Traité des donations entre-vifs et testamentaires*, vol II, Paris: Rollin, 1754, 244, 484, 508, 510, 520, discussing the implementation of art 57 of the 1553 Ordinance in various regions, quoting Cambolas and d'Olive as above for Toulouse (and Maynard for a diverging opinion), and the provision is said not to be implemented at the Parliaments of Grenoble and Aix, but applied by the Parliament of Bordeaux.

D. CONCLUSION

In the context of peripheral regions such as the southern parts of Flanders
and Hainaut, and the highly symbolic Tournai territory, where during the
sixteenth and seventeenth centuries the borders between the French realm
and the Habsburg dominions had fluctuated, contrasting influences played a
role in moulding those regions' legal culture. A strong emphasis on particular
laws and institutions was one strategy for securing a degree of continuity and
security as, over time, a city or territory could be tossed from one sovereign to
another and back again. In those territories which eventually remained under
French rule, the French Crown pursued (as in other – peripheral – territories
around France) a sustained yet cautious policy of pressing the legal and judicial system into a more general French mould. Such an influence appears
more clearly when French royal institutions and laws were introduced and
strengthened in French Flanders. On the other hand, the continuing reliance
on particular customary laws, not unlike the attachment to regional and local
customs in other parts of the French *pays de coutume*, apparently did not contribute much to the development of a "common customary law" of the realm,
but applied occasionally rough techniques of comparative customary law if
that suited a reasoning reinforcing the Flemish practitioners' own customary
rules on a particular issue. By the beginning of the eighteenth century, an
extensive use of commentaries on customs was a common feature of that comparative approach. The connections with Flemish and other Netherlandish
customs in the territories which remained under Habsburg rule, but also in the
provinces of the Dutch Republic, justified continuing comparative references
to those customs and their commentaries. Such comparisons would inevitably
weaken any effort towards incorporating Flemish customs into the construct
of common French customary law. The use of law reports, both French and
Netherlandish (and, by the end of the seventeenth century, to a much lesser
extent to reports from other foreign jurisdictions) followed the same pattern,
which is also a feature of many French-Flemish law reports from that period.
In that context, the subsidiarity of the civil law, much differentiated from one
area of the law to another, comes even more strongly to the foreground. By
the time the *Parlement de Flandre* was established, the paradox is that within
its jurisdiction, *ius commune* was often used as an instrument for reinforcing
or consolidating the particular local or regional legal culture. The Parliament
and its law reporters played an important part in combining their own particular legal culture with the civil law culture and a practical comparative method
focused on customs and statutes from, mainly, France and the Low Countries.

2 Paradigms of Authority in the College of Justice in Scotland

J D Ford

A. HOW WERE AUTHORITIES USED IN THE COLLEGE OF JUSTICE?

B. WAS THERE AN *USUS MODERNUS SCOTICANUS*?

The College of Justice was founded in 1532 as a new embodiment of an existing court, where judges known as "lords of session" decided cases debated before them by lawyers known as "advocates".[1] Throughout the period covered by this collection of essays, the court played a significant role in both the application and the development of the private law of Scotland. Indeed, after the creation of the United Kingdom of Great Britain in 1707, when Scotland ceased to have its own legislature and the British parliament was discouraged from legislating on matters of "privat right", the College of Justice became the only forum in which the law governing such matters was actively developed.[2] But how was it developed? How did the advocates who appeared before the lords of session seek to identify applicable law, and what effect did they expect their efforts to have on the law they were identifying? The first part of this chapter considers the use of authorities in debates before the court by examining a case heard shortly before the union and by relating it to other cases heard during a wider period. The second part moves beyond a review of the records and reports of decided cases and, taking into account discussions of the use of authorities in treatises written by practitioners, asks whether a settled con-

---

1 A M Godfrey, *Civil Justice in Renaissance Scotland: The Origins of a Central Court*, Leiden: Brill, 2009.

2 Records of the Parliaments of Scotland (www.rps.ac.uk) [RPS], 1706/10/257. Although cases were heard on appeal by the British Parliament after 1707, it was not until the nineteenth century that these decisions began to be treated as a source of law. Note that throughout this chapter the original spelling of primary sources is adhered to, but not their capitalisation or punctuation.

sensus informed the practice of the court.[3] In the end, it is suggested, the practice of the court is better understood in terms of competing paradigms of authority.

A. HOW WERE AUTHORITIES USED IN THE COLLEGE OF JUSTICE?

In the autumn of 1699 Teilman Gooden, a Huguenot serving under Lord Polwarth in the army of William of Orange – who, ten years earlier, had replaced James VII and II on the separate thrones of Scotland and England – received permission to visit his home in Cambrai.[4] In search of a ship to take him across the North Sea, he travelled to Kirkcaldy on the coast of Fife, where he lodged overnight at an inn run by William Murray.[5] On the following morning he discovered that someone had removed his clothes and personal effects, along with a bag containing money and other items, from the room in which he had slept. After learning that Murray had been banished from Edinburgh for spreading "false news" about William's government, Gooden decided to raise an action against him before the privy council – a judicial as well as executive body, which would also cease to exist after the union.[6] His decision may have been affected by awareness that both Lord Polwarth and his father, the Earl of Marchmont, were members of the council, for his case was formally presented there by Polwarth's brother, Sir Andrew Hume of Kimmeringhame, who had been an advocate for just three years, probably as directed by another kinsman, Sir Patrick Hume of Lumsden, who had been an advocate since 1667.[7] Understandably, however, the council was persuaded by Murray's representatives – Sir David Thoirs of Inverkeithing, an advocate since 1661, with William Hogg and

---

3 The significance of treatise writing itself as a contribution to the development of the law is touched on but not examined directly.

4 On the political background see, for instance, T Harris, *Revolution: The Great Crisis of the British Monarchy, 1685–1720*, London: Penguin, 2006. For Polwarth's enlistment in William's forces, prior to the "Glorious Revolution" of 1688, in which William was accompanied to Britain by the earl of Marchmont, see M Glozier, *Scottish Soldiers in France in the Reign of the Sun King: Nursery for Men of Honour*, Leiden: Brill, 2004, 87–88.

5 National Records of Scotland [NRS], CS167/89.

6 *Extracts from the Records of the Burgh of Edinburgh*, 2nd series, 9 vols, ed M Wood and H Armet (Edinburgh, 1927–1967), vol VIII, 184.

7 F J Grant, *The Faculty of Advocates in Scotland, 1532–1943*, Edinburgh: Scottish Record Society, 1944, 103–104 and 106. Although the younger advocate's name appears first in the privy council records, the order is reversed in the records of the session, and the likelihood is that the older advocate took the lead from the outset.

Robert Whyte, advocates since 1680 and 1696 – that a criminal complaint of "robbery and spuilzie" should not be heard unless the king's advocate granted his concurrence, and that a civil claim for compensation should be heard instead by the lords of session, since "ane intricat debate may arise".[8] A month later the case was brought before the session by Gooden's lawyers, who were belatedly joined by the king's advocate, Sir James Stewart of Goodtrees – the draftsman of legislation establishing the presbyterian form of church government favoured by Polwarth and Marchmont after William became king.[9] Murray's lawyers objected that, as a matter of law, he was not responsible for the security of property brought into his inn unless it was deposited with him personally, and that, as a matter of fact, Gooden's property had not been lost in the way alleged on his behalf. The lords of session found the pursuer's allegations to be legally relevant and instructed him to produce appropriate evidence, about which there was further argument.[10] One of the judges, Sir John Lauder of Fountainhall, considered the case sufficiently interesting to be worthy of inclusion in a collection of reports that he was writing.[11]

One argument advanced by Gooden's advocates was that the lords of session had already decided, in a case raised by Patrick Steill against the master of Forbes in 1686, that a vintner who opened his house to the public was responsible for the loss of a cloak belonging to one of his customers. In reporting decisions, a central aim of writers like Lauder was to facilitate the recollection of previous cases in this way.[12] Precedents often were cited by advocates, who were sometimes asked by the judges whether "they had any practiques to alledge, either *pro* or *contra*".[13] It helped if reports were available, for otherwise advocates had to rely on their memories and trace any

8 NRS, PC4/2, 19 December 1699, and PC2/27, ff 290v–2r; Grant, *Faculty of Advocates*, 103, 206 and 219.

9 H C G Matthew and B H Harrison (eds), *Oxford Dictionary of National Biography*, 61 vols, Oxford: Oxford University Press, 2004, vol LII, 695–697.

10 Although the decision was not recorded in the registers of acts and decreets (NRS, CS18/134/1, CS22/190 and CS26/131), a draft of the act of litiscontestation is included among the process papers (CS167/89).

11 *The Decisions of the Lords of Council and Session*, 2 vols, Edinburgh: Printed for C Hamilton and J Balfour, 1759–1761, vol II, 82–83 and 103–104.

12 Previous cases were also cited in the debate on the proof presented in Gooden's case. For a fuller discussion of the aims of reporting in Lauder's time, see J D Ford, *Law and Opinion in Scotland during the Seventeenth Century*, Oxford: Hart Publishing, 2007, 281–371.

13 Sir Alexander Gibson of Durie, *The Decisions of the Lords of Council and Session*, Edinburgh, 1690, 740. Although printed under the title "Decisions", reports were generally known, and circulated in manuscript, as "practiques" or "practicks".

decisions that they remembered in the court records.[14] There was an expectation that precedents would be followed, if only because it was thought "fit our practiques were uniform", but sometimes a "practique was obtruded and not respected".[15] A previous case would certainly not be followed if it was shown that it "clearly differed" from, or did not "meet" or "quadrat" with, the case in hand.[16] In Gooden's case it was argued by Murray's advocates that there was "a great difference" between the situation in a tavern, where customers who dropped in for a drink or meal could hardly be expected to hand over their belongings for safe-keeping, and an inn, where it was "most ordinary" for bags to be deposited with the staff.[17] A previous decision would also be ignored if "there appeared to be a singularitie in the case mentioned", or if it had involved "circumstances" that prevented it from genuinely serving as "a precedent or leading case".[18] According to Lauder, Murray's advocates also argued that Steill's case "had sundry specialities".[19] Moreover, it was a commonplace that the court was not strictly bound to follow "a single practique", as opposed to "the custom of the lords by current decisions".[20] Again according to Lauder, Murray's advocates argued further that Steill's case was "but a single instance", to which it was replied that the liability of "taverners and innkeepers" for the loss of goods on their premises had also been "found by the lords in other cases".

The other cases that might have been cited will be returned to later, but they were not identified in the reports and records of Gooden's case, nor was

---

14 Lauder, *Decisions*, vol I, 196. See too J Finlay, "*Ratio decidendi* in Scotland, 1650 to 1800", in W H Bryson and S Dauchy (eds), *Ratio decidendi: Guiding Principles of Judicial Decisions*, Berlin: Duncker and Humblot, 2006, 117–135, at 122–123.

15 Gibson, *Decisions*, 203, 253, 332 and 578–579; Sir John Gilmour of Craigmillar, *The Decisions of the Lords of Council and Session*, Edinburgh: James Watson, 1701, 6–7; Sir David Falconer of Newton, *The Decisions of the Lords of Council and Session*, Edinburgh: James Watson, 1701, 55; Sir John Nisbet of Dirleton, *The Decisions of the Lords of Council and Session*, Edinburgh: George Mosman, 1698, 19, 108 and 116; Sir James Dalrymple of Stair, *The Decisions of the Lords of Council and Session*, 2 vols, Edinburgh: Heir of Andrew Anderson, 1683–1687, vol I, 393–394 and 601, and vol II, 123–124, 672, 728 and 796–798; Sir John Lauder of Fountainhall, *Historical Notices of Scotish Affairs*, 2 vols, Edinburgh: T. Constable, 1848, vol I, 48, and vol II, 840.

16 Gilmour, *Decisions*, 76–77, 93, 103 and 123; Stair, *Decisions*, vol I, 528, 585, 706 and 759, and vol II, 43–44, 95, 234–235, 471 and 825.

17 NRS, CS167/89. An attempt was also made to distinguish the cases cited in relation to the proof produced.

18 Nisbet, *Decisions*, 104; Lauder, *Decisions*, vol I, 218 and 227.

19 Lauder, *Decisions*, vol I, 83. There is no trace of this argument, or the one mentioned next, in the process papers, but Lauder may have been reporting accurately something said when the advocates debated the case orally *in praesentia dominorum*.

20 Gilmour, *Decisions*, 132–133; Stair, *Decisions*, vol I, 356, and vol II, 152–154, 160–166, 206, 558, 603, 727–728, 738–739 and 796–798; Lauder, *Decisions*, vol I, 343.

reference made to any earlier decisions in the reports and records of Steill's case – noted by no fewer than three reporters, including Gooden's senior counsel, Sir Patrick Hume.[21] The debate had centred there on "how farre a taverner should be obleist for the theft of what is inbrought", in accordance with "the edict *Nautae, caupones* or the comon law". Steill's advocates had contended that the edict was not applicable to the alleged theft from his tavern, for three reasons.[22] In the first place, they had argued that a tavern was not a *caupona*, "not being for accommodating of the leidges", to which it had been replied that this "imaginarie distinction" should not be drawn since it was "not to be founde in law", on the principle that *non est distinguendum, ubi lex non distinguit.* In the second place, they had argued that a *caupo* could not be held liable under the edict unless it was shown that a theft had been committed by his servants, whereas in this case "it was verie probable the cloak might have bein stollen by some other person". To this it was replied by Forbes' advocate that his opponents had made a "mistake in poynt of law", for the praetor's edict furnished "ane twofold actione", and while a claim in "quasi-delict" might have required proof of theft by an innkeeper's servants, a claim in "quasi-deposit", of the type Forbes was making, required no more than proof that goods had been lost in an inn. In the third place, Steill's advocates had argued that he could not be held liable unless it was shown that "the cloack lybelled wes actually delivered", to which it was replied that this was "also a mistake in lawe". In the *Digest* title on the edict, Ulpian had explicitly stated that there was no need for goods to be delivered to (or even drawn to the attention of) a *nauta*, while Gaius had equiparated *nautae* with *caupones*, and "the reasone that is rendered for this by all doctors is that the pairty, by express delyvery of his goods, obliges the taverner by depositatione to restore, wherby the pairty tacitly passes from the

21 National Library of Scotland [NLS], Adv MS 24.3.4(2), fols 187v–8r; Sir Roger Hog of Harcarse, *Decisions of the Court of Session*, Edinburgh: Printed for G Hamilton and J Balfour, 1757, 261; Lauder, *Decisions*, vol I, 448. No act or decreet has been found in NRS, CS18/102, CS22/11 or CS26/79, but the process papers survive as CS98/1054, and an incomplete copy of an "information" submitted on behalf of Forbes also survives separately as GD52/75. Claire Allen and Alan Borthwick kindly provided assistance in searching for the remainder of the document. Although Stewart, incidentally, had become an advocate before Hume, he had been unable to practise for many years.

22 Steill was represented by Alexander Birnie and George Alexander, and Forbes by David Forbes, a distant kinsman, as the son of John Forbes of Culloden (Grant, *Faculty of Advocates*, 73). As will become apparent in a moment, it may be significant that Birnie had struggled to pass his examination in Roman law before being admitted to the bar (J W Cairns, "Advocate's hats, Roman law and admission to the Scots bar, 1580–1812", (1999) 20 *Journal of Legal History*, 24–61, at 56).

benefite of the edict".[23] This third line of argument was revisited in Gooden's case, where (as has been seen) it was said to make more sense for goods to be deposited with the staff of an inn than a tavern, and where the "intricat debate" anticipated before the privy council was in relation to "how farr that edict of the Roman pretors *Nautae, caupones, stabularii &c.* is, or ought to be, sustained or receaved in this kingdome".

As recounted so far, the arguments advanced before the lords of session appear to have rested on an assumption that the edict had indeed been received into Scots law, for they revolved around interpretation of the *Digest* texts on the topic. However, there were other dimensions to the discussion of how far the edict ought to be sustained. Steill's advocates warned the lords that his case was "off ane universall and generall concerne", since if he were found liable, "all inkeepers might be with ease ruined". Customers might pretend to have lost property on their premises, or to have lost more than they had. On the other hand, Forbes' advocate pointed out that thefts were an all too frequent occurrence in Edinburgh taverns, and maintained that, while there was a risk of fraud on either side, "that which burdens the taverners is rationally dispensed with as the leist of two evils". In Gooden's case it was again warned that if Murray were found liable, "ther would be a foundation laid down for ruining the haill innkeepers in Scotland", who might easily be defrauded by travellers, "among whom there are not a few *improbi homines*". Out of fairness, Murray's advocates maintained, "the doctors" had come to regard many forms of theft as instances of *casus fortuitus*, which excused innkeepers from liability under the edict, and the delivery of bags and other items to innkeepers had effectively become a condition of their strict liability in "the custome of the far greater part of the nations in Europe". As support for this line of argument reference was made to Joannes Voet's commentary on the *Digest*, to a *consilium* by Regnerus Sixtinus, and to reports of *decisiones* by Jean Grivel and Jean Papon.[24] According to Lauder, reference was also made to the works of Petrus Peckius, Arnoldus

---

23 D.4.9.1-2. The translation follows *The Digest of Justinian*, 4 vols, ed A Watson, Philadelphia: University of Pennsylvania Press, 1985. Although no particular doctors were named here, the idea that liability for *receptum* was quasi-contractual in nature can be found in several of the sources mentioned below.

24 Ioannes Voet, *Commentarius ad Pandectas, in quo, praeter Romani iuris principia ac controversias illustriores, ius etiam hodiernum et praecipuae fori quaestiones excutiuntur*, 7 vols, Halle: Joan Jac Curtii, 1776–1780, vol I, 715–716; Hermannus Vulteius, *Consilia sive responsa doctorum et professorum facultatis iuridicae in Academia Marpurgensi*, 4 vols, Marburg: Paulus Egenolphus, 1606–1614, vol I, 15–16; Jean Grivel, Sr de Perrigny, *Decisiones celeberrimi sequanorum senatus Dolanus*, Antwerp, 1619, 155–157; Jean Papon, *Recueil d'arrests notables des cours souveraines de France*, Paris: Jean Houzé, 1584, 707.

Vinnius and Reinhardus Bachovius, as support for the argument that inn-keepers could in one way or another restrict their liability to the loss of property deposited with them.[25] Reference was similarly made in Steill's case to the works of Petrus Gregorius Tholosanus, Ioannes Schneidewinus and other "doctors", but these authors seem to have had less influence on the court's decision than the concerns raised about the prevalence of theft in the city.[26] According to one reporter, the lords considered the case care-fully as a "preparative" for others, and according to another they resolved, mindful of losses suffered by their friends and acquaintances, "to make an example" of Steill.[27] Although they may also have been mindful in this case of their authority to regulate business activity in Edinburgh, where the court sat, it is striking that they were not discouraged from deciding the later case in Gooden's favour by arguments that to do so would be contrary to the con-sensus of the continental doctors and of most neighbouring nations.[28]

In questioning the extent to which the praetor's edict should be sustained in Scotland, Murray's advocates were in fact challenging more fundamen-tally the assumption that it had been received into Scots law. The edict had originally been introduced, they explained, because in Rome innkeepers were often suspected of being complicit in thefts committed on their prem-ises, "whereas in Scottland, scarse will any instance occurr in ane age of any such collusion betwixt innkeepers and theeves". Given that it appeared to recede "far from equity" for people to be held liable without any proof that they were personally at fault, this "singular and exorbitant edict", which was "evidently accomodat to the peculiar exigencies and circumstances of the Romans", could not "in reason be followed in Scotland". Gooden's advocates

---

25 Since these references do not appear in the process papers it is not entirely clear what was being referred to, or whether these works were actually cited, but reference could have been made to Petrus Peckius, *Commentaria in omnes pene iuris civilis titulos ad rem nauticam pertinentes*, Louvain: Petrus Colonaeus, 1556, 47–49; *V Cl Petri Peckii in titt. Dig et Cod ad rem nauticam pertinentes commentarii, quibus nunc accedunt notae cum ampla dote variorum circa rem nav-alem observationum, beneficio Arnoldi Vinnii*, Leiden: A Wyngaerden, 1647, 60–62; Reinhardus Bachovius, *Commentarii in primam partem Pandectarum*, Speyer: Ioannes Bernerus, 1630, 1300.

26 Since the information submitted on Forbes' behalf breaks off just as reference to these works was beginning to be made, it is not clear who all the doctors cited were, but reference was certainly made to Petrus Gregorius Tholosanus, *Syntagma iuris universi, atque legum pene omnium gentium et rerum publicarum praecipuarum*, Orleans: Philippus Albert, 1611, 688, and Ioannes Schneidewinus, *In quatuor Institutionum imperialium D Iustiniani libros commentarii*, Strasbourg: Casparus Dietzelius, 1632, col 1096.

27 Hog, *Decisions*, 261; Lauder, *Decisions*, vol I, 448.

28 Cf *The Acts of Sederunt of the Lords of Council and Session, 1553–1790*, Edinburgh, 1790, 103, 153–154, 174–175, 192–193, 198–200, 201 and 203.

replied that the edict "was both just and necessary", as had already been accepted in Steill's case, where it had been argued that the praetor had "most rationally made taverners lyable in the termes of the edict". As has been mentioned, however, no previous decision had been cited in Steill's case, and the lords of session had declared on an earlier occasion that "their power reached not safely to them to make any new law, where there was no practique thereanent before".[29] When a new law needed to be made, the lords would sometimes decline to decide a case until legislation on the matter was passed in Parliament, yet more frequently they asked to have a point debated "out of the common law, in regard their was nothing yet in our law to be a rule theirfor".[30] As had been reported by Sir John Nisbet of Dirleton, a lord of session in the 1660s and 1670s, some of the judges believed that "when we have not a municipal law nor custom to the contrary, we ought to follow, tho not the authority, yet the equity of the civil law, which is received everywhere where there is no custom to the contrary".[31] If it were recognised that the civil law was binding *non ratione imperio, sed imperio rationis*, then it might be maintained that "where we have no statute law of our own, the Roman law is our rule".[32] On this view, in following the civil law when it was found to be rational or equitable, the court would not be making new law so much as finding existing law. Yet Nisbet had also reported that in the opinion of other judges the civil law was merely "the municipal law of the Romans, and is not of force with us until it become our law, either by a statute or custom authorizing the same".[33] In reports written during the same period by another lord of session, Sir James Dalrymple of Stair – who was to return to the court at the end of the 1680s as the first Viscount Stair, after he sailed back to Britain from exile with William of Orange – it was repeatedly stated that "the civil law oblieges not us, but only we ought to consider the equity and expediency thereof", that it was "not a rule to us further than our customs have allowed the same", and that it was "not a law, but an example we follow freely when we find it just and fit".[34]

---

29 Gibson, *Decisions*, 819.
30 NLS, Adv MS 24.4.1, f 104v; Gilmour, *Decisions*, 45–47; Nisbet, *Decisions*, 115; Lauder, *Decisions*, vol I, 248 and 273.
31 Nisbet, *Decisions*, 140.
32 Lauder, *Decisions*, vol I, 257.
33 Nisbet, *Decisions*, 111–112.
34 Stair, *Decisions*, vol I, 49–50 and 280, and vol II, 314–315 and 489–491. As suggested in Ford, *Law and Opinion in Scotland*, 356–361, Stair may have been creative in reporting these cases, but the crucial point for present purposes is that this view was held by someone in the court. See too Gilmour, *Decisions*, 38–39.

On this view, when the court decided a case in accordance with the civil law, it was not finding existing law but contributing to the creation of a new "custom of the lords by current decisions".[35]

As was also mentioned earlier, by the time that Gooden's case was heard in 1700 there were other reported decisions that could have been cited along with Steill's case. Six years earlier Lauder had reported a decision in which it was found that people who let out rooms in their homes to lodgers "were in the same case with innkeepers and taverners".[36] By then the keeper of the park adjacent to Holyrood House had twice been found liable as a *stabularius* for the disappearance of horses put out to grass there.[37] Despite some uncertainty over the effectiveness of a notice that the keeper had erected in an attempt to exclude liability for the loss of horses, no one seems to have questioned whether he would otherwise have been liable under the edict. In the same year as Steill's case was decided the court had even found a carter liable *de receptis* for the loss of money from a pack he had been given to transport from Ayr to Kilmarnock.[38] Presumably the carriage of goods by land was thought to be analogous to the carriage of goods by sea.[39] There were certainly cases in which it was found that shipmasters would be liable for the loss of (or damage to) goods they were carrying unless it could be shown to have resulted from "stress of weather", "naufrage", "piracy" or some other *casus fortuitus*.[40] According to Stair's reports, it was claimed in two of these cases that shipmasters were strictly liable "by the custom of all maritim courts", and that the praetor's edict was "in vigour by our custom", although no trace of these claims appears in the other reports. Similarly, according to Stair's account of the first reported case concerning an innkeeper, which had been decided as far back as 1661, the court found that he was liable for the loss of money on his premises "according to the law *Nautae, caupones, stabularii &c.*, which is observed in our custom", although no mention of Scottish custom was made in two other reports of

---

35 It may not be coincidental that most of the references to judicial customs found and cited in n 19 above come from Stair's reports.

36 Lauder, *Decisions*, vol I, 610 and 627–628. See also P J du Plessis, "Innkeeper's liability for loss suffered by guests: *Drake v Dow*", (2007) 11 *Edinburgh Law Review*, 89–94.

37 Nisbet, *Decisions*, 43; Stair, *Decisions*, vol I, 486–487; NLS, Adv MS 24.4.1, fol 313r.

38 Hog, *Decisions*, 261.

39 As is pointed out in A Rodger, "The praetor's edict and carriage by land in Scots law", (1968) 3 *Irish Jurist*, 175–186, at 176, the brief report does not make the court's reasoning apparent.

40 Stair, *Decisions*, vol II, 130–131, 463–464, 471–472, 553–555 and 791; NLS Adv MS 24.1.12, fols 192r–v and 340r–v; *The Decisions of the Court of Session, from Its First Institution to the Present Time*, 22 vols, ed W M Morison, Edinburgh: Bell and Bradfute, 1801–1804, vol XII, 10109–10110. See also Gibson, *Decisions*, 821–822.

the case.[41] By 1700, at least nine previous decisions could thus have been cited in support of the general proposition that the praetor's edict had been received into Scots law by "the current of the lords decisions", or *praxis forensis* as it was sometimes called, though earlier reports have not been found to show that a forensic custom was already in existence in 1661.

An alternative interpretation of the references to custom in Stair's reports might be that advocates were taken to have based their pleadings on the established practices of the hospitality and shipping trades.[42] Advocates often did draw attention in their pleadings to the practices of particular trades, towns or territories, offering to prove the existence of "an inveterate custom, time out of mind", and maintaining that "such immemorial customes have the strength of law".[43] Evidence was adduced from the records of other courts and testimony was taken from relevant experts, but as well as being "proved", it was believed that practices also had to be "approved" by the lords of session, who might find an established practice "unlawful" and declare that "in time coming they would have no regard to that unwarrantable custome".[44] By the 1660s and 1670s, moreover, it was sometimes argued that no custom could be considered binding unless it was shown that "the lords by their decisions did approve the same, which decisions can only make a custom equivalent to law", and that "customes here are only such as are judicial, by the kings ministers of justice".[45] One lawyer who repeatedly argued along these lines when he appeared at the bar was Nisbet, who complained in the reports he wrote as a judge about the tendency of Stair and some of his other colleagues to "assert" or "pretend" that a practice had been established when nothing had been "instanced to verify the custom".[46] As there is no indication in Stair's reports of the cases involving innkeepers and mariners that efforts had actually been made to prove their customary

---

41 Stair, *Decisions*, vol I, 63–64; NLS, Adv MS 24.3.9, fol 66v, and Adv MS 24.4.1, fol 51r.

42 For evidence that maritime practice had fallen into line with the praetor's edict before this time see *Alexander King's Treatise on Maritime Law*, ed J D Ford, Edinburgh: The Stair Society, 2018, 289–290.

43 Gibson, *Decisions*, 72, 202–203, 227, 300, 428–429, 582, 627–630, 753 and 771; Gilmour, *Decisions*, 67; Nisbet, *Decisions*, 110; Stair, *Decisions*, vol I, 243, 264–265, 413–414, 465, 502–505 and 699, and vol II, 23–25, 313 and 397; Lauder, *Historical Notices*, vol I, 9 and 176, and *Decisions*, vol I, 52–53.

44 Gibson, *Decisions*, 567; Stair, *Decisions*, vol I, 159 and 732–733.

45 Gilmour, *Decisions*, 132–133; Stair, *Decisions*, vol I, 356, 446–447, 473–474 and 561–562, and vol II, 208–210.

46 Nisbet, *Decisions*, 135–136, 169 and 177–178. Nisbet sometimes appeared at the bar in his capacity as king's advocate, being the last person to hold this office while also sitting on the bench.

acceptance of responsibility for the safety of goods, it may be that he was indulging in the tendency condemned by Nisbet, who insisted that reference ought at the very least to be made to "a decision, which may be the foundation of a custom", and that even a practice that had been proved and approved "ought not to be put in the balance with express laws founded upon good reason and common law".[47] What he disliked especially was the assertion of customary practices as a means of avoiding or limiting learned debate on the "principles of law". In reporting a case in the 1670s in which someone disputed a point of law "lookt upon as a principle wheirin their could be no controversie", Lauder remarked on the "wofull divisions" in the court, where some judges favoured Stair's approach to deciding cases while others preferred Nisbet's.[48] Advocates appearing before the court faced a difficult task. As the pleadings surviving from the cases raised by Gooden and Steill reveal, in the closing decades of the seventeenth century they still had to be prepared to assist the judges both in finding learned solutions to problems and in making exemplary decisions to guide future practice.

B. WAS THERE AN *USUS MODERNUS SCOTICANUS*?

To self-styled doctrinal legal historians, the conclusion to be drawn from the first part of this chapter may seem obvious. In one way or another, it may be supposed, the praetorian edict *Nautae, caupones, stabularii*, or at least the provisions it contained on responsibility for the security of property, had been "received" into Scots law, so that the liability of innkeepers was governed by the "common law" of Europe.[49] If the aim is to take a long view of the law's development, to look backwards to see where today's law came from, then this response may be adequate. Indeed, if this is the aim, making out the broad contours of a wood from a distance may be preferable to investigating the varieties of tree that it contains. Yet for those who make it their business to visit the past as if it were a foreign country, and to present their contemporaries with accounts of what they find there that are both intelligible to them and true to the sources examined, the matter is bound to seem more complicated. Was the praetorian edict considered authoritative

---

47 Another possibility, however, is that the customs referred to were considered too notorious to require proof.

48 Lauder, *Decisions*, vol I, 40. Lauder was still at the bar when he reported this case.

49 R Zimmermann and P Simpson, "Strict liability", in K Reid and R Zimmermann (eds), *A History of Private Law in Scotland*, 2 vols, Oxford: Oxford University Press, 2000, vol II, 548–583, at 570–571.

as a written statement of reason, or had the lords of session followed it freely as an example in a series of decisions from which a forensic custom emerged, or had it somehow informed customary practices that the lords were prepared to endorse?[50] There appear to have been different views of how the civil law might be received into Scots law, corresponding to different views of how it might be regarded as the *ius commune*. If a genuinely historical understanding of what was happening is to be achieved, and if the sources on which any historical account of Scots law must be based are to be used reliably, then sense will need to be made of the different views encountered in the reports and records of decided cases.

Perhaps it would help to take not so much a long as a broad perspective on the Scottish sources. In the earliest reports of decisions delivered in the College of Justice, written by John Sinclair in the 1540s, there is evidence of copious reference being made to the literature of the *mos Italicus* before judges who consciously adhered to the principles that *statuta sunt stricti iuris, quae sunt contra dispositionem iuris communis*, and that *casus omissi manent in dispositione iuris communis*.[51] By the seventeenth century, however, as the cases already discussed illustrate, the basic texts of the civil law were being read more critically by lawyers who appreciated that they often dealt with laws suited to the peculiar needs of an ancient people. If the influence of the *mos Gallicus* is discernible here, the approach taken was not founded on the essentially humanist assumption that the civilisation of ancient Rome ought to be recovered and imitated.[52] The works of the civilian doctors continued to be studied as a repository of solutions to current issues, which has been taken to typify the *usus modernus Pandectarum* rather than the *mos Gallicus*.[53] Where the *usus modernus* has been taken to

---

50 The essay referred to in the previous note goes too far in concluding from the mention of the edict in William Welwod's *The Sea-Law of Scotland*, Edinburgh: Robert Waldergrave, 1590, sig B4v, that "it had certainly arrived" by his time. If due account is taken of Welwod's approach to writing about maritime law, the only thing that can be deduced with certainty from his handling of the topic is that he had been reading the *Digest*, as might have been expected of a professor of civil law. See J D Ford, "William Welwod's treatises on maritime law", (2013) 34 *Journal of Legal History*, 172–210.

51 G Dolezalek, "The Court of Session as a *Ius commune* court, witnessed by 'Sinclair's Practicks', 1540–49", in H L MacQueen (ed), *Stair Society: Miscellany IV*, Edinburgh: Stair Society, 2002, 51–84.

52 The extent to which there really were any legal humanists, as opposed to humanistic lawyers, is considered in an earlier collection of essays in this series: P J du Plessis and J W Cairns (eds), *Reassessing Legal Humanism and Its Claims: Petere Fontes?*, Edinburgh: Edinburgh University Press, 2016.

53 G C J J van den Bergh, *The Life and Work of Gerard Noodt*, Oxford: Oxford University Press, 1988, 133–135 and 263–264.

differ from the *mos Italicus* is not only in its critical treatment of the basic texts but also in two other respects.[54] In the first place, a concerted effort was made to combine learned with local sources, with the result that each jurisdiction formed its own understanding of the relevance of the *ius commune*.[55] In the second place, texts were read and cited when the legal topics they dealt with arose for discussion, not whenever they touched on broad ideas that seemed to be of interest. It is a notable feature of the pleadings submitted in the cases raised by Gooden and Steill that the learned references they contain were confined to texts on the praetorian edict and to discussions of those texts in books written during the sixteenth and seventeenth centuries, two of which were devoted to the discussion of maritime law.[56] The limited range of these learned references, the critical reading of the basic texts, and the willingness of the judges to deviate from an apparent consensus among the doctors and other nations may all be considered indicative of an *usus modernus Scoticanus*. So may it be concluded that Scotland was participating in a movement affecting most of Europe? One concern could be that historians have appropriated a label used in Germany towards the end of the seventeenth century and applied it to earlier times and other places, even though it is taken to denote a movement characterised by variability.[57] Whether there was more diversity than similarity in the ways authorities were used in different parts of Europe during the early modern period is a question that the essays in this volume should help to answer. Another concern, however, could be that to talk of an *usus modernus Scoticanus* would be to ignore the divergence within Scotland between those who attributed the quality of *observabilitas* to the civil law, regarding it as binding insofar as it was equitable, and those who viewed it as a foreign law, the example of which might or might not be followed when new law was being made.[58]

---

54 A Wijffels, "Early-modern literature on international law and the *usus modernus*", (1995) 16 *Grotiana*, 35–54, at 35–42.

55 See too H Mohnhaupt, "La discussion sur *theoria et praxis* aux XVIIème et XVIIIème siècles en Allemagne", in *Confluence des droit savants et des pratiques juridiques*, Milan: Giuffre, 1979, 277–296.

56 As noted, vague reference was also made to other "doctors", and some of those named discussed the views of the medieval glossators and commentators. In general, though, advocates seem to have relied primarily on more modern authors by the latter half of the seventeenth century.

57 M Schmoeckel, "Holy Roman Empire of the German Nation", in H Pihlajamäki, M D Dubber and A M Godfrey (eds), *The Oxford Handbook of European Legal History*, Oxford: Oxford University Press, 2018, 358–377, at 363.

58 P G Stein, *The Character and Influence of the Roman Civil Law: Historical Essays*, London: Hambledon Press, 1988, 125.

Whether this divergence of opinion should be passed over is the question addressed in the remainder of this chapter.

Another characteristic feature of early modern legal practice, it has been suggested, was an endemic vagueness in the way that authoritative sources were handled in relation to one another.[59] As far as Scotland is concerned, this cannot be taken to mean that there was no agreement about how authorities should be used. In treatises court practitioners wrote for the benefit of their colleagues – often for the instruction of novice advocates – it was generally maintained that the sources of Scots law should be investigated in the order prescribed in a famous *Digest* text, where Julian had observed that when *scriptae leges* were unavailable, recourse should be taken to *quod moribus et consuetudine inductum est*, failing which to *quod proximum et consequens ei est*, failing which to the law *quo urbs Roma utitur*.[60] Everyone agreed that the first source to be investigated was the legislation enacted in the Scottish Parliament, but there was less agreement about the authority of statutes passed by other bodies, and there was a major disagreement about the authority of various medieval texts known as the "auld lawes".[61] Moreover, even when a relevant act of parliament was available, and even though some lawyers felt uncomfortable with Julian's notion that *scriptae leges* could lose force by falling into desuetude, there was no denying that many Scottish statutes had been deprived of effect in this way.[62] Acceptance of the notion of *desuetudo* made the boundary between *lex* and *consuetudo* imprecise, and the imprecision was increased by the uncertainty over the relationship between popular and forensic customs already outlined.[63] Julian's reference to *quod proximum et consequens ei est* was also construed ambiguously, mostly as approval of analogous reasoning, but also as an invitation to draw upon the experience of neighbouring nations.[64] His reference

---

59 A Watson, *Sources of Law, Legal Change and Ambiguity*, Edinburgh: T & T Clark, 51–75.

60 D.1.3.32; Thomas Craig of Riccarton, *Ius feudale tribus libris comprehensum*, tr L Dodd, Edinburgh: The Stair Society, 2017, 172–181; Sir John Skene of Curriehill, *Regiam maiestatem, Scotiae veteres leges et constitutiones*, Edinburgh: Thomas Finlason, 1609, sig A3r; *Hope's Major Practicks, 1608–33*, 2 vols, ed J A Clyde, Edinburgh: The Stair Society, 1937–1938), vol I, 1–5; Sir George Mackenzie of Rosehaugh, *The Institutions of the Law of Scotland*, Edinburgh: John Reid, 1684, 3–8; NLS, Adv MS 25.6.1, fols 8r–9v.

61 In addition to the works just cited, see Sir James Dalrymple of Stair, *The Institutions of the Law of Scotland*, Edinburgh: Printed by the heir of Andrew Anderson, 1681, 14 and 96, and British Library, Sloane MS 3828, fol 133r.

62 Mackenzie, for instance, felt bound to reach this conclusion repeatedly in his *Observations on the Acts of Parliament*, Edinburgh: Printed by the Heir of Andrew Anderson, 1686.

63 This point will be returned to in the next paragraph.

64 Sir John Nisbet of Dirleton, *Some Doubts and Questions in the Law, Especially of Scotland*, Edinburgh: Printed by George Mosman, 1698, 134; Sir James Stewart of Goodtrees, *Dirleton's*

to the law *quo urbs Roma utitur* was taken to mean that when no statute or custom could be applied directly, extended by analogy or supplemented from the laws of comparable nations, attention was to turn at last to the civil law. While this left room for discussion of the relative standing of the civil, canon and feudal laws, it was usually agreed that their ranking depended on which area of law was under investigation.

Although reminiscent to some degree of how lawyers were taught to handle their sources in the medieval universities, the instruction provided by early modern writers on Scots law was significantly different. "In this kingdom", wrote Thomas Craig, in a hugely influential book completed at the start of the seventeenth century, "we are bound by the laws of the Romans to the extent that they agree with the laws of nature and correct reasoning".[65] This meant that instead of the civil law being treated as a standard of *ratio scripta* against which other laws could be appraised, it had itself to be appraised against another standard.[66] It also meant that while assistance could be derived from the works of modern doctors who read the Roman texts more critically than their predecessors had done, it was Scots lawyers themselves who were ultimately responsible for the appraisal of their sources. Since the Scottish universities were not to develop active faculties of law until the eighteenth century, it seemed important to writers like Craig for the College of Justice to be conceived of as a centre of learning in which a consensus could be formed on whether particular provisions of the civil law were reasonable or equitable.[67] It was as an admirer of Craig that Nisbet urged his colleagues to scrutinise the learned laws. "As to lawyers and jurisconsults", he wrote, *"turpe est sine lege loqui, et ubi leges silent,* they cannot but be silent".[68] The significance of learning in the civil law for him was that it enabled advocates and judges to express opinions in the absence of local sources, for "by reason of the great equity of it, in questions *de iure privato*, tho it has not the force of law with us, yet it is of great authority and use in cases not determined either by statute or custom".[69] Even if Roman

---

Doubts and Questions in the Law of Scotland Resolved and Answered, Edinburgh: J Watson, 1715, 217.

65 *Ius feudale*, 52–53.

66 Scottish thinking was influenced especially by the writings of practitioners in France, where prospective advocates tended to study law until the 1670s. After that they studied increasingly in the Netherlands (J W Cairns, "Importing our lawyers from Holland: Netherlands influences on Scots law and lawyers in the eighteenth century", in G G Simpson (ed), *Scotland and the Low Countries, 1124–1994*, East Linton: Tuckwell Press, 1996, 136–153).

67 *Ius feudale*, 52–55.

68 *Some Doubts and Questions*, 138.

69 That Nisbet took a contrary view of "questions of state and government" is consistent with the

law was only "the municipal law of that people", when found to be equitable it was something on which properly legal opinions could be based. It was because Nisbet hoped to see the law developed through the exchange of such opinions that he believed new customs ought to be fashioned exclusively through decisions founded on learned disputation.[70] Stair also emphasised the importance of forensic debates in a treatise he wrote, but he did not believe their purpose was to find existing law in the equitable principles of the civil law.[71] As he saw it, the civil law provided no more than a particularly impressive example of how natural equity might be manifested in positive law. Presenting a Hobbesian account of the need for laws to be made through the exercise of sovereign authority, he maintained that the lords of session exercised the requisite authority in deciding the cases brought before them, and that if their decisions received approval, they would give rise to new customs. For Stair, the law of Scotland would ideally take shape through a combination of either judicial decisions and popular approval or popular customs and judicial approval.[72]

The divergence between the approaches to legal research and reasoning encouraged by Nisbet and Stair may seem to resemble the divergence sometimes discerned between an earlier and a later *usus modernus* in Germany, where Hermann Conring is credited with making the pivotal discovery that the civil law had never been authoritative simply as imperial law.[73] Whatever may have been happening in Germany, however, there was no linear progression in Scotland from an earlier to a later approach. The situation there resembles more closely the periods of "revolutionary science" described in a justly celebrated work by Thomas Kuhn.[74] In periods of "normal science",

comment in Wijffels, "Early-modern literature in international law", 42, that discussion of public law was "largely abandoned" in the *usus modernus*.

70 Those who thought like Craig and Nisbet tended to associate the reference in the *Digest* to *consuetudo aut res perpetuo iudicatae* (D.1.3.38) with the reference to *disputatio fori* (D.1.2.2.5), and to take the statement that approval of local customs should first be looked for in *iudicia contradicta* (D.1.3.34) to mean that they should be treated as law only if approved in court decisions.

71 This reading of Stair's *Institutions* is worked out, at perhaps inordinate length, in Ford, *Law and Opinion in Scotland*.

72 This view of how laws should be made was consistent with a political theory expounded in several treatises by presbyterian authors, including James Stewart, who had been Stair's apprentice at the bar.

73 J Schröder, "Legal scholarship: The theory of sources and methods of law", in Pihlajamäki, Dubber and Godfrey, *Oxford Handbook of European Legal History*, 551–565, at 562–563.

74 T S Kuhn, *The Structure of Scientific Revolutions*, 3rd edn, Chicago: University of Chicago Press, 1996. "Whatever the merits of his later work", it has aptly been remarked, "the early Kuhn is still worth mining for insights" (T Nickles, "Kuhn, historical philosophy of science and case-based reasoning", (1998) 6 *Configurations*, 51–85, at 52).

Kuhn explained, research is conducted within communities that are both institutionally and intellectually homogeneous. Not only do scientists work in the same laboratories, publish their findings in the same journals and so on, but they also conduct their research in accordance with the same "paradigms", recognising certain models of how research ought to be conducted and grounding their endeavours on shared assumptions.[75] In revolutionary periods scientists may continue to deal with shared data, and to work in the same institutional settings, but they develop new paradigms that are incompatible with each other and compete for acceptance. Intellectual divisions tend to emerge in times of crisis, when scientists are troubled by anomalous data, become dissatisfied with working practices and presuppositions, and begin to devise alternatives. A scientific revolution will occur if a new paradigm achieves dominance, but before this happens other paradigms may also emerge and gain adherents.[76] Although in retrospect it may seem that one dominant paradigm replaced another, historians will often find that the transition was a great deal more complicated, and that any appearance of continuous advance towards the present, accelerated by occasional breakthroughs, is in reality an illusion.[77]

A sense of crisis can be seen to pervade a series of attempts to reform the law of Scotland. As early as 1426 the three estates assembled in Parliament, concerned that cases raised before the courts were being "prolongit wranguisly in scath and prejudice of the party and fraude of the law", appointed a commission to "se and examyn the bukis of law of this realme".[78] The commission seems to have proposed legislation designed to prevent the pleading of "frivolus and fraudful excepciounis", but half a century later the need was still felt for "the mending of the lawis".[79] The particular problem

---

75 I Hacking, "Paradigms", in R J Richards and L Daston (eds), *Kuhn's Structure of Scientific Revolutions at Fifty: Reflections on a Science Classic*, Chicago: University of Chicago Press, 2016, 96–110. The term "paradigm" is used in a Kuhnian sense in both van den Bergh, *Life and Work of Gerard Noodt*, 328, and A Wijffels, "Early-modern scholarship on international law", in A Orakhelashvili (ed), *Research Handbook on the Theory and History of International Law*, Cheltenham: Edward Elgar Publishing, 2011, 23–60, at 45.

76 Since Stair was committed to the presbyterian cause that triumphed in 1690, and Nisbet to the episcopalian establishment it displaced, it may be significant that paradigm shifts have been likened to changes of religious belief (T S Drønen, "Scientific revolution and religious conversion: A closer look at Thomas Kuhn's theory of paradigm-shift", (2006) 18 *Method and Theory in the Study of Religion*, 232–253).

77 D Hollinger, "T S Kuhn's theory of science and its implications for history", (1973) 78 *American Historical Review*, 370–393.

78 RPS 1426/13.

79 H L MacQueen, "Pleadable brieves, pleading and the development of Scots law", (1986) 4 *Law and History Review*, 403–422, at 414.

perceived then was "the gret diverseite now fundin in diverse bukis put in be diverse persones that ar callit men of law", and the solution proposed was to have copies of the "auld lawes" and of "statutis" passed more recently "put in a volum", with those who "will use practik" informed that they must "use nane uthir lawis as for the lawis of this realme bot thai that ar fundin in that buke".[80] No authorised version of the written laws of Scotland was produced at this time, yet almost a century was to pass before demands for reform resurfaced, perhaps because in the meantime the lords of session had effectively reduced the relevance of local "practick" by comparing it critically with the "theorick" taught in the schools of civil and canon law.[81] It was surely no coincidence that the next appointment of a commission "to see and examinat the bukis of law" occurred at the same time as papal authority was abrogated in Scotland.[82] Although an authorised edition of parliamentary legislation was then printed, two further commissions were appointed in the later sixteenth century "anent the sichting, collectioun and reformatioun of the lawis of this realme".[83] The problem perceived by this stage was "the harme quhilk this commoune weill sustenis throw want of a perfyte writtin law, quhairupoun all jugeis may knaw how to proceid and decerne", and the commissioners were instructed to examine not only "the bukis of law" and "actis of parliament" but also the "decisionis befoir the sessioun", from which they were to "draw the forme of the body of oure lawis, alsweill of that quhilk is alreddy statute as thay thingis that were meit and convenient to be statute". Notwithstanding the printing of both an updated edition of parliamentary legislation in 1597 and editions of the old books of law in 1609, several further commissions were appointed to reform the law during the seventeenth century.[84] In view of the continuing need for "ane

---

80 RPS 1469/34 and 1473/7/17. See too RPS 1450/1/21.

81 A L Murray, "Sinclair's Practicks", in A Harding (ed), *Law-Making and Law-Makers in British History*, London: Royal Historical Society, 1980, 90–104.

82 *The Actis and Constitutiounis of the Realme of Scotland*, ed Edward Henryson, Edinburgh, 1566, sig A2; *The Acts of the Parliaments of Scotland*, 12 vols, ed T Thomson and C Innes, Edinburgh, 1814–1875, vol III, 140. It is suggested in J W Cairns, T D Fergus and H L MacQueen, "Legal humanism and the history of Scots law: John Skene and Thomas Craig", in J MacQueen (ed), *Humanism in Renaissance Scotland*, Edinburgh: Edinburgh University Press, 1990, 48–74, at 51, that attempts to codify the local law, in Scotland as in France, were inspired by the *mos Gallicus*, though how this could have been true of a movement that started, in both places, in the fifteenth century is not explained.

83 RPS, A1575/3/7 and 1578/7/18. See too RPS 1587/7/156 and 1592/4/67.

84 *The Register of the Privy Council of Scotland*, 2nd series, 8 vols, ed D Masson and P Hume Brown, Edinburgh: General Register House, 1899–1908, vol IV, 137–139; *The Earl of Stirling's Register of Royal Letters Relative to the Affairs of Scotland and Nova Scotia from 1615 to 1635*, 2 vols, ed C Rogers, Edinburgh (printed for private circulation), 1885, vol II, 592 and

certane and constant course in all the supreme courts and justice seats",
and of "the many prejudices which arise from the great number of useless,
indistinct and undigested laws", the commissioners were to examine the old
books, acts of parliament and decisions of the supreme courts, were to weed
out "such actes and statuites as ar abrogat or become in desuetude", and
were "to collect and sett downe the haill customes and generall consuetudes
inviolablie observit". Nevertheless, the law remained unreformed in 1707,
when it was understood that there would be no further opportunity to codify
the private law of Scotland.[85]

There is little evidence that lawyers shared the desire of laymen to have
the whole law set down in legislation. Although they gave priority to legislation in their research, and assisted in the production of editions of written laws, their response to the recurring concerns about the obscurity and
uncertainty of Scots law, and about the apparent arbitrariness of judicial
decisions, was to draw attention to their handling of unwritten laws in the
books they produced primarily for their colleagues.[86] It is scarcely surprising
that laymen found these books less than reassuring, and continued to call for
the codification of the law, given that different lawyers recommended different approaches to legal research, and that they all expected legal development to involve phases of uncertainty. On the one hand, while lawyers like
Nisbet maintained that decisions were not arbitrary when grounded on the
equitable provisions of the civil law, because they had abandoned the notion
that the civil law was by definition equitable, there was room for disagreement about the binding force of particular provisions until lawyers arrived at
a consensus about their equitable character.[87] On the other hand, while lawyers like Stair maintained that "a fixed and known custome" could be "wrung
out from their debates upon particular causes", they expected it to take
time for the decisions of the lords of session to give rise to rules recognised
as laws by litigants.[88] For lawyers like Nisbet, when questions could not be

639–640; RPS A1630/7/49, A1630/7/59, 1633/6/47, 1649/1/306, 1681/7/52, 1695/5/31 and
1695/5/192.

85 J D Ford, "The legal provisions in the acts of union", (2007) 66 *Cambridge Law Journal*, 106–
141, at 126–127.

86 As is pointed out in Ford, *Law and Opinion in Scotland*, 37–38, 44, 48–49, 53–54 and 374–379,
legal literature was often produced or published in response to the appointment of reform
commissions.

87 J D Ford, "Conciliar authority and equitable jurisdiction in early-modern Scotland", in A M
Godfrey (ed), *Law and Authority in British Legal History, 1200–1900*, Cambridge: Cambridge
University Press, 2016, 140–169.

88 *Institutions*, 11. As he explained more fully in a second edition of his treatise, published in
1693, Stair took the willingness of litigants to take advantage of the developing practice of the

answered through recourse to the learned laws, there was no option but to wait for Parliament to create a new law.[89] For lawyers like Stair, the lords of session had the sovereign authority to make arbitrary decisions, based on considerations of "expediency" as much as "equity", which they had to do whenever they lacked a local statute or custom to apply.[90] Stair himself believed that the edict *Nautae, caupones, stabularii* had been received into the customary law of Scotland for its "utilitie" or "expediencie", which had remained open to discussion until the custom became fixed and known, whereas for Nisbet and his followers the edict could only have been given effect to begin with in the belief that it was equitable, which meant for them that it was already being recognised as a binding law.[91] Although superficially similar, the approaches taken by these lawyers were not merely inconsistent but were, in Kuhn's terms, incommensurable with each other.[92] Lawyers used the same vocabulary in talking about the same sources, yet they tended to "talk through each other", which resulted in debates of the type reviewed in the first part of this chapter.[93] Lay observers had reason to complain that the handling of the disputes they raised before the lords of session was so confused as to be incomprehensible, and it must be wondered whether it would increase the comprehension of observers today if the label *usus modernus* were applied to the thinking of all the lawyers who practised in the early modern court. The views of Stair and his followers were as different from those of Nisbet and his followers as those were from the views of Sinclair and his followers in the early sixteenth century. If the *usus modernus* needs to be distinguished from the *mos Italicus* then, by the same token, distinctions need to be drawn between different modern perspectives, and it is actually arguable that Stair differed more in his thinking from Nisbet than Nisbet did from Sinclair.[94] A pattern familiar to legal historians may be taken to run from a customary paradigm – in which the law was essentially what people believed it to be – through a learned paradigm – in which the law was essentially what experts believed it to be – towards a legislative

court to provide the *tacitus consensus populi* from which customary law derived some of its authority.

89 Nisbet, *Some Doubts and Questions*, 134.
90 Stewart, *Dirleton's Doubts and Questions*, 217.
91 *Institutions*, 143–145.
92 I Demir, "Incommensurabilities in the work of Thomas Kuhn", (2008) 39 *Studies in the History and Philosophy of Science*, 133–142.
93 For a clear example, compare the uses of the expression *sustinendum iudicium* in the passages cited supra, this chapter, notes 89–90.
94 The response in Ford, *Law and Opinion in Scotland*, was to restrict use of the label to lawyers like Nisbet, although this may not be consistent with usage elsewhere.

paradigm – in which the law was essentially what lawmakers declared it to be.[95] Whereas Nisbet and Sinclair promoted different kinds of learned paradigm, Stair firmly rejected the idea that law could be found in the consensus of experts and insisted instead that there could be no law without the exercise of sovereign authority. Yet Stair did not promote a legislative paradigm, for he expressed a strong preference for customary over statutory law making.[96] A legislative paradigm would eventually be established in the nineteenth century, but the views of early modern lawyers cannot be plotted neatly on a continuum from the medieval to the modern.[97] It was a competition between a customary and a learned model of legal research and development that remained to be played out during the eighteenth century.[98]

95 The history of Roman law, for example, clearly followed this pattern, which does not mean that custom gave way to jurisprudence which then gave way to legislation, but that the ways in which these sources were related to each other changed as each type of law achieved dominance over the rest.

96 Custom was certainly more important in early modern Scotland than is suggested in R Houston, "Custom in context: Medieval and early modern Scotland and England", (2011) 211 *Past & Present*, 35–76, at 38–45.

97 Not only was the absolute authority of the British Parliament recognised, but *rationes decidendi* came to be regarded as strictly binding rules, and juristic opinions expressed in certain books (including, ironically, Stair's *Institutions*) were taken to enjoy a similar authority.

98 The institutional setting is explored in J Finlay, *The Community of the College of Justice: Edinburgh and the Court of Session, 1687–1808*, Edinburgh: Edinburgh University Press, 2012, but much remains to be done in exploring the intellectual commitments of practitioners in the court.

3 Legal Authorities in Castilian Courts' Practice: *Decisiones* and *Consilia* to Study the *Arbitrium Iudicis*

*Javier García Martín**

* Proyectos de investigación DER 2017-83881-C2-1-P, and DER 2017-84733-R. I would like to thank Professors Carlos Garriga and Remedios Morán and Doctor Dámaso de Lario for having read and commented upon this text.

A. CASTILIAN *DECISIONES* AND *CONSILIA* IN THE EARLY MODERN PERIOD: AN EXCEPTION TO THE RULE?

A positive judgment about *decisiones* (law reports), such as Muratori's regarding Italy, cannot be found among Castilian legal authors of the Enlightenment. Although critical of legal literature in general, he shows himself to be more favourable to Italian books on supreme courts' *decisiones* than on *consilia*.[1] The genre was so unusual in Castile that it was likely to have been rarely considered. Nevertheless, it would be unfair to say that lawyers in eighteenth-century Castile did not take into consideration legal comments of the type, particularly, those written in the seventeenth century by two prominent authors, Juan Bautista de Larrea (1589–1645) and José Vela de Oreña (1588–1643). They were law professors at the University of Salamanca and then magistrates at the *Chancillería* [High Court] of Granada,[2] who wrote two outstanding doctrinal works on Granada Court's *decisiones*, reprinted several times.[3]

---

1 "Quanto poscia alle decisioni, queste senza fallo meritano più stima e riverenza, che i consigli e le allegazioni de i Consulenti", Muratori, Ludovico Antonio, *Dei difetti della giurisprudenza*, Venezia, Giambattista Pasquali, 1743, 52. See M G Renzo di Villata, "Tra consilia, decisiones e tractatus . . . Le vie della conoscenza giuridica nell'età moderna" (2008) 81 *Rivista di Storia del Diritto Italiano*, 15–76, at 48.

2 M P Alonso Romero, "Catedráticos salmantinos de Leyes y Cánones en las Chancillerías y Audiencias regias durante el siglo XVII", in M P Alonso Romero (ed), *Salamanca, escuela de juristas. Estudios sobre la enseñanza del Derecho en el Antiguo Régimen*, Madrid: Universidad Carlos III, 2012, 375–398, at 381, names Larrea but does not mention Vela. On Larrea, see P Volpini, *Lo spazio politico del "letrado". Juan Bautista Larrea magistrato e giurista nella monarchia di Filippo IV*, Bologna: Il Mulino, 2004, and J A López Nevot, "The *Visitatio Generalis Magistratuum* in the *Decisiones* of Juan Bautista Larrea (1639)", in I Czeguhn, J A López Nevot and A Sánchez Aranda (eds), *Control of Supreme Courts in Early Modern Europe*, Berlin: Duncker & Humblot, 2018, 149–173; I Merino, "Larrea y Tablares, Juan Bautista" in *Notitia Vasconiae. Diccionario de historiadores, juristas y pensadores políticos de Vasconia*, Madrid: Marcial Pons, 2019, vol I, 387–389. We have less information about Vela de Oreña: J A López Nevot, "Literatura jurídica y tribunales superiores en la Andalucía del Barroco" in M L López-Guadalupe and J J Iglesias Rodríguez (eds), *Realidades conflictivas. Andalucía y América en la España del Barroco*, Seville: Universidad de Sevilla, 2012, 429–456. Larrea was a doctor of laws from the University of Salamanca and had held a temporary chair in civil law, while Vela had held it in canon law: Nicolás Antonio, *Biblioteca Hispana Nova*, Martriti: apud Joachinum de Ibarra, 1783–1788, vol I, 648 and vol II, 822–823; José Rezábal y Ugarte, *Biblioteca de los escritores que han sido individuos de los seis Colegios Mayores: de San Ildefonso de la Universidad de Alcalá, de Santa Cruz de Valladolid, de San Bartolomé, de Cuenca, San Salvador de Oviedo y del Arzobispo de la de Salamanca*, Madrid: Imprenta de Sancha, 1805, 180 and 411. I would like to thank Dr Dámaso de Lario for his references and information about these authors.

3 Juan Bautista de Larrea, *Novae decisiones Sacri Regii Senatus Granatensis*, Lugduni: Iacobi et Petri Prost, 1636, and *Novarum decisiones Sacri Regii Senatus Granatensis Regni Castellae*, Lugduni: Jacobi et Petri Prost, 1639. They were reprinted several times (Turnoni, 1647 (vol I), Lugduni, 1658 (vol II), 1679 and 1729), but always outside Spain. For the first volume (*Novae decisiones*) I am using the first edition of 1636, but for the second volume (*Novarum decisiones*)

On the other hand, in the second half of the eighteenth century, the priest and lawyer Juan Francisco de Castro (1721–1790) – the Spanish Muratori so to speak, – still found it useful to collect case laws in a book so that they could be found easily "among legal norms and many other books". The main reason for doing so, according to him, was that case law was increasing by the day.[4] However, in so admitting, Castro did not hesitate to quote Larrea, among other authors, to criticise lower-court judges who did not issue sentences according to *allegata et probata*; only the prince and the supreme courts could judge exceptionally *cum arbitrium*, provided they did not diverge much (*"con discretos rompimientos"*) from what had been alleged and proved earlier. For Castro, the problem with law reports was the misunderstandings that they caused in those less-instructed jurists who tended to consider the authors' arguments as the main raison for a judgment.[5]

Larrea was not the only one to receive attention from eighteenth-century Castilian lawyers. Vela de Oreña's work, for instance, was considered by Agustín Fernando Sanz y Constanzo, a lawyer at the Royal Council, as a good guide for understanding the differences between *ius commune* and Castilian law.[6] Nevertheless, it is a fact that we have found only a small number of law reports from Castile in the Modern period.[7] Although words

I opted for a later edition (*Novarum Decisionum Granatensium Pars secunda, editio postrema*, Lyon: sumptibus Deville Fratrum et Ludov. Chalmette, 1736), as it is digitised and therefore more easily accessible to the reader. José Vela de Oreña, *Dissertationum juris controversi in Hispalensi Senatu*: Granatae: apud Vicentium Aluarez à Mariz, 1638, and *Dissertationum juris controversi tam in Hispalensi quad Granatensi Senatu secundus tomus* . . . Granatae: apud Baltasarem de Bolibar, 1653. Vela's work was then reprinted in Lyon (1675) and Geneva (1726 and 1761). For Vela de Oreña, I am using the 1726 Geneva edition.

4 Cfr Juan Francisco de Castro, *Discursos críticos sobre las Leyes y sus intérpretes en que se demuestra la incertidumbre de éstos y la necesidad de un nuevo y metódico cuerpo de Derecho para la recta administración de Justicia*, Madrid: Joachim Ibarra, 1765, lib II, disc 7, 279–282. Previously, Gerardo Ernesto Frankenau [*sed* Juan Lucas Cortés], *Sagrados Misterios de la Justicia hispana* [Sacra Themidis Hispaniae Arcana, 1703], Madrid: Centro de Estudios Constitucionales, 1993, 208–209.

5 Ibid, lib III, disc 2–10. Other references to Larrea can be found in lib II, disc 7, 282 and 289.

6 Cfr Agustín Fernando Sanz y Costanzo, *Glosa expedita ó índice general de la Nueva Recopilación en la qual se demuestran por el orden y método de la glosa puesta en las ediciones de 1745, 1772 y 1775 las leyes y autos acordados*, Madrid: Joachim Ibarra, 1779, xvij.

7 Other authors can be added to those that we are taking into consideration. Thus, the lawyer Gómez de León, *Informationum decisionum et responsorum juris Centuria*, Hispali: excudebat Petri Martínez, 1564; Lorenzo Matheu y Sanz, *Tractatus de re criminali sive controversiarum usufrequentium in causis criminalibus cum earum decisionibus* . . ., Lugduni: sumptibus Petri Anisso, 1672, on the basis of judgments from the *Sala de Alcaldes de Casa y Corte* as a part of the *Council of Castille*; for Spanish America see Juan Francisco de Montemayor, *Excubationes semicentum ex decisionibus Regiae Chancellariae Sancti Dominici insulae, vulgo dictae Española, totius Novi Orbis primates compaginatas*, Mexici: apud Franciscum Rodriguez Lupercio, 1667 (the last one being just legal records and not law reports).

do not always condition contents, Larrea and Vela de Oreña were two of the few Castilian magistrates who used *"decisions"* in the titles of their books. Even historians disagree as to whether Larrea's book should be properly regarded as *decisiones* literature. Thus, if some authors describe Larrea's *Novae Decisiones* as the only single law report book in Castile,[8] J M Scholz, who does not define such books on the basis of their titles, places Larrea's work among the *questiones forenses*. In his view, *decisiones* were collections based on case law, while q*uestiones forenses* were disputable questions for which different judgments come to be quoted.[9]

Despite the intense historiographical debate about law reports as a genre, the term will be used here in a broad sense. It has been pointed out that the collections of *decisiones* and *consilia* all over Europe are case-law books which, while clearly an expression of different traditions, had no official *status* and were conceived for the private use of judges, law students and legal practitioners.[10] That is why we will not make a distinction between *reports* and *decisiones* on the basis of the role assigned to precedent.

However, beyond these historiographical debates, a question remains: why was the genre so unsuccessful in Castile during the seventeenth century, unlike in the kingdoms and territories of the Crown of Aragon and Spanish Italy? Perhaps it can be explained by the success of other genres such as *comments* on statutes (*lex*), particularly the so-called *"Leyes de Toro"* (1505), a collection of eighty-three laws dealing mostly with property and inheritance and, as such, the very basis of private law in Castile until the Civil Code (1889).[11] According to D Ibbetson and A Wijffels, case law "might have been admitted as a source of law only where other sources (the learned laws, local statutory laws, custom) were silent or inconclusive".[12]

---

8 A M Barrero, sv "Decisionistas", in M Artola (ed), *Enciclopedia de Historia de España*, Madrid, Espasa Calpe, 1988, vol VII, 390. Neither Barrero nor Scholz take into consideration Vela de Oreña's work. The same discussion is held, in any case, about Vela. For Barrientos Grandón, Vela's work should be considered among the *questiones disputatae* (J Barrientos Grandón, "Derecho común y derecho indiano en el reino de Chile", *Memoria X Congreso del Instituto Internacional de Historia del Derecho Indiano*, vol I, México, 1995, 133–159, at 151), while for López Nevot he should be considered as a law-reports author (J A López Nevot, "Literatura jurídica" 436, n 40].

9 J M Scholz, sv "Spanien" in H Coing (ed) *Handbuch der Quellen und Literatur der neueren Europäischen Privatrechtsgeschichte*, vol II: *Neuere Zeit (1500–1800). Das Zeitalter des Gemeinen Rechts*, München: C H Beck'sche Verlagsbuchhandlung, 1976, 1299–1302, at 1301.

10 D Freda, "'Law Reporting' in Europe in the Early-Modern Period: Two Experiences in Comparison" (2009) 20 *Journal of Legal History*, 263–278, at 269–270.

11 J García Martín, "*Leges de Toro*. Construcciones interpretativas e historiográficas" (2006) 1 *e-Legal History Review*, 1–70.

12 D Ibbetson and A Wijffels, "Case law in the Making: The Techniques and Methods of Judicial

Nevertheless, it cannot be accidental that both Larrea and Vela were sanctioned by the government while fulfilling their responsibilities as magistrates before they wrote their *decisiones*. We can infer, therefore, that they wrote their books in defence of both the work of the *Chancillería* of Granada, repeatedly inspected throughout the seventeenth century,[13] and of their own work as judges of the tribunal. That could explain why they decided to write on a subject so difficult to deal with, since only those magistrates that had nothing to prove about their own science were supposed to be able to write such works.[14] In fact, for the seventeenth-century librarian Pedro Coello, to write his *Novae Decisiones* was the main reason for Larrea's success in the last years of his career, as he was promoted to the Council of Castile, the highest court of justice.[15]

By and large, magistrates in the high courts, who usually owned large libraries – and not only of legal books – were considered role models for the *letrado* (legal expert) of sixteenth and seventeenth-century Castile, unlike in the following century, when the model was the practising lawyer.[16] In early modern times, magistrates were supposed to be the only ones who did not need to follow either the advocates' *allegationes* or the *consilium sapientes* in

Records and Law Reports", in A. Wijffels (ed), *Case Law in the Making* vol I: *Essays*, Berlin: Duncker & Humblot, 1997, 13–35, at 35.

13 J A López Nevot, "Visitatio", 155 and 158. After a *visita* (inspection) carried out on the Chancillería of Granada in 1628–1629, Larrea was convicted on six counts, mainly related to the seduction of a maiden and a widow, which – the inspector argued – had influenced his judgment as a judge. See P Volpini *Lo spazio*, 29–34, and doc n 1, 291–296. It is significant that, in Dec 98 of Larrea's second volume (*Novarum Decisionum*), devoted to the *visita*, Larrea argued against a secret and irregular trial (*pesquisa* of *residencia*) carried out against a magistrate for his private behaviour beyond the public exercise of his function (ibid, 221, nr 15). The text was translated into Spanish and spread over as a printed paper. See P Volpini, "Por la autoridad de los ministros: observaciones sobre los letrados en una alegación de Juan Bautista Larrea (primera mitad del siglo XVII)" (2005) 30 *Cuadernos de Historia Moderna*, 63–84, esp 351. For his part, Vela de Oreña was condemned between 1623 and 1632 for having revealed information about court decisions and the votes of the judges. Cfr J A López Nevot, "Literatura jurídica", 437–438, and J A Pérez Juan, "La visita de Ramírez Fariña a la Audiencia de Sevilla (1623–1632)" (2002) 29 *Historia, Instituciones, Documentos*, 357–405, at 391.

14 M N Miletti, *Stylus Judicandi. Le raccolte di "decisiones" del Regno di Napoli in età moderna*, Napoli: Jovene editori, 1998, 103–106.

15 Cfr Pedro Coello, "Al Doctor Don Ivan Bautista de Larrea", in F de Pradilla, *Suma de las leyes penales*, Madrid: en la imprenta del Reyno, 1639, *proemium*. This dedica disappeared in the second edition of 1644: P. Volpini, *Lo spazio*, 37.

16 J P Dedieu, "La muerte del letrado", in F J Aranda Pérez, *Letrados, juristas y burócratas en la España moderna*, Toledo: Universidad de Castilla-La Mancha, 2005, 479–512, and J García Martín, "Las bibliotecas y las alegaciones jurídicas impresas de los abogados en Castilla (siglos XVII y XVIII). El problema de la *communis opinio*", in S Muñoz Machado (ed), *Historia de la abogacía española*, Pamplona: Aranzadi, 2015, vol I, 717–765.

their sentences, as J Menocchio (1532–1607) has pointed out.[17] That is why, being part of the king's supreme courts (where only the best jurists would reach), their works enjoyed a higher authority.

No doubt political power in Castile played a role in promoting some books over others, insofar as censorship was a main feature of the Spanish Catholic Monarchy since the Reformation.[18] But is this the main reason why law reports are so scarce in Castile? Or should an explanation be looked for in the Castilian hierarchy of legal sources?

We must not lose sight of the fact that two of the main legal norms in that kingdom – the *Ordenamiento de Alcalá* (1348) (l. 28.1) and the *Leyes de Toro* (1505) (l. 1) – gave priority to royal laws (*pragmáticas* and *leyes*) over local customary laws (*fueros*), conferring moreover to the Castilian kings – as the "heirs" of the Visigothic kings – the right to finally decide in a case law for which there was no royal or customary law (i.e. *ley* or *fuero*), the so-called *"ius interpretandi"*. If that has been traditionally the main reason put forward by Spanish historiography for establishing a central difference between the Crown of Castile (more normative and without motivated sentences) and the Crown of Aragon (more judicial and open to *ius commune*), the claim has been losing force in recent times.[19]

Legal historians have proved that the king's *ius interpretandi* in Castile did not lead to the "expulsion" of the *ius commune* from the courts to the benefit of royal law.[20] On the contrary, in the countries ruled by the *ius commune*, the fundamental basis for interpretation was the *argumentum ab auctoritate*. However, not every judge had the same authority. Hence the distinction recently proposed by some scholars between necessary authorities – the prince, the emperor, among others – and probable authorities, among which should be placed interpretation by judges and lawyers as learned men.[21] This

17 "iudice iudicare posse non expectato sapientis consilio", *Iacobi Mennochii . . . De arbitraris Ivdicvm Qvaestionibvs et cavsis*, Francofurti ad Moenum: apud Petrum Fabricium, impensis Sigismundi Feyrabend et Petri Longi, 1576, *quaestio* 23, n 4, fol 17r.

18 D de Lario and J García Martín, "La *impermeabilización ideológica* de Felipe II: cronología de una coyuntura (1558–1571)" (2014) 40 *Estudis*, 31–69.

19 See J M Pérez-Prendes, *Historia del Derecho español*, Madrid: Universidad Complutense, 2004, vol II, 1478–1479. As the author points out, it makes little sense to keep talking about "decisionismo" for the Crown of Castile and "pactismo" for the Crown of Aragón.

20 C Garriga, "La trama jurídica castellana a comienzos del siglo XVI (Notas y materiales)", in B González Alonso (ed), *Las Cortes y las Leyes de Toro de 1505*, Salamanca: Junta de Castilla y León, 2006, 299–379; and C Petit, "Derecho común y derecho castellano. Notas de literatura jurídica para su estudio" (1982) 50 *Tijdschrift voor Rechtsgeschiedenis*, 157–196.

21 D Ibbetson, "Authority and precedent", in M Godfrey (ed), *Law and authority in British Legal History*, Cambrige: Cambridge University Press, 2016, 63–69.

distinction was generally put forward by Castilian lawyers with regards to the
ius interpretandi from the beginning of the sixteenth century and continued
to be accepted during the seventeenth century as the lawyer F Bermúdez de
Pedraza (1576–c 1655) declared in his seventeenth-century *Arte legal*.[22]

Scholars invoked the distinction between necessary interpretation – that
only the king could establish – and probable interpretation, in which the
communis opinio doctoris could be sufficient to rule on a case, without
having to consult the king continuously.[23] Moreover, Castilian kings tried to
avoid "interpreting" the laws because the judgments they made based on the
ius interpretandi had retroactive effects.[24]

Thus, insofar as *decisions* – even in Castile – reflect the way in which
supreme courts interpret cases without a specific legal rule, it could be said
that they do not always follow the hierarchy of sources politically defined in
each kingdom. As happens all over Europe, they tend to follow some of the
rules established by the *ius commune* in support of the *arbitrium iudicis*.[25]

Arbitrium, no doubt, is linked to the word *interpretatio*. But only the
prince, as legislator, has the prerogative of transforming it in a legal norm,
thus, equating, as it were, *lex* and *arbitrium principis*. Otherwise, *arbitrium*
should be "regulated and adjustable", inasmuch as judicial discretion was
conditional upon a just and equitable resolution. In other words, the power
of a judge under *ius commune* was limited by three main parameters: *aequitas*, *iustitia* and *ratio*.[26] That does not mean, of course, that supreme court
decisions were free from political purposes. Larrea, for instance, mentions
an undated judgment about a *mayorazgo* (an entailed estate on the basis
of primogeniture) in which the *Chancillería* of Granada, *"nisi expresse de
judicio disponentis apparent"*, moved away from its previous interpretations
in favour (*voluisse*) of the *real* statute against the personal one. The Court,

22 Bermúdez de Pedraza, Francisco, *Arte legal para estvdiar la iurisprudencia*, Salamanca, En la
    Emprenta de Antonía Ramirez, viuda, 1612, 73. The distinction would have been established for
    the first time by the first commentators of the *Leyes de Toro*, Juan López de Palacios Rubios and
    Diego del Castillo. See J García Martín, *"Leges"*, 9–10 and 22.
23 J García Martín, "Las bibliotecas", 721–722.
24 Id, *"Leges* de Toro", 12 ff.
25 *"Iudex in dubiijs debet illam opinionem sequi quae pie causae, animae et conscientiae favet"*,
    states Rodrigo Suárez, judge of the Chancillería of Valladolid at the beginning of the sixteenth
    century. On the point that he followed, among others, the *Proemium ad Leges Fori* of Johannes
    Andreae (*Excelentissimae allegationes et consilia*, Vallisoleti: excudebat Didacus Fernández a
    Córdoba Bibliopolae (Colofón, Salmanticae: apud Ioannem et Andraeam Renaut), 1588), fol
    85r–v, n 28.
26 M Meccarelli, *Arbitrium. Un aspetto sistematico degli ordinamenti giuridici in età del diritto
    comune*, Milano: Giuffrè, 1998, 49, 53 and 71–72.

thus, decided to take into account goods instead of persons in order to establish the succession to that *mayorazgo*. The aim was to respect the founder's will – the judgment estates – but also, as Larrea himself explained, to look for the profit of the Spanish treasury.[27]

At any rate, although magistrates had decision-making *authority*, it should be noted that the word *authority* must be identified, at that moment, with the latin word *autoritas* and not with *auctoritas* – as E Spagnesi has pointed out – as *decisiones* under the *ius commune* were a part of *iurisprudentia* (an *art* and not a *science* as a form of interpretation) able to generate *stylus*, from which *authority* comes.[28] Thus, if it is true that *decisiones* developed as a gender without the personal *subtilitates* of a lawyer's *consilium*, they were not to be considered as official judgment collections, but as interpretations written by authors in their private capacity. In fact, they do not always mention records, data or the real name of the parties in the dispute.[29] In conclusion, all these books were legal doctrine not disconnected from academic exercises.[30] Continental-type law reports were, in the end, doctrinal works – *observationes*, according to Machado Cabral[31] – written by judges, normally considering a wider range of sources than other types of work, particularly collected judgments from the high courts that they could easily consult. However, they are not the only practice-oriented legal literature quoting supreme courts judgments in Castile. A number of magistrates like Diego de Covarrubias (1512–1577) or Juan Castillo de Sotomayor (1563–1640) did as much. They did not write law reports but their work had plenty of references to judgments.[32] Not to mention other practical works, such as

---

27 "et cum id respiciat bona, inde gravamen reale existimabitur, quia in ipsam dispositionem, ut salva sit, dirigitur" (Larrea, *Novarum Decisionum*, vol II, Dec 51, n 16–17, 4).

28 E Spagnesi, "Iurisprudentia, stilus, au(c)toritas" in Sbriccoli, Mario and Bettoni, Antonella (eds) *Grandi tribunali e Rote nell'Itala di Antico Regime*, Milano, Giuffrè, 1993, 574–604, 601–603.

29 Larrea, *Novarum Decisionum*, vol II, Dec 54, 24, normally uses common names like "'ex filiam Joannem nepotem' and 'filius Petrus testatoris'" (24). Also Dec 53 "Titius", 20, n 14.

30 Professors at the University of Salamanca in the sixteenth century included Diego de Covarrubias, J Castillo de Sotomayor, J Bautista Larrea, J Vela de Oreña and Gil de Castejón. Moreover, A Acevedo and J Gutierrez had also studied there. Cf S de Dios, "Tendencias doctrinales en la época de la jurisprudencia clásica salmantina" (2002) 47 *Salamanca. Revista de Estudios*, 285–311.

31 G C Machado Cabral, *Os decisionistas portugueses entre o direito comun e o direito patrio*, doctoral dissertation, Universidade de São Paulo, 2013, 79–80. See also Machado Cabral's contribution to this volume.

32 Diego de Covarrubias, *Practicarum quaestionum*, Salmanticae: Andreas à Portonarijs, 1556, and Juan Castillo de Sotomayor, *Quotidianarum Controversiarum Iuris*, 8 vols, Ludguni: sumptibus Lavr Anisson et Io Bapt Devenet, 1658. See S de Dios, "La doctrina regalista en el doctor Juan del Castillo Sotomayor" in *Facultades y Grados. X Congreso Internacional de Historia de las Universidades hispánicas*, Valencia: Universidad de Valencia, 2010, 303–350.

the collections of *allegationes* and *consilia sapientis judicialis* – the former *pro parte* and latter never *contra ius*[33] – written by some of the most prestigious magistrates[34] and lawyers[35] in Castile.

It is far more significant, however, that sometimes supreme courts did not hesitate to follow a *consilium* as *intepretatio*. Unsurprisingly, the authors underlined such an event in their works to demonstrate their recognised creativity.[36] For instance, we can find some examples in Juan Gutiérrez's (1535/40–1618) *consilia* and *allegationes* dealing with testamentary law and criminal law, successively reprinted until the first half of the seventeenth century.[37] Alfonso de Acevedo's (1518–1598) *consilia* seem also to be relevant, insofar as some of them carried an influence even in the *decisiones* of the closest court to the king in the realm, the Council of Castile.[38] Larrea himself recalled another of Acevedo's *consilium* with regards to the rights of natural sons as an authoritative argument for judgment in the *Chancillería*.[39]

Both, Gutiérrez and Acevedo , as well as M Salón de Paz (c 1565†) were, in any case, lawyers, not judges, promoted by royal power. It is interesting to note, however, that they were going to be remembered not for their *consilia* but for their commentaries on royal statutes: Salón de Paz on the *Leyes de Toro* and Acevedo and Gutiérrez on the *Nueva Recopilación* (*NR*), the official collection of Castile royal laws in early modern times (1567); commentaries always written in support of the royal laws.[40] Thus, Gutiérrez's *consilia*

---

33 A Romano, "Letteratura consiliare e formazione dei diritti privati europei: l'esperienza del diritto di famiglia siciliano tardomedievale" in M Ascheri, I Baumgärtner and J Kirshner (eds), *Legal Consulting in the Civil Law Tradition*, Berkeley: The Robbins Collection, 1999, 255–291, at 261, n 11.

34 See Martín de Azpilcueta, *Consiliorum et responsorum libri quinque iuxta ordinem decretalium*, Romae: ex Typographia Aloysi Zannetti, 1595 (1st edn, Methimnae Campi, 1555); Juan Bautista Valenzuela Velazquez, *Consilia sive juris responsa*, 2 vols, Coloniae Allobrogum: sumptibus Marci-Michaelis Bousquet et Sociorum, 1727 (1st edn, Naples 1618–1634).

35 See Marcos Salón de Paz, *Consilia seu iuris responsa decisiva*, Methymnae Campi, 1576; Alfonso de Azevedo, *Consilia sive responsa, post obitum autoris . . . congesta*, Vallisoleti: excudebat Ioannes a Bostillo, 1604; Juan Gutiérrez, *Consilia varia*, Salmanticae: excudebat Petrus Lasus, 1595.

36 L Lombardi, *Saggio sul diritto giurisprudenziale*, Milano: Giuffrè, 1975, 126.

37 I have consulted Joannis Gutiérrez, *Operum, Tomus octavus, seu repetitiones VI. Allegationes XIV: et consilia sive responsa LII*, Lugduni: apud, Ant Servant et socios, 1730, *alleg* 1, 182, n 31 (on a 1567 testamentary case in Plasencia), who explains how this *allegatio* was followed at each stage of the complex legal proceedings, and *alleg* 2, 185, n 16 (another *allegatio* that was only used in the first level of the lawsuit). See also ibid, cons 2, 219, n 30 (on testamentary law).

38 I have consulted Alfonso Azevedo, *Consilia*, Vallisoleti: Excudebat Ioannes à Bostillo, 1607, cons 35, n 55, fol 221v. However, his *consilium* on ecclesiastical benefit limits was approved only in part by the *Chancillería* of Valladolid.

39 Larrea, *Novae decisiones*, vol I, Dec 32, n 54, 256.

40 M P Alonso Romero, "Lectura de Juan Gutiérrez (c 1535/40–1618), un jurista formado en Salamanca" in id, *Salamanca*, 119–164.

would be reprinted as a part of his commentary to *NR*, the book that should define the legal order in Castile, while Acevedo's main commentary would be quoted for the promotion of royal statutes against customary law.[41]

According to P Gilli, it was only when the most important jurists started to join the supreme courts that the importance of *consilia*, compared to *decisiones*, began to decrease in Italy.[42] Certainly, in Castile, references to *consilia sapientes* tended to disappear in scholars' quotations but that did not mean that law reports replaced them as a more authoritative interpretation – the *communis opinio fori*.[43] It is an important difference.

A good way to check whether an author continued to be quoted at the end of seventeenth-century Castile would be to test the number of times – and the subjects – that he is mentioned in Castejón's *Alphabetum juridical* (1678). Gil de Castejón, a member of the Council of Castile and a former professor of law at the University of Salamanca, wrote a two-volume *commonplaces* book, as a dictionary and easy-to-consult work (*promptuario*) which was very successful.[44] However, as his entries were devoid of any reference to previous debates, they condemned any author not cited to oblivion.[45] Unsurprisingly, law reports – among them Larrea's and Vela's – but seldom *consilia*, continued to be quoted in the *Alphabetum*. Even so, in the first half of the eighteenth century, Larrea and Vela continued to be mentioned in Pedro Nolasco de Llano's comments on the *Leyes de Toro*, as an adapted Castilian version of a previous commentary written in Latin by Antonio Gómez (1501–1561) in the sixteenth century.[46]

By the end of the eighteenth century and beginning of nineteenth the situation, however, was very different. Sancho de Llamas Molina (1744–1829), the main *commentator* on the *Leyes de Toro*, quoted Larrea to contradict

41 In fact, A Azevedo declared himself opposed to accept any present or future customs contrary to royal statutes, *Commentariorum juris civils in Hispaniae Regias Constitutiones* (1583), Lyon: apud fratres Deville, 1737, vol I, *Nueva Recopilación* 2.1.3, n 17–20, 125.

42 P Gilli, "Les *consilia* juridiques de la fin de Moyen Âge en Italie: sources et problèmes" (2000) *Reti medievali*, available at: www.rmoa.unina.it/2102/1/RM-Gilli-Consilia.pdf (last accessed 28 January 2020), 1–11, at 9–10.

43 M Ascheri, *Tribunali, giuristi e istituzioni dal medioevo all'età moderna*, Bologna: Il Mulino, 1989, 89–93.

44 I have used Aegidio Castejón, *Alphabetum Juridicum, Canonicum, Civile, Theoricum, Practicum, Morale atque Politicum*, Matriti: ex Typographia Regia Joannen García Infançon, 1678, 2 vols. There are many references to Larrea and Vela on private and criminal law entries.

45 A M Hespanha, "Form and content in early modern legal books" (2008) 12 *Rechtsgeschichte*, 12–39, at 27.

46 Pedro Nolasco de Llano, *Compendio de los comentarios extendidos por el Maestro Antonio Gómez a las ochenta y tres Leyes de Toro*, Madrid: En la Imprenta de D Joseph Doblado, 1785. Larrea is quoted at 8, 39, 181, 237 and 279; Vela at 276, 295 and 327.

him. It so happens, for instance, in relation to *lex* 63, in which a ten-year period for the prescription of personal obligations was established but was increased to thirty years if a mortgage had also been set up. The debate between Castilian jurists was about the very moment that time should start accruing. According to Larrea[47] – and previously to A Acevedo – the period prescribed had to be reckoned from the moment that the obligation arose, not from the moment the debt was acknowledged in a written document. This meant that if the recognition came ten years after having set up the mortgage, it was not worth executing the debt as the deadline had already expired. If the acknowledgment was made fifteen years later, the prescription period could last up to twenty-five years, although, according to *lex* 63, that period should end after twenty years. Larrea informs us that there were dissenting decisions on the issue at the *Chancillería* of Granada.[48]

Given that uncertainty, Llamas Molina declares himself in favour of the principle *"non exemplis sed legibus judicandum est"*.[49] By so doing he accepted Vela's position to let the time accrue from the moment of the recognition of the debt.[50] According to Llamas, Larrea, following Donellus, had based his position on the intention of the parties, but at the end of the eighteenth century the only possible argument, Llamas argues, could be the statute (*lex*). However, Vela did not hesitate to take into account other statutes that had not been considered (*NR* 4.21.5).

It seems reasonable to conclude that Castilian *decisiones* literature is but the outcome of a period – mainly of the first half of the seventeenth century – in which the development of this type of legal literature in Aragon, Catalonia and Portugal (under the Spanish monarchy until 1640) had a significant importance.[51] In any case, Larrea's and Vela's works continued

---

47 Larrea, *Novae decisiones*, vol I, Dec 49, n 7, 413.
48 "Senatus visis actis decisione ad aliam Aulam ex discordia remissa, tandem decreuit in hoc casu non posse habere locum executionem post quindecim annos transactos à schedulae confectione . . . etsi nunc à debitore recognitio fieret", ibid, n 18, 415.
49 Sancho Llamas Molina, *Comentario crítico-jurídico-literal a las ochenta y tres leyes de Toro*, Madrid: Imprenta de Repullés, 1827, vol II, 207–208.
50 Vela de Oreña, *Dissertationum juris controversi*, vol I, disc 26, n 19.
51 Among the early Aragonese authors on *decisiones* mention should be made of Miguel del Molino (1513), Martín Monter de la Cueva (1598), Luis de Casanate (1606) and José Sesé y Piñol (1610–1612). Among the Catalan jurists, see Miguel Ferrer (1580), Jaime Cáncer (1594–1608), Luis de Peguera (1605), J P Fontanella (1639) and José Ramón (1628). As to the Portuguese ones see, for example, Antonio de Gama (1578), Álvaro Valasco (1588–1601), Jorge Cabedo (1602–1604), Belchior [Melchior] Febo (1619–1623) and Gabriel Pereira de Castro (1621). See A Pérez Martín and J-M Schulz, *Legislación y jurisprudencia en la España del Antiguo Régimen*, Valencia: Universidad de Valencia, 1978, 317–322; and G C Machado Cabral, *Os decisionistas*, 111–112.

to be quoted, at least until the end of the eighteenth century, as part of the Castilian legal authors whose innovative approaches were to be considered to confirm or reject *communis opinio*.

The interest in studying such works is twofold. On the one hand, to analyse the way in which the development of other types of legal *comments* made law reports less authoritative to define local law (*ius proprium*) – within, of course, the *ius commune*. On the other hand, to find out to what extent "foreign" authors – for *Chancillerías*' judgments ought only to be applied within the kingdom of Castile – came to be quoted in relation to *iura propria* and in which subjects.[52] In that respect, although continental-type law reports intend to justify *arbitrium juris* without paying much attention to precedents, as English ones did,[53] they provide a good source for the study of judicial changes throughout the period. We should look first, however, at the structure and image of Castilian High Courts.

B. CASTILIAN SUPREME COURTS AS "THE KING HIMSELF": THE ROYAL COUNCIL OF CASTILE AND THE *AUDIENCIAS* AND *CHANCILLERÍAS*

By and large historiography agrees that the peculiarity of the Castilian system at the beginning of the early modern times was the diversity of its supreme courts.[54] From the fourteenth century onwards there was a court council, the Royal Council of Castile, with both administrative and judicial functions, as well as a High Court, the so-called "*Corte y Chancillería*" (court and chancery) – or *Chancillería* – of Valladolid (1371), split into two at the beginning of the sixteenth century, when setting a *Chancillería* at Granada (from 1505). In the following years, other high courts, less important than the *Chancillerías*, were created: the *Reales Audiencias* of Galicia, Seville and the Canary Islands; and ten more in the Spanish Kingdoms of America.

This plurality was to be consolidated only from the beginning of the sixteenth century, after the *Comuneros* revolt of 1520–1521 that demanded a decentralised judicial system. No doubt, the Royal Council of Castile

---

52 A Wijffels, "*Orbis exiguus*, Foreign Legal Authorities in Paulus Chrisianeus's Law Reports", in S Dauchy, W Hamilton Bryson and M C Mirow (eds), *Ratio decidendi. Guiding Principles of Judicial Decisions*, vol II, Berlin: Duncker & Humblot, 2010, 37–62.

53 In England, the status of judicial precedents as a source of authority only began in the early Tudor period, and even then the courts were not considered bound to follow precedents. See, for example, N Duxbury, *The Nature and Authority of Precedent*, Cambridge, University Press, 2008, 33–35; and David Ibbetson, in this volume.

54 I Czeguhn, *Die kastilische Höchstgerichtsbarkeit*, Berlin: Dunker and Humblot, 2002, 82 ff.

remained the highest court of justice in the whole system, as it was the closest institution to the king, taking up most of the so-called "Court cases" (*casos de corte*),[55] as well as the most important lawsuits.[56] The tendency, however, from the end of the fifteenth century and the beginning of the sixteenth century (*Cortes de Madrid*, 1528, pet 5),[57] was to curtail the Royal Council's jurisdiction in favour of the *Chancillerías*, so as not to delay lawsuits. To that end, King Charles I of Castile issued a statue in 1533 to prevent the Royal Council from claiming jurisdiction on legal proceedings pending before the *Chancillerías*.[58] Curtailing the jurisdiction of the Royal Council was the starting point of the institutional development of the *Chancillerías* in Castile.

This legal change was quickly noticed by Castilian legal scholars, who did not hesitate to identify the *Chancillerías* with the king himself, giving them scope to judge beyond *allegata et provata*. In doing so, they took advantage of the first European *decisiones* authors. Already in the fifteenth century, Guy Pape (d 1477) had used the Roman concept of *"praetor"* to ascribe the French *Parlement* the capacity to create law *loco principis* and, at the beginning of the sixteenth century, Matteo d'Afflitto defined the Neapolitan Council as a *Senate*, to reinforce its authority.[59] Thus, we should not be surprised to see that, in the middle of the sixteenth century, the Castilian lawyer P Núñez de Avendaño (c 1490–c 1560), following

55 The so-called "Casos de corte" were lawsuits reserved to the royal jurisdiction. They were cases of particular gravity or significance (e.g. treason, murder, rape, counterfeiting of currency or documents, and so on). Initially, they were only criminal cases, but their scope expanded significantly over time (including, e.g., cases concerning widows and orphans), as a means of asserting royal power. See M P Alonso Romero, "El proceso penal en la Castilla moderna" (1996) 22 *Estudis. Revista de Historia Moderna*, 199–216.

56 C Garriga, "Iudex perfectus. Ordre traditionel et justice de juges dans l'Europa del *ius commune* (Couronne de Castilla, XVe–XVIIIe siècles)", in *Histoires des justices en Europe*, vol I: *Valeurs, representation, symboles*, Toulouse: Université Capitole, 2014–2015, 79–99, at 88–89.

57 "[Q]ue los de su Consejo real no entiendan en pleitos ordinarios e que los remitan a las chancillerías" (*Cortes de los Antiguos reinos de León y Castilla* [henceforth, CLC], Madrid, Establecimiento tipográfico de los Sucesores de Rivadeneyra, 1882, vol IV, 450).

58 "Instrucciones de Carlos I al presidente y los del Consejo que no avocasen pleitos frente a las Chancillerías" (the entire document is in S de Dios, *Fuentes para el estudio del Consejo Real de Castilla*, Salamanca: Universidad de Salamanca, 1986, 95 and 99), to be supplemented by a *ley* issued in the Cortes de Valladolid of 1548, pet 200, later collected in the *Ordenanzas de la Chancillería de Valladolid* (1566), fols 196v–198v. See C Garriga, "La consolidación de la jurisdicción suprema en Castilla", in I Czeguhn, S Lopez Nevot, A Aranda and J Weizen (eds), *Die Höchstgerichtsbarkeit im Zeitalter Karls V Eine vergleichende Betrachtung*, Baden-Baden: Nomos Verlagsgesellschaft, 2011, 133–176, at 151–158, and Id, "Estudio preliminar", in *Recopilación de las Ordenanzas de la Real Chancillería de Valladolid (1566)*, Madrid, Consejo General del Poder Judicial-Tribunal Supremo, 2007, 7–125, at 32–33.

59 U Petronio, "I Senati giudiziari" in *Il Senato nella storia. Il Senato nel Medioevo e nella prima età moderna*, Roma: Instituto Poligrafico e Zecca dello Stato, 1997, 268–451, at 385–390.

d'Afflitto – and also the humanist Bartholome de Cassiano in his *Catalogo Gloriae Mundi* (Lyon, 1546) – holds that the *Audiencias* (*"que vulgo apellatur Chancillerías"*) enjoyed such *plenitudo potestatis* that *"aequalis cum ipso Rege videtur"*, because *"Rex non potest de plenitudine potestatis tollere quod iussit Cancellaria"*.[60]

Since then, the *Chancillerías* began to be considered by Castilian scholars like the Council of Castile, the Senate of Milan or the *Sacro Regio Consiglio* of Naples – all of which were under Spanish rule – but also, the Roman Rota, the *Reichskammergericht* and the French *Parlements*.[61] The *Chancillerías* in fact acted as courts of first instance in both civil and criminal cases, in a variety of matters recorded in the *Ordenanzas*,[62] and also as appellate courts in claims against judgments rendered by local judges, mainly the *corregidores* (territorial judges with police responsibilities).[63] Thus, they were "de facto" High Courts.

According to Vela de Oreña, the Court (*Curia Principis*) – including both the Council of Castile and the *Chancillerías* within the concept – had to be thought of as *"locum patria communis"*, not because the Prince lived there but because they represented his person and his majesty "and everything is issued under his royal seal".[64] Nonetheless, there was an important difference between the two *Chancillerías*. Thanks to the report of the royal inspector (*visitador*) Francisco Sarmiento, sent by the king in 1575 to examine the *Chancillería* of Valladolid, we learn that this tribunal was considered to be above the *Chancillería* of Granada. The former was placed, as Sarmiento explains, closer to the king's court: due to this proximity, it was supposed to have a better *stylus*. Besides, the *Chancillería* of Valladolid

---

60 Pedro Nuñez de Avendaño, "Dictionarium Hispanum . . ." in Id, *Quadraginta responsa, qvibus qvam plurimae leges regiae explicantur*, Madrid, Apud Petrum Madrigal, 1593, fols 92r and 174r–v, sv "Canciller". Significantly, Nuñez de Avendaño was likely considered an authority by Neapolitan lawyers in the seventeenth century, see M N Miletti, *Stylus*, 128–129.

61 U Muessig, "Superior Courts in early-modern France, England and the Holy Roman Empire" in P Brand and J Getzler (eds), *Judges and Judging in the History of the Common Law and the Civil Law*, Cambridge: Cambridge University Press, 2012, 209–233.

62 *Recopilación de las Ordenanzas de la Real Audiencia y Chancillería de su Magestad, que reside en la villa de Valladolid (1566)* [hereinafter, OChV] *Estudio preliminar de C Garriga*, Madrid: Consejo General del Poder Judicial, 2007, book 4, titles 9–10, fols 160r–164v, and *Ordenanzas de la Real Chancillería de Granada (1601)* [hereinafter, OChG], Granada: Diputación, 1007, book I, title 11, fols 89r–90v, and book II, title 4, fols 176r ss.

63 C Garriga Acosta, "La Real Audiencia" in Payo Hernán, René and Sánchez Domingo, Rafael, *El Régimen de Justicia en Castilla y León: de Real Chancillería a Tribunal Superior. XXV Aniversario de Tribunal Superior de Justicia de Castilla y León*, Burgos: TSJCL-Junta de Castilla y León, 2014, 13–96, at 42.

64 Vela de Oreña, *Dissertationum juris controversi*, vol II, diss 39, n 49, 102, quoting the Castilian jurists Rodrigo Suárez (1440/60–1500/20) and Juan Yañez Parladorio (XVI cent).

dealt with more lawsuits than the *Chancillería* of Granada.[65] This could be a perfectly good reason to explain the development of a *decisiones* literature connected to the *Chancillería* of Granada – located farther away from the central power – instead of the *Chancillería* of Valladolid. That would be the case too for Lisbon, Milan or Naples.

At any rate, the increase in the number of cases tried by the *Chancillerías* from the mid-sixteenth century onwards made them both appear as if they were invested with a "sacred authority" to judge.[66] That of course would also apply to their magistrates, who were generally members of the lower nobility, completely loyal to the monarchy and with years of legal training in the elite colleges (*colegios mayores*) of the Castilian Universities.[67]

According to Larrea and also to Matheu y Sanz, those who offended or killed a magistrate ought to be considered convicts of a crime of *lèse-majesté*.[68] Furthermore, magistrates could even decide not to apply a royal statute. That was the case, according to Vela, for *NR* 4.3.10, a norm that forbade magistrates to advocate or to judge a case in the *Chancillería* when they themselves or their wives or children were involved. Vela, taking himself and Larrea as an example, proves by a judgment in the *Chancillería*, that the practice in Granada was the opposite:

> Nevertheless, in our Court it was rightly decided a suit which I myself, [acting] in my wife's name, brought against one circuit judge of this circuit . . . There, among other reasons, it was alleged that a case involving a member of the Royal Senate could not possibly be heard by the Senate itself: and however it was judged in my favour in court by the very distinguished and erudite nobleman D Juan Bautista de Larrea, with other not less erudite and learned magistrates.[69]

But it was also, he argued, the practice at the *Chancillería* of Valladolid, where another similar judgment that he quotes in detail had been ren-

---

65 Cfr Garriga Acosta, "La Real Audiencia", 38.

66 R L Kagan, *Lawsuits and litigants in Castile 1500–1700*, Chapel Hill: University of North Carolina Press, 1981, 182.

67 D de Lario, *Escuelas de imperio. La formación de una elite en los colegios mayores*, Madrid: Dykinson, 2019, esp 215 ff.

68 Juan Bautista Larrea, *Allegationum fiscalium*, Ludguni: sumptibus Petri Borde, Joannis et Petri Arnaud, 1699, alleg 102, n 10, 127. "[A]d crimen laease Majestatis . . . pertinenere, quod adversus Magistratum fuerit, attentatum, cum nomine Regis justitiam administraret" and Matheu y Sanz, *Tractatus de re criminali*, contr 14, 81–84.

69 "*Sed contrarium nihilominus in Senatu nostro merito judicatum est in causa, quam in eo ego nomine uxoris meae movi adversus Praetorem quendam huius districtus, in quo et illud concurrit, quod in hac curia fuit repertus; pro quo inter alia allegabatur, Regio Senatori adversus eum nullo modo casum curiae competere; et nihilominus pro me judicatum est in aula viri praestantissimi ac eruditissimi Don Joannis Baptistae de Larrea, conjudices habentis non minus doctos ac eruditos viros . . .*", Vela de Oreña, *Dissertationum juris controversi*, vol II, diss 39, n 50, 103.

dered.[70] For Vela, who had no doubts about the justice of a sentence to protect fellow magistrates – unlike A de Acevedo who (*"ingenue"*) was in favour of the strict application of the norm – such a *decisio* should be considered as *Chancillería stylus* (*"quod solum exemplum sufficiebat, ut Granatensis curia illud secuta eodem modo judicaret"*). The reason for that was that magistrates could thus clarify the content of statutes when needed, said Vela, following Guy Pape as *"in specie magna est eorum authoritas"*.

This change in favour of the magistrates' *arbitrium* was clearly noticed at the end of the sixteenth century by the judge J Castillo de Bovadilla. In his treatise for *corregidores* (lower judges) he explains how *arbitrium* (*alvedrío*) was far more common among magistrates than in previous times.[71] Nevertheless, this was a distinct feature of supreme courts only, as the lower judges were obliged to follow the *communis opinio doctorum*[72] in their sentences, lest they could be accused of incompetence or negligence. On the contrary, magistrates who represented the king could judge "like God on earth" and according to their "conscience", going even beyond the statutes.[73]

As public persons and members of a "college", magistrates of Castilian *Chancillerías* were supposed, like A Monti points out for the Senate of Milano, to judge *tamquam Deus*,[74] based on the *ius commune arbitrium*. That is the reason why M Salón de Paz, in two of his *consilia* (1576), argues that the magistrates at his *Chancillería* in Valladolid, as *iudices supremos*, *"debent sola facti veritate inspecta et cognita iudicare sine alij juris apicibus"*, because that court was a *Regium praetorian* (*Pinciano similem*).[75] He based his *consilia* on two sources: (i) some legal norms collected in the NR (4.17.10, 2.4.22 and 2.5.6); and (ii) two main *decisiones* (mere authors' opinions at the time) by Guy Pape and Thomas Grammatico (1473–1556),

---

70 Ibid, n 51, 104.
71 Jerónimo Castillo de Bovadilla, *Política para corregidores y señores de vasallos en tiempo de paz y guerra . . . expurgada según el expurgatorio de MDCXL*, Madrid: en la Imprenta de la Gazeta, 1775, vol I, lib 2, cap 10, n 9, 368.
72 Ibid, vol I, lib 2, cap 7, n 26, 346: *"la opinión común se tiene por ley"*. In criminal cases, supreme courts would often reduce the penalties inflicted by lower judges. See P Ortego Gil, "El arbitrio de los jueces inferiores: su alcance y limitaciones" in J Sánchez-Arcilla, *El arbitrio judicial en el Antiguo Régimen (España e Indias, siglos XVI–XVIII)*, Madrid, Dykinson, 2013, 133–220.
73 Bovadilla, *Política para corregidores*, vol II, lib 5, cap 3, n 58, 641. The magistrates *"representan a la persona Real, y como el Rey, juzgan según Dios en la tierra, la verdad sabida y por presunciones, aunque no concluyan, y según les dicta su conciencia y pueden exceder de las leyes"*. Cfr Garriga, "La Audiencia", 61.
74 A Monti, *Iudicare tamquam Deus. I modi della giustizia senatoria nel Ducato di Milano tra Cinque e Settecento*, Milano: Giuffrè, 2003, 116–117.
75 Salón de Paz, *Consilia*, cons 19, n 36, fol 91r: *"et hoc facere debent servata equitate"*.

who argued in favour of the court judging *ultra petita*. As for the *NR*, Salón de Paz tried to match the selected norms with earlier ones contained in the *Ordenamiento de Montalvo* (1484), a private compilation. However, this method of interpreting sets of laws on the basis of earlier ones was to disappear in the seventeenth century.

The point is whether that image of a magistrate was generally accepted in Castile.

C. *STYLUS* AND HIGH COURTS' *ARBITRIUM* – THE ROLE OF PRECEDENT

The clause *"secundum conscientiam"*, according to A Monti, was originally conceived for the summary proceedings of the ecclesiastical courts in the fourteenth century, as Roman Rota *decisiones* prove.[76] Although, in the thirteenth century, Jacques de Revigny was the first author to accept such a possibility in royal courts of justice, including of course the *Parlement de Paris*.[77] It was Guy Pape, in the following century, who enlarged the concept – although not without controversy.[78]

The consequence of that interpretation, widely disseminated, would be that magistrates did not need to motivate their judgments. Like in the case of the Roman Rota, there was a significant reason for this: to avoid the risk of being condemned, if a legal error (due to an unfair or a false cause) occurred. While different solutions were adopted across Europe (including the kingdoms of the Spanish monarchy), the *communis opinio* was for judges not to motivate their sentences, as a matter of prudence.[79] The Crown of Castile was quick to adhere to that practice.[80] As such, in early modern times, justice in Castile is not to be found in precedents, but in the magistrates' conscience; hence, the reasoning of a judgment was not based on sentences but on the magistrates themselves, responsible for rendering their judgments.[81]

---

76 A Monti, "Between Case Law and Legislation: the *Senato* of Milan, a Supreme Court during the *Ancien Régime*", in B Feldner, and others (eds), *Ad Fontes. Europäisches Forum Junger Rechtshistorikerinnen und Rechtshistoriker Wien 2001*, Frankfurt am Main, Peter Lang, 2002, 303–318, 309, n 17.

77 A Padoa Schioppa, "Sulla coscienza del giudice nel diritto comune", in *Ivris vincula. Studi in onore di Mario Talamanca*, Napoli: Jovene, 119–162, at 143.

78 A Monti, *Iudicare tamquam Deus*, 115–118.

79 G Massetto, "Sentenza (diritto intermedio)" in *Scritti di storia giuridica*, Milano: Giuffrè, 2017, vol II, 1007–1052, at 1009.

80 Bermúdez de Pedraza, *Arte legal*, 70.

81 No doubt the obligation to maintain the secrecy of magistrates' votes in Castile (cf *Nueva Recopilación*, 2.5.43) encouraged keeping courts' decisions unmotivated, but in the end the lack

That is why their backgrounds as fellows of the *colegios mayores*, where their souls and minds were forged, is so important, as recently shown.[82]

Diego de Covarrubias was one of the first Castilian authors to talk about the duty for a judge to sentence according to his *conscience* – on the basis of Pope Innocent III's *Per venerabilem* [X, 4.17.13], but also Deuteronomy (cap 7) and Exodus (cap 23)– insofar as he should not ignore anything that he might know beyond *allegata* et *probata*. In saying as much, however, he did not hesitate to argue against Guy Pape, to conclude that high courts could not judge against royal statutes, presumed to be issued for *utilitas publica*.[83] Only the prince could change a statute *"propriam et particularem Scientia"*. In theory, this could be an important limit against the *arbitrium juris* in Castile. But was it so in practice? No doubt, a court's own *stylus* – the body of procedural rules developed by the court on the basis of its own case law – and the publication of *decisiones* as a criterion for certainty in judicial decisions, could both be considered as "limits" to the *arbitrium iudicis*, particularly for lower-level judges.[84] But it was not the same for high-court magistrates.

With regards to *stylus*, at the beginning of the seventeenth century, the Castilian lawyer F Bermúdez de Pedraza claimed that *stylus* was different from one court to another, but where a court decision was confirmed by the prince, then it would become universally binding.[85] This principle began to appear at least one century earlier, for, according to M Salón de Paz, a high court represented the king himself and its *stylus judicandi* (*usus fori*) was supposed to be approved by him.[86]

The growing importance attributed to *stylus* in Castile during the first half of the sixteenth century let the *Cortes de Madrid* in 1551 ask the king to pronounce on "what is to be respected, if the *stylus* or the statute [*si se ha*

---

of motivation in the decisions was considerably more a custom than a legal principle. C Garriga, "Aritmética judicial. Las operaciones de la justicia española (siglo XVIII)", in J R Lima Lopez and A Slemian (eds), *História das justiças 1750–1850*, São Paulo: Alameda, 2018, 109–201, at 126–135 and 154–156; Garriga Acosta, "La Real Audiencia", 61.

82 Lario, *Escuelas*, 211 ff.

83 "*[U]nde falsum est quod Guido Papae scribit, ut posse supremi senatus iudices ferre sententia contra allegata et probata, ex propia et privata scientia*", Diego de Covarrubias y Leyva, "Variarum resolutionum" in Id, *Omnium Operum tomus secundus*, Frankfurt: apud Ioan Feuerab, 1583, lib 1, cap 1, n 3, 2–3. It is interesting to note that Salón de Paz, in his *consilia*, does not speak about the judge's consciousness but only about "veritate inspecta".

84 G Massetto, "Sentenza", 1009; P Ortego Gil, "El arbitrio", 200–201.

85 Bermúdez de Pedraza, *Arte legal*, 70.

86 Marcos Salón de Paz, *Ad leges Taurinas insignes commentario*, Pinciae: apud Franciscum Ferdinan à Corduba Regal Typogra, 1568, proem, n 227, fol 34v.

guardar el estilo o la ley] so that both judges and litigants would know what
to do [*para que los jueces e partes sepan que han de hacer*]".[87] Again, it is
M Salón de Paz who informs us on the actual practice. In his comments on
the *Leyes de Toro*, he tells us how in the mid-sixteenth century it was not
unusual for high courts ("*in quibus iudices non juris ignari, sed sapientes
creantur*") to use different interpretations on statutes and on a variety of
"*doctorum sententiae*", just like it happened before the existence of those
laws ("*prout contingent ante harum legum constitutiones et hodie frequen-
tissime*"). In such cases, magistrates – Salón de Paz explains, according to
Johannes Andreae and Jason de Mayno – could even change a previous
stylus to establish a new one, should they think that the former was against
ius and *ratio*, something which happened frequently in difficult cases.[88]

That does not tell us, however, what was a *stylus*' nature and its scope of
application. In the late Middle Ages, the dispute between scholars was on its
nature – procedural or substantive – and the differences between customary law and *stylus*. From the late fourteenth century and the first half of
the fifteenth century (i.e. with Antonio de Butrio and Nicolò de' Tudeschi
(Panormitanus)), however, *stylus* came to be considered both procedural and
substantive, and the differences regarding custom were reduced.[89] Finally,
at the beginning of the sixteenth century, in the context of a growing trend,
the Neapolitan Matteo d'Afflitto, who sustained that interpretation, assigned
to *stylus* legal force (*vim legis*), and even considered that *stylus contra ius*
would be valid when restricted to the court jurisdiction that established it.[90]

In sixteenth-century Castile, according to the well-known practising
lawyer Gonzalo Suárez de Paz (†1590) it was common opinion that *stylum
facit ius* (that was the best way to interpret a legal norm, as a judgment
rendered by a lower-level judge against a notorious *stylus*) should be considered null and void. *Stylus*, therefore, could be alleged in Castile both as
procedure and as substance ("*cum ad litium ordinationem, tam ad earum
decisionem*").[91] Legal scholars who made comments on royal norms agreed,
however, in considering *stylus* (*exemplum, observantia*) as a last resort to
produce a judgment only if a legal norm was lacking, or there were doubts
regarding the interpretation of a privilege or of another norm. "*Deficiente*

87 CLC, V, pet 108 (bis), 547–548.
88 "*[S]olet quidem et stylus ex iustis causis in curijs frequenter mutari, volubilis que est*" Salón de
    Paz, *Ad leges Taurinas*, proem, n 225 and 233, fol 35v.
89 C Lefebvre, *Le pouvoirs du juge en droit canonique*, Paris: Recueil Sirey, 1938, 229–233.
90 G Vallone, *Le "decisiones" di Matteo d'Afflitto*, Lecce: Milella, 1988, 75–82.
91 Gonzalo Suárez de Paz, *Praxis ecclesiastica et saecularis*, Palthen, 1613, proem, fol 1r–v, n 4–5.

iure expresso exemplis esse iudicandum censens", stated both M Salón de Paz[92] and Juan Gutiérrez in line with Lorenzo Silva, Antonius de Butrio, Jacobus Menocchio and other Italian authors, for whom "previous decisions on a same issue are to be followed all the more in cases dealing with privileges or other doubtful legal norms interpretation".[93]

The main reason was that *stylus* could not be considered an *interpretatio necessaria*, an exclusive attribute of the prince, as M Salón de Paz argues, quoting Alberico da Rosate; that is why magistrates could change it from one time to another. *Stylus*, just like *consuetudo* – says Salón de Paz citing G Nevizzano – should be proved;[94] it was not enough to quote it, as on the contrary it would be the case with legal norms. Even the oldest customs (*longa consuetudine*), if notorious, did not need to be proved – the key point in the conflict between customs and *stylus*, as we shall see.

As *interpretatio probabilis*, *stylus* would even be sometimes questioned by *consilia* authors in Castile as did the bishop and magistrate J Valenzuela Velázquez (1574–1645), who not only challenged some *exempla*, as opposed to natural law, but also supreme courts' judgments in general, as far as, with regards to *senatus consultum* authority [D. 48.10.14 and Nov 74] unlike *ius commune* – he stated – *"jus nostrum non tribuit* [to Senate's judgments] *legis condendae authoritatem"*.[95] In supporting such an argument, Valenzuela Velázquez quoted a *decisiones* author, the Portuguese Alvaro Valasco (1526–1593), fond of considering Portugal as a part of *"Hispania tota"* on the basis of royal legislation and not of high courts' judgments.[96]

However, far from any criticism, seventeenth-century Castilian *decisiones* authors insisted upon the relevance of *stylus*. In line with Matteo d'Afflitto, for both Larrea and Vela *stylus* had force of law. On his part, Vela de Oreña did not hesitate to assert that despite C.7.15.13 did not confer force of law to *stylus* (*"cum non exemplis sed legibus sit iudicandum"*), for a supreme court like the *Chancillería* of Granada, *"solum exemplum sufficiebat"*.[97] In the final instance, then, magistrates were to judge in *principis loco*, and they were

92 Salón de Paz, *Ad leges Taurinas*, proem, n 230, fol 35r.
93 *"[Q]uando agitur de privilegii vel alterius dubiae dispositionis interpretatione, observantia precedens in eodem casu maxima attendenda est"*, Juan Gutiérrez, *Practicarum questionum, super prima parte legum novae collectionis regia Hispaniae – liber tertius et quartus*, Matriti: apud Pedrum Madrigal, 1593, lib III, *quaestio* 16, n 76, 168.
94 Salón de Paz, *Ad leges Taurinas*, fol 35r, n 231 and 232.
95 Valenzuela Velázquez, *Consilia*, vol I, cons 69, n 218, 452.
96 G C Machado Cabral, *Os decisionistas portugueses*, 160–195.
97 Vela de Oreña, *Dissertationum juris controversi*, vol II, diss 39, n 51, 104, and also diss 36, n 10 and diss 6, n 10.

supposed to have enough *authoritas* to solve any legal doubt. Vela de Oreña, however, did not quote almost any Castilian author in support of his argument except J Castillo de Sotomayor. Nearly his whole comment was based on civil law (C.7.45.13 and C.9.2.14) and *decisiones* authors from different origins (G Pape, P Rebuffi, U Zasius, A d'Afflitto, Antonio da Gama and A Barbosa, among others).

Likewise, Larrea mentions different sentences of the *Chancillería* of Granada to prove the need for the parties to accept a pre-agreed purchase price, should a new tax law change the rules, as it had happened in Castile at the begging of the seventeenth century. In doing so he quotes three main decisions that would have become *stylus*;[98] for him, one of the most authoritative sources in Castilian law to be followed, as argued, both in procedure and in substance (*"praxim recepta Tribunalium omnino servandam sive . . . tendat ad litem ordinanda sive ad decidenda"*).[99] It was all right to invoke *stylus*, but it was up to the court to gauge its pertinence, as *stylus* should not be followed if it was against reason (*"ubi non curandi de style quod offendit rationem . . . poties valeat ratio quam stylus"*) – a way to introduce the *arbritrium iudicis* in the legal system. Within the context outlined above, it remains to be seen how the role played by *precedent* in Castilian law in the seventeenth century should be considered – but to what extent?

In general, it could be said that literature on *decisiones* adds new cases to the reservoir of knowledge of a jurist – commentaries on particular legal norms and treaties – or sanctions earlier solutions that continued to be invoked. In Continental *ius commune* precedent case law – *praeiudicia* – were interpreted as a value-oriented guide but they were not legally binding, as the basis for the actual decision could change.[100] When this happened, however, the decision would be compared with the earlier and opposing one, so as to make clear that what brought about the change was the court's *arbitrium* – based, in its turn, on *aequitas*, reason (*ratio*) or public utility.

For Larrea, the best *interpretatio* was the one based on a plurality of

---

98 Larrea, *Novae decisiones*, vol I, Dec 11, n 52, 54 and 59, 172, 173 and 174 respectively.

99 On procedural *stylus* see the same Larrea, *Novarum Decisionum*, vol II, Dec 53, n 16, 20–21, on the refusal to let allegations of documentary falsehood interrupt the main trial.

100 M N Miletti, *Stylus*, 111–113. Also, in England, during the civil wars the binding force of precedent was rare and based much more on law records than on law reports: I Williams, "Early-modern Judges and the Practice of Precedent", in P Brand and J Getzler (eds), *Judges and Judging in the History of the Common Law and the Civil Law*, Cambridge: Cambridge University Press, 2012, 51–66, at 53–54.

decisions,[101] as he argued in a lawsuit on an uncle's right to receive alimony from his nephew in a primogeniture succession. Larrea mentioned three judgments in which both *Chancillerías* and the Royal Council of Castile had granted that right:

> and though similar decisions do not compel [to judge according to them], because [a case] should be judged according to legal rules and not after *exempla* [C.7.45.13], however, a great number of a Supreme Court judgments on the same kind of cases constitute a practice and a *stylus*, from which it is not lawful to move away [D.1.3.32 and C.8.52(53)].[102]

Hence these sentences (*decreta*) should be considered *stylus*. Nevertheless, Larrea was aware that the case at stake was a difficult one, having been a matter of dispute between magistrates at the *Chancillería* of Granada. Besides, the sentence that he decided to comment on in this *questio* denied an uncle such a right, and he indirectly showed his disagreement "because often different and opposed judgments on this question do not mention the reasons that could have moved magistrates".[103] According to him, a change of interpretation had to be based on *aequitas* within the framework of the Catholic religion.[104]

The conclusion to be drawn is clear: precedent, in Castile, did not have binding force and magistrates in supreme courts did not have to explain the reasons for their change of minds (*conscience*). However, if such a change were to take place, that would mean that the court decided to start defining a new *stylus*. In the end, precedents are but "favourable presumptions" to be changed with good reasons only.[105] That was the basis for the *arbitrium iudicis* in Castile.

D. LEGAL AUTHORITIES IN FAMILY AND CONTRACT LAW THROUGH *DECISIONES* LITERATURE

As has been argued before, *decisiones* literature show that statutes (legal norms) were not always applied in Castilian courts' practice according to the same hierarchy of legal sources as established in nineteenth-century

101 *"[E]t quantumuis similes sententiae non adstringant, quia non exemplis, sed legibus iudican-dum* [C.7.45.13], *tamen decreta et multiplicia Supremi Senatus in eodem genere causarum consitutuunt practicam et stylum, quo recedere non licet* [D.1.3.32 and C.8.52(53)]", Larrea, *Novae decisiones*, vol I, Dec 47, n 10, 609: " *optima oit intorprotatio quod oummitur ex plurali-tate sententiarum . . ."*

102 *"[C]um saepius diversae et contrariae sententiae in has quaest[iones] ne liqueat de rationibus quae possent movere iudices"*, ibid, n 13, 610.

103 Ibid, n 52 and 53.

104 Ibid, n 60.

105 M Kriele, "Il precedente nell'ambito giuridico europeo-continentale e angloamericano", in *La sentenza in Europa. Metodo, tecnica e stile*, Padova, CEDAM, 1988, 515–528, at 517.

legal codes. Although throughout the seventeenth century the *Nueva Recopilación* was the main legal source quoted – as it defined the sacred order of the *ius proprium* in the realm – the *arbitrium* of the supreme courts would also contribute to update the law. In doing so, however, magistrates did not act "arbitrarily" but under *ius commune* categories.[106] Beyond the emphasis on the king's willingness to issue new laws (*"voluntas domini regis facit ius in regno"*) – a point on which French historiography has repeatedly insisted – we should bear in mind that magistrates, as "priests of justice", were obliged – just like the king himself – to act according to a number of higher values: reason, truth, public utility and equity (*ratio, veritas, utilitas publica, aequitas*),[107] because the main aim of *arbitrium* in early modern times was the search of justice beyond legal norms.[108]

For the purpose of this section we will consider here only private law – not criminal law – and Larrea's and Vela de Oreña's work. Although, in general, both authors deal with several common issues, there are important differences between them. Thus, Larrea describes first two conflicting views, before quoting "briefly" the court's judgment, to put forward after his own reasoning, sometimes quoting himself – like Vela does – as a member of the court that judged the case (*"me iudice"*).[109] Vela, instead, quotes several *Chancillería*'s *decisiones* on the same subject and in a more detailed way, collecting data, facts and real names, and so paying far more attention to precedents. On the other hand, Larrea always argues alleging *civil law* norms, that he tries to reconcile with royal laws. Vela, on his part, underlines far more the differences between *ius commune* and *ius proprium*. In any case, both mention a wide range of Castilian and foreign authors – as well as foreign *decisiones* – to sustain their arguments as part of a sort of a Catholic *ius gentium*, ultimately identified with *ius naturale*.[110]

(1) Statutes

No doubt legal norms were the most authoritative source of law in Castile in the early modern period. Thus, Larrea himself states, with regard to *ley 27 de Toro*:

---

106 M Meccarelli, *Arbitrium*, 56–60.
107 J Krynen, "Droit romain et état monarchique. A propos du cas français", in J Blanchard (ed), *Représentation, pouvoir et royauté à la fin du moyen âge*, Paris: Picard, 1995, 13–23, at 22–23.
108 Pérez-Prendes, *Historia del Derecho español*, vol I, 52–54.
109 *"Haec nostri Praetoris sententia ultra quam satis suscita fuit argumentis, quae proxime pro hac parte retulimus"* (Larrea, *Novarum Decisionum*, vol II, Dec 54, n 11, 27).
110 I Birocchi, *Alla ricerca dell'ordine. Fonti e cultura giuridica nell'età moderna*, Torino: Giappichelli, 2002, 89–90.

"non licet disputare de legibus, sed iudicare secundum eas".[111] Nevertheless, unlike in the sixteenth century, when authors tried to reconcile previous legal norms (*lex antica*) and collected ones in their comments, both Larrea and Vela took into consideration *Nueva Recopilación* as a single reference. Years later, as a royal prosecutor, Larrea, in his *Allegationes*, would insist upon the fact that previous legal norms not included within the *Nueva Recopilación* should be considered not in force (*"nullam eius fosse observantia"*).[112]

Given the religious context, after the Council of Trent, in which legal norms were issued, these were supposed to be part of a sacred order that the Catholic monarch was obliged to keep; this is why legal interpretation could become *a matter of conscience*. Thus, sixteenth-century *consilia* authors had to insist on the necessity to interpret legal norms should they not be clear enough. M Salón de Paz, for instance, as a lawyer at the *Chancillería* of Valladolid draws on canon law rules to prove that magistrates – *iuris non ignori sed sapientes* – do not sin, when adapting an obscure legal norm to a case law in which a variety of interpretations was possible;[113] moreover, to support his point, he quotes, as an authority, Rodrigo Suárez, an earlier magistrate at the same *Chancillería*, who, taking Baldus as a reference, had proved that was an *"antiqua praxis"*.[114]

During the seventeenth century, *decisiones* literature will clearly advocate the necessity to update legal norms through interpretation: as circumstances change, so does the *interpretatio* and so high courts create *ius novum* too.[115] As a part of the *ius gentium, ius commune* served a wider purpose than local law: *ad aequalitatem in judicius servandam*.

A true case was brought to bear by Larrea on that point: the requirement of equality among heirs would be guaranteed by the written promise made by a father not to favour one of his children in his reserved portion (*legítima*) at the expense of the others, as he argues in relation to Dec 65. Consequently, all the children, if such a promise was made, would have an acquired right (*ius quaesitum*) from their father. He argued, however, beyond the limits of the case law, not only quoting Castilian legal norms, so that *ius commune* could be thought of as *universalitas in unicum corpus* [D.18.7.3].[116]

---

111 Larrea, *Novae decisiones*, vol I, Dec 32, n 55, 256.
112 Larrea, *Allegationes*, vol I, *quaestio* 37, n 34, 193.
113 That was a common practice in Castile at the time. Cfr Salón de Paz, *Ad leges taurinas*, proem, n 224–225, fol 34v: *"male intelligentem legem obscuram et varijs modis intelligibilem, mortaliter non peccare"*.
114 Ibid, n 225.
115 Larrea, *Novae decisiones*, vol I, Dec 62 74.
116 Larrea, *Novarum Decisionum*, vol II, Dec 65, n 8, 87.

In any case, an extensive *interpretatio* of a legal norm by a judge was possible only if there was the same *ratio* for the case as for the legal norm.[117] Only in such cases, the *arbitrium iudicis* could apply extensively *"ex qualitatite, necessitate, et quantitate"*.[118] But what is the difference between an extensive interpretation of a legal norm and judging in fairness (*aequitas*)? Larrea – like Vela – makes an interesting distinction between written *aequitas* (a judge is entrusted by a legal norm to apply *aequitas* in some cases) and unwritten *aequitas* (for which there is no legal norm). But would the *aequitas canonica* be the main reference for these authors? According to Larrea, not at all – and that was an important change in the seventeenth century. For him, canon law should be thought as subsidiary to civil law. Furthermore, only if a written canonical legal norm existed, the *aequitas canonica* could be applied to the case.[119] For Vela, moreover, the *utilitas publica* (*"reipublica vel fisci utilitatis"*) – not *affectio* – was sometimes the criterion to maintain *aequitas*; for instance, in rental prices of lands, a criterium that could be transfered *"ad Ecclesiam"*, as he argued following canonists such as the Portuguese A Barbosa, J Papon and P Rebuffi in France and Paolo di Castro in Italy. *"Sola utilitatis ratio"* would be his main ground for defending public interests – the payment of taxes – over private ones (*affectio*): *"nam ... cesset affectionis ratio, quae in privatis consideratur, et militet illa altera aequitatis naturalis"* [D.39.3].[120]

(2) Customary law

By and large, in early modern times Castilian lawyers continued to accept the possibility for customary law to derogate a statute. A frequency of acts was required, however, to define a practice as customary law. In the last instance, it all depended on judges' *decisiones*,[121] but it was a widely disputed question whether those acts should be judicially or extrajudicially recognised.[122] It should be kept in mind that in the sixteenth century M Salón de Paz and Juan Gutiérrez had equated *custom* and *stylus*.

---

117 Larrea followed here the civil law [C.5.27.11] and Accursius' *intepretatio*.
118 Larrea, *Novarum Decisionum*, vol II, Dec 47, n 40, 404. *"Quod lex non dicit, nec nos dicere debemus"*, states Vela de Oreña, *Dissertationum juris controversi*, vol I, dis 12, n 9, 138.
119 Ibid, Dec 65, n 39, 404. Regarding the alimony asked by an uncle for a nephew, Larrea argues that only civil law – not canon law – was a norm in relation to the right of food [D.12.2].
120 Vela de Oreña, *Dissertationum juris controversi*, vol I, dis 13, n 55, 158.
121 G Massetto, "Sentenza", 1015–1017.
122 Hieronymus Caevallos (Jerónimo de Cevallos), *Speculum practicarum et variarum questionum communium contra comunes*, Toleti: apud Thomas Guzmanium Typographum, 1599, vol I, quaestio 350, 450–453.

Within that context, during the sixteenth century a much-debated question was the need to prove the use of a local statute (*fuero*) for it to be applied by a court. Be it written or not, for Rodrigo Suárez, the party that alleged the statue had to prove its use. The problem arose regarding Biscay law (*Fuero de Vizcaya* [*FV*]). Originally considered as customary law, *FV* was sanctioned as a territorial statute (*lex*) by King Charles I of Castille in 1527, under the name of Fuero Nuevo de Vizcaya (*FN*). Behind this new version of *FV*, however, was the privilege of "*hidalguía universal*", the lower nobility status that *FN* extended in 1527 to all of Biscay's population, even to those living outside the territory. The privilege was accompanied by the exemption of taxes.

By the middle of the sixteenth century, the *Chancillerías' stylus* seems to have been contrary to Biscay's claim not to need proving their nobility status, although for Biscay lawyers to be born there was proof enough to gain the status of *hidalgos*. The prosecutor J García de Saavedra lets us know of two judgements from the *Chancillería* of Valladolid (in 1545 and 1550) against such a presumption.[123] Nonetheless, a few years later the court *criterium* had changed: *FV* could be alleged without proving its use.[124] In the meantime, some Castilian authors had supported Biscay's claim. So did Juan Gutiérrez who, in his comment to *NR* 2.11.8-9, argued that "*communem reputationem et communem usum loquendi*" were enough to prove such *nobilitas*;[125] he even questioned the letter of the judgements mentioned by García de Saavedra and stressed the fact that they would be contrary to the applicable law in this case (i.e. *FV*).[126] As a rule, it was for magistrates to decide without the king's intervention.[127]

A major change had no doubt taken place in the literature on customary law. One of the most important arguments for it was the purity of Catholicism

---

123 Juan García de Saavedra, *De hispanorum nobilitate et exemptionen sive ad Pragmaticam Cordubensem quae est l 8 tit 12 lib 2 Recopilationis Commentarij*, Valladolid: apud Haeredes Bernardi de Sancto Domingo, 1588, 197, n 25: "*Y por esos años de 45 y 50 se dudo como avia de probar la hidalguía el Vizcayno, se mando se consultasen los acuerdos de Valladolid y Granada, y el de Valladolid respondió que el vizcaíno no pudiese gozar hidalguía si no la probasse . . .*" ("And as in the [15]45s and [15]50s there was doubt as to the way for those born in Biscay to prove their 'hidalguía' [low nobility], it was ordered to check the court decisions of [the *Chancillerías* of] Valladolid and Granada, and that of Valladolid replied that the Biscay born could not enjoy 'hidalguía' unless he proved it . . .").

124 J García Martín, "El Fuero de Vizcaya en la doctrina y la práctica judicial castellanas", in J Arrieta, X Gil and J Morales (eds), *La Diadema del Rey. Vizcaya, Navarra, Aragón y Cerdeña en la Monarquía de España (siglos XVI–XVIII)*, Bilbao: Universidad del País Vasco, 2017, 53–168.

125 Gutiérrez, *Practicarum*, lib III, quaest 16, n 78 and 82, 96–97.

126 Ibid, *quaestio* 17, n 220–227 [*NR*, 2.11.8].

127 Ibid, *quaestio* 31, n 9.

in Biscay as, from 1512 descendants of Jews, Muslims and Converts were banned from settling in Biscay. Moreover, in 1590 King Philip II would order García de Saavedra's work to be expurgated from the paragraphs arguing against Biscay nobility.[128] One century later, Vela continued to admit the extrajudicial way of proving *consuetudines generales "per duos actos inductos"* (*dis* 12). While Larrea, on the same line, thought that an important condition was required: not to find any contradiction between the alleged acts.[129] In this reasoning customary law – territorial but not local – could replace a legal norm, in the same way that a new legal act replaces and repeals an earlier one; thus, customary law was a way to create new law (*ius novum inducere*).[130] But custom, like *stylus*, could not go against *ratio* (religion).[131] In the last analysis, it was for the high courts to decide on customary law in relation to *lex*.

(3) Legal literature

As regards doctrine (i.e. *ius commune* as a Catholic *ius gentium*), I will now focus on two main subjects: subsidiary law and the concepts of *communis opinio* and *ratio*.

(a) Canon law and civil law: their relationship with Castilian law

In the early sixteenth century, due to the magistrate Juan de Palacios Rubios's (1450–1524) influence, Castilian lawyers followed the tradition to consider statutes and the customary law applied by high courts as "common law of the kingdom" (*derecho común del reino*).[132] It was, however, debatable whether the subsidiary law should be canon law or civil law. Most authors (D Pérez de Salamanca, A Acevedo and J Gutiérrez among them) aligned themselves with Palacios Rubios's position in considering canon law as supplementary/complementary to royal law.

Some of Gutiérrez's *consilia* dealing with the payment of default inter-

---

128 J García Martín, "El Fuero de Vizcaya", 66–67.

129 Larrea, *Novae decisiones*, vol I, Dec 2, n 20, 28.

130 "[I]n consuetudine speciali . . . quemadmodum lex posterior aliam legem antiquam potest abrogare, ita et consuetudo legitime praescripta jus novum inducere, et antiquo detrahere", Larrea, *Novarum Decisionum*, vol II, Dec 62, n 54, 74.

131 Ibid, Dec 98, n 23, 223–224: "*stylo et consuetudine recedere debemus quando ratio certa aliud suadet*".

132 J García Martín, "En los orígenes del derecho comparado. Pierre Rebuffi (1487?–1557) y la creación de una tradición jurisprudencial salmantina en el comentario del Derecho regio", in S de Dios, J Infante and E Torijano (eds), *Juristas de Salamanca, siglos XV–XX*, Salamanca, Universidad de Salamanca, 2009, 13–79, at 21.

ests prove it; unlike civil law, that did not give the creditor the possibility to stop the consequences, the canonical *aequitas* did. Thus, Gutiérrez did not hesitate to state that usually at the *Chancillerías* "*deficiente juris regio potius recurrendum ad ius canonicum quam ad leges imperatorum*".[133] That position would, however, be clearly opposed by Salón de Paz, who, against Palacios Rubios and his followers ("*sequaces*") claimed that, in practice, the *Chancillerías* normally preferred *ius ciuile* as "*ius regni municipale esse: et non ius universale*".[134]

In this way, in the seventeenth century Larrea argued for the use of civil jurisdiction against the ecclesiastical jurisdiction in an inheritance case, in which a cleric was in possession of the estate; he recognised that this type of case was disputable, inasmuch as the *Chancillería* of Granada had produced contradictory judgments ("*discutiendum recte*") whenever a declinatory plea for ecclesiastical jurisdiction had been asked by a cleric. Nevertheless, it was Larrea's view that if a cleric possessed a *mayorazgo* estate, any claim about it should be admitted in the civil jurisdiction (i.e. the Royal Council of Castile and the *Chancillerías*).[135]

Both Larrea and Vela seem to have been in favour of the Count Duke of Olivares's attempt to reduce the influence of ecclesiastical jurisdiction in the kingdom, for which the Council of Castile and the *Chancillerías* had been vested with specific functions.[136] It should be remembered that, after Larrea's death in 1646, the first volume of his *Allegationes fiscales* was included in the Roman Index of forbidden books – not in the Spanish one – on condition of *donec corrigatur* for *alleg* 37 (about the Royal Patronage) and *alleg* 64 (about a member of a Military order) thought to be against the ecclesiastical jurisdiction.[137] On the other hand, it should also be noted that Vela's *decisiones* were dedicated to Olivares.

Regarding *civil law*, one of the main themes that our authors dealt with is

---

133 Gutiérrez, *Consilia*, cons 33, num 5, fol 104v, and *cons* 43, n 20, fol 127r–v ("*practicatum iam in regali cancellaria Vallisoleti*"), in both cases the main reference was Juan de Palacios Rubios.

134 "[E]t contra Ioan[nes] Lup[us] et sequaces praxis quotidiana est, singulis que diebus supraemi iudices, alij que inferiores (iure canonico omisso) iuris civilis legibus (iure quidem canonico omisso) lites deciduntur", Salón de Paz, Marcos, *Ad leges Taurinas*, l. I, n 592–593, fol 140r.

135 Larrea, vol I, Dec 10, n 25, 95. In the case in point, the *Chancillería* decided against the declinatory plea after changing Chambers, the second one sentencing that "*non posse in hoc casi fori declinatoriam locum habere, recte decrevit*".

136 OChV 1.1. fols 10v ss; and OChG, 1.2, fols 6r–v ss. Explicitly, Gregorio López, *Las Siete Partidas del sabio Rey don Alonso el nono*, Salamanca, Andrea de Portonaris, 1555, P 2.13.13, gl. *nin fuerça*, fol 37v.

137 P Volpini, *Lo spazio*, 87–90; and R Savelli, *Censori e giuristi. Storie di libri, di idee e di costumi (secoli XVI–XVII)*, Milano: Giuffrè, 2011, 219–220.

the conflict between local statutes – *lex municipalis* – not only within Castile but also in the relationship between Castile and the other kingdoms, where different laws were in place. Law-report authors formulate some rules in order to solve them. The main trend would be to favour real statutes as opposed to personal ones, as happens in France – the main author of which being Bertrand d'Argentré (1519–1590).[138] Clearly Larrea's opinion, like d'Argentré's, was essentially territorially minded and closely related to property and tax payment.

Marriage was one of the main issues regarding *collisio statutorum*, as very often the local statute (*fuero*) of the place in which the marriage was celebrated (*lex loci celebrationis*) was different from the one where the couple was to live (*lex domicilii*). For instance, in Dec 62 Larrea deals with the problem of determining whether the matrimonial assets of a marriage should be decided according to the place in which the marriage contract was concluded or to the husband's domicile. In this case, he declares himself in favour of the husband's domicile – the one that the wife was submitted to, according to Castilian law – regardless of whether the Royal Court where the wife lived was considered *patria communis* of all Spaniards, or the priority the judgment gave to custom (*ex more regionis*) over status.[139]

Statute theory was also applied to contract law to solve that type of conflict. In this case, Larrea would be against the freedom of the parties to change their domicile should a previous agreement be established for the purpose;[140] his arguments were based both in the Roman sources and their medieval and early modern interpretation (C.3.13.2, D.46.3.6, Bartolus, Alciatus, Mascardus and Menocchio). On his part, Vela makes a real exercise in comparative law between countries under *ius commune*, with references to Portugal, Catalonia and Brittany – mentioned by d'Argentré in his work – as examples in which local or municipal laws were particularly relevant.[141] Vela's references to *utilitas publica* and *local statutes* make him appear closer to Enlightened aims, although in his arguments he is far more

---

138 H Coing, *Europäisches Privatrecht*, 2 vols, Munich: C H Beck, 1985–1989; in Spanish, *Derecho privado europeo*, 2 vols, Madrid: Fundación Cultural del Notariado, 1996, vol I, 188–190.

139 The case has been studied by M M Pérez-Victoria de Benavides, "La teoría estatutaria como solución al conflicto entre el derecho histórico de los distintos reinos (A propósito de una sentencia de la Chancillería de Granada en el s XVII)', (2001) 6 *INITIUM*, 445–468. Also, A Barbosa and Caldas Pereyra, following some contemporary Portuguese authors, placed in the domicile the *ratio decidendi*.

140 Larrea, *Novarum Decisionum*, vol II, Dec 94, 204.

141 Vela de Oreña, *Dissertationum juris controversi*, vol I, diss. 1, n 18 and 74, at 5 and 10 respectively.

in line with the Castilian tradition of *"concordantiae"*, a genre in which *ius proprium* would always be considered as a part of *ius commune*.[142]

Be that as it may, the *Chancillería* of Granada did not always produce its judgements in accordance with the legal norms. Thus, Vela de Oreña would argue in favour of *justice* beyond what seemed to be a common legislation in different countries, allowing, for instance, a minor under the age of twenty-five to reach his majority when married, ending at that moment his guardianship or his curatorship (*NR* 5.1.8). Against that, *aequitas* and *ius gentium*, according to him, would have been the criteria adopted by the *Chancillería* of Granada for non-application in such a case a legal norm.[143]

(b) *Communis opinio doctorum* versus *ratio* as grounds for *arbitrium iudicis*

The lawyer Jerónimo de Ceballos (1560–1641), who published in 1599 a successful treatise on the subject, considered *communis opinio doctorum* as having the force of a *lex* that could be alleged before a court of justice. To support his position, he quoted several Italian (Baldus, Angelus, Felinus and Jason de Mayno) and Castilian authors (Avilés, Matienzo and Martín de Azpilcueta), who argued that a judgment contrary to the *communis opinio* should be considered *"iniquo"*.[144] That is the way it doubtlessly worked for lower-level judges. Castillo de Bovadilla explains that a *corregidor* who sentenced against *communis opinio* "sins against his duty" and could be sanctioned in a *juicio de residencia* (an inspection at the end of his tenure).[145] But it was the opposite for the high courts.

Although most of the *decisiones* authors (Nevizziano, Corazzi) agreed in considering that high courts took *communis opinio* into account, at least in doubtful cases (*casus dubii*), in the early sixteenth century the Neapolitan Matteo d'Afflitto strongly opposed that position. According to d'Afflitto, it was the high court's judgment to have force of law by itself, not as a reflection of *communis opinio*. That is why, in some of his *decisiones*, he did not hesitate in contradicting *communis opinio* or deciding to use only a part of

---

142 In this regard, three main authors connected to Salamanca should be quoted: Juan Bautista de Villalobos, *Antinomia juris Regni Hispaniarum ac ciuilis*, Salamanca, 1569; Juan Martínez de Olano, *Concordia et novum reductio antinomiarum iuris communist ac Regi Hispaniarum*, Burgos, 1575 (with references to the law of Navarra); and Sebastián Jiménez, *Concordantiae utriusque iuris ciuilis et canonici cum legibus Partitarum*, Toleti: typis Petri Roderici: expensis Michaelis de Vililla, 1596.

143 Vela de Oreña, *Dissertationum juris controversi*, vol I, diss. 1, n 18, 32 and 72 at pp 5, 6 and 10.

144 J de Caevallos, *Speculum practicarum*, vol I, praefatio, n 31 and 35, 7–8.

145 J Castillo de Bovadilla, *Política*, vol I, lib 2, cap 7, n 25–26, 346.

it;[146] for him, like for Caravita, the Neapolitan *Sacro Regio Consiglio* could rectify *ius commune* through its judgements.[147]

For his part, Cevallos, following Gómez de León, admitted too that, in Castile, Roman Rota's sentences *"dicitur opinio communis"*; because of the collegiate nature of the court and the quality of its judges (*"viri doctissimi"*). Furthermore, and in line with Decius, *"decisio Rotae est maioris auctoritatis quam communis opinio doctors"*.[148] Cevallos based his view on the relevance of canon law at the time; an argument that was not shared by other authors. There are of course many references to *communis opinio* in Larrea's and Vela's works, for specific subjects like *mayorazgo* or illegitimate children, based on Castilian lawyers, and on *tractatus* and *decisiones* authors from other countries (Fabio, Nevizziano, Thesauro and Grammatico, among others). However, it is not unusual to find judgments rendered by the *Chancillería* of Granada against the *communis opinio doctorum*; in such cases Larrea declares himself against *decisiones* based on the agreement of a number of authors (*"semper ego de hac opinione dubitaui, vt non immerito mirandum sit tot interpretes in id conspirasse, nec pondere rationes, sed numero authors meriti"*). The judgment should be based, he argued, in *"sciendi causas"*;[149] in that case, authors like Cicero or Seneca are often quoted by him in search of moral grounds. Larrea, as the humanist jurist that he was, seems to be looking for arguments outside the *corpus juris civilis*.[150] However, on the other hand, he often also quoted, indirectly through *decisiones* literature, sentences from other high courts outside Castile (Venice, Naples, Catalonia and Portugal).[151] In doing so, Larrea would question, for instance, a Venice Senate's judgment compiled by Menocchio, in which the succession for an estate was established in favour of a nobleman from a female parental line. Although many scholars (Decio, Menocchio, Farinacci, Acevedo and J Castillo de Sotomayor) and some supreme courts' judgments agreed with it (*"similium imitandas"*), Larrea highlights as more authoritative a Council of Castile's judgement in favour of male blood relatives.[152]

---

146 G Vallone, "Le *decisiones* di Matteo d'Afflitto", in J H Baker (ed), *Judicial Records, Law Reports, and the Growth of Case Law*, Berlin: Duncker & Humblot, 1989, 143–179, at 177–178.

147 M N Miletti, *Stylus*, 119–121.

148 Caevallos, *Speculum*, vol I, *quaestio* 1, n 25–27, 6–7.

149 Larrea, *Novae decisiones*, vol I, Dec 10, n 27–28, 147. Also, against the *communis opinio*, Id, *Novarum Decisionum*, vol II, Dec 56, n 10, and cons 68, n 16, 108–109.

150 Ibid, *Novae decisiones*, vol I, Dec 10, n 28, 147–148; for Seneca (*epistula* 44), see M M Pérez-Victoria de Benavides, "La teoría estatutaria", 458.

151 Larrea, *Novae decisiones*, vol I, Dec 34, n 10–11, 433.

152 According to Larrea, while *"Senatus decreta plurimum authoritative habent"*, most scholars had mistakenly interpreted the main *ius commune* rule on the point (i.e. D.48.10.14), as they

Finally, he sometimes resorted to more authoritative authors (e.g. L de Molina with reference to the *mayorazgo*), to maintain a restrictive interpretation allowing him not to judge on the basis of *communis opinion*.[153] These cases are clearly based on *arbitrium iudicis*, in which *aequitas*, *publica utilitas* and *ratio* should be considered by the courts as a limit within the framework of the *ius commune*. The main resource to contradict *communis opinion* is, in any case, the appeal to *ratio* (*aequitas*). As M Miletti has pointed out, that was usually a way to introduce a change regarding precedents, a sort of Senatus' "freedom to contradict" – as d'Afflitto again would argue – based on discussion and consensus between the magistrates as a collegiate institution.[154] Thus, Larrea often used the term *"ex ratione"* to add value to another opinion expressed against the *communis opinio*,[155] or the term *"ex aequalitatem"*, always on the basis – and that should be stressed – of the *ius commune* (*"iure commune ad aequalitatem in judiciis servandam, pactum et aequalitatem"*).[156] For his part, Vela resorts both to *ius commune* and to royal norms as a criterion to distinguish between *aequo* and *iniquo* (*"adeo iustam naturalique rationi conformem judicat, ut contrariam juris communis velut iniquam et irrationabilem damnet"*).[157] In short, those were ways for the *arbitrium iudicis* to evolve, according to the *ordo iuris* – insofar as permitted by the *ius commune*.[158]

E. CONCLUSION

Muratori's *Dei difetti della giurisprudenza* was first translated into Spanish at the end of the eighteenth century by Vicente María de Tercilla, a lawyer practising before the Royal Council of Castile. He added, however, a surprising note to his translation: the so-called *"autos acordados"* – collected

were giving such an authority to a *senatusconsultum* instead of a *Senatus* sentence (ibid, Dec 34, n 10, 433).

153 For instance, in order to refuse the payment to the widow of the interest accrued on the entailed estate (*mayorazgo*), which was customary with regard to dowry restitution. Larrea, like Molina, thought it would be akin to usury, and therfore forbidden. Ibid, Dec 37, n 15–16, 312.

154 M N Miletti, *Stylus*, 173–174.

155 For instance, when he assigns to the second-born son the capacity to inherit a *mayorazgo* estate in the place of the offspring of the first-born son, that was declared legally incapable. In so doing, he opts for the *lex rei sitae*, taking the *ius commune* as the main reference. See Larrea, *Novarum Decisionum*, vol II, Dec 52, n 10, 3. Larrea also refers to Dec 31, n 41, 238, regarding contract: *"fieri pactum in rem, quando eius causa fit, et ad successorem transit"*.

156 On the breaking of a contract, ibid, Dec 65, n 7, 87.

157 Vela de Oreña, *Dissertationum juris controversi*, vol I, diss 2 n 75–76, 10–11.

158 M Meccarelli, *Arbitrium*, 76.

judgments by the Royal Council printed in 1745 as an addition to *NR* – "were the most appreciated".[159] Tercilla did not speak of *Chancillerías* nor of *decisiones* literature; the Royal Council had recovered its pre-eminent position; in fact, the number of civil cases dealt with at the *Chancillería* of Granada plummeted from the mid-seventeenth until the end of the eighteenth century.[160]

One of the *autos acordados* in 1713 (*NR* 2.1.1) would limit the number of authors – preferably Spanish – to be alleged by lawyers in their cases; *decisiones* literature, full of references to foreign authors, in addition to Castilian ones, was no longer considered a suitable guide. Unsurprisingly, the lawyer and scholar J Berní y Catalá (1712–1787) did not include Larrea or Vela among the authors that he recommended for a lawyer's training; rather, he suggested studying the scholars' commentaries to legal norms – *NR*, Leyes de Toro and Fuero Real in Castile – in every part of the kingdom.[161] Furthermore, he conferred solely to the monarch the competence for interpreting laws.

The growing importance of the Royal Council's *decreta* and the key role the Enlightenment authors assigned to legal norms – theoretically "opposed" to *ius commune*, though not in daily practice – as a guide for interpretation, made *decisiones* disappear as a genre to be considered by the royal power. That does not mean, however, that Larrea and Vela disappeared from the legal literature in the eighteenth century. Castilian *decisiones* literature was representative of a period – the seventeenth century – in which (i) decentralisation of courts became operational through the role played by *Chancillerías'* judgments – at times even against *communis opinio doctorum*; (ii) the *letrado* (magistrate) *status* was thought of as a model for science and justice; and (iii) a new generation of legal experts coming from the lower nobility, and mostly trained at the University of Salamanca, struggled to achieve the confidence of political power. Castilian law reports were

---

159 *"Defectos de la jurisprudencia. Tratado utilísimo para todos los que se dedican al estudio de esta Facultad, y llegan al honor de actuar como Abogados, ó decidir como Jueces en los Tribunales. Escrito en idioma italiano por Luis Antonio Muratori . . . y traducido al castellano con varias ilustraciones y Notas segun el Derecho real de España por el Lic D Vicente Maria de Tercilla."* Madrid: en la Imprenta de la Viuda de D Joachim Ibarra, 1793, 51, n 1. At the beginning of that century, the *Actos Acordados* had been already commented as *Decreta Senatus Castellani*, by Manuel Arredondo Carmona, *Senatus Consulta Hispaniae illustrata*, 2 vols, Matriti: ex typographia Ildephonsi à Riego, 1729–1732.

160 I Gómez González, *La justicia, el gobierno y sus hacedores. La Real Chancillería de Granada en el Antiguo Régimen*, Granada: Comares, 2003, 182.

161 J Berní y Catalá, *Disertación la La Llave de la Jurisprudencia Española que escrive a sus pasantes*, Valencia: Josef Estevan y Cervera, 1774, 9 ff.

born out of this context. Influenced by the success in other kingdoms of the Catholic monarchy – and France – they were used by some members of this generation to update legal interpretation.

Consequently, the contrasts between sixteenth-century *consilia* – written by authors known for their comments on legal norms – and *decisiones* were significant: the latter (i) gave more relevance to collected legal norms (mainly *NR*); (ii) put at arm's length canon-law norms as much as possible; (iii) built up *ius proprium* mainly out of Castilian family law; and (iv) in their legal reasoning appealed to reason (*ratio*) as opposed to *communis opinio*. However, these authors did not think of *ius proprium* and *ius commune* as beign opposed to one another. On the contrary, they found in *ius commune*[162] a sort of Catholic *ius gentium* to guide *arbitrium juris* to solve dubious cases based on *aequitas* (*ratio*). Precedent was an element to be considered, provided that it was to be applied to case law according to *ratio* but with no binding force – as was then the case in England. The reason was that Castilian high courts could apply *probable interpretatio*, but not *necessaria interpretatio*, an exclusive competence of the monarch.

From the mid-eighteenth century the change would be paramount. Several elements contributed to it: the assertion of the royal law and of the *interpretatio necessaria*; the strengthening of the Royal Council as the Supreme Court of the kingdom; and the reprint and update of several commentaries to compilations of sixteenth-century laws. All of it ended up making the *decisiones* literature in Castile a failed project against the existing royal laws and their commentaries.

---

162 Significantly, in Larrea's *decisiones* the greatest number of quotations comes from civil law. On Larrea's sources see the interesting figures of M M Pérez-Victoria de Benavides, "La teoría", 459, n 55.

4 Law Reporting, Authority and Precedent: the Common Law Paradigm

David J Ibbetson

A. INTRODUCTION
B. THE MEDIEVAL BACKGROUND
C. THE END OF THE YEAR BOOKS: PRINTING AND MANUSCRIPTS
D. AUTHORITY AND PRECEDENT

A. INTRODUCTION

Writing in the middle of the fifteenth century, Sir John Fortescue, Chief Justice, described the English common law as being based upon custom.[1] More than a century later the same could be said, contrasting with an admittedly caricature picture of the legal systems known from continental Europe which were based on the law of Justinian.[2] Roman law had no formal part to play in English law, and consequently English law lacked any formally binding text which was seen as its foundation. But, as elsewhere in Europe, in the sixteenth century (probably because of the rise of the circulation of printed texts) there was a move towards greater predictability in the law than was possible in a purely customary system. Before the middle of the seventeenth century this formal predictability was to be grounded in the authoritative status of decided cases. The purpose of this chpater is to describe the way in which this occurred from the interplay between the reporting of decisions – and the printing of those reports – and the theorising of a doctrine of precedent.

---

1 *De Laudibus Legum Anglie*, ed S B Chrimes, Cambridge: Cambridge University Press, 1949, 39.
2 Sir Thomas Smith, *De Republica Anglorum*, ed L Alstone, Cambridge: Cambridge University Press, 1906, 142.

B. THE MEDIEVAL BACKGROUND

It has been said that, at least since the late thirteenth century, English law was always in some sense a system of case law.[3] There is, undoubtedly, a grain of truth in this: from the middle of the thirteenth century the English common law was developed by judges, who sat together in Westminster Hall (then just outside London) and would have known each other very well. Insofar as there was an idea that "like cases should be decided alike", it would almost inevitably follow that a decision made in one case would influence a decision made in a subsequent case on similar facts. Moreover, not only did judges sit in Westminster Hall, but all significant legal argumentation took place in Westminster Hall. While we cannot say for certain that any successful legal argument would have to fall within the parameters of previous decisions, we can be fairly sure that a heterodox argument which departed from previous decisions – from what was generally accepted to be the law – would have relatively little chance of success. We might see the development of case law in this way as something that was locked in place by the precocious English practice of law reporting, in what eventually came to be known as the "Year Books".[4] Reporting in this form began in the latter part of the thirteenth century and continued until the last year book was printed sometime after 1535.[5]

But this is only a partial picture. Before the middle of the fourteenth century there had been established what might be thought of as an alternative focus for legal thinking in the Inns of Court, hostels which brought together senior and junior lawyers and which may have had from the start an educational function.[6] Formal lectures, readings on important areas of law, took place in the Lent and summer vacations in each of the four Inns of Court, and moots – stylised lawsuits designed to teach young lawyers the rudiments of legal argument – would have constituted a major part of the education of a lawyer. In addition, in bringing together lawyers of different levels of experience, the Inns of Court functioned as places where informal discussion of the law would have taken place on a daily basis. It has been

3 J Baker, *Introduction to English Legal History*, 5th edn, Oxford: Oxford University Press, 2019, 207.
4 P Brand, "The Origins of English Law Reporting", in C Stebbings (ed), *Law Reporting in Britain*, London: Hambledon, 1995, 1–14, at 1.
5 Baker, *Introduction*, 190–192.
6 J Baker, "The Third University of England" (2002) 55 *Current Legal Problems*, 123–150, now in Id, *Collected Papers on English Legal History*, Cambridge: Cambridge University Press, 2013, 143–167, at 143.

strongly argued, therefore, that these types of legal discussion and education in the Inns of Court were at least as important as, and probably more than, decisions reached in Westminster Hall.[7]

This centralising role of the Inns of Court means that we do not have to worry about the difficulty of the circulation of manuscript law reports nor of their reliability. We need not doubt the accuracy of the statements made in the middle of the fifteenth century, that the Year Books existed for the erudition of future generations[8], but need not suppose that every aspiring lawyer would have been expected to learn his law from the Year Books, nor that every advocate would have been expected to leaf through the Year Books every time he had to argue a case.

C. THE END OF THE YEAR BOOKS: PRINTING AND MANUSCRIPTS

Printing changed this.[9] From the 1480s older Year Books began to be printed from manuscripts, and it seems that the printers themselves were creating some new Year Books containing more recent cases.[10] Printing continued apace in the early sixteenth century and around the middle of the century there had emerged something like a fixed canon of Year Book texts running from the middle of the fourteenth century up until 1535, although it would not be until the edition of 1678–1680 that the canon was definitively fixed.[11] The ending of the series of Year Books was once thought to have been significant; however, we know that the practice of individuals keeping reports for themselves did not come to an end, but if anything accelerated, so that the explanation of the ending of the Year Books must lie in the economics of the commercial production of manuscript and printed texts rather than in any development within the legal system. The frequency with which older editions of the Year Books were reprinted[12] makes it unlikely that the old style of Year Books had ceased to be relevant. Stylistically, there was little

---

7　J Baker, *The Law's Two Bodies: Some Evidential Problems in English Legal History*, Oxford: Oxford University Press, 2001, 73–79.

8　Fortescue, *De Laudibus*, 115; Baker, *Law's Two Bodies*, 67, note 29.

9　E Ives, "The Purpose and Making of the Later Year Books", (1973) 89 *Law Quarterly Review*, 64–86; Baker, *Introduction*, 191–192.

10　Ives, "Purpose and Making", 76–78.

11　Baker, *Introduction*, 191.

12　J Baker, "The Books of the Common Law", in L Hellinga and J B Trapp (eds), *The Book in Britain: Volume III, 1400–1557*, Cambridge: Cambridge University Press, 1999, 411–432, and now in Id, *Collected Papers*, 611–636, at 631.

difference between individuals' notes of cases and the more recent Year Book texts.

Year Book texts themselves were decidedly unwieldy. The cases were in chronological order, or at least appeared to be so, and it was thus no easy task to find the answer to any question. Importantly, therefore, alongside the Year Books there began to appear Abridgements, collections of cases arranged under alphabetical headings. The first of these was printed in 1490 and attributed to Nicholas Statham, but by far the most important was that of Anthony Fitzherbert, the so-called "Grand Abridgement", which was printed between 1514 and 1516.[13] It was perhaps this Abridgement, more than anything else, which opened up access to the Year Books, and it may even be the case that the appearance of the Abridgements effectively brought an end to the printing of the Year Books: if we see the Abridgement as an index, then any volumes of reports that were printed after this would fall outside the index; and unless there were to be regular updated reissues of the Abridgement – which would not in fact have been commercially practicable – any such works would have fallen outside what amounted to the definitive canon.

The printed text, whether of a Year Book or Fitzherbert's Abridgement, might have an effect on the development of the substantive law. One example will suffice.[14] Throughout the fifteenth century it had been a matter of controversy whether an action of assumpsit – what we might see as an action for breach of contract – would lie in cases of pure non-performance, as well as in cases of misperformance. The answer which was normally given was that the action was inapplicable, although there might have been a degree of flexibility on the borderline between non-performance and misperformance. In 1499 chief justice Fyneux stated in Gray's Inn that the action would lie. So far as we can see there was no warrant for this, either in decisions of the courts or in the doctrine of the Inns of Court, but his statement was reproduced both in Fitzherbert's Abridgement and in the printed Year Book of 1505 (misdating was not uncommon at this time), and it seems to have triggered a major change in the operation of the action of assumpsit. We may doubt whether his remark would have gained as much currency or as much weight if it had not been so publicised.

---

13 For Abridgements generally, see Baker, *Introduction*, 195–197; for Fitzherbert, "The Book that 'made' the Common law: The First Printing of Fitzherbert's 'La Graunde Abridgement', 1514–1516", (1958) 51 *Law Library Journal*, 100–116, and F Boersma, *Introduction to Fitzherbert's Abridgement*, Abingdon: Professional Books, 1981.

14 J Baker, *The Oxford History of the Laws of England, Volume VI: 1483–1558*, Oxford: Oxford University Press, 2003, 841–860; Fitz Abr, Action sur le Case, 45, YB M.21 Hen VII f 41 pl 66.

Except in the rare case where there was a relevant statute, there was little or nothing which could act as a counterbalance to judicial authority. English law had nothing equivalent to Justinian's *Corpus Iuris* and the later comments on that, and nothing to parallel the authoritative texts of the canon law. The earliest synthetic works of common law to be printed were either high-level overviews of the law of real property (most notably Thomas Littleton's *Tenures* and William Perkins' *Profitable Book*)[15] or largely out-dated texts on pleading which had been composed two centuries or more earlier.[16]

The printing of Year Books and Abridgements brought about a change in legal method. It was now possible to formulate arguments on the basis of specific reports, especially of legal decisions, whether the reports were found in the Year Books or in an Abridgement. Already by the 1530s lawyers were framing arguments in this way, both in court and in more discursive legal writing.[17] Moreover, legal practice was changing too. Whereas in the middle ages most legal argument was focused on pleading and took place before the case went to the jury (the principal mechanism in the common law for the elucidation of facts), with the judges relatively rarely being required to reach a formal decision, in the sixteenth century pleading was largely a matter for the parties without any judicial oversight, and legal arguments took place after the jury's verdict had been given.[18] The judges now had no choice but to decide cases, even if they remained reluctant to reach a final decision where there was any judicial disagreement. The reporting of cases coupled with this change in legal practice led to the crystallisation of legal rules outside the common erudition of the Inns of Court. John Baker has rightly remarked that by the middle of the sixteenth century we have moved into a world in which legal reasoning looks very like the legal reasoning of the nineteenth or twentieth century.[19]

They remained a major problem – not a problem within the law itself, but a problem within the economics of printing. We may take Fitzherbert's Abridgement as an example. It was first printed, as we have seen, between

---

15 Thomas Littleton, *Tenures*, London: Lettou and Machlinia, c 1481 (some sixty editions before 1600); William Perkins, *Perutilis Tractatus*, London: Redman, 1528 (fourteen editions before 1600).

16 For example, *Novae Narrationes*; see Joseph Beale, *Bibliography of Early English Law Books*, Cambridge, MA: Harvard University Press, 1925; supplement by Robert Anderson, Cambridge, MA: Ames Foundation, 1943, 123–124.

17 Baker, *Oxford History*, vol VI, 488–489.

18 Ibid, 35–44, 393–397.

19 Ibid, 489.

1514 and 1516 and was sold at a price of 40 shillings. By way of comparison, a respectable country clergyman at the time might have an annual income of only two or three times this, and although a successful lawyer would have earned well in excess of this amount, a price of 40 shillings would have been well beyond the capacity of a young lawyer beginning to make his way.[20] Even if every successful lawyer arguing in Westminster Hall and every judge possessed his own copy, the number sold in any year remained low; it was perhaps to take fifty years for the copies that were originally printed to sell out.[21] Individual Year Books would have been less expensive; there must have been a significantly bigger market for these since they were reprinted several times in the sixteenth century. However, it is not clear that there would have been a similar market for new reports if the Abridgements are seen to have been functioning as an effective index to the Year Books dating from before the publication of Fitzherbert. This was exacerbated by the grant of a monopoly to print law books to Richard Tottell in 1553 (renewed in expanded form in 1555 and 1559).[22] The market for law books was therefore free from competition and Tottell could afford to produce works which he could be confident would sell. Only two new sets of reports were published before 1600, the date at which Sir Edward Coke's Reports first began to appear. 1571 and 1578 saw the publication of the commentaries of Edmund Plowden, and 1585 the reports of Sir James Dyer. It is significant that the publication of neither of these was the initiative of the publisher himself: Plowden saw his own Commentaries through the press – for fear, he said, of corrupt copies of his manuscript getting into circulation – and Dyer's Reports were published on the initiative of his relatives after his death.[23]

This might have led, and to some extent did lead, to a tension within the law. Legal argument was beginning to be based upon texts, but the printed texts which were available were largely the Year Books which were

---

20 E Ives, *The Common Lawyers of Pre-Reformation England. Thomas Kebell: a case study*, Cambridge: Cambridge University Press, 1983, 321–325. William Staunford, who started to practise in 1539, after some ten years preparation, earned £35 in his first year, rising to well over £100 in his third: N Ramsay, "The Fees they Earned: the Incomes of William Staunford and Other Tuydor Lawyers", in D Ibbetson, N Jones and N Ramsay (eds), *Legal History and its Sources: Essays in Honour of Sir John Baker*, Cambridge: Cambridge University Press, 2019, 139–158, at 144.

21 A second edition appeared in 1565 and a third in 1577.

22 Baker, "Books of the Common Law, 1400–1557", 630–632.

23 Edmund Plowden, *Commentaries*, London: Richard Tottell, 1571, Prologe, iii; James Dyer, *Cy ensuont ascuns nouel cases, collectes per le iades tresreuerend iudge, Mounsieur Iasques Dyer*, London: Richard Tottel, 1585, ii L W Abbott, *Law Reporting in England 1485–1585*, London: Athlone, 1973, 159, 206–207.

becoming increasingly outdated. Although this was to some extent allevi-ated by the publication of Plowden's and Dyer's reports, these did not add a great deal to the amount of material in print. At a time when the law was changing rapidly, responding to the major social and economic shifts of the sixteenth century and reflecting the changes in legal practice which had triggered a massive increase in judicial decision making, the legal materials available were in danger of ossifying. Moreover, the number of practising lawyers was increasing,[24] and even if it is the case that the most important legal work was in the hands of men who were right at the top of the profes-sion, it would have been increasingly difficult to revert to the medieval world in which the Inns of Court were the places in which doctrinal legal think-ing was anchored.[25] But individuals were keeping their own notes in their own manuscript books, and increasingly in the second half of the sixteenth century manuscript reports began to circulate. Many hundreds of volumes of these reports survive, and we may guess that many thousands would once have existed. Some lawyers, no doubt, would have laboriously copied out others' manuscripts for themselves, but others would have resorted to scriveners to copy out texts for them, and it seems clear that some series of reports circulated in commercial copies.[26]

The paucity of printed reports of cases before 1600, therefore, contrasts markedly with the sheer volume of manuscript reports of the reign of Queen Elizabeth I. We must not be misled by the couple of dozen volumes of reports from the sixteenth century which were to be published in the seven-teenth century. The publication of these was almost certainly an attempt by publishers to profit from printing texts from a century earlier which would have been easily available in a world in which authority was increasingly being ascribed to printed texts.[27] The small number of printed reports of cases was hardly supplemented by discursive literature. It is true that some books were written and published, but to a large extent the law which they contained was the law which was derived from the Year Books and other printed reports. It is not difficult to see why this should have been. English law was not taught in the universities, and in so far as it was taught at all this

---

24 W Prest, *The Rise of the Barristers*, Oxford: Clarendon Press, 1988, 7.
25 Above, 85.
26 D Ibbetson, "Law Reporting in the 1590s", in C Stebbings (ed), *Law Reporting in Britain*, 73–88, at 73; Id, "Report and Record in Early-Modern Common Law", in A Wijffels (ed), *Case Law in the Making. The Techniques and Methods of Judicial Records and Law Reports*, vol I: *Essays*, Berlin: Duncker & Humblot, 1997, 55–69, at 55.
27 Below, 91, 93.

took place in the Inns of Court and was focused very much on legal practice. Significantly, there was no basic structure to English law such as was provided in continental Europe by Justinian's institutes. By the 1590s attempts were being made to remedy this,[28] but the case law of the courts remained the dominant source of law.

Although there was no shortage of legal material in manuscript, the use of this material was problematic. Few manuscripts had indexes arranged by subject matter, although of course individual lawyers might have made such indexes for themselves or selected cases from the reports to include in their commonplace books; as had been found with the Year Books, an index was crucial. But manuscript reports took many forms, from individuals' own notes of cases which they had appeared in or had heard, to volumes of reports of what might have been thought to be important cases and which were designed to be circulated.[29] They were, therefore, of very variable quality. Most of them were anonymous, so there was no warrant that the author of any report could be trusted to have understood what was going on in the case. Moreover, reports of the same case might differ from each other or differ from one of the printed reports. There were no clear criteria making it possible to justify the use of one report rather than another. Fairly frequently a report of a case would be linked to the court's record of that case, the plea roll. But plea rolls were not easily accessible to the profession and they were highly formalistic in their contents; comparison with the plea roll would only rarely enable a later lawyer to determine whether the earlier report was in fact accurate.

The bedrock of legal argument therefore remained the printed reports, that is to say the Year Books as supplemented by Plowden and Dyer.[30] It followed that the law had a lack of historical perspective: a case from the mid-fourteenth century was just as relevant as a case in Dyer or Plowden (although the citation rate increases with the recentness of the case). Even where the law had been developing significantly in the sixteenth century,

---

28 A Watson, "Justinian's Institutes and Some English Counterparts", in P Stein and A Lewis (eds), *Studies in Justinian's Institutes in Memory of J A C Thomas*, London: Sweet & Maxwell, 1984, 181–186.

29 Ibbetson, "Report and Record", 56–62. Two examples of reports which seem to have been designed to be circulated are the reports of Thomas Coventry (Id, "Coventry's Reports" (1995) 16 *Journal of Legal History*, 281–303), and the anonymous collection of reports from the Exchequer Chamber (Id, "Errores in Camera Scaccarii", in D Ibbetson, N Jones and N Ramsay (eds), *Legal History and its Sources: Essays in Honour of Sir John Baker*, Cambridge: Cambridge University Press, 2019, 23–43).

30 Ibbetson, "Report and Record", 63–66.

reliance was being placed substantially on earlier material. In *Slade's Case*, for example, argued between 1596 and 1602 and recognised at the time as a lawsuit of the greatest importance,[31] not a single case known only from the manuscript was cited by any of the lawyers on either side. Yet this case was seen at the time as being a case of paramount importance, so much so that we have detailed reports of all of the arguments, and the legal point involved could not have arisen directly in the two centuries covered by Year Book reports.

It is worth pausing for a moment to consider the model of law which is being assumed at this time. If old law was just as good as new law, it must have followed that the law had not changed – except in so far as statute had intervened. The common law was timeless,[32] and there was no sense that it was being made by judges rather than being simply articulated by them. Decisions were evidence of what the law was, they did not produce it.

A major turning point occurred after 1600. In that year the first volume of Sir Edward Coke's Reports was printed, and a further ten volumes followed in the next decade or so.[33] Although the reports were rooted in the tradition of the Year Books, they provide a more modern interpretation of the older law. Coke was Attorney General and later chief justice of, first, the Common Pleas and, then, the King's Bench, so that his interpretations of the law carried very great weight. It would be wrong to think that his reports necessarily recorded the reasons which the judges had for reaching any particular decision; and they were to be criticised by one of his great rivals, Thomas Egerton, Lord Ellesmere, for their lack of fidelity to judicial reasoning.[34] We may assume that Coke was aware of this, and that his reports, like the continental *decisiones*, were meant rather to explain the "true" basis of decisions which had been reached. Comparison of his printed reports with his own manuscripts show that at least sometimes he edited them considerably before publication, not merely with a view to clarifying their mode of expression but no doubt intentionally formulating the reasons for the deci-

---

31 Ibbetson, "Law Reporting in the 1590s", 84–85; for the reports of this case, see J Baker, "New Light on Slade's Case" (1971) 29 *Cambridge Law Journal*, 51–67 and 213–236, and now in Id, *Collected Papers*, 1129–1175.

32 This seems to have been the position taken in the prefaces of Edward Coke's *Reports*, discussed by George Garnett, "'The Ould Fields': Law and History in the Prefaces to Sir Edward Coke's Reports", (2013) 34 *Journal of Legal History*, 245–284.

33 Two further volumes were published posthumously.

34 "The Lord Chancellor Egertons Observations upon ye Lord Cookes Reportes", (1615), ed L A Knafla, *Law and Politics in Jacobean England: The Tracts of Lord Chancellor Ellesmere*, Cambridge: Cambridge University Press, 1977, 297–318.

sions in a different way.[35] He might simply reproduce his own argument in the case, taking no notice of the arguments which had been made on the other side.[36] At a time when carefully reasoned judicial decisions were the exception rather than the rule – it is noteworthy that the words of judges were described as their arguments and not their judgments – we should perhaps not criticise him for this too much, and his reports were undeniably a commercial success in so far as we can judge from the speed with which they were reprinted, but as greater weight began to be placed on the rea-soned decision[37] this style of reporting became somewhat anachronistic, to be replaced by a style of reporting more faithful to the reasons put forward by the judges.

The perceived inadequacies of manuscript reports, coupled with the high status in the legal profession of Plowden, Coke and Dyer, led in the early seventeenth century to a very clear shift of reliance upon printed reports rather than manuscripts.[38] Other factors may have contributed too: as early as 1553, for example, an attempt had been made to regulate the printing of law books,[39] and although this does not appear to have affected their rate of publication there did develop a practice of seeking the approval of judges for the publication of volumes of reports; in 1622 chief justice Hobart demanded to know by what warrant certain reports attributed to William Dalison had been put in print, and when it appeared that their publication had not been authorised the lawyer who had been citing them immediately ceased to rely on them.[40] A lawyer might still have some manuscripts in his own private library,[41] but in framing arguments in court it was the printed text which mattered.

35 See for example D Ibbetson, "Edward Coke, Roman Law, and the Law of Libel", in L Hutson (ed), *Oxford Handbook of English Law and Literature, 1500–1700*, Oxford: Oxford University Press, 2017, 487–506.

36 As in his report of *Slade's Case* (1602) 4 Co Rep 91.

37 Below, 96.

38 I Williams, "He Creditted More the Printed Booke: Common Lawyers' Receptivity to Print, c 1550–1640", (2010) 28 *Law and History Review*, 39–70.

39 Baker, "Books of the Common Law, 1400–1557", 631.

40 *Wade's Case* (1622) Cambridge University Library MS Ii 5.34, f.123.

41 J Baker, "English Law Books and Legal Publishing, 1557–1695", in J Barnard and D F McKenzie (eds), *The Cambridge History of the Book in Britain*, vol IV (1557–1695), Cambridge: Cambridge University Press, 2002, 474–503, and now in Id, *Collected Papers*, 637–669, at 638–639.

D. AUTHORITY AND PRECEDENT[42]

At the same time as this change in practice was occurring, English law was developing its theory of the authority of judicial precedents. Both the terms "authority" and "precedent" were ambiguous, and it is necessary to try to unpick this ambiguity.

So far as authority is concerned, we should distinguish between having authority and being an authority.[43] A king might have authority within his kingdom, a sheriff might have authority within his county, in the sense that they might have power to command. Within the scope of his authority an instruction given by a King or sheriff to a person subject to that authority rendered the person instructed liable to obey. Looking from the point of view of the common law, the power to command was vested in Parliament, so an act of Parliament would be determinative of a legal rule; although it might be argued, ultimately unsuccessfully, that an instruction issued by the monarch might be similarly determinative. Being an authority must be understood in terms of the language of medieval dialectic, traceable back to Cicero's *Topica*.[44] An authority was a legitimate source of argument based on what some other person had said or written, based on an idea that a person who was expert in his field ought in principle to be believed, *expertus in sua scientia credendum est*. It might be necessary or it might be merely probable; if it was the latter it could be countered by other probable arguments, but if it was the former it could not be countered at all.[45] A probable argument had weight, while a necessary argument was determinative. All of this was well understood in the sixteenth century, and arguments from authority were ubiquitous in English discourse in the early modern period.[46] In a legal context, arguments from authority were clearly described by the Dutch writer Nicolaus Everardus (Nicolaas Everaerts), whose *Topicorum seu Locorum Legalium Opus de Inventione* looks to have been influential in England in the second half of the century. In the common law context, a decision in a case, or even an argument in a case, was authority, in the sense that it could be used in a subsequent legal

---

42 This section is substantially derived from D Ibbetson, "Authority and Precedent", in M Godfrey (ed), *Law and Authority in British Legal History, 1200–1900* (Cambridge 2016), 60–84.

43 Ibid, 71.

44 *Topica*, 4.24; and behind this, Aristotle, *Topics*, 1.1.

45 John Buridan, *Summulae de Dialectica*, 6.5.10, ed G Klima, New Haven: Yale University Press, 2001, 482.

46 Ibbetson, "Authority and Precedent", 69–73.

argument. But, unlike a statute, it was not a necessary authority and was not determinative.

Precedent, literally speaking, was something which had gone before; in an English legal context it was strongly focused on something in writing. It might be a form of conveyance, it might be a form of pleading, it might be a form of judgment.[47] If that which had gone before had been accepted without criticism, there was reason to believe that it was acceptable and could therefore be followed. Its weight was all the stronger if the earlier example was the work of someone worthy of respect, such as a judge or sergeant at law, an expert in his science who ought to be believed. In the language of dialectic, it was probable authority,[48] although its distant roots were found in the work of Quintilian rather than Cicero. In the middle of the sixteenth century continental European works on legal dialectic began to assimilate authority and precedent; hence the second edition of Everaert's *Topica* referred to the "argument from authority or, if you prefer, from precedent".[49] The Latin word for precedent was *praejudicium*, literally something which had been adjudged before. Although the meaning of precedent as any form of written text continued – and indeed continues today – and in the latter part of the sixteenth century it came to be focused more on a previous judgment, in particular a judgment that had been reasoned.

This trend towards assimilating the ideas of authority and precedent, in the sense of previous reasoned judgments, was consolidated around 1600. It might have been influenced by the establishment of the court of Exchequer Chamber to hear writs of error from the more radical King's Bench, but the evidence suggests that at the time the King's Bench did not see itself as being absolutely bound by these decisions;[50] or some part might have been played by the *mitior sensus* rule in defamation, according to which words had to be taken in their most benevolent sense, so that it might have been thought that there was no room for any assessment of the context of the words or the intention with which they had been

---

47 *Grendon v Bishop of Lincoln* (1577) Plo 493, 503 (charter); *Buckley v Thomas* (1555) Plo 118, 128 (pleading); *Anon* (1588) BL MS Lansdowne 1076 fol 129 (counsel relying on prior judgment as precedent).

48 *Charnock v Worsley* (1589) 1 Leon 114, 116 per Egerton S-G: "Presidents are not so holy, *quod violari non debeant*".

49 Everardus, *Loci argvmentorvm legales* . . . Lvdgvni: apvd Gvliel. Rovillvm, 581. Clearer still, treating the two terms as essentially interchangeable, is Claudius Cantiuncula, *Topica Legalia* . . . Basileae: Apvd Hieronymnm Cvrionem . . . 1545, 5–8.

50 Ibbetson, "Errores in Camera Scaccarii".

spoken.[51] William Fulbecke's *Direction, or Preparative to the Study of Law*[52] may have played a part: relying on the Oxford Professor Alberico Gentili's *Lectionum et Epistolarum quae ad Ius Civile Pertinent*,[53] and probably through him referring to the Italian humanist Alciatus, he distinguished carefully between reasoned opinions and *obiter dicta* in describing the force of judgments. But of central importance, so far as we can see, were the works of Sir Edward Coke.[54] His printed report of *Slade's Case*, decided in 1602 and published in 1604, contains a disquisition on the force of precedent,[55] despite the fact that there had been no hint of this in the arguments which had been put forward in the case. Furthermore, whereas in the arguments in Slade's Case "precedent" was being used in its widest sense, in the printed report all of Coke's focus is on *judicial* precedent. There are very close linguistic similarities between Coke's writings and the works of legal dialectic published in continental Europe, so much so that it is almost impossible not to believe that he had been strongly influenced by these. His younger contemporary John Dodderidge was quite explicit in citing them in his work on legal method dating from the late 1620s.[56] By this time the authority and precedent of case law were being treated as equivalent, although it must be stressed that in terms of the theory of dialectic cases remained merely probable authority and not necessary authority: later courts should, in principle, follow cases when similar facts arose, but they were not absolutely bound to do so. It was this that put weight on the reports of cases; the official record of the case, the plea roll, did not give reasons, it was only a report that did that. Noticeably, therefore, reliance would have to be placed on the report even though it was the judgment itself which was, in theory, the precedent. So, for example, in the case of *Wright v Swanton* in 1604, dealing with the same point as had been decided in *Slade's Case*, it was not so much the judgment in *Slade's Case* that was treated as being authoritative but expressly Coke's report of it, which had just been published.[57]

---

51 Baker, *Introduction*, 471–472.

52 London: Thomas Wight, 1600, 84.

53 London: Wolfius, 1584, lib III, cap 17 (= 217).

54 Ibbetson, "Authority and Precedent", 76–77.

55 4 Co Rep 91.

56 John Dodderidge, *The English Lawyer. Describing a Method for the Managing of the Lawes of this Land*, London: Printed by the Assignees of I More Esq, 1631, 61, citing as well as Everardus and Cantiuncula, Hegendorphinus, Fregius, Gambraeus, Apellus, Bellonus, Oldendorpius, Nevisanus and Grammara.

57 (1604), in J Baker, *Baker & Milsom Sources of English Legal History*, 2nd edn, Oxford: Oxford University Press, 2010, 479.

It was this confluence of the practice of relying upon reports of reasoned arguments and judgments and the theory that these arguments and judgments, judicial precedents, were probable authorities that led to English law's emergence as a system of case law, although it was not until the nineteenth century that its theory of binding precedent was fully formulated.

5 Legal Authorities in the Making of Portuguese Private Law: Emphyteusis and Majorat in Practical Literature

Gustavo César Machado Cabral

A. PORTUGUESE LAW IN THE SIXTEENTH AND SEVENTEENTH CENTURIES: POLITICS, INSTITUTIONS AND LEGAL STRUCTURE

This chapter examines a period from the sixteenth century until the beginning of the eighteenth century, when Portugal was a maritime empire whose territories extended over four continents that were connected by maritime routes allowing for the circulation of people, goods and ideas. As the focus of this discussion is the centre of the empire and not its periphery, the kingdom – the form by which the European peninsular area was known – is in the spotlight.

The dynasty of Avis was founded after the so-called "Avis Revolution" between 1383 and 1385, resulting in the coronation of King John I. From previous political experience during the Borgonha dynasty (1139–1383) onwards, the king played an important role in the law making that was exercised in the *cortes*, assemblies with noblemen, high clergymen and the attorneys of the villages.[1] Some of these legislative acts were published in the twentieth century,[2] but since the fifteenth century many of these acts have been gathered with other orders enacted by the king after being counselled by jurists. These compilations were named *Ordenações do Reino* (Ordinances of the Kingdom) and were officially published during the reigns of Afonso V (1445), Manuel I (1521) and Philip II (1603) – the last one enacted during the so-called "Iberian Union" (1580–1640), an age when the Spanish Habsburg kings held the Portuguese Crown following the succession crisis of 1580. Unlike the modern codes, these compilations were not intended to be complete or applied in any case, but to be the common law of the kingdom (*ius communi regni*),[3] which meant that they were applicable whenever a particular norm did not exist or was unsuitable for a specific case.

While the *Ordenações do Reino* were the highest source of law, they were not the only source. This chapter will focus on two others – legal literature and case law. Before that, however, some introductory remarks are needed. Portuguese learned legal culture relied on the only law school of the entire kingdom, Coimbra University, where the professors were under the influence of traditional *mos italicus* and, from the second half of the sixteenth century until the reformation of the university during the reign

---

1 See I Graes, *Contributo para um estudo histórico-jurídico das cortes portuguesas entre 1481– 1641*, Coimbra: Almedina, 2005; P Cardim, *Cortes e cultura política no Portugal do Antigo Regime*, Lisboa: Cosmos, 1998.

2 N J Espinosa Gomes da Silva (ed), *Livro de leis e posturas*, Lisboa: Universidade de Lisboa, 1971.

3 "Ius regium, ius commune est in regno". Antonio da Gama, *Decisiones Supremi Senatus Regni Lusitaniae*, Barcinone: Lelij Marini, 1597, Dec 50, n 5, 55–56; "Nostrum ius regium est nostrum ius commune". Gabriel Pereira de Castro, *Decisiones Supremi eminentissimique Senatus Portugalliae ex gravissimorum patrum responsis collectae*, Ulyssipone: Petrum Craesbeeck, 1621, Dec 2, 10.

of King Joseph I and the ministry of the Marquis of Pombal in 1772, of the Society of Jesus and scholastic thinking.[4] Throughout the chronological framework of this chapter, Portuguese legal literature takes a prominent role thanks to the influence of some particularly important authors and the huge number of editions of certain books, as will become clear later.

Case law, on the other hand, depended on the existence of high courts. Royal jurisdiction had a multilevel organisation that included ordinary judges elected in the villages (*juízes ordinários*) and erudite judges appointed by the king to act in the juridical space of the village (*juízes de fora*) and *ouvidores* responsible for appeals in the term of a *comarca* (which extended across many villages), but also the *Tribunais de Relação*, collegiate courts of appeal with jurisdiction over large areas, and the *Casa da Suplicação*, the highest court with jurisdiction over the entire empire. In the early modern age, the *Tribunal da Relação* of Oporto was the only one in the peninsular area of the Portuguese Empire and, since the justice reformation of 1582, it had jurisdiction over the northern part of Portugal; in other areas of the peninsula, the *Casa da Suplicação* filled that role. In the overseas territories, the *Tribunal da Relação* of Goa was installed in India in the sixteenth century and in Portuguese America, others were installed in Bahia (1609 and, after been closed during the Dutch occupation of the Brazilian Coast, reinstalled in 1652), Rio de Janeiro (1751), Maranhão (1812) and Pernambuco (1820). For the purpose of this chapter, I will emphasise the court of Oporto. Particular jurisdictions – such as the corporative and seigneurial-like – and other relevant but specialised courts – such as the *Desembargo do Paço* or the *Mesa de Consciência e Ordens* – are not part of this study. Most of the cases reported here were originally decided by the *Casa da Suplicação* and a few by the *Tribunal da Relação* of Oporto.

Bearing in mind the distinction highlighted by John Baker between "records" and "reports",[5] the non-existence of official publications of the court rulings in Portugal is worth mentioning, particularly if, according to the *Ordenações do Reino*, the judges were required to give a reason for their decisions.[6] Most of the continental courts in Europe did not publish records,

---

4 For an overview, see G C Machado Cabral, *Direito natural e iluminismo no direito português do final do Antigo Regime*, Fortaleza: Universidade Federal do Ceará, 2011.
5 J H Baker, "Preface", in Id (ed), *Judicial records, Law reports and the growth of case law*. Berlin: Duncker & Humblot, 1989, 7.
6 Lib III, tit 66, 7.

thus giving an aura of secrecy to the deliberations of the courts.[7] Practical literature filled this gap.

Many questions about the practice of the Portuguese high courts remain unanswered, probably due to the lack of monographic studies on the *Casa da Suplicação*.[8] Others, such as the enforceability of previous decisions of the court to subsequent cases, are clearer thanks to recent scholarship.[9] However, most of the huge number of documents of this Court, (particularly lawsuits) – preserved in the National Archive of the *Torre do Tombo* in Lisbon – have yet to be properly explored, which is why this chapter focuses more on what case law can be found in legal literature. It aims to contribute to the understanding of the tangled relations between legal literature and case law, looking specifically at private law. Practical books had a prominent role that must be better understood.

B. THE SOURCES

Until the end of the *Ancien Régime*, there was no official publication of court decisions in Portugal. However, in their Lisbon workshops, editors unofficially printed books of juridical literature from the sixteenth century – both royal ordinances and further legislation. Unlike many other European states,[10] in Portugal court rulings were not secret, and reasoning was mandatory for all judges since a royal ordinance dating from 1521.[11] However, having access to these rulings was not easy, because of the absence of an official collection of decisions published by the Portuguese courts. At the

---

7 See S Hocks, *Gerichtsgeheimnis und Begründungszwang: zur Publizität der Entscheidunsgründe im Ancien Régime und im frühen 19 Jahrhundert*, Frankfurt am Main: Vittorio Klostermann, 2002.

8 António Manuel Hespanha acknowledged this deficiency in the historiography and indicates a few paths towards a monographic study on the *Casa da Suplicação*. A M Hespanha, *As vésperas do Leviathan. Instituições e poder político, Portugal – século XVII*, Coimbra: Almedina, 1994, 228–236. For other issues, particularly related to the reasoning of the sentences, see G C Machado Cabral, *Literatura jurídica na Idade Moderna. As decisiones no Reino de Portugal (séculos XVI e XVII)*, Rio de Janeiro: Lumen Juris, 2017, 60–72.

9 A P Barbas Homem, *Judex Perfectus: função jurisdicional e estatuto judicial em Portugal, 1640–1820*, Coimbra: Almedina, 2003, 296–307.

10 For an overview, see Cabral, *Literatura jurídica*, 52–60.

11 "Mandamos, que daqui por diante todos os Nossos Desembargadores, Corregedores das Comarcas, e todos os Ouvidores, e Juízes de Fóra, posto que cada huum dos sobreditos Letrados nom sejam, e quaisquer outros Julguadores, que Letrados forem, que sentenças (assim na primeira instancia, como na causa d'appellaçam, ou agravo, ou na causa da revista) a causa, ou causas, per que se fundam a condenar, ou absolver, ou revoguar, dizendo especificamente o que é, que se prova, e por que causas do feito se fundam a darem suas sentenças". *Ordenações do Reino (Ordenações Manuelinas)*, lib III, tit 50, 6

end of their books, Jorge de Cabedo and Belchior Febo had sections for the transcription of *arrestos*, which were decisions taken by the *Casa da Suplicação*. In terms of size, however, these transcripts take up only a comparatively small part of the whole work of both authors.[12]

If direct access to the courts' decisions was difficult, indirect access was considerably simpler, thanks to the availability of practical literature. Probably the best description of its role in disseminating case law in early modern Portugal was made by an ironic book entitled *Demetério Moderno ou o bibliografo jurídico portuguez* ("Modern Demetrius, of the Portuguese juridical bibliophile"): "They [scil, the jurists] do not say 'the *Tribunal da Relação* (Royal Court), the *Desembargo do Paço* (Palatine Council), the *Conselho da Fazenda* (Fiscal Council), the *Mesa da Consciência* (Court of Conscience) and the *Conselho Ultramarino* (Ultramarine Council) decided so'; but they affirm 'Pegas, Silva, Gama, Portugal, Guerreiro, Paiva, Barbosa, Mendes a Castro claim so'".[13] This sarcastic tone tells us something important: the litigant parties knew of the Portuguese courts' decisions through the practical literature.

Recent legal historical studies have highlighted the role of legal literature in the early modern period both from a dogmatic perspective[14] and in a kind of "sociology of literature", focusing on the production and circulation of books and their authors.[15] Following this perspective, the present contribution divides Portuguese juridical books in different literary genres, not to separate them but to examine their common features. This way, the three most important genres can be distinguished – commentaries, monographs and practical literature. In this last group, *decisiones*, *consilia* and *allega-*

---

12 In the first volume of the 1699 edition of Jorge de Cabedo's book, the transcription of *arrestos* has only 16 pages, while the *decisiones* reaches 194 pages. In Belchior Febo's (1625), *arrestos* has 78 pages against the 370 pages of the *decisiones*.

13 António Barnabé de Elescano Barreto e Aragão, *Demétrio Moderno, ou o bibliografo jurídico portuguez*, Lisboa: Officina de Lina da Silva Godinho, 1781, 112.

14 A M Hespanha, *Como os juristas viam o mundo. Direitos, estados, pessoas, coisas, contratos, ações e crimes*, Lisboa: CreativeSpace Independent Publishing, 2015.

15 F Ranieri "Juristische Literatur aus dem Ancien Régime und historische Literatursoziologie. Einige methodologische Vorüberlegungen", in C Bergfeld (ed). *Aspekte europäischer Rechtsgeschichte: Festgabe für Helmut Coing zum 70. Geburtstag*, Frankfurt am Main: Vittorio Klostermann, 1982, 292–322; C. Reske, *Die Buchdrucker des 16 und 17 Jahrhunderts im deutschen Sprachgebiet: auf der Grundlage des gleichnamigen Werks von Josef Benzing*, Wiesbaden: Harrassowitz Verlag, 2007; J-M Scholz, "Legislação e jurisprudência em Portugal nos séculos XVI a XVIII: fontes e literature" (1976) 25 *Scientia Juridica*, 512–587; Id, sv, "Portugal", in H Coing (ed), *Handbuch der Quellen und Literatur der neueren europäischen Privatrechtsgeschichte. Zweiter Band: Neuere Zeit (1500–1800), das Zeitalter des Gemeinen Rechts. Zweiter Teilband: Gesetzgebung und Rechtsprechung*, München: C H Beck, 1977, 1319–1342.

tiones are included because of their focus on practical matters, particularly on law courts' decisions.[16]

As previous works have made clear,[17] there are many similarities among these genres, especially the interest in a forensic practice. In the *decisiones*, each *decisio* was on a specific problem decided by a certain court. In the *consilia*, a specific problem was addressed to a jurist that was responsible for answering the consultation. In the *allegationes*, the author was usually a counsel who would publish the arguments that he had presented in court for his client. Finally, a final group that may be called "practical literature in a strict sense" is particularly concerned with providing the litigants an overview of the most relevant forensic practice, including the *resolutiones* and what Portuguese legal scholarship[18] has called *"praxe"* or *"praxística"*. While all four categories ultimately allowed the readers to get to know case law, this aim is all the more apparent in the final group. This is why this chapter will rely mainly on practical literature, notably on the *decisiones* written by António da Gama, Álvaro Valasco, Jorge de Cabedo, Belchior Febo, Gabriel Pereira de Castro, António de Sousa de Macedo and Diogo Guerreiro Camacho de Aboim, as well as the *allegationes* and the *resolutiones* by Manuel Álvares Pegas, and finally the *observationes* by Miguel de Reinoso.

C. PRIVATE LAW IN PRACTICAL LITERATURE: WHY *MAJORAT* AND *EMPHYTEUSIS*?

When analysing the contents of the Portuguese *decisiones* literature, I have classified each *decisio* into four groups according to the fivefold internal division of the *Ordenações do Reino* (1603).[19] Parts one and two (public law and ecclesiastical law) are in the first group of my classification, and the

---

16 This group was inspired by the idea of *Entscheidungsliteratur*, which was described by Heinrich Gehrke. In his text, Gehrke referred to *decisiones* and *consilia* as *Entscheidungsliteratur*, but I have added the allegationes to this category due to the similarities among them. H Gehrke, *Die privatrechtliche Entscheidungsliteratur Deutschlands: Charakteristik und Bibliografie der Rechtsprechungs- und Konsiliensammlungen vom 16 bis zum Beginn de 19 Jahrhunderts*, Frankfurt am Main: Vittorio Klostermann, 1974, 3–4; G C Machado Cabral, "Pegas e Pernambuco: notas sobre o direito comum e o espaço colonial" (2018) 9(2) *Direito & Práxis*, 704–706.

17 Cabral, *Literatura jurídica*.

18 A M Hespanha, *História das instituições. Épocas medieval e moderna*, Coimbra: Almedina, 1982, 518–524.

19 The *Ordenações do Reino* were divided into five books, but in my analysis the *decisiones* on public law and ecclesiastical law come together.

three other branches (civil procedural law, private law and criminal law) have their own group. For the purpose of this chapter, what is called "private law" gathered together *decisiones* devoted to the subjects treated in Book 4 of the *Ordenações* – the classical matters of private law, such as the law of the persons (including personal status and secular effects of marriage), law of obligations, contracts, successions and property law. Private law had an unquestionable prominence: 44 per cent of the *decisiones* in the book of Jorge de Cabedo (1602) deal with private law; in that of António de Sousa de Macedo (1660) the figure increases to nearly 46 per cent. In the other practical books, the number of *decisiones* on these matters is even higher: 56 per cent in Belchior Febo (1619–1625); 65 per cent in Miguel de Reinoso;[20] 72 per cent in Álvaro Valasco (1588); 78 per cent in Gabriel Pereira de Castro (1621); 81 per cent in Diogo Guerreiro Camacho de Aboim (1738); and 84 per cent in António da Gama's (1578). Clearly, practical literature focuses more on private law than on other branches of the law.

Among the many possible topics on private law, this chapter will focus on *majorats* and *emphyteusis*. Both institutes are related to property law and are connected to other issues such as obligations, contracts and successions. Focusing our attention on them as examples regarding private law is useful both because of their close association with other private-law subjects and, moreover, because of their great importance among Portuguese practical literature (see Figure 5.1). Apart from *decisiones*, in the other major source discussed here, the *resolutiones* of Pegas, three out of twenty *resolutiones* deal with both topics. These topics are relevant for Pegas, as he published a four-volume treatise specifically devoted to *majorats* (*Tractatus de exclusione, inclusione, successione, & erectione maioratus*, 1685).

António Manuel Hespanha defined *majorat* as way of settling some real estate so as to ensure that the succession *mortis causa* would always follow a particular order established by the owner through a will or a contract in terms that could differ from the order of succession established in the *Ordenações do Reino*.[21] Manuel Álvares Pegas highlighted the effects of *majorat* on real estate in terms of indivisibility, integrity and conservation

---

20 The book of Reinoso, entitled *Observationes practicae in quibus multa quae in controversiam in forensibus judiciis adducuntur*, is not properly considered *decisiones* literature, despite its interest in forensic questions. It is structured in 74 *observationes* that deal with practical matters, but in a different way from how *decisiones* did. For further clarification, see Cabral, *Literatura jurídica*, 114–118.

21 Hespanha, *Como os juristas*, 435–436.

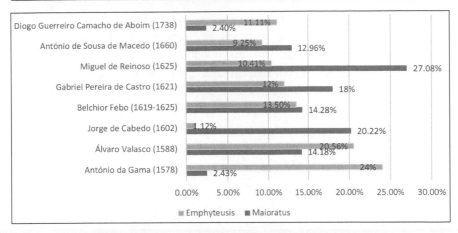

Maioratus and *emphyteusis* in *decisiones* on private law

of the estate.[22] Primogeniture is a fundamental element in Luís de Molina's concept of *majorat*, as a means to ensure that the land would remain within the same family.[23] Thus, the person who establishes a *majorat* would be able to control the future of the family's estates, since the deed creating the *majorat* would also establish the rules governing the succession, including the prohibition to divide the estate in full or in part.

Emphyteusis, in its turn, is the right (whether perpetual or temporary) to enjoy land and its fruits against the payment of a sum to the landowner. Being a real right, the landowner would be left with the "direct ownership" over the land, whereas the *emphyteuta* would have the so-called "useful ownership" of the same land, as well the obligation of tendering it back to the landowner whenever the *emphyteuta* wanted to sell it, due to the right of first refusal of the landowner. Only if the landowner did not avail himself of such right could the *emphyteuta* sell to a third party, but in such case he also had to pay a sum to the landowner.[24] Portuguese early modern legal literature highlights the importance of *emphyteusis* in the country. Writing in the sixteenth century, Francisco Caldas Pereira, the author of one of the most relevant monographs on this topic, described the kingdom as "a single and universal emphyteusis".[25]

22 Manuel Álvares Pegas, *Tractatus de exclusieve, inclusione, successione, & erectione maioratus. Pars prima*, Ulyssipone: Michaelis Deslandes, 1685, 4.
23 Ludovico de Molina, *De hispanorum primogeniorum origine ac natura libri quatuor*, Coloniae: Ioannis Baptistae Ciotti Senensis, 1588, 1–7 (lib I, cap 1).
24 Hespanha, *Como os juristas*, 379.
25 "... quid est regnum hoc, nisi vna, & vniuersalis emphyteusis?", Francisco Caldas Pereira,

Both *majorats* and *emphyteusis* were trending topics in early modern Portugal, as the statistics above attest (see Figure 5.1). The popularity of these subjects in practical literature would suggest that they were frequently debated before the royal courts. Indeed, both legal literature and royal courts sought to clarify each and every issue arising from the definition of these institutes in the *Ordenações do Reino*. Thus, the two subjects provide a very good example of the interplay between different legal sources in the early modern period, a time in which royal statutes, forensic literature and case law mutually influenced each other.

D. ANALYSING THE WORKS

We shall now proceed to examine how Portuguese practical literature used court decisions in discussions on private law. This line of enquiry will be based on quantitative analysis so as to answer questions about the use of case law, the court where the case was decided, and how the same case appeared in the text. As previously explained, the analysis is based on the writings on *majorat* and *emphyteusis* in the selected works mentioned above, which provide a good sample of all kinds of practical literature (as specified in B. THE SOURCES).

(1) *Decisones*

The *decisiones* literature was the most important kind of practical literature in Portugal, not only because of the significant number of books published over a long period – seven books published between 1578 and 1738[26] – but also because of its editorial success. All the books except the final one (published by Diogo Guerreiro Camacho de Aboim) had at least four editions in different cities, including many of the principal printing centres of early modern Europe (e.g. Antwerp, Frankfurt am Main and Venice). In his incomplete (and perhaps not entirely reliable) inventory,[27] Johannes-Michael Scholz[28] listed, for example, nineteen editions of Antonio da Gama's

Commentarivs analyticvs, de renovatione emphyteutica. Ulyssippone, Emmanuel de Lyra Typo, 1585, *quaestio* 11, n 21, 87.

26 This chapter does not analyse the volumes of Manuel Themudo da Fonseca's (1589–1652) *Decisiones et quaestiones senatus archiepiscopalis metropolis Olysiponensi* because of its ecclesiastical nature, which falls outside the scope of the present work.

27 A discussion about the editions of these books and the list made by Scholz (which is highly relevant despite some specific shortcomings) can be found in Cabral, *Literatura jurídica*, 126–127.

28 Scholz, "Legislação e jurisprudência em Portugal", 1335–1336.

Decisiones Supremi Senatus Lusitaniae, printed between 1578 and 1734, and eleven editions of Jorge de Cabedo's *Practicarum observationum sive decisionum Supremi Senatus Regni Lusitaniae*, printed between 1602 and 1734.

Instead of focusing on the individual analysis of each work, I shall concentrate on the structure and the content of the cases discussed in the books in order to understand whether there was a clear pattern in the use of *decisiones* as a legal source. Bearing in mind the inappropriate equivalence between *decisiones* literature and law reports, which was the main reason of criticism by Portuguese jurists in the Enlightenment,[29] the following topics will clarify the role of case law in this kind of literature.

(a) Presence of case law

First, it is important to identify the effective use of case law in *decisiones* literature, and this can be clarified only by verifying each decision in every book. A thorough analysis of the books proves that case law was one of the three kinds of authority invoked, alongside legal literature and statutory law, but it is not easy to establish a hierarchy among them. Even a superficial examination of all the books leads to the conclusion that some *decisiones* did not even mention a case decided by a court, and that case law was used less than legal literature. Taking the case of Belchior Febo's *Decisiones Senatus Regni Lusitaniae* as an example, only twelve out of 220 *decisiones* do not mention court decisions – a lower number in comparison to the thirty-eight that do not mention the *Ordenações do Reino*, but four times higher than the three *decisiones* that do not invoke the *auctoritas* of a single author.

Looking at all cases on *emphyteusis* and *majorat* in the seven books, most relied heavily on case law in their arguments. All of the eleven *decisiones* on *emphyteusis* and *majorat* in Diogo Guerreiro Camacho de Aboim's (1738) mentioned case law, as well as the twenty present in Belchior Febo (1619–1625) and the five found in António de Sousa de Macedo (1660). Seventy-eight out of eighty *decisiones* in António da Gama (1578) and eighteen of the twenty-one in Gabriel Pereira de Castro (1621) mentioned case law; a proportion that is higher than the slight majority (twelve out of twenty-one) found in the work of Jorge de Cabedo (1602). Only in Álvaro Valasco (1588) do the vast majority of the cases (thirty out of thirty-one) not mention case

---

29 For a reconstruction of the Portuguese historiography on the *decisiones* literature, particularly the criticism on this kind of literature, see Cabral, *Literatura jurídica*, 118–121.

law. These figures seem to prove the relevance of case law in the eyes of the authors of collections of *decisiones*.

(b) Ways of using case law

More important than verifying the presence of case law in a collection of *decisiones* is understanding the way in which case law was used, and especially the relationship between the cases invoked before the court and the court's decision. There are two ways of using case law in this kind of literature. First, case law may appear as the basic element of the *decisio* discussing a specific legal issue. In this case, the solution depends on the *decisio* itself, which thus provides the answer for the specific issue. The central argument is by no means reduced to the reference of the court's decision because of the strong presence of the learned jurists supporting the author's opinions. Even so, the final resolution is based on a case quoted either at the beginning or at the end of the *decisio*.

To give an example from Jorge de Cabedo's work, let us take a case discussing whether the passage of time would terminate the pension for *emphyteusis*. At the beginning of the *decisio*, the author mentioned a decision of 1575 (without explicit reference to the specific court that rendered it).[30] In another *decisio*, focused on whether a donation required the consent of the party who had the direct ownership of the thing, Cabedo referred to the case of the *Crown v Miguel de Noronha*, judged by the *Casa da Suplicação* (no date) at the end of the *decisio*, after the opinion of jurists like Álvaro Valasco, Aymon Cravetta, Jason de Mayno, Johannes de Imola and Bartolus de Saxoferrato.[31] António da Gama likewise concluded some *decisiones* referring to a single court decision, such as the cases of *António Gonçalves v Manuel Ferraz*[32] and *Francisco de Leiria v António Luís*.[33] On another occasion he began a *decisio* about pending fruits in the succession of a *majorat* with reference to the case of Miguel Cabral in Madeira Island[34] and, immediately thereafter, he would provide his argument.

If initially jurists preferred short *decisiones*, after the example of Matteo d'Afflitto or Joachim Mynsinger von Frundeck, seventeenth and

---

30 Jorge de Cabedo, *Practicarum observationum, sive decisionum Supremi Senatus Regni Lusitaniae*, Antuerpiae: apud viduam et filium Joannis Baptistae Verdussen, 1699, Dec 110, 113–114.
31 Ibid, Dec 104, 107–108.
32 Gama, *Decisiones Supremi*, Dec 113, 106.
33 Ibid, Dec 274, 239.
34 Ibid, Dec 350, 328.

eighteenth-century authors wrote longer *decisiones* that sometimes performed another role. In Belchior Febo's book, for instance, some *decisiones* are actually a detailed case report. It is the case of a discussion about a usufruct clause in the constitution of the *emphyteusis* and the subsequent transfer of possession. There, the author basically discusses the case of the *Count of Linhares v D Jerônimo Pereira de Sá*, decided by the *Casa da Suplicação* (again, no date), with a thorough report about the suit, including the transcription of documents, the reconstruction of facts of the case, the arguments of the judges – one of which was the reference to another (dateless) court decision – and the information of the success of D Jerônimo Pereira de Sá against his brother and contender in another lawsuit.[35] Some pages later, discussing the succession of a *majorat*, the same Belchior Febo wrote about a case decided by the *Casa da Suplicação* in 1622, transcribing a clause in the institution of a *majorat* and naming as *"primus iudex"* the judge Nuno da Fonseca Cabral, which seems to point to the fact that Febo translated into Latin the most relevant arguments written by the judge who delivered the court's verdict.[36] This is the form chosen by Diogo Guerreiro Camacho de Aboim in his work, which may be clearly seen when he argues that, if the *emphyteuta* would rent out the land for a long time without the consent of the person with direct domain, he could also initiate a lawsuit without his assistance. In this *decisio*, Aboim, who was judge at the *Tribunal da Relação* of Oporto, first explains his opinion using legal authorities, and then concludes by mentioning that he was the *iudex relator* of the appeal of *Antônio Rodrigo v Pantaleão da Costa Pereira*, decided by this court on 16 January 1702[37] – a case where the legal issue was identical to the one in the *decisio*. Gabriel Pereira de Castro did the same when discussing the succession in a *majorat* and the issue of lack of evidence of blood relation in the case of the *majorat* of Loba, another clear case in which the author's arguments as *iudex relator* in the court were translated into Latin.[38]

Second, case law is defined by the absence of any link between a case and the *decisio*, which is concerned on a juridical issue whose answer is discussed in both legal authorities and the *decisio* itself. In other words,

---

35 Belchior Febo, *Decisionum Senatus Regni Lusitaniae*, Olysippone: Petrum Craesbeeck, 1625, Dec 105, 40–51.

36 Ibid, Dec 142, 279–284.

37 Diogo Guerreiro Camacho de Aboim, *Decisiones, seu quaestiones forenses ad amlissimo, integerrimoque Portuensi Senatu*, Ulyssipone: ex officina Bernardi Antonii de Oliveira, 1759, quaestio 44, 260–264.

38 Castro, *Decisiones Supremi eminentissimique Senatus*, Dec 25, 122.

in these cases, court decisions are treated just like any other authorities. This approach is used in many *decisiones* on *majorat* and *emphyteusis* in António da Gama's volume. Arguing whether a father who constitutes an *emphyteusis* for himself, his wife and his son could sell it without the consent of the others, Gama referred to a few cases both in favour and against the opinion that he favoured – three cases at the beginning of the *decisio*, one in the middle and one at the end.[39] Dealing with the renewal of ecclesiastical *emphyteusis*, he began the *decisio* with the concrete example of the Monastery of Odivelas, which seemingly inspired the whole discussion, and thereafter he mentioned three other cases without then returning to the original example.[40] The use of this structure denotes that the central issue of the *decisio* would not depend on the court's judgment, which is referred to simply as an argument to strengthen the author's opinion. Looking at the first way of using case law, on the other hand, it would seem that decisions could have been used by the authors both as the basic element for their comments on a practical issue and as an element in favour or against the author's own opinion. This would point to a plurality of possible uses of case law in this kind of literature.

(c) Relevant information

Different authors referred to court decisions in very different ways. The most complete references include the names of the parties, the place where the litigation took place, the court responsible for the decision, the judges, the notary that wrote the sentence and the year of the decision, but only a few cases contain all such information. More frequent is the combination of "parties-court-year", and this is what we are going to focus on.

Two authors (Castro and Macedo) do not mention the year in any *decisio*. Aboim mentions it in eight out of eleven *quaestiones*. In Febo, sixteen out of twenty *decisiones* mention the year; in Cabedo, seven out of twelve; and in Gama, forty-two out of seventy-eight. The only *consultatio* directly mentioned by Valasco was dated. Most cases in Gama's book were decided after 1549, when he was appointed to the *Casa da Suplicação*, and many of them date to the last years before the publication of his work (1578). Cabedo was appointed to the same court in 1583, and four of the seven bearing a

---

39 Gama, *Decisiones Supremi*, Dec 8, 15–17.
40 *Nicolau Migens v Monastery of St Mary of Espinheiro in Évora* (sd); *Manuel Teles v Agnete Gaga* (sd); Pedro Antunes v Lourenço de Brito Nogueira (1563). Gama, *Decisiones Supremi*, Dec 326, 299–300.

date were decided after that. All eight dated cases in Aboim's volume were decided between 1701 and 1702. The period is hardly fortuitous, as he was appointed to the *Tribunal da Relação* of Oporto in 1701 and was then nominated to the *Casa da Suplicação* at the beginning of 1703, thus terminating his relationship with the court that inspired his book.

Extracting data from these sources is not an easy task. Personal details of the litigants are quite rare and most of the information about them is derived from indirect elements. The nature of the discussion is one of them: considering that the *decisiones* deal with land issues, even when there is no mention of precise monetary figures or the value of the contentious goods, it may be safely assumed that the parties were quite well off. In other cases, the limited information about the parties is enough to determine their social status, mainly when nobility and religious orders are mentioned – the higher classes of the *Ancien Régime*. Middle or lower social classes are not easily identified in the cases reported in *decisiones* literature, but this does not necessarily mean that they did not litigate.

(d) Courts

Only a few cases mention expressly the court responsible for the decision. In such a case, the authors would use some Latin expressions such as *"senatus lusitaniae"* or simply *"senatus"* to refer to the *Casa da Suplicação*. These references also appear in the title of the books, suggesting a relation between the court and the content of the book a relation that scholars have not yet worked out. It is possible to argue that most of the cases reported in a book might have been decided by the court named in the title of the book, even when this is not explicitly stated. This is a reasonable assumption, which should however be proved with archival work.

Six of the seven works on *decisiones* analysed here are related to the *Casa da Suplicação*, where all of the authors but Belchior Febo served as judges. The only exception is the volume by Diogo Guerreiro Camacho de Aboim, on the *Tribunal da Relação* of Oporto (*"senatus portuensis"*), which reports cases decided during his short spell in that court before his appointment to the *Casa da Suplicação* in 1703.

In the discussions on *majorats* and *emphyteusis*, the authors do not refer to decisions of foreign courts, at least not explicitly. The content of foreign courts' judgments might derive from the familiarity of the authors with foreign books on *decisiones*. Considering the link between literature and court practice, it is not unreasonable to envisage the influence of foreign courts on Portuguese *decisiones*. In other subjects, foreign courts are mentioned, but always mediated by a learned author. António da Gama, for example, mentioned decisions of the *Sacro Regio Consiglio* of Naples through the book of Matteo d'Afflitto, and decisions of the *Parlement de Paris* through the work of Nicholas Bohier[41] in his discussion on succession and on matrimonial regimes, respectively. Valasco referred to a decision of the *Parlement de Paris* through the work of Pierre Rebuffi[42] when discussing the duty of the father in educating his son and the duties of the Portuguese noblemen in the countryside. If, however we were to consider only explicit references to foreign courts in the discussions of *majorat* and *emphyteusis*, not a single one has been found.

(2) *Consilia* and *allegationes*

The *consilia* literature was widespread in late medieval and early modern Italy, where the most influential jurists engaging in this genre wrote and published collections of their *consilia*. In the Holy Roman Empire, where the opinion of jurists was highly prestigious, writing *consilia* turned into a very lucrative activity for their authors.[43] Classical *consilia* writers such as Alexander Tartagnus, Filippo Decio and Baldus de Ubaldis used the same structure in their *consilia*, a structure based on short texts about the specific legal issues which they were called to solve. The authors were contracted by one party to make a statement on the case – hence the lack of impartiality of *consilia*. The same partiality features in the *allegationes*. The *allegatio* was written by the counsellor advising a party in a specific case. Both *consilia* and *allegationes* share the aim of convincing the court about the reasons of the party that paid the author of the text and relying on previous cases was key to achieving that.

In contrast to the Italian Peninsula, in Portugal the amount of published *consilia* is very low, and for the purpose of this chapter the most relevant text was Diogo de Brito's (–1635) *Consilium in causa maioratus regiae coronae Regni Lusitaniae*.[44] There, the author discusses the succession of a Portuguese *majorat* settled by the first Duke of Pastrana between his grand-

---

41 *Decisiones* I and IX for the Court of Naples and CCCLVII for the Court of Paris.
42 *Consultationes* XCIX, in the first volume, and CVII, in the second.
43 For this consiliar "market", see U Falk, *Consilia. Studien zur Praxis der Rechtsgutachten in der frühen Neuzeit*, Frankfurt am Main: Klostermann, 2006.
44 Diogo de Brito, *Consilium in causa maioratus regiae coronae Regni Lusitaniae*, Olysiponae: ex officina Petri Crasbeeck, 1612.

son D Rodrigo or Ruy da Silva (Rodericus a Silva), first-born of the second Duke of Pastrana of the same name, and D Diego da Silva (Didacus a Silva), Count of Salinas and Ribadeau and Duke of Francavilla. As arguments in favour of the Count of Salinas, Brito transcribed excerpts of the *Ordenações do Reino* and mainly legal literature, most importantly *consilia* literature. However, in almost 200 pages aimed at persuading the *Casa da Suplicação* – where the author was appointed judge the year after the publication of that book – not a single decision of this court is nominated, and the only time that case law appears is merely an indirect reference through Jean Corsier's *Decisiones capellae Tholosanae*.[45]

On the other hand, the Portuguese *allegationes* are more numerous and diverse in the subjects they cover. Manuel Álvares Pegas (1635–1696), probably the most successful Portuguese lawyer in the seventeenth century, published some of his *allegationes*, most of them about private law and land issues, and two of them specifically centered on *majorats*. The *Allegaçaõ de direito por parte do excellentissimo senhor Dom Pedro de Menezes sobre a successam do titulo, e estado de Villa-Real, e Morgados de dita Casa, e bens patrimoniaes, que a ella pertencem, e ao ditto Senhor successor della* refers to a judgment at the *Casa da Suplicação*, to which the *allegatio* was meant.[46] That is the only reference in that whole *allegatio*. In the other *allegatio* on *majorat*, *Allegaçaõ de direito por parte de D Luiz Angel Coronel Ximenes de Aragão sobre a successão dos morgados, que instituiraõ Antonio Gomes Angel, e sua mulher Joanna Hieronyma*, Pegas did not report a single previous case.

(3) *Resolutiones forenses*

A well-known author of *allegationes*, monographs and the vast commentaries on the *Ordenações do Reino* (a work in fourteen volumes), Manuel Álvares Pegas also published in 1682 a book named *Resolutiones Forenses practicabiles*. This work is both a late addition to the Portuguese practical literature and, especially, a rather peculiar one, because it uses decisions taken by Portuguese judges and courts of many jurisdictional levels rather than focusing only on the *Casa da Suplicação* – as all the other works on *decisiones* did. The practical aims of the work are made clear both in the title and particularly in the content of the chapters, which aim to provide the

---

45 Ibid, 79.

46 *Casa de Aveiro v Crown*, 14 March 1668, judges Luiz Gomes do Basto, Luiz Fernandes Teixeira, João Velho Barreto and Cristóvão Pinto de Paiva. Manuel Álvares Pegas, *Allegaçoens de Direito*, Lisboa: Officina de Antonio Isidoro da Fonseca, 1738, 63–64.

jurists with instruments for their professional activities. In short, this book intends to sum up how the courts ruled the most frequent issues in judicial practice. The general structure is quite similar in all the chapters: Pegas introduces the general question and thereafter deals with particular issues, using both juridical literature and case law to underpin his opinion. Unlike with the *decisiones* literature, this book is heavily influenced by practice; in the 1188 pages of the 1682 edition, the author mentioned 1272 decisions.

Pegas' work is in two volumes, divided into twenty chapters in total. Only three chapters deal with *emphyteusis* and *majorats*. Of those chapters, Chapter 4 is the only one to report cases on *majorat*, particularly the succession of the last possessor, while Chapters 9 and 10 deal with different aspects of *emphyteusis*, mainly alienation and transfer. In those three chapters, Pegas referred to 200 decisions in total (thirty in Chapter 4; 148 in Chapter 9; and twenty-two in Chapter 10) – the following sections examine in detail the use of case law.

(a) Ways of using case law

Unlike *decisiones*, *consilia* and *allegationes*, the chapters of Pega's *Resolutiones Forenses* are not based on a concrete case. The practical use of the *resolutiones* is shaped in the first paragraphs of the chapter, when Pegas describes a problem that calls for a solution. If, for authors like Gama, Febo or Aboim, this concrete situation would usually originate in a case decided by a court, and their *decisiones* were meant to provide a solution to such situation, in Pegas the main question seems to consist of a set of specific issues to be answered individually with the use of every relevant source of law. Case law is therefore one of these sources, but here its relevance is explained by the declared intention to provide the readers with a useful tool for their forensic practice.

A comparative analysis of the case law used in the three sections above denotes a pattern of punctual references to cases alongside numerous references to legal literature – especially *decisiones*, *consilia* and monographs – and then, in the middle of the chapter, a strong presence of more detailed information about the cases. Let us take Chapter 4 as an example. There, the first mention to case law comes only in paragraph 51, when Pegas denies in a specific case the liability of the successor in a *majorat* for the damage caused to third parties by the previous incumbent in it;[47] it is only after

---

47 *D Diogo de Menezes v Henrique Nunes Faya*, 1663. Manuel Álvares Pegas, *Resolutiones Forenses practicabiles in quibus multa, quae in utroque foro controversa*, Ulyssipone: typographia Michaelis Deslandes, 1682, cap 4, n 51, 307.

some punctual references to other kinds of source does he focus more on case law. Unlike the writers of *decisiones*, Pegas transcribes the salient parts of a court's ruling to clarify what was exactly enforced by it, as in the suits of *Baltazar de Lemos Castro v D Luiza de Figueiredo* (12 July 1672)[48] and *Count of Soure v Counts of Palma* (17 March 1676; appealed in 21 July 1676),[49] among many other cases.

At other moments, Pegas transcribes the judicial decisions in the original vernacular and thereafter provides the salient parts of the ruling in Latin with the formula "haec sententia fuit fundata in deliberationibus sequentibus".[50] The case of *Bartolomeu Fernandes Pereira v Pedro Ribeiro Esmeraldo* is a very good example; the appeal against the decision in the first degree, and the arguments for the rejection were thoroughly described in a way that even references to documents used in the suit and their respective pages can be found.[51] This construction reveals that this commentary seems to be the Latin translation of the arguments used by the judge who delivers the opinion of the court to make stronger the decision, which was based on legal literature and the reconstruction of the facts that prompted the suit and with no references to previous decisions of the court.

Throughout Pegas' book, the frequent use of case law has different functions and features. Despite the corroborative role described above, case law is sometimes used in different ways.[52] Sometimes it is used as a (generic) reference to the argument, at other times it is a Latin transcription of the arguments of the decision. Transcriptions are more frequent (at 113, 56.5 per cent of the total) than generic references (at eighty-seven, 43.5 per cent of the total). The point is important: these transcriptions can be seen as true court records. The transcriptions were never checked and were considered by jurists as genuine accounts of the decisions.

(b) Relevant information (year and parts)

This section and the next one deal with the combination "parties-court-year" – the essential elements to pinpoint the case. The indication of the parties and the date of the decision are usually mentioned to identify the judicial dispute despite, even if Pegas often left out the date. Only three out of 200

48 Ibid, 314.
49 Ibid, 321–322.
50 *Anna Oliveira de Carvalho v D Helena Soares de Macedo*, ibid, 343.
51 Ibid, 314–321.
52 See, for example, *Countess of Redondo v Marchioness of Arronches*, 1679, ibid, cap 9, 607; *Manuel de Sousa Pinheiro v Manuel Baldaya*, ibid, cap 9, n 136, 616.

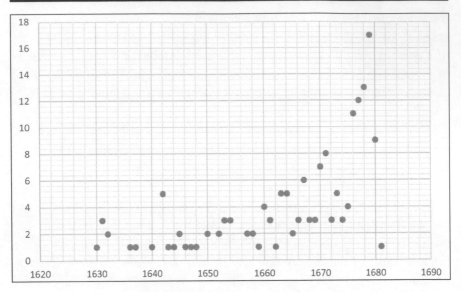

Year of the cases in Pegas' *resolutiones*

cases do not mention the parties: in these cases, it is possible to identify the case by reference to date and court. The number of cases without any mention of the date is comparatively higher (thirty-five out of 200), yet still low with regard to the total number of cases. The following chart displays the years of the decisions:

Most of the cases (130 out of 165) were decided after Pegas received his Bachelor of Laws ("leitura de bacharel") in 1658, the exam that allowed law graduates to practise as a lawyer or to be nominated for a judicial office. Considering the extension of the book, the year of publication (1682) and the high number of cases judged in the years immediately before its printing, it is inevitable to conclude that the author's intention was to provide the reader with the most recent and up-to-date information about the subjects discussed in his book. Excluding 1681, which is probably the year in which the manuscript was ready for publication, almost half of the cases (sixty-three out of 130) were decided between 1676 and 1680. As the title of the book suggests, the author aimed to deal with the latest forensic decisions rendered in Portugal.

When Pegas transcribed a decision, he always included the reference to the city, the full date, and the mention of both judges and the notary. For instance, in the case of *João Mendes v Pedro Fernandes* he writes: "The defendant was thus declared not guilty, but he must pay the plaintiff what he owes to the Princess. And the plaintiff must pay the costs of this suit in which he was convicted. Oporto, 11.29.1679."[53] Simpler references, on the other hand, only contain the year of the decision, in a structure such as this: "And that was judged in the case of *Ioannis Gonsalves v Francisco Vieira and Maria Antonia*, in 1670."[54]

Despite the high number of cases mentioning the parties, the limited information about them does not allow us to draw any conclusions. Some indications can be extracted from indirect elements, particularly the subject matter. For instance, land disputes would normally involve a very specific segment of the Portuguese society of the time. In most instances, litigation on *emphyteusis* and *majorats* would predominately involve nobility and clergy. Pegas also mentions some of the most important noble houses of the kingdom, such as the House of Bragança, involved in a case of 1642[55] (just one year after the acclamation of its head, João, as King of Portugal and consequently its transformation into the Portuguese royal house), and the House of Aveiro[56]. The Duchess of Torres Novas was the tutor of the Duke of Aveiro in a case against D Maria de Mello[57], and the Count of Villa Verde was represented by Pegas in a lawsuit.[58] Nobles litigated among themselves, such as in the cases of *Count of Soure v Count of Palma*,[59] *Count of Castelo Melhor v Duke of Cadaval*, *Count of Figueiredo v Countess of Castelo Melhor* and *Countess of Redondo v Marchioness of Arronches*.

The way religious orders or institutions litigated could take two forms. Sometimes the head of the monastery appeared with the clergymen, such as in the cases of the Abbot and the clerics of the Monastery of Saint Bernard[60] and the Abbot and the clerics of Saint John of Tarouca[61] or the Abbot and the clerics of the *Royal Convent of Alcobaça v Captain Antonio Velho do Souto*;[62] or nuns, as in the case of *the nuns of the Convent of Vialonga v Francisco Ribeiro*.[63] In other situations the clerics appear as a collectivity, such as the

---

53 "Portanto, absoluem o R do pedido pello A com tal declaraçam, que o ditto R pagará ao A a parte do foro deuido à Senhora Princesa. E pague o appellado as custas dos autos de huma, & outra instance, em que o condenão. Porto, 29. de Nouembro de 679. Lacerda. Magalhães. Motta. Fui presente, Lemos." Ibid, cap 10, n 48, 777.

54 "Et ita judicatum fuit in causa Ioannis Gonsalues, com Francisco Vieira, & Maria Antonia, anno 1670, apud Notarium Emmanuelem de Goes Pinheiro." Ibid, cap 9, n 334, 700.

55 Ibid, 670.

56 Ibid, cap 4, 308.

57 Ibid, cap 9, 672.

58 Ibid, 610.

59 Ibid, cap 4, 321–322.

60 Ibid, cap 9, 629–630.

61 Ibid, 657–659.

62 Ibid, cap 10, 778.

63 Ibid.

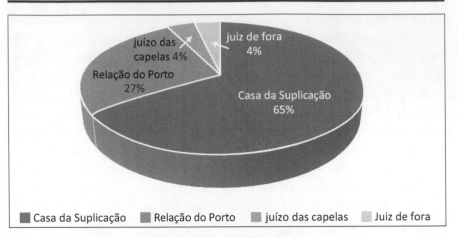

Courts mentioned in the cases in Pegas' *resolutiones*

Brothers of Mercy of Oporto,[64] the clergymen of the Monastery of the Holy Cross of Coimbra,[65] the clergymen of the Convent of Saint Eligius[66] and the case of *the Convent of Saint Anne v the Convent of Chelas*.[67]

(c) Court

None of the elements reported in Pegas' *Resolutiones Forenses* is so particular as the data that he provides about the courts. Whereas case law in *decisiones* literature is focused mostly on high courts, in Pegas the sampling is wider, touching many levels of Portuguese royal jurisdiction. Except for the *decisiones* of Camacho de Aboim, which were based on the decisions of the Court of Oporto, all the other volumes of *decisiones* were based on decisions of the *Casa da Suplicação*. In the *Resolutiones* of Pegas, from the lower judge nominated by the king to act in local spheres (the so-called "*juiz de fora*", who was a learned judged appointed by the king to act in the villages alongside the ordinary judge, who was elected by the people and might not be learned) to the *Casa da Suplicação*, it is possible to find references to decisions of different jurisdictional offices. Most of the cases do not indicate directly the court responsible for the decision – it is mentioned in only fifty-five out of 200 cases.

The clear predominance of the *Casa da Suplicação* is due to its impor-

64 Ibid, cap 4, 345–346.
65 Ibid, cap 9, 651–652.
66 Ibid, 731.
67 Ibid, 701.

tance as the Portuguese highest court in the early modern period, and to the author's choice to report all the decisions in the lawsuit – and therefore any appeal, thus often leading to the *Casa da Suplicação* itself. Despite the difficulties of providing conclusive evidence on the point, it seems highly likely that most of the cases with no indication of the court were decided by the *Casa da Suplicação*. Pegas might have had access to this privileged information thanks to his close relationships with that court. Among the other courts, more than one quarter of cases refer to the Court of Oporto, and some exceptional cases mention decisions taken by the *juiz de fora*. Equally rare are the decisions of the *juízos das capelas*, judges with jurisdiction only on chapels, a figure established by the Crown with the statute of 23 October 1604.[68]

Sometimes Pegas reported the whole path of the lawsuit, encompassing two[69] or even three[70] rounds of appeal, followed by a mention of the final decision by the *Casa da Suplicação*. Most of the reported decisions of the *Tribunal da Relação* of Oporto were then confirmed by the *Casa da Suplicação*. On other occasions (such as the case of the *Count of Prado v the Marquis of Montalvão and the Count and Countess of Serem*), the court of Oporto was called to decide in appeal on a previous decision, which Pegas would also mention.[71] References to decisions of the *Tribunal da Relação*, without mention to any previous or further appeal (as the case of *João Dias v Domingos Pires*[72] in 1678), were exceptional.

Some particularities emerge from this data, which is one of the few sources about special jurisdictions such as the above-mentioned judge of the chapels (*juízos das capelas*)[73] and the other in charge of the mint (*juízo dos moedeiros*).[74] He transcribed two sentences by *juízes de fora* of the villages of Covilhã (judge Gonçalo da Cunha Vilas Boas, 4 February 1677)[75] and

---

68 I would thank to António Manuel Hespanha for this information. For information about the legal regime of the chapels, see Hespanha, *Como os juristas*, 454–455. Such as is the case for many of the inferior magistrates with specific jurisdiction, there is no monographic work on the *juízo das capelas*.

69 *Mathias Lopes v Rev Simão Álvares Pereira*, the Abbot of Lamas, Tribunal da Relação of Oporto (8 July 1677) and *Casa da Suplicação* (3 December 1678). Pegas, *Resolutiones Forenses*, cap 9, n 496, 739–741.

70 *Fray Antônio Rodrigues v Brothers of Mercy of Oporto*, ordinary judge of Oporto (31 December 1677), *Tribunal da Relação* of Oporto (20 May 1679) and *Casa da Suplicação* (7 May 1680). Ibid, cap 4, n 241, 345–347.

71 Ibid, cap 9, n 292–294, 683–685.

72 Ibid, n 168, 621.

73 Ibid, cap 10, n 29, 774, and n 54, 780.

74 Ibid, cap 11, n 236, 960.

75 *Manoel Botelho v Domingos Francisco*, ibid, cap 9, n 520, 746–747.

Amarante (judge João Fernandes de Carvalho, 31 August 1667);[76] decisions like these are not easy to find.

Pegas had direct access to the suits reported in the book. This may be clearly appreciated in the instances where he gives a summary of the proceedings and then provides a transcription of the decisions. This is the case of *D Francisco de Azevedo v Fathers of Carmel*, first decided in Lisbon on 26 August 1661, and the appealed before the *Casa da Suplicação* on 1 February 1663. In this case, Pegas listed five decisions and their respective appeals.[77]

E. CONCLUSION

In early modern Portugal, case law had a prominent role in the making of veritable national legal systems. Decisions of high courts such as the *Casa da Suplicação* were relevant for legal practitioners, whose main purpose was to persuade lower judges about their arguments. The lack of official publications of high courts' decisions was somehow made up by practical literature. In this sense, *decisiones, consilia, allegationes* and *resolutiones forenses* were useful tools for jurists to get information about important decisions issued within the kingdom and to use them in support of their cases in their work as counsel.

The idea of authority is a central concept in both case law and legal literature. A text based on the arguments of famed jurists was appreciated and respected both in the late-medieval and in the early modern times, but as time went by references to case law became even more prestigious. The growing number of practically oriented works in the sixteenth and seventeenth centuries is revealing of the growing interest in this kind of argument. As a result, among early modern Portuguese jurists the authorities held in highest regard were those who dealt better with case law. The influence of authors such as Pegas, Gama and Cabedo cannot be fully separated from their connections with court practice. In other words, the authority of the most prominent Portuguese jurists of the seventeenth century depended on the authority of case law. At the same time, of course, the high prestige of those decisions also depended to their widespread circulation, which in Portugal occurred through practical literature. Thus, the interaction between case law and legal literature contributed to make them valuable in the eyes of contemporary jurists.

---

76 *Antônio Francisco v Francisco Antônio*, ibid, n 551, 754–755.
77 Ibid, n 441, 728–731.

This mutual influence in the growing importance of case law and legal literature can be observed particularly in early modern private law, a branch of the law that relied more on them than, for instance, on statutes. This analysis of the way that legal literature dealt with *majorats* and *emphyteusis* has shown that the close relationship between case law and practical literature, both immersed in a concept of authority strong enough to inhibit a clear separation between them as sources of law independent of each other, played a fundamental role in the making of private law. In this regard, Portugal was no different from most regions of Western Europe.

6 *Iura scripta* and *Operae iurisperitorum* in Municipal Courts of the Kingdom of Poland (Sixteenth to Eighteenth Centuries)

Maciej Mikuła

A. SOURCES OF *IUS MUNICIPALE POLONICUM* – ADAPTATION OF SAXON-MAGDEBURG LAW IN POLISH TOWNS

The wave of migrants from overpopulated Western Europe that poured into the lands east of the River Elbe during the thirteenth century brought a law that proved attractive both to the new settlers and the old landlords. The popularity of *ius Teutonicum* – as the new law came to be called in the Kingdom of Poland – rested on its three fundamental traits. First, it guaranteed the personal freedom of the residents of a newly founded settlement; second, it contained a precise catalogue of the rights and duties of the settlers and the landlord; and third, it upheld the idea of self-government of the new urban and rural communities.[1] These basic principles, which at first applied locally to the settlers (*hospites*), were soon adopted by the landlords as a general standard. The latter, by committing themselves to clear rules and assurances of personal freedom to the settlers, were able to recruit more migrants and thus accelerate the economic development of their domains. The noble landlords need not have been averse to the idea of local government, inclusive of judicial autonomy, because it relieved them of the duties connected with the administration of justice without any diminution of income from fines or forfeitures decreed by local courts.

The core and, in retrospect, the most important law collection of *ius Teutonicum* in the Kingdom of Poland, was the Magdeburg Law, which has been the object of intense study for at least two hundred years.[2] Apart from the *ius commune*, and before the adoption of the Napoleonic Code of 1804, *ius Teutonicum* was in use throughout large parts of continental Europe.[3] It supplied the foundation for thousands of town and village charters from the Elbe in the west to the Dnieper in the east. Its extraordinary career was already noted by the author of the thirteenth-century *Constitution of the Magdeburg Courts*, a collection of the provisions of Magdeburg Law to be used alongside the most popular version of the Saxon-Magdeburg Law, the Magdeburg *Weichbild*.[4] Of prime importance in the history of its reception was the territory of the Kingdom of Poland and the Grand Duchy

---

1 Cf K Tymieniecki, "Prawo niemieckie w rozwoju społecznym wsi polskiej" *Kwartalnik Historyczny* (1923) 37, 39, 41, 60–64, 68–70; Id, "Prawo czy gospodarstwo?" *Roczniki Dziejów Społecznych i Gospodarczych* (1946) 8/2, 289–291; B Zientara, "Das Deutsche Recht (ius teutonicum) und die Anfänge der städtischen Autonomie", in K Fritze, E Mueller-Mertens and W Stark (eds), *Autonomie, Wirtschaft und Kultur der Hansestädte*, Weimar: Böhlaus, 1984, 94–100; J Matuszewski, "Prawo sądowe na wsi polskiej lokowanej na prawie niemieckim", *Studia z Dziejów Państwa i Prawa Polskiego* (1995) 2, 54–59; J Matuszewski, "Rodzaje własności gruntu we wsi lokowanej na prawie niemieckim", in K Iwanicka, M Skowronek and K Stembrowicz (eds), *Parlament, prawo, ludzie. Studia ofiarowane Profesorowi Juliuszowi Bardachowi*, Warszawa: Wydawnictwo Sejmowe, 1996, 158–164, at 158, 160–162, 164.

2 See I Bily, W Carls and K Gönczi, *Sächsisch-magdeburgisches Recht in Polen. Untersuchungen zur Geschichte des Rechts und seiner Sprache*, Berlin/Boston: De Gruyter, 2011 (Ivs Saxonico-Maidebvrgense in Oriente, vol II); K Gönczi, W Carls, *Sächsisch-magdeburgisches Recht in Ungarn und Rumänien. Autonomie und Rechtstransfer im Donau- und Katpatenraum*, Berlin-Boston: De Gruyter, 2013 (Ivs Saxonico-Maidebvrgense in Oriente, vol II).

3 I would like to thank Professor Dirk Heirbaut for drawing my attention to this historical comparison.

4 Art 113: ". . . *Eapropter omnes de Polonia ac de Bohemia, qui sub iure locati sunt Teutonico ac de marchia et de Myssenensi provincia, et de marchia Luziciensi, hii omnes ius suum in Hallis recipere debent, et de civitatibus, que in hiis districtibus locati sunt.*" Edition of MS from Archidioecesian Archive in Gniezno, MS 104: M Mikuła, *Prawo miejskie magdeburskie (Ius municipale Magdeburgense) w Polsce XIV–pocz XVI w Studium o ewolucji i adaptacji prawa*, 2nd edn, Kraków: Jagiellonian University Press, 2018, 350.

of Lithuania, first joined by the person of the ruler, and later, from 1569, forming a personal union *aeque principaliter* (a Commonwealth of Two Nations).[5]

The proliferation of the foundation formula modelled on the Magdeburg Law (including the three principles just mentioned) did not mean, however, an automatic copying of provisions in the field of criminal law, private law or judicial procedure. The degree to which the original provisions of the Saxon-Magdeburg Law (i.e. both the *Weichbild* and the *Sachsenspiegel*) were adopted in Polish charters varied considerably on the basis of a number of factors, some of which are worth looking into.

The *ius Teutonicum* as used in the Kingdom of Poland was by no means uniform. Whereas the north followed a variant of the Magdeburg Law known as the Chełmno Law, the southern parts of the Kingdom held on to a "purer" form of the code, which succeeded in ousting the *Środa* Law (Latin: *ius Novi Fori*; German: *Neumarkt-Magdeburger Recht*) that used to be popular in the thirteenth and fourteenth centuries. The Magdeburg Law proper and its Chełmno variant did not rely on the same catalogue of sources of law. One major difference was the admission of the case law of the Magdeburg Lay Bench (German: *Schöffengericht, Schöffenbank*) as a valid source of law by the adherents of the Magdeburg Law in southern Poland. While traces of the Magdeburg judgments (Polish: *ortyle*; German: *Urteile*) can still be found in the judicial practice of the early sixteenth century, the extent of their influence on the administration of justice in Polish towns throughout that period is still in need of closer study. Meanwhile, in the north, in the territory ruled by the Teutonic Knights (*der Ordensstaat*), the town of Chełmno (Kulm) was incorporated under a charter which provided for the creation of a municipal court analogous to the Magdeburg Lay Bench. The Chełmno Bench thus became a lawmaking institution in its own right, with competence to modify and develop the case law that came from Magdeburg. By 1466, when large parts of Western Prussia were annexed to the Kingdom of Poland after the Thirteen Years' War (1454–1466), the differences between these of branches of the Magdeburg Law had grown considerably. The breach deepened in the sixteenth century as the Chełmno Law was successfully modernised and codified,[6] while

5 W Uruszczak, *Historia państwa i prawa polskiego*, vol I (966–1795), 2nd edn, Warszawa: Wolters Kluwer, 2013, 189. Cf R Frost, *The Oxford History of Poland-Lithuania*, vol I: *The Making of the Polish-Lithuanian Union*, 1385–1569, Oxford: Oxford University Press, 2018, 57.

6 On criminal law in the *ius Culmense*: D Janicka, *Prawo karne w trzech rewizjach prawa chełmińskiego z XVI wieku*, Toruń: Towarzystwo Naukowe w Toruniu, 1992; on inheritance law:

similar efforts to codify the main branch of the Magdeburg Law ended in failure.[7]

In the case of towns incorporated under the Magdeburg Law, a detailed catalogue of sources of law was much longer. Apart from the Magdeburg Law itself, it also included a number of other sources. The former was represented by the Magdeburg *Weichbild*, the *Sachsenspiegel*, the Magdeburg judgments (*ortyle*), as well as answers to judicial questions produced by the Magdeburg Lay Bench. In the sixteenth century, the corpus of the Saxon-Magdeburg Law in Poland became stable. The practice of looking for instructions or *ortyle* from Magdeburg came to an end (it was formally banned in Poland in 1356, and in the Kingdom of Bohemia in 1547). The appearance of revised, printed editions of the *Weichbild* and the *Sachsenspiegel* (1535) was a watershed. Their texts differed from the medieval collections and were glossed with numerous references to Roman Law.[8] A very important factor in the development of urban law was the impact of other kinds of law, in particular royal and parliamentary (*Sejm*) legislation and the laws adopted by individual towns (town councils). The latter, known as *wilkierze* (German: *Wilkur*) often reflected customary norms that functioned alongside the Saxon-Magdeburg Law.[9] Thus, in practice, the Saxon-Magdeburg Law was just one element of Polish urban law – *ius municipale Polonicum* (the first to make this assessment was the sixteenth-century jurist Bartłomiej Groicki)[10] and its provisions were adapted and modified to local needs at the point of selection for translation from German into Latin and during the process of translation.[11] To describe that process – which depended on pragmatic selection of material that was attractive or indispensable – I suggest using the term "adaptation".[12]

P Kitowski, *Sukcesja spadkowa w mniejszych miastach województwa pomorskiego w II połowie XVII i XVIII wieku: studium prawno-historyczne*, Warszawa: Neriton, 2015.

7 J Reszczyński, *Sądownictwo i proces w kodyfikacji Macieja Śliwnickiego z 1523 roku: o wpływach prawa rzymskiego i praw obcych na myśl prawną polskiego Odrodzenia*, Kraków: Jagiellonian University Press, 2008, 549–553; M Mikuła, "Prawo miejskie magdeburskie", 188.

8 See B Kannowski, *Die Umgestaltung des Sachsenspiegelrechts durch die Buch'sche Glosse*, Hannover: Hahn 2007 (Monumenta Germaniae Historica. Schriften, vol LVI).

9 The significance of the customary law in municipal courts is underlined by G M Kowalski, *Zwyczaj i prawo zwyczajowe w doktrynie prawa i praktyce sądów miejskich karnych w Polsce XVI–XVIII w*, Kraków: Jagiellonian University Press, 2013, 167–168.

10 B Groicki, *Porządek sądów i spraw miejskich prawa majdeburskiego w Koronie Polskiej*, in K Koranyi (ed), *Biblioteka Dawnych Polskich Pisarzy-Prawników*, vol I, Warszawa: Wydawnictwo Prawnicze, 1953), 6.

11 M Mikuła, "Prawo miejskie magdeburskie", 180–183.

12 The presence of a foreign law is described in many ways and with many terms. With regard to the "reception" of the Magdeburg Law, see, for example, R Lieberwirth, "Einführung oder

The complex nature of the early phase of Poland's urban law is made even more complicated by the changes in its socio-historical environment. In the course of time, some norms that were taken over from the Saxon-Magdeburg Law at the very beginning of the process tended to lose relevance, or, in the sixteenth century and later, to become outright obsolete. The perception of the law as anachronistic prompted various efforts to reform it – some successful, as in the case of the Chełmno Law or the reform of criminal law in Hungary (which consisted of the adaptation of a revised code from Austria), and some unsuccessful, as in the case of Polish attempts to codify the Magdeburg Law. The latter led in turn to a search for other solutions, in particular drawing on the work of contemporary authorities in the field of law.

B. RECORDS OF THE CRACOW CRIMINAL COURT

The successful codification and modernisation of the Chełmno Law in the sixteenth century gave the towns of Pomorze (Western Prussia), Gdańsk (Danzig) and Toruń (Thorn) a solid foundation for judicial decisions.[13] Things were different in the south of the country where the traditional collections of the Saxon-Magdeburg Law (1535) could not compensate for the lack of an updated code of law. The situation favoured the reliance of legal practice on acclaimed judicial authorities. One of them, which will be at the centre of the discussion in this chapter, was the Municipal Criminal Court of Cracow. Although at the turn of the sixteenth century Cracow ceased to be Poland's capital city, it remained a major urban centre. What is also important is that its archives have been for the most part preserved in good condition, and some of the criminal court records have even been published in critical editions. Over the past few years, four volumes containing transcripts of the early modern criminal case records from Małopolska have been published in the series *Fontes Iuris Polonici*. Three of them contain mate-

---

Rezeption? Mittelalterlich deutsches Recht in slawischen Herrschaftsgebieten. Das Beispiel: Polen", in E Eichler, H Lück and W Carls (eds), *Rechts- und Sprachtransfer in Mittel- und Osteuropa. Sachsenspiegel und Magdeburger Recht. Internationale und interdisziplinäre Konferenz in Leipzig vom 31 Oktober bis 2 November 2003*, Berlin: De Gruyter, 2008, 167–179 (Ivs Saxonico-Maidebvrgense in Oriente, vol I); H Lück, "Aspects of the transfer of the Saxon-Magdeburg Law to Central and Eastern Europe" (2014) 22 *Rechtsgeschichte – Legal History*, 79–89 (where recent literature may also be found).

13 For example, inheritance law: T Maciejewski, *Zbiory wilkierzy w miastach państwa zakonnego do 1454 r. i Prus Królewskich lokowanych na prawie chełmińskim*, Gdańsk: Wydawnictwo Uniwersytetu Gdańskiego, 1989, 134–135.

rial from Cracow for the years 1554–1625,[14] 1589–1604,[15] and 1630–1633 and 1679–1690.[16] The fourth is a transcript of the Book of Criminal Case Records of the town of Dobczyce from 1699–1737,[17] which is used here only in a supplementary role.[18]

As shown by Marian Mikołajczyk, the early modern urban criminal trial in the Kingdom of Poland was adversarial, although with some elements of an inquisitorial approach.[19] So many of the main proceedings had the character of a contest in which either of the opposing sides was trying to present a more convincing argument. The lawyers representing them brought into the debate both quotations from the text of the law (i.e. *Speculum Saxonum* and *Ius municipale Magdeburgense*) and references to legal doctrine (Bartłomiej Groicki, Benedict Carpzov, Jodocus Damhouder, Andrzej Lipski and Giulio Claro). However, the form of the records says little about the manner in which the judicial proceedings changed over time. All that can be said on this point is that the courts developed a habit of turning to Groicki's treatise when they felt the need to buttress their sentences with an appropriate citation. Cracow's sixteenth-century records of criminal proceedings against defendants arrested in the city itself usually include no justification of the ruling nor any reference to the argument presented in court on behalf of the litigants. From the second half of the seventeenth century, the records grew in size as they include the written pleadings submitted by counsels, protocols of surgical examinations and other documents relevant for the

14 W Uruszczak, M Mikuła and A Karabowicz (eds), *Księga kryminalna miasta Krakowa z lat 1554–1625*, Kraków: Wydawnictwo Uniwersytetu Jagiellońskiego, 2013 (Fontes Iuris Polonici. Prawo Miejskie, vol I).

15 W Uruszczak, M Mikuła and K Fokt (eds), *Księgi kryminalne miasta Krakowa z lat 1630–1633, 1679–1690*, Kraków: Wydawnictwo Uniwersytetu Jagiellońskiego, 2016 (Fontes Iuris Polonici. Prawo Miejskie, vol IV) (heraftt, FIP IV).

16 M Mikuła (ed), *Księga kryminalna miasta Dobczyc 1699–1737*, Kraków: Wydawnictwo Uniwersytetu Jagiellońskiego, 2013 (Fontes Iuris Polonici. Prawo Miejskie, vol II) (hereinafter, FIP II).

17 W Uruszczak, M Mikuła, K Fokt and A Karabowicz (eds), *Księga kryminalna miasta Krakowa z lat 1589–1604*, Kraków: Wydawnictwo Uniwersytetu Jagiellońskiego, 2016 (Fontes Iuris Polonici. Prawo Miejskie, vol III).

18 Grounds for decisions in early modern criminal municipal courts were analysed, in particular, by M Mikołajczyk, *Proces kryminalny w miastach Małopolski XVI–XVIII wieku*, Katowice: Wydawnictwo Uniwersytetu Śląskiego, 2013, 473–477; Id, "'Stosując się do prawa wyraźnego ...'. Podstawy prawne wyroków kryminalnych grodziskiego sądu miejskiego w latach 1702–1756" (2013) 19 *Studia Iuridica Lubliniensia*, 201–216, at 202–203, G M Kowalski, "Zwyczaj i prawo zwyczajowe", and M Mikuła (who looked, in particular, at decisions from Cracow and Dobczyce), "Na marginesie edycji miejskich ksiąg kryminalnych. Prawo pisane i dzieła prawnicze w praktyce sądu krakowskiego i dobczyckiego" (2017) 20 *Studia z Dziejów Państwa i Prawa Polskiego*, 427–439.

19 M Mikołajczyk, *Proces kryminalny*, 568, 570–573.

court. The pleadings were studded with argument based on formulas found in contemporary legal authorities. Indeed, by the end of the seventeenth century the treatises of acclaimed jurists supplied the groundwork for the pleas of both the plaintiff and the defendant in nearly all criminal cases heard by the court.

C. BARTŁOMIEJ GROICKI

Bartłomiej Groicki (1519/1534–1605), a citizen of Cracow, was a leading Polish urban lawyer of the sixteenth century.[20] He established his renown with the publication of a multivolume corpus of urban laws, some of which had been in use in Cracow.[21] The number of reprints of his treatises is a good indicator of their popularity. The great demand for his work may also have resulted from the fact that they were written in Polish, while the standard sixteenth-century treatises on urban law by Johannes Kirstein (Jan Cerasinus) and Jan Cervus Tucholczyk (Ioannes Cervus Tucholiensis) were in Latin. Groicki also translated the *Constitutio Criminalis Carolina* of 1532, the first general code of criminal law and criminal procedure of the Holy Roman Empire. Groicki's translation was in fact a selection and adaptation of those provisions of the Imperial code that he considered applicable in Poland; moreover, he interspersed it with his own commentaries, most notably a condemnation of the use of torture.[22]

Groicki's works were a favourite quarry for the defence attorneys appearing in the Cracow court. Attorney Rogaleński therefore turned to Groicki's magisterial *Code of Urban Court Proceedings* (*Porządek sądówi spraw miejskich*) for help in constructing an argument to dissuade the court from the use of torture in a case of theft.[23] He pointed out that the defendants were minors under 14 years of age and that the evidence of their involvement in

---

20 See G M Kowalski, *Bartłomiej Groicki. Prawnik polskiego Odrodzenia. Wystawa w 400-setną rocznicę śmierci. Biblioteka Jagiellońska 5–29 kwietnia 2005*, Kraków: Księgarnia Akademicka 2005; G M Kowalski and Z Pietrzyk, "Testament Bartłomieja Groickiego (1603)" (2005) 55 *Biuletyn Biblioteki Jagiellońskiej*, 219–226; K Koranyi and M Patkaniowski, sv "Groicki Bartłomiej", in *Polski słownik biograficzny*, vol VIII, Wrocław: Zakład Narodowy im. Ossolińskich – Wydawawnictwo Polskiej Akademii Nauk, 1959–1960, 628–629.

21 K Estreicher, *Bibliografia polska*, vol XVII, Kraków: Drukarnia Uniwersytetu Jagiellońskiego pod zarządem Józefa Filipowskiego, 1899, 403–413; S. Kutrzeba, *Historia źródeł dawnego prawa polskiego*, vol II, Lwów: Zakład Narodowy im. Ossolińskich, 1926, 278–282.

22 L Dargun, "O źródłach prawa miast polskich w wieku szesnastym. I. O źródłach przepisów karnych w dziełach Groickiego" (1888) 22 *Rozprawy Akademii Umiejętności. Wydział Historyczno-Filozoficzny*, 11–16.

23 FIP IV, n 310, 26 March 1685.

the offence was shaky at best. In these circumstances, he argued, the use of torture was unlawful.[24] The argument must have been accepted by the Cracow court as the records of the case make no mention of torture. All they say is that the court, taking account of the boys' ages, sentenced them to pillory and expulsion from the city. The sentence was carried out.[25] The popularity of Groicki's work is further attested by handwritten notes in the margins of the extant copies of his treatise *Postępek praw skrócony*[26] [*Concise Legal Proceedings*] (a condensed version of *Constitutio Criminalis Carolina*) in the Jagiellonian Library collection. Remarkably, in one of the copies there are notes written in the same hand in sections referring to torture and theft.[27] The question of authorship of those notes cannot be resolved: there are no clues to suggest that they were written by the attorney Rogaleński.[28]

In Małopolska's small towns, Groicki's treatises – written in clear, straight-forward Polish – became the most popular handbook of law.[29] That must have been true of Dobczyce, where the local court on two occasions based its sentence on the provisions of *Constitutio Criminalis Carolina*, although without express mention to Groicki. In the first case, the killing of a town clerk (deputy mayor) was punished by a qualified death sentence – that is execution involving severe pain.[30] Groicki's text mentions torturing with pincers and drawing. The Dobczyce court found these punishments exemplary, but in the case at hand chose the cutting off the culprit's hand as more suitable for the crime of assault and laying hands on a person in authority. In the other case, involving a woman charged with infanticide, the judges handed down an optional sentence – that is the combined punishment of premature burial and impalement or drowning.[31] While these options are also mentioned by Groicki, their practical execution would be impossible. The conundrum was resolved, as the Dobczyce Book of Criminal Case Records reports, when the landlady of the village where the convicted woman lived remonstrated with the court and the death sentence was commuted to

---

24 M Mikołajczyk, *Proces kryminalny*, 216.
25 FIP IV, n 310, 2 April 1685 and n 311, 3 April 1685.
26 Bartłomiej Grociki, *Ten Postępek wybran iest z Praw Cesarskich* ..., Cracoviae: Lazarus Andreae, 1562.
27 Jagiellonian Library in Cracow (hereinafter, BJ), Stare Druki, Cim 5008 (fol 1582r), Art XXXI and XC.
28 Another copy with notes in margin may be found in BJ, Stare Druki, Cim 6326. The notes are found on Art XIIII, XXXII, XXXIII, XLIIII; BJ, Stare Druki, Cim 6429, Art IIII, VI, VII, XII, XXXI, XXXVIII; BJ, Stare Druki, Cim 6432, Art IV, XXXVII, LXXIX.
29 M Mikołajczyk, *Proces kryminalny*, 475.
30 FIP II, n 8, 13 December 1700.
31 FIP II, n 15, 15 April 1704.

whipping and banishment. It seems most likely that this was the outcome intended from the outset: the Dobczyce judges proceeded in accordance with the law, and the owner of the village intervened, by virtue of her dominion rights, to spare the convict's life.

D. GIULIO CLARO, JODOCUS DAMHOUDER AND ANDRZEJ LIPSKI

The renowned jurist and historian Andrzej Lipski (1572–1631)[32] made a synthesis of urban law in his hefty treatise *Practicarum Observationum ex Iure Civili et Saxonico collectarum* (1602), in which he also used legal authorities and *Constitutio Criminalis Carolina*. In 1679 this work was cited by the prosecutor[33] when the Cracow municipal court had to determine whether the defendant was to be charged with aggravated assault or attempted murder.[34] Lipski's authority tipped the scales in favour of the latter; it meant that the woman in the dock was condemned to death by beheading.[35] During the same trial the prosecution also invoked Jodocus Damhouder's *Praxis rerum criminalium* (1554).[36] It seems that on the point under discussion, Lipski followed the opinion of his elder colleague. It was fairly common to cite both Damhouder and Lipski. Especially in cases of theft, the counsel for the defence buttressed his reasoning with the authority of both jurists – for example, when the defendant claimed that she had purchased the stolen goods in good faith and asked permission to swear an oath to establish the point[37] (although the court had her whipped instead).

---

32 K Estreicher, *Bibliografia polska*, vol XX, Kraków: Drukarnia Uniwersytetu Jagiellońskiego pod zarządem Józefa Filipowskiego, 1906, 315–317; W Czapliński, sv "Lipski Andrzej", in *Polski słownik biograficzny*, vol XVII, Wrocław: Zakład Narodowy im. Ossolińskich – Wydawnictwo Polskiej Akademii Nauk, 1972, 415–417.

33 FIP IV, n 49 (7 October 1679): "Triplicando, instigator producit, iuxta [praescripta] reverendissimi Lipsii et Damuderii, [that] qui animo occidendi vulnerat, pro homicida censetur" – and more than that: she did want to kill, but was not able to.

34 "Nam occidendi animo vulneraverit, dubium non est, quod puniatur ut homicidia", Andrzej Lipski, *Practicarum Observationum ex Iure Civili et Saxonico. . . centuria prima*, Rigae: Nikolaus Mollyn, 1602, obs LXXXVI, n 2, 402.

35 FIP IV, n 53 (31 October 1679).

36 "Veluti si quis hominem non occidat, sed tantum vulneraverit, eo tamen animo, ut occidere posset, is pro homicida damnandus est . . ." Joos de Damhouder, *Praxis rerum criminalium*, Antwerp: apud Ioannem Bellerum sub Aquila aurea, 1570, cap 67, n 13, 161.

37 1693: Joos de Damhouder, *Praxis rerum criminalium*, cap 16, "De Receptatoribus furtorum", and cap 17, "*De Repertis*"; Andrzej Lipski, *Practicarum Observationum . . . centuria prima*, *obs. 92, n 7, "Apellatio a remissione quomodo differat"* (National Archive of Kraków, City Records of Kraków (*Archiwum Narodowe w Krakowie, Akta Miasta Krakowa* – hereinafter, ANK, AMK), MS 869, fol 243r–v).

In the records of the criminal trials at Cracow Court, the names of Damhouder and Lipski appear in various deliberations – for example, about the admissibility of torture in cases of sacrilege,[38] on the issue of whether a single act of theft (*simplex furtum*) should warrant the death penalty,[39] about punishment for adultery (treated differently in secular and canon law)[40], and in cases of libel[41] and blasphemy.[42] The authority of Andrzej Lipski and his abridgement of the *Constitutio Criminalis Carolina* was usually invoked in typically procedural issues such as the requirement of giving sureties by the plaintiff against his appearance in court.[43] Jodocus Damhouder's manual of criminal law was also used extensively in a 1690 murder trial of a man accused of poisoning of his wife.[44] The prosecution made much of Damhouder's provision that this type of crime should be punished by beheading with a sword,[45] and indeed the man was condemned to death by beheading.[46] Further support for this form of capital punishment was drawn from *Sententiae receptae* by Giulio Claro (1525–1575),[47] a treatise, which, like Damhouder's manual, was looked up to argue for and against the use of torture in the course of the trial.[48]

38 1691: Joost de Damhouder, *Praxis rerum criminalium*, cap 35 (ANK, AMK, MS 869, fol 5r).
39 1696: Andrzej Lipski, *Practicarum Observationum . . . centuria prima*, obs. 62, n 2, "Furtum simplex jure civile poena capitali non punitur" (ANK, AMK, MS 869, fol 535v).
40 1695: Joos de Damhouder, *Praxis rerum criminalium*, cap 79 (*sed* 97), n 18 "Aliae poenae de vi publica in Iure civili: alia in Iure Canonico", ANK, AMK, MS 869, fol 491r.
41 1697: Joos de Damhouder, *Praxis rerum criminalium*, cap 125, n 1, "De injuria quae sit scripto, seu de famosis libellis"; Andrzej Lipski, *Practicarum Observationum . . . centuria prima*, obs. 81, "*De injuria quae sit scripto, seu de famosis libellis*" (ANK, AMK, MS 870, fol 4v).
42 1695: Joost de Damhouder, *Praxis rerum criminalium*, cap 106 (ANK, AMK, MS 869, fol 485r).
43 1694: Andrzej Lipski, *Practicarum Observationum . . . centuria prima*, obs. 15, n 3 "Inscriptio non requiritur ex Imp. Caroli constitutione" (ANK, AMK, MS 689, fol 341r).
44 "Ideo eundem inculpatum poenis in legibus descriptis morte puniendum esse, nimirum pro atrocitate criminis in exemplum aliorum ad deterrendum a similibus facinoribus, per equum trahendum ad locum supplicii deducendum et morti damnandum rotisque implicandum, licet rigor legum antiquarum in tales parricidas cuti cum gallo, cane, symia et cato includendos et in profundis maris sive cuiusvis aquae mittendos et praescribant autoritateque legum, ut pote Jodoci Damhouderis atrocius esse crimen extingere hominem veneno quam gladio, in *Praxi Rerum Criminalium* C. 74 descibentis, et Julii Clarii, eo in casu, si maritus uxori venenum dederit, licet quae evaserit, ut parricidam poenam demereri, petens ut supra ex agnitione facti puniri." (FIP IV, n 524, 20 VI 1690).
45 Joos de Damhouder, *Praxis rerum criminalium*, cap 73, "De Homicidio per Venenum", 170.
46 FIP IV, n 535, 17 VII 1690.
47 "Et ita iudicavit senatus in causa cuiusdam medici, qui uxori venenum dederat, et fuit ei caput imputatum." *Iulii Clari patritii Alexandrini, iurisconsulti longe clarissimi, et serenissimi Philippi Hispaniarum regis Catholici in Prouincia Mediolanensi supremi consilliarii, ac regentis dignissimi. Receptarum Sententiarum Opera Omnia: quae quidem hactenus per auctorem in lucem edita sunt . . .*, Francoforti: ex officina typographia Nicolai Bassaei, 1596, lib V, sv "Homicidium", 46, n 13.
48 1695: Joos de Damhouder, *Praxis rerum criminalium*, cap 35, n 12, "Quaestionibus nullus damnandus est, nisi crimen patratum in maleficos exercentes" (ANK, AMK, MS 869, fol 420v).

E. BENEDICT CARPZOV

No legal authority was as popular with lawyers as the Leipzig jurist Benedict Carpzov (the Younger) (1595–1666), author of *Practicae novae imperialis Saxonicae rerum criminalium*, which went through several revised editions until the end of the seventeenth century.[49] References to this magisterial treatise recur in a number of debates between prosecution and defence in criminal trials at the Cracow municipal court. In a case of infanticide (a capital crime) from 1683[50] the prosecutor demanded that the decapitation of the female culprit be preceded by torture.[51] He pressed his point by citing Carpzov's distinction between three types of child abandonment and the appropriately graded retribution. The most abhorrent of them, *expositio* – leaving an infant in a wild and deserted place where it would be sure to die of exposure – deserves to be punished by death. As Carpzov stated, his view of the matter was no different from that of the ancient Roman *lex Cornelia*.[52] In the 1683 case the woman accused of infanticide swore that the baby she abandoned was already dead. After some discussion, the court sentenced the woman to sixteen lashes and banishment from the city. In another trial held in 1683,[53] the prosecutor obviously took a cue from Carpzov when he tried to expand the basis of the indictment in a case of theft. He argued that in determining the punishment for a servant accused of robbing his master – after having been found in possession of the key to a casket, which contained the stolen valuables – the court should also take into account the fact that the man was apprehended after escaping from prison. Carpzov examined with great care the problem of prison escape as an aggravating factor in conjunction with other charges. In this case, two of his observations were

---

49 W Uruszczak, "Model procesu karnego według Practica nova imperialis Saxonicae rerum criminalium Benedykta Carpzowa (†1666)", in J Czapska, A Gaberle, A Światłowski and A Zoll (eds), *Zasady procesu karnego wobec wyzwań współczesności. Księga ku czci Profesora Stanisława Waltosia*, Warszawa: Wydawnictwa Prawnicze, Państwowe Wydawnictwo Naukowe, 2000, 154–165; H Lück, "Benedict Carpzov (1595–1666) und das 'römisch-sächsische Recht'. Zu Seinem 350. Todestag am 31 August 2016" (2016) 4 *Zeitschrift für europäisches Privatrecht*, 888–927.

50 FIP IV, n 190, 11 September 1683.

51 "Actor replicando adduxit auctoritatem legis ex Carpzovio, [that when an infant is found] in cloaca vivus, [so she should be] subiici torturis, [and] meretur poenam gladii, [because] pro indaganda veritate petit eandem torturari."

52 "Primus casus est, quando infantes in locum solitarium, et a conspectu hominum remotum, abjiciuntur, ea intentione et proposito, quo inedia consumantur et moriantur; tunc eventu subsequuto, exponents poena legis Corneliae de sicariis, nempe gladio, puniendi sunt." Benedict Carpzov, *Practicae novae Imperialis Saxonicae rerum criminalium pars prima*, Lipsiae: apud Johannem Fridericum Gleditschium, 1739, cap 10, n 5, 40; cf also 6–9 and 40–41.

53 FIP IV, n 200, 11 September 1683.

of special importance – the escape was an aggravating circumstance and torture was permitted in such cases.[54] The counsel for the defendant also invoked Carpzov's authority in their attempts to save the defendant from being subjected to torture. They pointed out that Carpov, while commenting on an edict of Emperor Augustus, found torture permissible only in the investigation of crimes that were both grave and obvious, and when there was no other way of clearing doubts.[55] The defence counsel then argued that there was no certain proof of the servant having actually stolen the valuables, which meant that (his involvement in) the crime was far from obvious. Such certainty, however, was absolutely necessary for the court to allow the use of torture, the most drastic probatory means at its disposal.[56] The defence entered the fray resolutely, yet with little success. The court records leave us in no doubt: torture remained the order of the day. In this final example, an appeal to Carpzov was made[57] by the defence counsel in a case of adultery in which the wife (plaintiff) decided to withdraw her suit against her husband.[58] The court rejected the counsel's plea for abatement, arguing that since the adultery in question was overt, the action could not be quashed even if it was the plaintiff's wish. The adulterous husband (defendant) was therefore sentenced to humiliating public exposure. The authority of Benedict Carpzov

---

54 "Etsi enim fuga per se suspicionem criminis perpetrati contra fugientem faciat" (CXL, 49) and "Septimum indicium oritur ex fuga: quae fugentem accusat, et in suspicionem sceleris adducit, adeoque et indicium ad torturam facit" (CXX, 60). Benedict Carpzov, *Practicae novae imperialis Saxonicae rerum criminalium*, pars III, Wittenberg: typis excusa Matthæi Henckelii, 1665, *quaestio* CXX, n 60, 182; *quaestio* CXL, n 49, 331; and subsequent passages of *quaestio* CXX (n 61–66) and CXI (n 35).

55 "Quae regula, ex verbis Edicti Divi Augusti desumpta, tria potissimum denotat: 1. Ut causa sit criminalis et delictum atrox. 2. Vere perpetratum. 3. Quod desint aliae probationes, nec veritas aliter haberi queat." Ibid, *quaestio* CXIX, n 2, 169.

56 "Ad torturasque non posse destinari, ex quo supplicium pro crimine non manet, quae non nisi ibi locum habent, dum adest crimen commissum, pro quo maneat suplicium vel poena corporis afflictiva authoritate Benedicto Carpzov parte 3, quaestio 119 se tuendo, libertatem expetiit." (FIP IV, n 548, 25 August 1690). Cf also FIP IV, n 532, 10 July 1690.

57 ". . . conjugi, uxorem aut virum adulterum recipere volenti, hoc concedendum, ac poenam mortis eo casu reo remittendam esse." Benedict Carpzov, *Practicae novae Imperialis Saxonicae rerum criminalium*, pars II, Wittenberg: typis excusa Mathæi Henkelii, 1670, *quaestio* LV, 35.

58 ". . . quod consors inculpati eundem intercedat et de sua instantia remittat, intulit ipsoque supplici libello eiusdem consortis suae ad spectabilem Magistratum super eliberationem mariti sui e carcere et ab ipsa causa supplicantis porrecto docuit non constare quoque de crimine et delicto corporis, nam et testes nonnulli, ut pote mulieres depositiones suas iuramento non comprobaverant ideoque earum testimonia non possunt operari et quoniam consors eidem marito ex parte sua remittit, ideo poena cessare debet, id authoritate Benedicti Carpzovii parte 2 . . ." (FIP IV, n 534, 15 July 1690).

was usually sought in cases involving adultery,[59] bigamy[60] and minor abuse.[61] His popularity with Cracow Criminal Court lawyers is all too evident.

F. JUSTIFICATION OF JUDICIAL DECISIONS OF THE CRACOW COURT: THE MAGDEBURG *WEICHBILD*, THE *SACHSENSPIEGEL* AND PARLIAMENTARY LEGISLATION

In the rulings of the Cracow Criminal Court there is no direct reference to works of contemporary jurists. This should not be surprising if we bear in mind that that the treatises of Benedict Carpzov, Giulio Claro, Jodocus Damhouder and Andrzej Lipski did not have the status of official sources of law. The case of Bartłomiej Groicki was somewhat different, at least in smaller towns. The respect with which the provincial courts treated his translation of *Constitutio Criminalis Carolina* was probably coupled with the belief that the provisions of that code were authorised by the Polish king. The fact that there was no such official authorisation shows the recognition of another handy digest of laws by a legal profession accustomed to work with multiple sources of law. Judging by the frequency with which his name appears in the records, Groicki – whose work was available to courts and litigants all over the country – was held in higher esteem in smaller towns than in the city of Cracow. Be that as it may, the sixteenth-century shift in favour of contemporary jurists was in the first place the result of the obsolescence of the old Saxon-Magdeburg Law, especially in the field of criminal law and the criminal trial where the parties could not help but reach out for more appropriate tools to make their case. The court, by ruling in favour of one of the parties, *de facto* endorsed the manner in which it presented its case, using the works of contemporary jurists. In this way the latter were given a tacit seal of approval, and the legal arguments underpinning them were allowed to complement the outdated formulas of the Saxon-Magdeburg Law. The works of the jurists, however, did not eliminate it: in particular, the rulings continued to be bound to the provisions of the Magdeburg *Weichbild*, the *Sachsenspiegel* and parliamentary legislation. The most frequently mentioned legislative acts of the Parliament were the Statute of 1519, which set down the composition of a court authorised to hear suits

---

59 1692: ANK, AMK, MS 869, fol 61r; 1693: ANK, AMK, MS 869, fol ante 197 (the numbering of the manuscript skipped a folio).
60 1698: ANK, AMK, MS 870, fol 127r.
61 1695: Benedictus Carpzov, *Practicae novae*, Pars II, *quaestio* LXXV, n 56 "Quomodo puniatur conatus stupri violenti" (ANK, AMK, MS 869, fol 444v).

against noblemen accused of committing crimes in the territory under urban jurisdiction, and the Statute of 1593 for preventing urban tumults and punishing the rioters. In a sentence handed down in 1633, the Cracow municipal court refers directly to Article 85 of the *Weichbild* concerning a brawl in which the combatants wielded knives and swords. The Cracow Court kept using as its reference book of law either the 1581 Polish translation by Paweł Szczerbic[62] or the authorised Latin edition of the Saxon-Magdeburg Law by Mikołaj Jaskier, published in 1535.[63] In a criminal case of bigamy heard in 1698, the court sentenced the defendant to beheading with a sword, echoing the plaintiff's plea based on Article 60 of the *Sachsenspiegel*.[64] Thus, both the *Weichbild* and the *Sachsenspiegel* continued to play a part, if a less prominent one, in the argument of the counsel.

G. CONCLUSION

From the sixteenth century onwards, the treatises of contemporary jurists played an important role in the legal practice of Polish towns incorporated under the Magdeburg Law. In the sixteenth and seventeenth centuries their influence grew as a consequence of the failed attempts to update and codify the municipal law based on the Magdeburg Law. The most notable of such projects was Maciej Śliwnicki's (d c 1551) code of municipal law entitled *Sigismundina* in honour of King Sigismund I. Published in 1523, it failed to secure official acceptance. The main reason for its rejection was the author's extensive adoption of Roman law, which had been hardly used by the town courts. Moreover, the Saxon-Magdeburg Law was too deeply rooted in the realities of a bygone age (even in the thirteenth and fourteenth centuries it already had some anachronistic traits) to provide an adequate template

---

62 Art 85: "Jeśliby się dwa spólnie, jeden mieczem a drugi nożem ranili, i obadwa by zaraz do sądu przyszli i na świeżym uczynku nakazano by szranki przez dekret, tedy za ranę nożową ma być gardło sądzon ten, który ją zadał". Paweł Szczerbic, *Ius Municipale, to jest prawo miejskie majdeburskie nowo z łacińskiego i z niemieckiego na polski język z pilnością i wiernie przełożone*, ed Grzegorz Maria Kowalski (Kraków 2011), 229 [Bibliotheca Iagiellonica. Fontes et Studia, 20]. See G M Kowalski, "Szczerbic Paweł", in *Polski słownik biograficzny*, vol XLVII, 2010–2011, 397–401.

63 Art 85: "Si duo vulneraverint se mutuo unus gladio et alter cultello, et ad judicium veniant, uterque conformiter, ac in recenti actione duellum comprobatum sit per veram sententiam, pro vulnere ex cultello judicatur in collum illius." Nicolaus Iaskierus, *Iuris Municipalis Maideburgensis Liber vulgo Weichbild nuncupatur . . .*, Cracoviae: Hiernonymys Vietor, 1535, fol 51r. See H Lück, "Jaskier Mikołaj", in *Handwörterbuch zur deutschen Rechtsgeschichte*, vol II, 2nd edn, Berlin: Erich Schmidt Verlag, 2012, col 1355–1356.

64 1698: ANK, AMK, MS 870, fols 127v and 130v.

for legal practice of the sixteenth century.[65] As a result, legal practitioners turned for guidance to legal manuals and treatises that were the product of a new generation of jurists, namely Bartłomiej Groicki, Andrzej Lipski, Joos Damhouder, Benedict Carpzov and Julio Claro. However, their approach and formulas were used in a selective manner. While the litigants in criminal cases heard by the Cracow Municipal Court borrowed freely from all of the contemporary authorities, the provincial courts seemed to have a decided preference for Bartłomiej Groicki. The records of the Cracow Court (which constitute a fairly complete database) offer very little information about the justification of judicial rulings. In those rare cases when the legal grounds of a decision are indicated, only the well-established sources of law (the Magdeburg *Weichbild*, the *Sachsenspiegel* and parliamentary legislation) is mentioned. Even so, there is little doubt that the court looked carefully at the legal argument taken form the works of contemporary jurists. By ruling in favour of one of the competing lines of reasoning it *de facto* recognised the authority of the jurists without admitting it explicitly in the justification of its closing judgment. In the last decades of the eighteenth century, after a long period of decline, the Polish-Lithuanian Commonwealth finally rose to the challenge of modernising all spheres of public life. The Constitution of 3 May 1791 and the Royal Cities Act of 18 April 1791[66] paved the way for the drafting of a modern urban law. Unfortunately, the partition of Poland by its neighbours, Russia, Prussia and Austria, put an end to that ambitious undertaking. After the fall of the Polish state, the patterns of reform of traditional urban law in Poland's cities and towns followed the models of modernisation pursued in each of the partitioning powers.

65 M Mikołajczyk, "Stosując się do prawa wyraźnego", 202–203.
66 W Uruszczak, "Ustawy okołokonstytucyjne Sejmu Wielkiego z 1791 i 1792 roku" (2013) 6(3) *Krakowskie Studia z Historii Państwa i Prawa*, 247–258, at 248–249.

7 Under the Legal Authority of the Senate of Milan (Sixteenth to Seventeenth Centuries)

Annamaria Monti

A. INTRODUCTION
B. ORDINARY PEOPLE AND THE JUDICIARY
C. THE SENATE'S CASE LAW: WAYS OF RETURNING A DOWRY
D. CONCLUSION

A. INTRODUCTION

The Senate of Milan was one of the most powerful European courts of justice in the early modern period, and its case law greatly influenced the development of substantive law.[1] Recent research on the problems of legislation, law and the role of judges has shone a spotlight on how case law impacts on sources of law. I believe this is an interesting opportunity to examine the issue by looking back on the institutional values and systems that society had in place during the *Ancien Régime*, of which the *Senate* itself was at once an expression and a guarantor.[2]

The Senate operated in a legal, political and even cultural climate that was eclectic but coherent. The *Milanesado* was part of the complex circuit of possessions falling under the *Monarquía Católica* in continental Europe. Indeed, it was one of the Spanish dominions' most loyal possessions: not a

---

1 U Petronio, *Il Senato di Milano. Istituzioni giuridiche ed esercizio del potere nel Ducato di Milano da Carlo V a Giuseppe II*, Milano: Giuffrè, 1972. In English, M Ascheri, "Italy from Medieval Times to 1800", in A Wijffels and C H van Rhee (eds), *The European supreme courts. A portrait through history*, London: Third Millennium Publishing, 2013, 46–48. See also G Gorla, "I tribunali supremi degli stati italiani fra i secoli XVI e XIX quali fattori della unificazione del diritto nello stato e della sua uniformazione fra stati", in Id, *Diritto comparato e diritto comune europeo*, Milano: Giuffrè, 1981, 543–617.
2 A Monti, *Iudicare tamquam deus. I modi della giustizia Senateria nel Ducato di Milano tra cinque e settecento*, Milano: Giuffrè, 2003, 65 ff.

single revolt in two-and-a-half centuries.[3] Following an initial adjustment period that coincided with the definitive passage of the Duchy of Milan to Habsburg Spain, membership in the Senate was reserved for exponents of the Lombard patriciate who had studied law at the University of Pavia.[4] The president of the Senate often had a privileged relationship with the Spanish sovereigns – and the local elite had the same ideals and lifestyles as the Spanish elite.[5]

However, the Senate was also keeper of Milan and Lombardy's juridical tradition, as well as of the town statutes in the Duchy and the Duchy's Constitutions (*Constitutiones*) of 1541, known as New Constitutions.[6] These Constitutions – which were the Prince's legislation – were a collection of laws and practices, much of which was based on late medieval decrees issued under Visconti and Sforza rule.[7] Specifically, Senate members jealously protected not only their own privileges, but also the administration of justice within their remit.

As the Senate rendered justice to the parties, it represented the Prince himself and therefore it enjoyed the power to decide according to its equitable power (*aequitas*), following its unobjectionable discretionary judgment (*arbitrium*).[8] The Court used to proceed and judge according to

3 D Sella and C Capra, *Il Ducato di Milano dal 1535 al 1796*, Torino: Utet, 1984. For further bibliographical reference, A Gamberini (ed), *A Companion to Late Medieval and Early Modern Milan. The distinctive features of an Italian State*, Leiden: Brill, 2015.

4 U Petronio, "Burocrazia e burocrati nel Ducato di Milano dal 1561 al 1706", in *Per Francesco Calasso. Studi degli allievi*, Roma: Bulzoni, 1978, 481–561: Id, "La burocrazia patrizia nel Ducato di Milano nell'età spagnola (1561–1706)", in *L'educazione giuridica*, pt IV. *Il pubblico funzionario: modelli storici e comparativi*, vol I, Perugia: Libreria universitaria, 1981, 253–328.

5 C Mozzarelli, "Nella Milano dei re cattolici. Considerazioni su uomini, cultura e istituzioni tra Cinque e Seicento", in P Pissavino and G Signorotto (eds), *Lombardia borromaica Lombardia spagnola 1554–1659*, vol I, Roma: Bulzoni, 1995, 421–456; A Álvarez-Ossorio Alvariño, *Milán y el legado de Felipe II. Gobernadores y corte provincial en la Lombardia de los Austrias*, Madrid: Sociedad Estatal para la Conmemoración de los Centenarios de Felipe II y Carlos V, 2001.

6 The Constitutions of the Duchy were in force until 1786. Here, I will quote the last edition: *Constitutiones mediolanensis Dominii jam primum illustratae decisionibus et annotationibus ab egregio jurisconsulto et advocato Pio Antonio Mogno Fossato*, Mediolani: ex typ J Marelli, 1764.

7 See M G di Renzo Villata, "Diritto comune e diritto locale nella cultura giuridica lombarda dell'età moderna", in *Diritto comune e diritti locali nella storia dell'Europa*, Milano: Giuffrè, 1980, 329–388; Ead, "Tra ius nostrum e ius commune. Il diritto patrio nel Ducato di Milano", in I Birocchi, A Mattone (eds), *Il diritto patrio tra diritto comune e codificazione (secoli XVI–XIX)*, Roma: Viella, 2006, 217–254. For extensive bibliographical references, see A Monti, " Constitutiones Dominii mediolanensis, 1541. Constitutions pour le Milanais (extraits relatifs à la procédure criminelle)", in J Hautebert and S Soleil (eds), *La procédure et la construction de l'État en Europe: XVIe–XIXe siècle. Recueil de textes, présentés et commentés*, Rennes: Presses universitaires de Rennes, 2011, 423–448.

8 M Meccarelli, *Arbitrium. Un aspetto sistematico degli ordinamenti giuridici in età di diritto comune*, Milano: Giuffrè 1998; Id, "Dimensions of Justice and Ordering Factors in Criminal Law

conscience (*secundum conscientiam*)[9] and its decisions were considered somehow divine in nature – *Senatus iudicat tamquam Deus* repeated local jurists and legal doctrine.[10]

The remarkable case law of the supreme court was a leading authority in the Duchy. The aim of this contribution is precisely to clarify how the supreme court influenced the development of substantive private law in the Duchy of Milan. First, the Senate did not give any reason for its judgments. All its activity was surrounded by secrecy, the so-called "mysteries of the Senate" (*"arcana Senatus"*). However, through indirect sources, mainly legal advisers (*consilia*) and reports of the Senate's case law, it was possible to understand how the supreme court enforced private substantive law through its judgments (i.e. *decisiones*), which consisted of the purview of the sentence and were pronounced in the name of the Spanish king, duke of Milan.[11] Second, the Senate was a supreme court which did not consider its own precedents as binding. However, the other judges of the Duchy, the lower jurisdictions which were called "inferior" judges, were bound to the Senate's judgments.[12] More precisely, *decisiones* were binding on the parties involved in the case, as well as on all lower judges as an authoritative example for similar cases (*consuetudo iudicandi*).[13] Indeed, the Senate had

from the Middle Ages till Juridical Modernity", in G Martyn, A Musson and H Pihlajamäki (eds), *From the judge's arbitrium to the legality principle: legislation as a source of law in criminal trials*, Berlin: Duncker & Humblot, 2013, 49–67.

9 K W Nörr, *Zur Stellung des Richters in gelehrten Prozess der Frühzeit. Iudex secundum allegata non secundum conscientiam iudicat*, München: Beck, 1967; A Padoa-Schioppa, "Sur la conscience du juge dans le jus commun européen", in J-M Carbasse and L Depambour-Tarride (eds), *La conscience du juge dans la tradition juridique européenne*, Paris: Presses Universitaires de France, 1999, 95–129; A. Cavanna, "La conscience du juge dans le stylus iudicandi du Sénat de Milan", ibid, 229–262.

10 Angelo Stefano Garoni, *Commentaria in tit de Senatoribus Novarum Constitutionum Status Mediolani*, Mediolani: apud Ph Ghisulphium, 1643, *Praeludia*; Giulio Cesare Calvino, *De aequitate tractatus novus usuque receptissimus*, Mediolani: ex typ F Vigoni, 1676, lib I, cap 5; Giulio Cesare Rugginelli, *Tractatus de Senatoribus sive Commentaria ad Novas Constitutiones Mediolani hoc titulo*, Mediolani: ex typ C I Quinti, 1697, § I, glos VI, cap 27. See also Ortensio Cavalcani, *Tractatus de brachio regio*, Venetiis: apud B Iuntam, 1608, *Pars prima* and *Pars sexta*.

11 See M Ascheri, *Tribunali, giuristi e istituzioni dal medioevo all'età moderna*, Bolgna: Il Mulino, 1995, 7–22 and 261–267.

12 Giacomo Menochio, *Consiliorum sive responsorum liber tertius*, Francofurti: sumptibus haeredum A Wecheli et I Gymnici, 1594, cons 282, n 36–38; Id, *Consiliorum sive responsorum liber quintus*, Francofurti: sumptibus haeredum A Wecheli et I Gymnici, 1594, cons 412, n 39; Id, *Consiliorum sive responsorum liber septimus*, Francofurti: sumptibus haeredum A Wecheli et I Gymnici, 1604, cons 676, n 2 ss; Id, *Consiliorum sive responsorum liber duodecimus*, Francofurti: sumptibus C Marnij, 1609, cons 1144, n 20-21; Id, *De praesumptionibus, coniecturis, signis, et indiciis commentaria*, Venetiis: apud haeredes F Ziletti, 1597, lib I, *quaestio* 1, n 14 and 27.

13 G P Massetto, sv "Sentenza (diritto intermedio)", in *Enciclopedia del diritto*, Milano: Giuffrè, 1989, vol XLI, 1,210.

strong control on these judges and received appeals and petitions against their judgments. Moreover, this control was also imposed through other mechanisms, which are key to understanding how, in practice, this supreme court influenced the development of substantive law, and specifically private law.

Every day the Senate's chancery received many supplication petitions from the people of the Duchy who were having problems with a specific judge or specific proceedings.[14] These requests were called *preces* and the Senate usually responded through its *rescripta*. In general, Senate *rescripta* were provisions through which the high court sent varied instructions to inferior judges on how to decide single cases.[15] An analysis of these provisions is essential to sketch a picture of case law in the Senate for the long period – almost three centuries – in which it administered justice. As stated by Giulio Claro – a well-known sixteenth-century Italian jurist – to learn what was the rule, what was the substantive law in force, one had to look at the Senate's case law,[16] which was the result of the Senate's different provisions, mainly *decisions* and *rescripta*.[17] What emerges is a complex and lively picture, closer to the everyday needs of the people than one could expect from a court judging as if it were god – *tamquam deus*.

Concerning the sources, I will refer to the sixteenth and seventeenth-century manuscript copies of the formularies of the Senate's record office, a

---

14 See C Nubola, "Supplications between Politics and Justice: The Northern and Central Italian States in the Early Modern Age", in L H van Voss (ed), *Petitions in Social History*, Cambridge: Cambridge University Press, 2001, 36, on the supplications, which put the subjects of the king in direct relationship with the development of authorities, as a privileged form of communication between the rulers and those ruled.

15 The granting of *rescripta* by the duke had been common practice in Milan Duchy since the fourteenth century: C Storti Storchi, "Giudici e giuristi nelle riforme viscontee del processo civile per Milano (1330–1386)", in *Ius Mediolani. Studi di storia del diritto milanese offerti dagli allievi a Giulio Vismara*, Milano: Giuffrè, 1996, 47–187. See also M N Covini, "La trattazione delle suppliche nella cancelleria sforzesca: da Francesco Sforza a Ludovico il Moro", in C Nubola and A Würgler (eds), *Suppliche e "gravamina". Politica, amministrazione, giustizia in Europa (secoli XIV–XVIII)*, Bologna: Il Mulino, 2002, 107–146. See also the German version in C Nubola and A Würgler (eds), *Bittschriften und Gravamina: Politik, Verwaltung und Justiz in Europa (14–18 Jahrhundert)*, Berlin: Duncker & Humblot, 2005.

16 Giulio Claro, *Volumen, alias liber Quintus*, Venetiis: expensis I A de Antonijs, 1570, *pars finalis*, *quaestio 38, Vidi aliquando*. See G P Massetto, "La prassi giuridica lombarda nell'opera di Giulio Claro (1525–1575)", in Id, *Saggi di storia del diritto penale lombardo (Secc XVI–XVIII)*, Milano: Led, 1994, 11–59; A Cavanna, *La codificazione penale in Italia. Le origini lombarde*, Milano: Giuffrè, 1975, *passim*.

17 For an overview, A Monti, "Between Case Law and Legislation: The Senate of Milan, a Supreme Court during the Ancien Régime", in B Feldner, V T Halbwachs, T Olechowski, J Pauser, S Schima and A Sereinig (eds), *Ad Fontes, Europäisches Forum Junger Rechtshistorikerinnen und Rechtshistoriker Wien 2001*, Frankfurt am Main [ua]: Peter Lang, 2002, 303–318.

kind of chancery manual: these collections of forms and instruments offer a wide perspective from which to appreciate the jurisdictional complexity of Milan Duchy as it was ruled by the supreme court.[18] Unfortunately, due to bombings during the Second World War, the Archives of the Senate were almost completely destroyed. However, through the collections of formularies and other different sources, both published and unpublished, mainly doctrinal and indirect or second-hand sources, it was possible to reconstruct the daily activity of this high court of Milan.

B. ORDINARY PEOPLE AND THE JUDICIARY

Each trial in front of the Senate began on request of a party. It meant that the supreme court intervened after a party had made a supplication. These specific supplications, which were a kind of petition-like document, had a particular technical name,[19] *preces*, and had to mention the ruler that they were addressed to: in the Milan Duchy they bore a specific title, "P R", which meant *Potentissime Rex* (His Majesty the King). They were in fact addressed to the Senate, which represented the king in rendering justice.[20]

"Petitions are demands for a favour, or for the redressing of an injustice, directed to some established authority. As the distribution of justice and largesse are important parts of ruling, rulers can hardly deny their subjects the right to approach them to implore them to exercise justice, or to grant a favour" – as Lex Heerma van Voss wrote some years ago to introduce a collective work on petitions studied as "a powerful historical source". He also added that "[w]riting petitions was a common human experience . . . humble (or not so humble) suppliants put them on paper . . . and the authorities to which these petitions were addressed took care to preserve them".[21]

The Senate's Archives were badly damaged over the centuries, especially during the Second World War; nevertheless, a number of these *preces* which were kept in other archives, mainly private or family archives, still survive

---

18 A Monti, *I formulari del Senate di Milano (secoli XVI–XIII)*, Milano: Giuffrè, 2001.

19 A Würgler, "Voices From Among the 'Silent Masses': Humble Petitions and Social Conflicts in Early Modern Central Europe", in van Voss (ed), *Petitions in Social History*, 14–15.

20 Consequently, Senate *rescripta* were granted in the name of the king, duke of Milan: see the forms in Milano, Biblioteca Ambrosiana, MS D 118 suss, *Formulae Senatus mediolanensis scriptae ab Iacopo Ivagnes fere anno 1610*, fol 1r and MS I 90 suss, *Inscriptiones litterarum quae nomine Senatus inscribuntur*, fol 8r, both edited in Monti, *I formulari*, 175 and 273.

21 L H van Voss, "Introduction", in Id, *Petitions in Social History*, 1.

today.[22] They testify to the intense exchange between the court, the people of the Duchy and their lawyers: it was a strict relationship, which was clearly reflected in the Senate's practice. In fact, in the Milan Duchy petitions were also "very flexible instruments", used by individuals or organised and recognised groups, which were sent to the Senate requesting intervention or calling attention to injustice and abuse.[23]

According to the definition given by the seventeenth-century Lombard jurist Giuseppe Oldradi, an expert on the subject, the technical word *rescripta* was reserved in his times to the letters written and sent by the Prince or the Senate. They were also called *litterae regiae et ducales* and were used mainly in administrating justice. As Oldradi explained, the Latin verb *rescribere* meant to concede, to order or to establish something.[24] One might think of the late Roman Empire provisions called precisely *rescripta* – as with most of Europe, it was very common in legal discourse to rely on Latin terms found in Justinian Code and Digest.[25]

The Constitutions for the Duchy of Milan of 1541 devoted a series of articles to these *rescripta* of the Prince.[26] Through these acts, which were given in the name of the Spanish king, duke of Milan, after examination of the petitions of the parties, the Senate could decide to examine and judge

22 For samples of supplications, see Milano, Biblioteca Ambrosiana, MS I 40 suss, *Formularium Civile manuscriptum ab Iurisconsulto . . . Domini Bernardini a Porta, cui nonnulla addita fuere ab Iurisconsulto . . . Joanne Maria Crotta* [post 1714?], 72–73, 127–128 and 141–144.

23 Nubola, "Supplications between Politics and Justice", 35, wrote that through petitions: ". . . it is generally possible to verify a number of fundamental forms and modes of communication between society and the institutions of the *ancien régime*, and to reconstruct the procedures of mediation, repression, acceptance, and agreement adopted by princes, sovereigns, or magistracies in response to social demands . . . These documents gave rise to legal proceedings administrative acts that led to proceedings in tribunals, magistracies, and chancelleries."

24 ". . . cum rescribere idem sit quod per literas quicquam concedere, iubere, mandare vel statuere": Giuseppe Oldradi, *De litteris et mandatis principum et praesertim excellentissimi sacrique regii Senatus Mediolanensis ac aliorum supremorum totius orbis Senatuum commentaria in tres partes digesta, in quibus Caesareae Provinciae Mediolanensis Constitutiones in tit. De rescriptis . . . explicantur . . . Pars prima*, Mediolani: ex typ I B Bidellij, 1630, *praeludium* III, n 4 and *praeludium* VIII.

25 See Nubola, "Supplications between Politics and Justice", 45: "*Rescritto*: the prince's written answer to a subject's request. If, in old canon law, the term was uniquely used for the Pope's written answers, beginning with the Middle Ages its use was expanded, insofar as the answers written by those who had legislative or jurisdictional power were also called *rescritti*." For the use of *rescripta* in canon law, see G Le Bras, C Lefebvre and J D Rambaud, "L'âge classique, 1140–1378. Sources et théorie du droit", in *Histoire du droit et des institutions de l'Eglise en Occident VII*, Paris: Sirey, 1965, 466–486.

26 *Constitutiones mediolanensis Dominii*, lib I, tit De rescriptis, et mandatis Principum, 4–5. See Angelo Stefano Garoni, *Observationes in Constitutiones Dominii Mediolanensis*, Mediolani: apud I B Bidellium, 1627, 6–11; Giulio Cesare Rugginelli, *Practicarum quaestionum rerumque iudicatarum liber singularis*, Venetiis: apud B Baretium, 1610, cap 29.

the case directly or send instructions to lower judges. If the Senate decided not to examine the case directly, it addressed this kind of letter to the judge concerned. *Rescripta* were usually issued by a single Senate member who could order lower judges to, for example, proceed according to the rules of the so-called "summary procedure" (*processum summarium*).[27] These proceedings, which were quicker, had been implemented for the first time by ecclesiastical courts during the thirteenth century and had been successively adopted by lay courts.[28]

In general, Senate *rescripta* were in fact provisions through which the high court sent varied instructions to lower judges. Therefore, *rescripta* also represented a relatively efficient instrument for the control and direction of other magistrates' activities.[29] If the inferior judge did not obey to the Senate's command, the high court sent another letter. The Senate granted another *rescriptum* at the party's request. At the same time, it imposed a three-day period on the disobedient judge to explain his actions.[30] The Senate's letter could be a simple order to proceed or it could contain more detailed instructions, concerning evidence, terms, appeal and resort procedures. Many kinds of these *rescripta* are illustrated in the collection of forms previously mentioned[31] and it is important to remark once again that these letters were conceded only if a party made a request.

Finally, *rescripta* were one of the everyday means through which the Senate exercised its daily control over the subordinate judges. As I have mentioned, the *rescripta* were conceded following petitions from ordinary people. These motivated requests and the reasons for them never went unanswered. Moreover, they actually opened new paths of intervention for the high court. As Andreas Würgler put it: "By confidently petitioning (and complaining) to the ruler, the subjects triggered expanding state action. The

---

27 Giovanni Antonio Zavattari, *De Fori Mediolanensis praxi, et nonnullis depravationibus ex eo tollendi dialogus*, Venetiis: apud H Polum, 1584, 116 and 148ff.

28 A Lattes, *Studi di diritto statutario I, Il procedimento sommario o planario negli statuti*, Milano: Hoepli, 1886; C Lefebvre, "Les origines romaines de la procédure sommaire aux XIIe et XIIIe s" (1956) 12 *Ephemerides iuris canonici*, 149–197; K W Nörr, "Rechtsgeschichtliche Apostillen zur Clementine Saepe", in C H van Rhee (ed), *The Law's delay: essays on undue delay in civil litigation*, Cambridge: Intersentia, 2004, 203–215; M Ascheri, "Between Statutory Law and Learned Law: Delay in the Early History of the Medieval Italian Communes (and Beyond)", in C H van Rhee (ed), *Within a Reasonable Time: The History of Due and Undue Delay in Civil Litigation*, Berlin: Duncker & Humblot, 2010, 40–42.

29 See G P Massetto, *Un magistrato e una città nella Lombardia spagnola. Giulio Claro pretore a Cremona*, Milano: Giuffrè, 1985, 125ff.

30 The collections of forms of the Senate testified of this procedure: Monti, *I formulari*, 52, 231 and 306.

31 Ibid, 47–52, 203 and 291.

numbers, recipients, contents, and resolutions of supplications may reveal channels of power. After all, the early modern state was partly the result of government reaction to popular petitions."[32]

C. THE SENATE'S CASE LAW: WAYS OF RETURNING A DOWRY

The sources give a picture of the Senate as the keeper of justice and the caring protector of the Lombard Duchy's subjects, who clearly felt that their sovereign "owed" them the justice he dispensed, very much in the sense so effectively described by Jacques Krynen. Indeed, the Senate represented the far-off sovereign and repaid the sovereign's "debt" by administering justice.[33]

In terms of private law, the Senate's most noteworthy solutions concerned family law and inheritance rights.[34] In judicial matters, it acted by either issuing *decisiones* or sending *rescripta* to the Duchy's judges.[35] Going even further, the Senate offered particularly interesting solutions to disputes over dowries, which were a fundamental part of families' assets and finances in the medieval and early modern period. A dowry was the property brought by a bride to meet the needs of the family.[36] The Senate dealt with dowry issues primarily in two critical moments: when the dowry was provided upon marriage; and when it was to be allotted following the dissolution of a marriage.[37]

The Senate was particularly active when addressing claims to dowries following the dissolution of a marriage – its case law in this area was more substantial. The court was perfectly aware of lawyers' opinions in its interpretation of town statutes or of the *ius commune*, and this helped to clarify unclear issues when it came to the obligation to return the dowry – an obli-

---

32 Würgler, "Voices From Among the 'Silent Masses'", 31–32.

33 J Krynen, *L'Empire du roi. Idées et croyances politiques en France XIIIe–XVe siècle*, Paris: Gallimard, 1993.

34 See M C Zorzoli, "Una incursione nella pratica giurisprudenziale milanese del Seicento e qualche riflessione su temi che riguardano la famiglia", in *Ius Mediolani. Studi di storia del diritto milanese offerti dagli allievi a Giulio Vismara*, Milano: Giuffrè, 1996, 617–657.

35 In non-judicial cases, the Senate also issued *dispensationes*, a kind of exemption, which were frequently issued to rule family and inheritance relationships, as well as contracts. In each single case the Senate dispensed the requesting party from the observance of a legal rule: see A Monti, "Fedecommessi lombardi: profili giuridici e riflessi privati delle dispense Senatorie" (2012) 124(2) *Mélanges de l'École française de Rome. Italie et Méditerranée*, 489–500.

36 M Bellomo, "Dote (diritto intermedio)", in *Enciclopedia del diritto*, vol XIV, Milano: Giuffrè, 1965, 8–32.

37 See C Valsecchi, "L'istituto della dote nella vita del diritto del tardo Cinquecento: i Consilia di Jacopo Menochio" (1994) 67 *Rivista di storia del diritto italiano*, 205–282.

gation that people often tried to avoid at all costs. Indeed, strong conflicting interests made real life complicated.[38] On the one hand, a woman had the right to have her dowry returned to her if her husband predeceased her; on the other, however, the deceased husband's family often wasted little time in – and had few scruples about – keeping the property that had been meant to support the marriage. If a wife predeceased her husband, claims to dowry property led to bitter clashes over money between the widower (favoured by local statutes) and the woman's family (supported by Justinian law). Things were even more complicated if children were involved.[39] Records indicate that the Senate's interpretation of the law tended to be either rigorous or founded on the concept of equity – it made its decisions based on the circumstances of the case and the personal qualities of the parties involved. In other words, at times it limited itself to simply applying the laws in force, whereas at other times it made use of its discretionary powers.

Unfortunately, the sources are few and far between, making it quite difficult to examine these topics in a comprehensive fashion. Indeed, only a few peculiar cases – brought before the Duchy's central court due to the importance of the assets at stake – have survived in any substantial form, and only because Lombard jurists referred to them in their writings. For example, a Senate clerk named Sadarini – in one of his *consilia* – shed light on the Senate's stance on the customary and legitimate claims that a woman could bring following her husband's natural death, reporting that the Senate consistently opted for a faithful application of the laws set out in Milan's statutes of 1498.[40] And the statutes conformed with the *ius commune* doctrine whereby the dowry was to be returned in its entirety to the widow, regardless of whether children were involved.[41]

Similar evidence could be found in the writings of another local jurist, Francesco Redenaschi, who was a careful observer of the Senate's practice. He reported – in its entirety – a Senate decision of 5 September 1646, handed down following lengthy legal proceedings brought by Costanza Sforza and her second husband, Venanzio Venanzi, against her children

---

38 For Venice, see P Lanaro, "La restituzione della dote. Il gioco ambiguo della stima tra beni mobili e beni immobili (Venezia tra Cinque e Settecento)" (2010) 135 *Quaderni storici*, 753–778.

39 G P Massetto, "Il lucro dotale nella dottrina e nella legislazione statutaria lombarda dei secoli XIV–XVI", in *Ius Mediolani*, 189–364.

40 *Statuta Mediolani cum appostillis clarissimi viri iureconsulti mediolanensis Domini Catelliani Cottae*, Mediolani: apud I A Castilionaeum, 1552, cap 291, "Qualiter mortuo marito, dos reddatur uxori, et quid lucretur uxor", fols 97v–98r.

41 F Sadarini, *Responsorum rerumque a Senatu iudicatarum liber primus* (Mediolani: apud F Agnellum et C I Quintum, 1671), resp 30.

(including Marco Antonio) and her brother Benedetto (her children's guardian), who were the heirs to her first husband, Clemente Bigaroli.[42] Sforza was awarded her dowry, which was returned with interest to be reckoned from the date of her new marriage.[43]

Although these two examples lack great detail, they nonetheless help to reveal the Senate's approach: resolving disputes equitably but without derogating too much from the law. This makes them worth considering. Fortunately, there is a much better record of the Senate's case law on the more technical issue of how dowries were returned to widows – indeed, it is even possible to discern evolution in the Senate's practice. If a party was to return a dowry but did not have enough money to do so, the lawyers' opinion was uncertain (on a theoretical level) as to whether normal laws of contract and obligation were to apply. This was especially true in the Duchy of Milan, where it was not a given that a dowry could be returned by transferring property to creditors in lieu of payment in accordance with the Prince's legislation in force (in which case, the transferred property was intentionally undervalued – by one third – in order to compensate for the debtor's failure to pay in cash).[44] This procedure of transferring property to creditors in lieu of payment was called *datio in solutum*[45] (in accordance with the Roman law concept);[46] and in the Duchy of Milan, it was regulated by the Prince's legislation.[47] The Senate, however, was initially inclined not to apply the Prince's legislation if a husband's family – following his death – did not have enough money to return the dowry. This was evidenced in a ruling of 1574 whereby

---

42 Francesco Redenaschi, *Consilia sive responsa*, Ticini Regii: apud I A Magrium, 1652, cons 94.

43 Another issue at stake was the estimation of the properties, goods and estates: M Martinat, "Chi sa quale prezzo è giusto? Moralisti a confronto sulla stima dei beni in età moderna" (2010) 135 *Quaderni Storici*, 825–856. See Giulio Cesare Giussani, *Tractatus de precio et aestimatione*, Mediolani: apud H Bordonum, 1615.

44 A Monti, "L'intervento pubblico nei rapporti contrattuali privati e la stima dei beni. La prassi lombarda della *datio in solutum* (Secoli XVI–XVII)", in M Barbot, M Cattini, M Di Tullio and L Mocarelli (eds), *Stimare il valore dei beni: una prospettiva europea* (Udine: Forum, 2018), 67–80.

45 Giovanni Maria Novario, *Tractatus de insolutum bonorum datione*, Neapoli: apud I Gaffarum, 1636; Giovanni Battista Asinio, *De executionibus tractatus*, Venetiis: apud J B Natolinum, 1589, *ad vocem*.

46 Nov 4.3 (= Auth Coll.1.4.3). See G Astuti, *Dazione in pagamento (storia)*, in *Enciclopedia del diritto*, vol XI, Milano, 1962, 732–733.

47 *Constitutiones mediolanensis Dominii*, lib II, tit *de bonis in solutum dandis aut ad hastam vendendis*, 170. See Giulio Cesare Giussani, *Commentarius in decretum novarum Constitutionum Mediolani. Liber secundus, de bonis in solutum dandis, aut ad hastam vendendis*, in O Carpani (ed), *In quatuor insigniores novarum Mediolani Constitutionum §§ . . . doctissimi commentarii*, Mediolani: ex typ B Somaschi, 1609.

the Senate confirmed what at that point had been consolidated practice:[48] when returning a dowry, a transfer of property in lieu of payment was not to be intentionally undervalued.[49]

Lombard case law began to change course, however, at the beginning of the following century. The Senate issued a ruling on 10 January 1608 in a case between Anna Cori, widow of a certain Ottavio Raverta, and Camillo Raverta, the deceased husband's brother and guardian of his children. The widow wanted her dowry back, and she was willing to accept property in lieu of cash – but only if the property was worth more than the sum due to her. Conversely, the counterparty was willing to return the dowry by transferring property in lieu of payment, but only if the property's value was appraised in accordance with the rules that had been consistently upheld by the Senate.[50]

The Senate was firmly intent on putting an end to these types of dispute, which were all too common and costly for the parties – as well as inappropriate. A number of proceedings of this sort were pending before the Senate at that time, so the Senate decided to issue a definitive ruling on the issue: from that moment onwards, the provisions of the Constitutions of 1541 – that is, the Prince's legislation – would apply. It was clear that, as the highest judge, the Senate wanted to decide once and for all about an issue that so far had been open to various interpretations – and doubtlessly it opted for a rigorous interpretation of the Prince's legislation on *datio in solutum*, extending its application to the provision of dowries as well. There was clearly a need to protect the size and substance of dowries themselves, which fell in line with the Senate's politics (as revealed in other rulings). At the same time, the Senate wanted to avoid appearing indifferent to debtors' financial predicaments – and indeed the court rarely left them to the mercy of their creditors. Nonetheless, the Senate's stance was not absolute in nature, meaning that it was not bound to rule in the same manner on each case. On the contrary, this supreme court – in the years to come – would continue to leave itself broad discretion so as to ensure equitable rulings. For example, if a family's property was lost or damaged due to war, the Senate did not think it

---

48 See the Senate *rescriptum* of 17 June 1574 in *Ordines excellentissimi Senatus Mediolani*, Mediolani: in Curia Regia, 1743, 07–09.

49 On the estimation of properties in the Milan Duchy, see M Barbot, "Between Market and Architecture: The Role of the College of Engineers, Architects and Land Surveyors in Real Estate Pricing in 16th–18th Century Milan", in R Carvais, A Guillerme, V Negre, J Sakarovitch (eds), *Nuts and Bolts of Construction History. Culture, Technology and Society*, Paris: Picard, 2012, vol II, 237–244.

50 The ruling is collected in *Ordines*, 198.

equitable to penalise the family further with a *datio in solutum*, which would only exacerbate the already heavy toll that war had taken on their property. In such cases, the Senate would thus order that the property be auctioned off, and that the money earned be used to return the dowry to the wife.[51]

It seems quite evident that a lack of money and the consequent inability to repay dowries in cash was a serious problem at that time. Indeed, *ancien régime* societies were continuously in debt, and not having any money was essentially the rule.[52] Thus, through its decisions, the Senate sought to strike a balance between keeping families together, honouring obligations to return dowries and respecting the applicable laws.

D. CONCLUSION

The Senate's decisions influenced how the law was applied in the Duchy of Milan, but their impact can be studied only through the sources available. This means that any study, whatever the place or the time, will inevitably be fragmentary in nature, besides the already fragmentary nature of court rulings themselves.

In this chapter, I have examined some concrete examples of how the Senate of Milan administered justice. I wanted to show how this central court was always willing to hear the pleas of the Duchy's subjects and to intervene through its decisions; be it by rendering final judgment or by instructing other judges on how to approach a given case. The Senate of Milan's case law was fuelled by the pleas of private individuals: by appealing to the Senate's office of the clerk, such pleas caused the Senate to react. Thus, the impact of the Senate's case law must be examined, so to speak, not only from the top down, but also from the bottom up.[53]

Disputes over dowries offer a particularly lively cross section of the law applied in the Duchy. The Senate was firm in its decisions when it heard such cases, and various aspects of life in the *ancien régime* – and thus in Milan – influenced its rulings. For example, families were frequently short on cash – thus, when the Senate ruled on how to return a dowry to a woman, it would order property to be transferred in lieu of payment. In European

---

51 Calvino, *De aequitate tractatus*, lib III, cap 263, n 14, 155.

52 See L Fontaine, *The moral economy. Poverty, credit, and trust in early modern Europe*, Cambridge University Press, 2014.

53 Würgler, "Voices from Among the 'Silent Masses'", 31: "By supplications, gravamina, and petitions, ordinary people forced their rulers to react to specific problems. They thus played a part in the setting of political agendas."

society of the time, it was vitally important to keep a family's wealth in the hands of agnates, as it was seen as a guarantee of the family's survival and indeed an expression of the family's power. Each of the Senate's rulings thus enforced town statutes, the Constitutions of 1541 or the *ius commune*, depending on the circumstances. This of course applies to other complex societal issues not examined here.[54]

Moreover, my study reveals how the Senate made broad use of its powers of equity – above all from a procedural point of view, and in particular when it came to preliminary investigations and fact-finding. It also used broad discretion when choosing which law to apply, be it town statutes, the Prince's legislation or the *ius commune*. This was no trivial matter, as the Senate was operating in a legal system with multiple sources of law – this way its decisions, while perhaps not taken as law themselves, were certainly seen as instructions on how to apply substantive law.

The Senate of Milan was thus a creative interpreter of the law, but we should not be misled: it was not "inventing" new laws, but rather adapting the substantive and procedural laws in force on a case-by-case basis. And it would even disapply some laws if the circumstances so required. As already said, the Senate was operating in the typical framework of continental Europe in the early modern period:[55] this supreme, Lombard court was thus a "lord" of the law, not the other way around. It responded to the pleas of subjects as if it were a good father, by taking the appropriate measures.

The Duchy's judges were required to abide by the Senate's consolidated practice. However, that practice remained valid only for as long as the Senate wanted it to. When the circumstances changed, so too did the Senate's interpretation. And it was when the Senate disapplied a law or deviated from its consolidated practice that perhaps its most meaningful powers emerged, elevating it to princelike – and indeed godlike – status.

---

54 For example, A Monti, "*L'immunitas duodecim liberorum* nella prassi Senateria lombarda di antico regime", in A Padoa-Schioppa, G di Renzo Villata and G P Massetto (eds), *Amicitiae Pignus. Studi in ricordo di Adriano Cavanna*, Milano: Giuffrè, 2003, vol II, 1509–1563.

55 See J Krynen, *L'idéologie de la magistrature ancienne*, Paris: Gallimard, 2009.

8 The Imperial Chamber Court and the Development of the Law in the Holy Roman Empire

Peter Oestmann

A. INTRODUCTION
B. THE DECISIONS OF THE IMPERIAL CHAMBER COURT AS LEGAL AUTHORITIES
C. AUTHORITIES IN THE OPINIONS OF THE IMPERIAL CHAMBER COURT
D. CONCLUSION

A. INTRODUCTION

In 1643, Hermann Conring, the well-known professor of the University of Helmstedt, published a book entitled *De origine iuris Germanici – On the origins of the German law*.[1] The volume became very famous because Conring refuted the so-called "Lotharian legend"[2] of the validity of the Roman law. Instead, he introduced a new term and said that the Roman law was received by the court practice. Conring's book gave an overview of more than 1,000 years of German legal history. In the chapters on modern history, Conring dealt with the *Reichskammergericht*, the Imperial Chamber Court. He said that the assessors of this court were obliged to obey the older decisions of their own court. They had to look at these judgments in the same

---

1 H Conring, *De origine iuris Germanici* (1643); German translation: H Conring, *Der Ursprung des deutschen Rechts* (1994); on Conring and his work M Stolleis (ed), *Hermann Conring* (1983), A Jori, *Hermann Conring* (2006).
2 For further details, Cf M Schmoeckel, "Lotharische Legende", in *Handwörterbuch zur deutschen Rechtsgeschichte* (henceforth, HRG), vol III (2016), col 1056–1058; P Oestmann, "Lotharische Legende", in *Enzyklopädie der Neuzeit* (henceforth, ENZ), vol VII (2008), col 1009–1011; N Jansen, *The Making of Legal Authority. Non-legislative Codifications in Historical and Comparative Perspective*, Oxford: Oxford University Press, 2010, 36–38.

way as at formally enacted laws and statutes.[3] However, some details in Conring's argumentations are not correct from a modern point of view. In addition, his footnotes are sometimes careless and inaccurate, but this is not a key issue. Conring did not study law, he studied philosophy, natural sciences and medicine.[4] He was later called a polymath – a professor of medicine, philosophy, political science and rhetoric. He was not a participant in the legal system but a careful observer. As an observer, Conring was sure that the decisions of the Imperial Chamber Court were legal sources like other laws, and that the highest courts of the Empire used the precedents of their own courts like other sources to solve legal problems and decide new cases. Conring believed that this was exactly what was prescribed in a law passed by the German *Reichstag* – the Imperial Diet – in 1570,[5] but he was wrong. As important as the result is the fact that the Imperial Chamber Court used its own precedents to decide cases and these precedents had the same quality as laws. In fact, there is little research on the specific German tradition of precedents in modern literature.[6]

From this point of reference, and inspired by Conring's observation, this chapter discusses two questions. On the one hand, I aim to demonstrate how the judgments of the Imperial Chamber Court influenced German legal practice and German law. On the other hand, I ask how the Imperial Chamber Court itself used precedents as authorities in its own forensic practice. So, there are two perspectives to the same question; both are quite new for German legal history. Of course, there is plenty of literature concerning the history of the Imperial Chamber Court;[7] however, when we ask whether the decisions of the court had any influence on the development of

---

3 Conring, *Der Ursprung des deutschen Rechts*, 229–230.

4 For a short overview on his CV, see G Kleinheyer and J Schröder (eds), *Deutsche und Europäische Juristen aus neun Jahrhunderten*, Tübingen: Mohr Siebeck, 2017, 104–107.

5 Conring, *Der Ursprung des deutschen Rechts*, 229. For the edition of the laws of the Holy Roman Empire see J J Schmauß and H C v Senckenberg (eds), *Neue und vollständigere Sammlung der Reichs-Abschiede*, Franckfurt am Mayn: Koch, 1747.

6 Focusing on the nineteenth century, C Günzl, "Germany's Case Law Revolution. Dealing with previous decisions in the 19th Century", in W Eves, J Hudson, I Ivarsen and S White (eds), *Common Law, Civil Law, and Colonial Law: Essays in Comparative Legal History, Twelfth to Twentieth Centuries*, Cambridge: Cambridge University Press, 2021, forthcoming.

7 The classical study is R Smend, *Das Reichskammergericht*, Weimar: Hermann Böhlaus Nachfolger, 1911; short overviews in English by P Oestmann, "The Law of the Holy Roman Empire of the German Nation", in H Pihlajamäki et al (eds), *The Oxford Handbook of European Legal History*, 2018, 748–752; A Baumann, "The Holy Roman Empire: the Reichskammergericht", in A Wijffels and C H van Rhee (eds), *European Supreme Courts*, London: Third Millennium Publishing, 2013, 96–103.

the substantive law, there is almost no research to be found.[8] One reason for this is easy to understand – clearly, it is impossible to make detailed statements about questions of influence.

Several years ago, there was a collaborative research group (*Sonderforschungsbereich*) in Munich which worked on authorities in general. As a member of this group, Thomas Duve wrote an essay entitled "With the authority against the authorities".[9] Duve said that thinking within the framework of the authorities had been a typical problem in the early modern period. In the nineteenth century, the authority of the law was generally considered to be the only authority, but I am uncertain whether this applies to modern law. Besides, in connection with early modern legal practice, there is significant consensus that we must reflect on a plurality of sources and authorities in modern research.

B. THE DECISIONS OF THE IMPERIAL CHAMBER COURT AS LEGAL AUTHORITIES

To evaluate the significance of the decisions it is first necessary to look at the sources of the substantive and procedural law as a whole. In early modern Germany, there was very little legislation in the field of private law.[10] For criminal law there was the *Constitutio Criminalis Carolina*, a penal code from 1532 which influenced many European countries.[11] However, for private law there was only the typical mixture of received Roman and canon law, statutes from the different territories, some police ordinances and a lot of customary law.[12] The procedural ordinances of the Imperial Chamber Court contained some sections which explained how the court had to apply the very different legal sources. In accordance with the late medieval theory of the statutes, there existed the so-called "*fundata intentio*" of the Roman and canon laws. The German statutes and customs were also accepted as sources of law, but it was not necessary for the assessors of the court to know

---

8 For some perspectives on this point, see A Amend-Traut, *Die Spruchpraxis der höchsten Reichsgerichte*, Wetzlar: Gesellschaft für Reichskammergerichtsforschung, 2008.

9 T Duve, "Mit der Autorität gegen die Autoritäten?" in W Oesterreicher et al (eds), *Autorität*, Münster: Lit Verlag, 2003.

10 P Oestmann, "The Law of the Holy Roman Empire", 744–746.

11 English translation of the main chapters by J Langbein (ed), "Prosecuting Crime in the Renaissance England, Germany, France", Cambridge, MA: Harvard University Press, 1974, 259–308.

12 An old but very helpful overview by O Stobbe, *Geschichte der deutschen Rechtsquellen*, Braunschweig: C A Schwetschke und Sohn, 1860/1864.

these laws. It was, however, the duty of the parties to produce those laws and to give evidence on the observance in practice. This principle was regulated in the ordinances from 1495 up to 1555,[13] but it was slightly modified in 1654.[14] However, there was never an explicit regulation saying that the decisions of the court themselves were legal sources or had a specific meaning.

So, when we ask how the Imperial Chamber Court influenced the German law, we must look at two fields of the law. It is easy to see the influence on the procedural law and the organisation of courts. The ordinances from 1495 to 1555 have been very important models for the courts in the different German territories. Many territories renewed their court system in the sixteenth century, often copying the ordinance of the Imperial Chamber Court for their own court of appeal.[15] By and large, territories had a president – a nobleman without expertise in the field of law – but the courts usually provided several educated assessors. The proceedings took place in written form without oral hearing. Sometimes, there existed a kind of audience (*Audienz*), but this was only a symbolic occasion for the procurators to give written statements to the members of the court. The courts' decisions provided no explicit motivation for the parties. When the territories wanted to get a *privilegium de non appellando*,[16] it was necessary to regulate the regional courts in accordance with the Imperial Chamber Court. This demonstrates that there was a kind of unification in the German court system, even when the Imperial Chamber Court was sometimes weak and worked very slowly.[17]

If we take a closer look and ask in what way the decisions of the Imperial Chamber Court influenced the German law, it is much more difficult to give a clear answer. First, it is important to emphasise that approximately 75

13 Ordinance of the Chamber Court of 1555, pt 1, title 13, section 1, in A Laufs (ed), *Die Reichskammergerichtsordnung von 1555*, Cologne-Vienna: Böhlau Verlag, 1976, 93; on this subject, P Oestmann, *Rechtsvielfalt vor Gericht*, Frankfurt: Vittorio Klostermann, 2002.
14 So-called *"Jüngster Reichsabschied"* 1654, section 105, in J J Schmauß and H C v Senckenberg, *Reichs-Abschiede*, vol III, Frankfurt: Ernst August Koch, 1747, 660.
15 The territorial courts have not been thoroughly studied. For some lines of enquiry see, for example, P Jessen, *Der Einfluß von Reichshofrat und Reichskammergericht*, Aalen: Scientia Verlag, 1986; B-R Kern, *Die Gerichtsordnungen des Kurpfälzer Landrechts von 1583*, Cologne-Vienna: Böhlau Verlag, 1991; T Süß, *Partikularer Zivilprozess und territoriale Gerichtsverfassung*, Cologne-Weimar-Vienna: Böhlau Verlag, 2017; F Lebküchler, *Die Grafschaft Tecklenburg und die Justizreform von 1613*, Münster: Aschendorff Verlag, 2019.
16 For a comprehensive note on this point, see U Eisenhardt, *Die kaiserlichen privilegia de non appellando*, Cologne-Vienna: Böhlau Verlag, 1980.
17 P Oestmann, *Wege zur Rechtsgeschichte*, Cologne-Weimar-Vienna: Böhlau Verlag, 2015, 180–182.

per cent of the cases were never decided by a formal final judgment.[18] The Imperial Chamber Court had several competences and tasks in the early modern court system; deciding cases was only one of them – and perhaps not the most important one.[19] However, if we want to look at the influence of the court on German law, we must concentrate on the 25 per cent of cases that were decided formally. The next point is a methodological problem. The Imperial Chamber Court did not motivate its decisions for the parties.[20] So, it was clear who won a case and who lost the lawsuit, but it was not easy to see why the court reached had this judgment. From the sixteenth century onwards, there were some assessors who published the decisions of the Imperial Chamber Court. The large series by Seiler and Barth contained more than 40,000 decisions in total, including interlocutory judgments.[21] However, these large volumes collected only the operative provisions (*Tenor, dispositif*) of the judgments. It was therefore impossible to know anything about the cases, legal problems and reasons. As a result, these collections of judgments were probably helpful for young advocates, procurators and judges to see examples of how to work in accordance with the *stilus curiae*; but regarding the influence on the law itself, we must look elsewhere.

I believe that the best sources for our goal are printed books from the so-called "literature of decisions" (in German, "*Entscheidungsliteratur*"). An important repertory by Heinrich Gehrke offers the best overview of this type of book.[22] Gehrke looked at more than 390 publications from the sixteenth to the eighteenth century, from several authors, many courts and several law faculties. Among them, the literature written by members of the Imperial Chamber Court is probably the most significant. In contrast to Seyler and Barth with their printed decisions, most of the other authors

---

18 Ibid, 164.
19 Consideration of the efficiency of work of the Chamber Courty by B Diestelkamp, "Das Reichskammergericht im Rechtsleben des 16 Jahrhunderts" in Id, *Recht und Gericht* (1999), 255–259.
20 On the history of the motivation of judgments, see S Hocks, *Gerichtsgeheimnis und Begründungszwang*, Frankfurt: Vittorio Klostermann, 2002; and C Günzl, *Auf dem Weg zur modernen Entscheidungsbegründung*, Doctoral dissertation, University of Münster, 2019, forthcoming.
21 R Seyler and C Barth, *Urtheil Und Beschaydt Am Hochlöblichen Kayserlichen Cammergericht*, Speyer: Melchior Hartmann, 1604/1605.
22 H Gehrke, *Die privatrechtliche Entscheidungsliteratur Deutschlands*, Frankfurt: Vittorio Klostermann, 1974; Id, "Deutsches Reich", in H Coing (ed), *Handbuch*, vol II (1976), 1343–1398; short information in English by U Müßig, "Superior courts in early modern France, England and the Holy Roman Empire", in P Brand and J Getzler (eds), *Judges and Judging in the History of the Common Law an Civil Law: From Antiquity to modern Times*, Cambridge: Cambridge University Press, 2012, 225–227.

worked in another style. They did not publish decisions but so-called "observations". These observations were very short treatises of one or five pages, collected in books called "Observationes". The oldest of these publications, written by Joachim Mynsinger, contained 400 observations in the first edition, and 600 observations in the later editions. It had been in print since 1563 and was one of the best known and most frequently quoted legal books in early modern Germany, perhaps even in Europe.[23] If Mynsinger did not quote decisions of the court, he provoked a scandal. And yet other members of the court complained that he had revealed the secrets of the consultations. However, Mynsinger was successful and the ice was broken. Fifteen years after Mynsinger, a second assessor of the court, Andreas Gail, published a book of the same name, "Observationes".[24] Many details found in his volume were highly similar to those in Mynsinger, leading Mynsinger to accuse his colleague Gail of plagiarism. In the end, this proved to be no disadvantage to Gail's book – his observations were more frequently printed than Mynsinger's and his book probably had the most editions of a legal book in early modern Germany. By the second half of the eighteenth century, Gail's text had been through nearly thirty editions.

Other authors from the Imperial Chamber Court published the written statements of the assessors, the so-called "relations" (in Latin: *Relationes*; in German: *Relationen*). In the years around 1600, these assessoes included Johann Meichsner[25] and an anonymous author using the pseudonym Adrian Gylmann.[26] These collections of relations were much more extensive than Gail's or Mynsinger's observations, more expensive and quite difficult to use. But with the help of these volumes it was possible to reconstruct the decision making of the Imperial Chamber Court in an authentic way. In the first half of the eighteenth century, the assessor Georg Melchior Ludolff[27] was

---

23 W Sellert, "Mynsinger von Frundeck, Joachim" in HRG, vol III (2016), col 1731–1732; S Schumann, *Joachim Mynsinger von Frundeck (1514–1588)*, Wiebaden: Harrassowitz, 1983.

24 P Oestmann, "Observationes" in S Dauchy et al (eds), *The Formation and Transmission of Western Legal Culture*, Cham: Springer (2016), 129–132; K v Kempis, *Andreas Gaill*, Frankfurt-Bern-New York-Paris: Peter Lang, 1988.

25 J Meichsner, *Decisionum diversarum in camera imperiali judicatarum, adjunctis votis et relationibus . . . tomus I–IV*, Frankfurt: Wolfgang Richter, 1603/1606. Reprinted several times up to 1693.

26 A Gylmann, *Symphorematis Supplicationum, pro processibus, super omnibus ac singulis imperii romani constitutionibus, in supremo Camerae Imperiolis Auditorio impetrandis*, 6 vols, Frankfurt: Wolfgang Richter, 1601/1608 (a very unclear collection with different titles for the seperate volumes).

27 For further details on his CV, see S Jahns, *Das Reichskammergericht und seine Richter*, vol II, pt 1, Cologne-Weimar-Vienna: Böhlau Verlag, 2003, 371–387.

the most prominent author of literature on the Imperial Chamber Court. He wrote observations, but also commentaries on the court's ordination and treatises on other subjects. In the second half of the eighteenth century, the assessor Johann Ulrich Cramer[28] published a series called *Wetzlarer Nebenstunden* – 128 small volumes of essays on cases decided by the Imperial Chamber Court.[29] These essays were often not written by Cramer himself; rather, he collected several hundred relations written by his colleagues. Eventually, this method enabled the readers to acquire knowledge of the judgments as well as of the motivations of the court.

It is unnecessary to provide all the details about the learned literature written by court members. For the purpose of this chapter, it is sufficient to note that many books of this so-called "chamber literature" (*Kameralliteratur*) were widespread and common for most of the judges, advocates and procurators and across all law faculties within the Holy Roman Empire. So, when we ask whether the decisions of the European central courts were authorities for the development of the law, we can give at least three answers. First, the judgments – the bare results – did not play such a big role. In modern German law, the decisions of the federal court are one of the most important authorities.[30] This was unthinkable in early modern times. Second, the learned literature written by court members was often used by other courts as authorities in the decision-making process. However, even this is not the central point. The most important result is the internal discussion within the legal literature of the time. Practitioners and professors wrote their books, and this very specific mixture of forensic practice and learned treatises formed the well-known German style of the *Usus modernus pandectarum*.[31] If we can agree that legal literature is a part of the law, especially in early modern times before codification, then the decisions of the Imperial Chamber Court were one of the most important sources of the *Usus modernus*, though admittedly an idirect one. The result is not new. In 1776, Johann Stephan Pütter, professor for public law at the University of Göttingen, wrote that in his time hardly any practical legal works were published that did not refer to Mynsinger or Gail.[32] Therefore, it seems clear that until

---

28 On his CV, S Jahns, *Das Reichskammergericht*, vol II, pt 1, 655–673.

29 J U v Cramer, *Wetzlarische Nebenstunden*, 28 vols, Ulm: Johann Conrad Wohler, 1755/1772.

30 Sometimes, they have binding force like formally enacted laws: § 31 Bundesverfassungsgerichtsgesetz.

31 Overview by K Luig, "Usus modernus" in HRG, 1st edn, vol V (1998), col 628–636.

32 J S Pütter, *Litteratur des Teutschen Staatsrechts*, vol I, Göttingen: Vandenhoek, 1776, 128. On this quotation, see Oestmann, "Observationes", 132.

the end of the Empire this "chamber literature" remained a central point of reference for German legal discussions.

It is not entirely clear whether the situation in different European territories was identical in this regard. At least in the Holy Roman Empire there existed two of the highest imperial courts: the Imperial Chamber Court and the Imperial Aulic Council (the *Reichshofrat*). This Aulic Council did not produce nearly as much literature as the Imperial Chamber Court. In the perception of its contemporaries, the Aulic Council was not so much a specialised court but rather a political institution; close to the Emperor and powerful, but not that interesting for the scholarship of law and jurisprudence.[33] Many law students went to Speyer or Wetzlar (the domiciles of the Chamber Court) to work there as young trainees. Remarkably fewer went to Vienna or Prague to study at the Aulic Council. It was only in the eighteenth century that the literature concerning the Aulic Council attained any considerable significance. By this time in the last century of the Holy Roman Empire, the contemporaries no longer spoke about the chamber procedural law, but spoke instead about the imperial procedural law, the *Reichsgerichtsprozess*.[34] However, even during this time, the chamber literature without doubt maintained its leadership.[35]

A few examples can illustrate what has been discussed so far. The first is a lawsuit in the city of Lübeck.[36] In the 1690s, Conrad Ludwig Heyer – a major in the army of Mecklenburg – fell in love with a very young, rich girl, Catharina Lefever, who was a member of a patrician family in Lübeck. The girl's father was dead and her brothers refused to agree to an engagement between their sister and the soldier. Eventually the major eloped with the girl to Mecklenburg, where they married just one or two days later. The brothers were outraged and went to the court of the city of Lübeck and sued both the major and their sister. They claimed that the abduction of a woman was a severe crime under Roman law, meaning that the soldier must be punished with the death penalty. Furthermore, they claimed that the sister should have lost all her stakes in the family assets and therefore

---

33 Overview of the Aulic Council by E Ortlieb, "The Holy Roman Empire: the Imperial Court's System and the *Reichshofrat*", in A Wijffels and C H van Rhee (eds), *European Supreme Courts*, London: Third Millennium Publishing, 2013, 86–95.

34 J F Seyfart, *Teutscher Reichs-Proceß*, Halle: Fritschische Buchhandlung, 1738.

35 Contemporary catalogue of this literature by E J K v Fahnenberg, *Litteratur des Kaiserlichen Reichskammergerichts*, Wetzlar: Phil Jac Winkler, 1792.

36 Case study by P Oestmann, "Lübecker Rechtspraxis um 1700: Der Streit um die Entführung der Catharina Lefever" (2000) 80 *Zeitschrift des Vereins für Lübeckische Geschichte und Altertumskunde*, 259–293.

be disinherited. Given the wealth at stake, the case was an important one. The sister eventually won the lawsuit before the city court of Lübeck, but the brothers filed an appeal against this judgment. At the Imperial Chamber Court, the sister also won the appeal. It was clear to everyone that a girl who married her lover must not be disinherited by her family when the guardian refused his approval without providing an objective reason.

The case caused a huge sensation in early modern Germany. At the trial in Lübeck the parties asked some well-known law faculties to give their opinion on the case. This way, the law faculty of Halle – at that time the best and most progressive German faculty – was involved in the lawsuit. It was Samuel Stryk, the author of the famous *Usus modernus pandectarum*,[37] who had to work out the statement of the faculty. He was in favour of the young couple and decided the case for the sister. This is unsurprising since the private "transmission of files" (*Aktenversendung*) was a kind of market,[38] and the consultant did not want to lose his clients for future occasions. However, Stryk did not, as a private person, give this opinion. He took his report back to the faculty and the faculty as a whole gave the statement. Afterwards, Samuel Stryk wrote a book entitled *De dissensu sponsalitio*,[39] in which he explained all the legal problems in this respect regarding marriage and elopement. As an appendix to his book, he added the statement of his own law faculty of Halle. It is clear that his personal experience in deciding the legal questions from Catharina Lefever and her husband encouraged Samuel Stryk to write this 370-page long treatise. The book was published in 1699. In that same year, the litigation before the city court of Lübeck was still in progress. Catharina Lefever and Conrad Ludwig Heyer's procurator changed his legal arguments and began often to quote Stryk's book. Eventually, the spouses won both lawsuits. This example leads us to a preliminary result: when we look at legal authorities, we can clearly see that the single case of a bride and her groom spurred the production of learned literature and that this very same literature became an important authority in the very same trial. At this stage of the *Usus modernus*, it is impossible and not useful to distinguish between theory and practice. For the sake of com-

---

37 On this collection, J Schröder, "Specimen Usus Moderni Pandectarum", in S Dauchy, G Martyn, A Musson, H Pihlajamäki and A Wijffels (eds), *The Formation and Transmission of Western Legal Culture. 150 Books that Made the Law in the Age of Printing*, Cham: Springer, 2016, 235–238.

38 U Falk, *Consilia. Studien zur Praxis der Rechtsgutachten in der frühen Neuzeit*, Frankfurt: Vittorio Klostermann, 2006.

39 S Stryk, *Tractatus de dissensu sponsalitio*, Wittenberg: Johann Wilhelm Meyer & Gottfried Zimmermann, 1699.

pleteness, it is worth adding that in this case Halle was not the only law faculty that was asked for a decision. Catharina's brothers asked the University
of Jena for an opinion, and the city court of Lübeck itself decided to make a
regular "transmission of the file" to the law faculty of Tübingen.

A further example comes from the mid-eighteenth century; again from
a lawsuit starting in the imperial free city of Lübeck. It was a litigation
between some relatives who quarrelled about an inheritance.[40] When the
rich wife of a senator died, one half of the property went to the husband,
and the other half to her relatives. One of these relatives was Johann Adolph
Krohn, who had studied law and was at that moment the mayor of Lübeck.
The other relative was Anna Maria von Spilcker. While Krohn was the uncle
of the deceased woman, and Spilcker her aunt, there was a crucial difference. Both of Krohn's parents were themselves actually the grandparents
of the deceased woman, but only Spilcker's mother was grandmother to the
deceased. Spilcker's mother had married twice – the first husband was the
grandfather of the deceased, while the second husband was the father of
Spilcker. Therefore, Spilcker was the aunt of the "defunct", but only from
one of her parents, not both. This situation was known as a "half birth"
(halbe Geburt). So, Krohn and Spilcker began to argue about the claims of
the half birth. It was quite clear that in Roman law a half-birth relative had
the same legal claim as a double-born one.[41]

In early modern statutory law, the solution was complex and varied from
city to city. In the statutes of Lübeck, this case was not clearly defined. There
was some discrimination against half-birth relatives, but there was no specific provision that said anything about aunts. Thus, it was unclear whether
a broad interpretation of the city law was allowed. The contemporary theory
of the statutes maintained that statutes had to be strictly interpreted, without
allowing for any extension.[42] However, in the mid-eighteenth century, the
law of several territories effectively had, in part, its own interpretation. As
such, according to the literature, it remained unclear as to whether the strict

---

40 The records were edited by P Oestmann, *Ein Zivilprozeß am Reichskammergericht. Edition
einer Gerichtsakte aus dem 18 Jahrhundert*, Cologne-Weimar-Vienna: Böhlau Verlag, 2009. Cf M
Doms, *Rechtsanwendung im Usus modernus. Eine Fallstudie zum Erbrecht der halben Geburt*,
Doctoral dissertation, University of Münster, 2010, available at: https://d-nb.info/1010264680/34
(last accessed 23 January 2020).

41 On the legal order of succession in the case without a last will, U Babusiaux, *Wege zur
Rechtsgeschichte: Römisches Erbrecht*, Cologne-Weimar-Vienna: Böhlau Verlag, 2015, 47–82.

42 P Oestmann, *Rechtsvielfalt vor Gericht*, 7–8; R Zimmermann, "Statuta sunt stricte interpretanda? Statutes and the Common Law: a Continental Perspective" (1997) 56 *Cambridge
Law Journal*, 315–328.

interpretation still applied, or whether it was necessary to allow for analogies in the statutory law. Of course, Spilcker wanted the case to be decided according to the Roman law, while Krohn argued that there was an old German tradition and custom in Lübeck to give preference to the double birth. An out-of-court settlement was unthinkable, and so Spilcker sued the mayor at the city court of Lübeck. During this lawsuit both parties started to produce legal literature. The son of the mayor, Hermann Georg Krohn, was a jurist and wrote a treatise entitled "The precedence of the double birth over the half birth".[43] He collected many examples from early medieval sources up to the Saxon Mirror (*Sachsenspiegel*) and published many court decisions to prove his own argument. On the other hand, Johann Christian Bacmeister, a nephew of Anna Maria Spilcker, was an assessor at the high court of appeal in Celle (*Oberappellationsgericht*),[44] and he also wrote a book on this subject, entitled "Refutation of the so-called 'precedence of the double birth over the half birth'".[45] Later, Hermann Georg Krohn wrote a second treatise to disprove Bacmeister's opinion.[46] The case proved complex and the court of Lübeck transmitted the file to the law faculties of Halle, Leipzig and Frankfurt/Oder.

In the end, this litigation became one of the most spectacular cases in Germany at that time. At the city court of Lübeck the mayor won his case, and the widow Spilcker and her nephew therefore appealed before the Imperial Chamber Court. After four years spent before the court of Lübeck, it took a further seven or eight years until the Imperial Chamber Court issued a decision on the long-lasting lawsuit. By this time, both parties were long since dead, but the legal question had been solved. The assessors in *Wetzlar* decided that the half birth had the same position in the law of succession as the double birth. This judgment was pronounced in May 1756.[47] Only one year later, the decision was printed together with the written opinion of the responsible assessor in *Wetzlarer Nebenstunden*, the above-mentioned series by Johann Ulrich Cramer.[48] The decision of

---

43 H G Krohn, *Versuch die Lehre von dem Vorrechte der vollen Geburth . . . in Richtigkeit zu bringen*, Lübeck: Jonas Schmidt, 1746.

44 On this court, one of the most important German courts of the eighteenth century, see S A Stodolkowitz, *Das Oberappellationsgericht Celle und seine Rechtsprechung im 18 Jahrhundert*, Cologne-Wiemar-Vienna: Böhlau Verlag, 2011.

45 J C Bacmeister, *Abhandlung von dem Recht der vollen und halben Geburt*, Hannover: Förster, 1748; reprinted in K G Krohn, *Abhandlung von dem Vorrechte der vollen Geburth*, Lübeck-Leipzig: Jonas Schmidt, 1748. The title in this second edition was "Refutation" (*Widerlegung*).

46 H G Krohn, *Weitere Ausführung des Versuchs*, Lübeck-Leipzig: Jonas Schmidt, 1748.

47 P Oestmann, *Ein Zivilprozeß*, 577.

48 J U Cramer, *Wetzlarische Nebenstunden*, vol VI (1757), 84–142, "Ob und wie weit die volle Geburth vor der halben ein Vorrecht bey der Erbfolge habe".

the Imperial Chamber Court had thus become part of the German legal literature.

In 1769, another twelve years later, a lawyer in Lübeck, Johann Carl Henrich Dreyer, published an overview of the laws of the city of Lübeck. The collection had a chapter concerning law books (*Rechtsbücher*) and decrees of Lübeck. In this chapter, we find the Imperial Chamber Court decision in the case of *Spilcker v Krohn*.[49] Dreyer, an author who wrote several books on the law and legal history of Lübeck, and who worked as a counsel of the city magistrates, wrote that a decision of the Chamber Court usually applied only to the two litigants of that lawsuit. However, in this particular case, he was certain that the 1756 judgment was a *beträchtliche Rechts-Urkunde*, a "substantial certificate of the law". Dreyer wrote that this judgment had settled the legal problems of the half birth for all time. He also quoted some aspects from the treatises of Krohn and Bacmeister, and informed the reader that even other scholars of the time wrote their essays on this very problem, among them Friedrich Esajas Pufendorf, one of the most prominent legal authors in Lower Saxony.[50] Therefore, plenty of literature existed on this important case. In his collection of the laws of Lübeck, Dreyer stated with certainty that the best treatise by far was the relation of the Imperial Chamber Court in the case of *Spilcker v Krohn*. He admired the diligence, profundity and strength of the opinion of the Wetzlarian assessor.

This example shows very clearly that the decisions of the Imperial Chamber Court were regarded as formal sources of the law and that at the same time they had the authority to change the substantive law in the German territories. Of course, this case is a stroke of luck because it is not at all easy to find such convincing sources. One must have a lawsuit with over-regional impact, a controversial legal question and reflections in the contemporary literature. One must also discover a final decision, and this decision must be printed in a contemporary collection. Nevertheless, I am sure that it is possible to find more of these examples. Presumably, it should be possible to also find such cases for regional courts or for some reports from law faculties (*Fakultätsgutachten*). However, the importance of the Imperial Chamber Court must not be overstimated. Especially in the eight-

49 J H Dreyer, *Einleitung zur Kenntniß der . . . von E Hochw. Rath der Reichsstadt Lübeck von Zeit zu Zeit ergangenen allgemeinen Verordnungen*, Lübeck: Christian Gottfried Donatius (1769), 319.

50 F E Pufendorf, *Observationes iuris universi*, vol II, 2nd edn (1779), *observatio* 192, "An ultra fratrum filios duplicitas vinculi in successione cognatorum jure Romano inspiciatur?", and *observatio* 193, "De Duplicitate vinculi in successione collateralium ex jure Germanico".

eenth century, a large part of the cases came from the small city of Wetzlar and the surrounding region.[51] The Chamber Court was not a powerful and brilliant court of justice,[52] such as the Lübeckian High Court of Appeal after 1820 or the *Reichsgericht* after 1879. In early modern times, the case law of the highest courts was not the leading factor in the development of new law. The contemporary *Usus modernus* was a mixture of written and unwritten laws, of theory and practice, of universities and courts, of noble-born and learned judges.[53] Therefore, we must be careful when we ask such modern questions concerning the influence of the court decisions for the modernisation of substantive law.

C. AUTHORITIES IN THE OPINIONS OF THE IMPERIAL CHAMBER COURT

In the second part of this chapter I will change my approach to look at legal authorities from another point of view: which authorities did the Imperial Chamber Court itself accept when it had to decide legal problems? The sources are once again the records of the appellate proceedings in the above-mentioned lawsuit *Spilcker v Krohn* concerning the half and full birth. As mentioned previously, the Imperial Chamber Court passed its final judgment in May 1756. The assessor Johann Wilhelm Summermann[54] was the consultant (*Referent*) and had to prepare the final decision. He worked out a statement of more than 100 pages, ending with the draft of the operating part of the decision (*Urteilstenor*). In his so-called "relation" (*Relation*) he decided the case in favour of the half birth. The starting point of his argumentation was the *fundata intentio* of Roman law.[55] Even in the mid-eighteenth century, the assessor Summermann assumed that the Roman law was received across the whole of Germany in such a way that the litigant who argued in accordance with it was to be preferred until the opposing party proved that a special law had to be applied. According to Roman law, the half and full birth were equivalent in cases of inheritance without testaments. So,

---

51 Repertory by J Hausmann, *Repertorien des Hessischen Hauptstaatsarchivs Wiesbaden*, section 1, vol III, Wiesbaden: Hauptstaatsarchiv, 1984–1986.

52 On some troubles in the eighteenth century, see A Denzler, *Über den Schriftalltag im 18 Jahrhundert. Die Visitation des Reichskammergerichts von 1767 bis 1776*, Cologne-Weimar-Vienna: Böhlau Verlag, 2016.

53 K Luig, "Usus modernus", col 628–636.

54 His CV in S Jahns, *Das Reichskammergericht und seine Richter*, vol II, pt 2, 1409–1426.

55 The relation is completely edited in Oestmann, *Ein Zivilprozeß*, 519–571, on the *fundata intentio*, see ibid, 539.

assessor Summermann had to show that the city of Lübeck had no divergent statutes. To reach this purpose, he examined all the arguments of the Lübeckian mayor and his son and rejected them. In this extensive explanation, he exemplified the value of each authority that Krohn and son used to demonstrate the precedence of the full birth. Assessor Summermann proceeded in seven steps.[56] The first was the natural law; the second, the medieval German law; the third, the old legal sayings; the fourth, the specific customary tradition in the city of Lübeck; the fifth, the analogy of the Lübeckian law; the sixth, the precedents of older court decisions; and the seventh, the opinion of the scholars.

Concerning the natural law, the mayor Krohn argued in his treatise that it should be obvious that one is not the same as two, and that the double birth had to be treated in another way than the half birth. The assessor of the Chamber Court interpreted the natural law in a way that meant that in general the full birth could have some advantages in comparison with the half birth, but that the half birth must never be excluded completely.[57] By this means, he did not explicitly deny the legal authority of the natural law because in the end Summermann's interpretation of the natural law was in accordance with his own decision.

After discussing the natural law, assessor Summermann arrived at the second argument, the so-called "old German law". He accepted that perhaps in ancient times the old Germans favoured full birth. However, he exclaimed: "But this does not concern us! *Laudamus veteres sed nostris utimur annis.*"[58] This was an unidentified quotation from the Roman poet Ovid, inviting praise for the old times, but to live for one's own times. In particular, the assessor criticised the *Sachsenspiegel*, the Saxon Mirror of the thirteenth century. This private work by Eike von Repgow was allegedly only a poorly patched compilation, in which its author had failed to understand the deeper meaning of the law of inheritance.[59] Ultimately, Summermann was certain that it was impossible to reconstruct a uniform and consistent medieval German law because the most important sources came from a period when the Roman law was already known in the Empire. In the eighteenth century there were some radical Germanists such as Christian

---

56 Ibid, 543–571.
57 Ibid, 543–547.
58 Ibid, 547.
59 Ibid, 548–549.

Thomasius[60] or the so-called "Legal Antiquarians" (*Rechtsantiquare*).[61] At least on this point, the Imperial Chamber Court distanced itself from this old German law. Medieval sources were no authority in disputed cases.

The third aspect was the legal sayings (*Rechtssprichwörter*). Allegedly, there existed such a saying in Westphalia that the half birth "had to go back". The defendant Krohn argued that this saying was part of the statute of the city of Soest and had come from Soest to Lübeck in the twelfth or thirteenth century. The assessor Summermann checked the details and used a collection of German statutes, edited by Georg Melchior von Ludolff, a former assessor of the Chamber Court in the first half of the eighteenth century.[62] In this collection he found exactly the opposite – meaning that in medieval Soest, half and full birth were treated in the same way. Thus, the simple allegation of a legal saying had no authority if the statutes of the same city said the contrary.[63]

In the next section, the chamber assessor considered the specific situation of the law of Lübeck. The mayor Krohn and his son had said that even in the centuries before the reception of Roman law, as well as in early modern times, all statutes in Lübeck had always privileged full birth. Assessor Summermann looked at the wording of several sections of the law books and tried to interpret them. In the final analysis, he was sure that the statute favoured the full birth in only a very few cases, not in general in the law of inheritance.[64] Statutory law was therefore indeed an authority for the decision of legal disputes in theory. However, the court maintained the possibility to interpret the law independently. Whether Summermann's approach was a strict interpretation of the technical meaning of the theory of the statutes is difficult to say. All in all, Summermann was persuaded that the Roman and the Lübeckian law matched each other on this point.

Afterwards, assessor Summermann looked at the precedents – some older judgments of the city council of Lübeck.[65] Krohn and his son had referred to about 20 decisions of the court of Lübeck on inheritance cases. Whether these judgments had to be considered as widely recognisd legal authori-

---

60 F L Schäfer, *Juristische Germanistik*, Frankfurt: Vittorio Klostermann, 2008, 84–92.

61 E Landsberg, *Geschichte der Deutschen Rechtswissenschaft*, vol III, pt 1, Munich-Leipzig: R Oldenbourg, 1898, 240–271.

62 G M v Ludolff, *Collectio quorundam statutorum provinciarum et urbium Germanicae cum praefatione*, Wetzlar: Nicolaus Ludwig Winckler, 1734, 791–810, "De Jure Susatensi Sivè Vom Recht der Stadt Söst".

63 Oestmann, *Ein Zivilprozeß*, 552–553.

64 Ibid, 553–559.

65 Ibid, 561–566.

ties was, however, unclear to the assessor. On two ocassions he explicitly wrote "whether we should recognise such precedents as decisive factors". Whether he was himself willing to follow these precedents is unclear, but we can look at other sources on this point. During the discussions with the other members of the court's Senate, three other assessors used the legal precedents as an argument. They all said that the most important precedents were in favour of the widow Spilcker and not the mayor Krohn.[66] Assessor Summermann was of the same opinion. He explained the inconsistencies among the twenty decisions to be due to the long period – three centuries – during which they had been given. All the decisions assimilated the full and half birth and ultimately followed the solution of the Roman law. Because of this consistency of the case law, the Chamber Court did not decide explicitly whether precedents had to be treated as legal authorities. Of course, the assessor used these arguments to strengthen his own decision. This, however, does not mean that those legal precedents would have had the authority to replace the Roman law had they favoured the opposite solution.

The last section of Summermann's statement was devoted to the learned literature. On this point Summermann had very clear ideas: "what matters is not the opinion of some doctors, especially if only a few of them, but the prescribed laws and the actual [legal] practice."[67] This is one of the few sentences that provides clear evidence for the authorities accepted by the Chamber Court. These were the laws in plural – so not only Roman law, but also the statutes and other sources. Beyond these laws, the court also looked at the actual legal practice. In the German tradition, this practice was sometimes called the "green observance" (viridis observantia) – green perhaps because the practice bloomed like a flower or a tree.[68] Even when the irrelevance of the learned literature was established as the starting point, assessor Summermann would accurately evaluate all the authors quoted by the defendant. Concerning David Mevius and Samuel Stryk, two important representatives of the Usus modernus,[69] he demonstrated that their opinion was neither accurate nor in fact closer to the Roman law. In one case, however, it was plain that the defendant had indeed referred to an author who

---

66 Transcript of the session of the Imperial Chamber Court in P Oestmann, Ein Zivilprozeß, 572–575.
67 Ibid, 566: "Allermaßen es nicht darauf ankomt, was einige und zumahl wenige Doctores dafür gehalten haben, sondern auf die vorgeschriebene Rechte und würckliche praxin."
68 Ibid, 320–322.
69 N Jörn (ed), David Mevius (1609–1670), Hamburg: Verlag Dr Kovač, 2007; J Schröder, "Specimen Usus Moderni Pandectarum", 235–238.

undoubtedly favoured the full birth. This was Joachim Lucas Stein, a well-known northern German scholar of Lübeckian law from the mid-eighteenth century.[70] Stein was still alive, and his book was the newest among all the relevant literature. Nevertheless, the Chamber assessor paid little attention to Stein's theory. He wrote that Stein's theory was only a single opinion in contrast to a wealth of other authors, and that he worked in an indiscriminate and haphazard way – and not without mistakes. According to assessor Summermann, Stein wanted to be a reformer rather than an interpreter of the law.[71] As such, reforming and improving the law was not the task of the literature. As a second argument Summermann mentioned several other authors whom the defendant had not quoted. This way he showed that his knowledge of the literature on the law of Lübeck did not need the help of the litigants, and that he was able to evaluate mainstream opinion. Summermann made frequent use of legal literature in all parts of his "relation". Very frequently, when quoting a phrase, he would also give a precise reference (e.g. "in my book on page . . .").[72] This makes clear that the assessor used the books that he quoted. Many early modern practitioners owned only one or a few textbooks or commentaries,[73] but the Imperial Chamber Court founded a court library in the first half of the eighteenth century.[74] It was therefore possible for the members of the court to use many erudite works. Whether all these books were authorities in a formal sense is unclear. In the court practice, solving legal questions without recourse to this kind of literature would have been unthinkable.

D. CONCLUSION

It is difficult to give a generalised answer to the question: Did the decisions of the highest imperial courts in the Holy Roman Empire leave some traces in the (substantive) law? Did the early modern jurisdiction have the power to modify and change the law? Were the highest courts regarded as authori-

---

70 J L Stein, *Gründliche Abhandlung des lübischen Rechts*, Leipzig, Rostock: J Schmidt, 1738/1746, vol II, tit 2.

71 Oestmann, *Ein Zivilprozeß*, 569–570.

72 Some examples ibid, 558, 561, 568–569 and 571. Summermann uses the Latin abbreviation *pm* = *pagina mea* or *pagina mihi*.

73 This is claimed about the *Iurisprudentia Romano-Germanico forensis* by Georg Adam Struve: G Kleinheyer and J Schröder, *Deutsche und Europäische Juristen*, 558.

74 I Scheurmann, "Wetzlarische Beiträge zu einer pragmatischen allgemeinen Rechtsgelehrsamkeit . . .", in W Speitkamp (ed), *Staat, Gesellschaft, Wissenschaft. Festschrift für Hellmut Seier zum 65 Geburtstag*, Marburg: N G Elwert, 1994, 229–244.

ties in scholarly discussions? And, asking the same question in the reverse, what kind of authorities did the highest imperial courts recognise when they had to solve controversial legal problems?

In contrast to modern law, when speaking about early modern times, it is not possible to differentiate between abstract discussions of the learned literature and practical decisions and motivations of the courts. In the period of the *Usus modernus*, the legal science in the Holy Roman Empire was a highly practical kind of scholarship. On the other hand, many judges published relations, observations, consultations and other written statements originating from internal discussions among the assessors or judges.

Examining single lawsuits can clarify some details. These two cases from the city of Lübeck show how thin and ambiguous the boundaries between literature and case law were. In fact, it is possible to prove some influence of the Imperial Chamber Court on the development of the German law. However, it is unclear whether specific, single case studies may be generalised. Even if the history of the Imperial Chamber Court has been well known for a long time, and even if early modern procedural law has been explored for many decades, there are still pieces missing from this puzzle. Some very important questions concerning the relation between court authority and the substantive law remain unanswered. This chapter has tried to clear a path through the jungle and to show some possibilities to offer approximate answers. But most of the work remains to be done.

9 Legal Authorities in the Seventeenth-Century Swedish Empire

Heikki Pihlajamäki

A. INTRODUCTION
B. LEGAL AUTHORITY IN SWEDEN: THE LAND OF WRITTEN LAW
C. LEGAL LITERATURE AS LEGAL AUTHORITY IN SWEDEN
D. LEGAL PRACTICE AS LEGAL AUTHORITY IN SWEDEN
E. LEGAL AUTHORITY IN SWEDEN'S OVERSEAS POSSESSIONS
F. COMPARATIVE CONCLUSIONS

A. INTRODUCTION

In older legal history, the meaning and contents of *auctoritas* was a disputed subject. Was it a "moral and political" concept only, as Siber[1] understood it to be, or did it also have a legal meaning, as Grant[2] would have it? Magdelain's position was *"vermittelnd"*:[3] the concept had evolved from a moral-political one to a legal concept. Kunkel, then, thought the term had no clearly determined legal meaning.[4] The concept of "authority" can thus have various meanings; some more legal, some less so. In most European countries during the early modern period, legal authority flowed from the prince – who was thought to hold such authority by God's authority. Some

---

1 H Siber, *Römisches Verfassungsrecht*, Lahr: M Schauenburg, 1952, 375.
2 N M Grant, *From Imperium to Auctoritas*, Cambridge: Cambridge University Press, 1946.
3 A Magdelain, *Auctoritas Principis*, Paris, Les Belles Lettres, 1947.
4 W Kunkel, review of A Magdelain, "Auctoritas principis" (1953) 70 *Zeitschrift der Savigny-Stiftung für Rechtsgeschichte* (Romanistische Abteilung), 437–445, at 438. See also N Jansen, *The Making of Legal Authority. Non-legislative Codifications in Historical and Comparative Perspective*, Oxford: Oxford University Press, 2010.

of God's authority was vested on the ecclesiastical courts of the Catholic Church, while in Protestant lands that particular piece of legal authority was, after the Reformation, transferred to the secular prince. Again, depending on time and place, part of that authority may have been vested on the estates convening in diets (constitutional or contractual monarchies). In the Middle Ages, the authority of law as a whole is often said to have rested on the emperor (*ratione imperii*), whereas in the modern age, law's legitimacy came to depend increasingly on reason (*imperio rationis*). Sweeping theoretical generalisations, however, tell little about practical legal authority: who really decided what the law was.

Let us start with legislation, or statute law, which in the early modern period emerged from the prince.[5] The ruler could either exercise the right to legislate himself or herself, or delegate (or at least allow) the power to legislate to other organs, such as parliaments or municipal authorities. The second typical source of legal authority was judiciary, again operating directly under the prince or with his active or passive approval. The legal authority of the judiciary typically stemmed from higher courts, such as the Imperial Chamber Court (*Reichskammergericht*) in the German Empire, the Great Council in Mechelin (*Grand Conseil des Pays-bas à Malines*) in the Burgundian Netherlands or *Rota Romana* of the Catholic Church. The third source of legal authority, historically as well as today, has been legal scholarship. Law professors have asserted their authority over legal questions through various ways. Learned advocates have used scholarship in their writings and speeches to courts. Courts themselves have relied on legal literature in their *rationes decidendi*. Scholars have given their expert opinions (*consilia*) at the request of parties to legal disputes and sometimes to courts themselves. In the sixteenth century in the German Empire, the practice of "transmission of acts" (*transmissio actorum, Aktenversendung*) even changed law faculties into *Spruchkollegien*. Acting as a *Spruchkollegium*, members of a law faculty drafted legal decisions (*responsum, consilium*) at the request of a court of law, in the name of which the final decision was given.

I will not dwell on early modern political theories but will instead focus on a particular early modern empire: Sweden. In the seventeenth century, as was typical for early modern empires, the Swedish Realm consisted of

5 Ultimately, secular rulers derived their authority from God. The point becomes even clearer when it comes to the canon law of the Catholic Church. Since here we are dealing with post-Reformation Sweden, canon law need not concern us. Neither will we dwell on the prince as God's representative on earth.

several parts, all with different legal traditions and social and political realities. When referring to early modern states of this type, historians often use
the term "composite state". The expression appeared in Pufendorf, but
was introduced with its modern meaning by H G Koenigsberger.[6] A composite state typically combines under one umbrella several polities, often
with distinct legal orders, administrative systems and differing degrees of
independence.[7] Composite states were often layered, in that their different
parts consisted themselves of several territories, held together by little else
than a common ruler, to whom the relationship of the different parts of the
composite state also varied.[8] All composite states share elements of indirect
rule, in which the local authorities enjoy some degree of autonomy over the
local affairs.[9] Conceptually, then, composite states differ little from empires,
which have been defined as "large political units, expansionist or with a
memory of power extended over space, polities that maintain distinction and
hierarchy as they incorporate new people".[10]

Early modern Sweden was a typical early modern composite state. Since
the middle Ages, Sweden proper – consisting of present-day Sweden and
Finland – was heavily dominated by statute law based on medieval customary law and with a slight touch of European learned laws. In Sweden
proper, legal literature or court practice had little importance. The parts of
the Holy Roman Empire of the German Nation which the Swedish kings
acquired through the Peace of Westphalia (1648) were ruled by German
gemeines Recht, over which Sweden attempted to gain control by establishing a high court in Wismar – a precondition for being granted appeals

---

6 H G Koenigsberger, "Monarchies and Parliaments in Early Modern Europe: *dominium
   regale* or *dominium politicum et regale*" (1978) 5 *Theory and Society*, 191–217 (also in Id,
   Politicians and Virtuosi: Essays in Early Modern History, London: The Hambledon Press, 1986,
   1–26).
7 See D H Nexon, *The Struggle for Power in Early Modern Europe: Religious Conflict, Dynastic
   Empires, and International Change*, Princeton: Princeton University Press, 2011, 70–71. See
   also H Spruyt, *The Sovereign State and its Competitors: An Analysis of Systems Change*,
   Princeton: Princeton University Press, 1994; C Tilly, *Coercion, Capital, and European States,
   AD 990–1992*, Cambridge, MA: Blackwell, 1992; J Muldoon, *Empire and Order: The Concept
   of Empire, 800–1800*, New York: St Martin's, 1999; J Burbank and F Cooper, *Empires in
   World History: Power and the Politics of Difference*, Princeton: Princeton University Press,
   2010.
8 H Gustafsson, "The Conglomerate State: A Perspective on State Formation in Early Modern
   Europe" (1998) 23 *Scandinavian Journal of History*, 189–213, at 194. Gustafsson uses the term
   "conglomerate" state. See also R Tuchtenhagen, *Zentralstaat und Provinz im frühneuzeitlichen
   Nordosteuropa*, Wiesbaden: Harrassowitz, 2008, 440–441.
9 Muldoon, *Empire and Order*, 119; Nexon, *The Struggle for Power in Early Modern* Europe,
   71–72.
10 Burbank and Cooper, *Empires in World History*, 8.

privileges (*prilegia appellationis*) from the imperial high courts, the Aulic Court and the Imperial Chamber Court. The third part of the realm was Livonia, which was also historically based on *gemeines Recht*, but less so than the more central parts of the German Empire. Since Livonia was small – and which the Swedes therefore hoped to be more "manageable" – the Swedish Crown tried to establish firm legal rule there.

This chapter discusses early modern legal authority in Sweden proper. I will first investigate the role of legislation as an embodiment of legal authority, then turn to legal scholarship and legal practice. Finally, legal authorities in Sweden proper are briefly compared to the situation in Sweden's overseas provinces, Livonia and the Swedish holdings in the Empire. Comparing the law courts and their attitudes towards legal authorities in these three parts of the Swedish empire, I wish to capture something essential about early modern European legal history in general.

Before continuing, one further observation should be put in place. We can observe the question of legal authorities from two slightly distinct viewpoints. We can treat the subject from the viewpoint of legal culture and observe how legal authority manifests itself generally in different social fields. But another way is to look at the subject specifically from the viewpoint of legal practice and ask from where legal decisions based on court decisions have drawn their authority. This chapter adopts the latter.

B. LEGAL AUTHORITY IN SWEDEN: THE LAND OF WRITTEN LAW

The array of legal sources in Sweden grew complex during the sixteenth and seventeenth centuries, as was the case in the regions of Western and Southern Europe. There was some learned *ius commune*, feudal law, town law and customary law. However, because of Sweden's simple social structure, the legal sources competing with royal statutory law never gained similar significance as elsewhere in Europe. The centralised royal power channelled some these features into the great Scandinavian codes, which summarised the legal changes of the sixteenth and seventeenth centuries. The main producers of legal authority in early modern Sweden, albeit not the only ones, were the public entities. The Crown, the Lutheran church and the towns also produced statutory law. This chapter will leave the church and the towns as norm-giving entities aside and concentrate on the Crown. Its legal authority was channelled into practical legal life through different norms: laws, privileges and police norms. A wave of legislative frenzy had swept across late medieval Europe, the Nordic countries included. The Catholic Church initiated the trend with its various collections, the first ones were of a private nature (e.g. the works of Ivo de Chartres of the eleventh century, or Gratian's Decretum of the early twelfth century), and the later ones (e.g. the *Liber Extra*, 1234) with an official sanction.[11] Secular legislation followed suit and combined customary law with royal legislation, canon law, feudal law and *ius commiue* in varying proportions and degrees. Examples of these laws include the Saxon Mirror, *Siete Partidas* and *Coutumes de Beauvaisis*, all from the thirteenth century.

The Norwegian early twelfth-century provincial laws (the laws of Gulating and Frostating) emerged among the first compilations in Europe,[12] and Iceland's *Hafliðaskrá* dates to the same period. Denmark's provinces – Scania, Jutland and Zealand – compiled their laws somewhat later, in the thirteenth century.[13]

The Swedish provincial laws were put into writing later than the laws of Denmark, Iceland and Norway. The Swedish laws were also much more numerous. Nine provincial laws remain to this day in manuscripts, either entirely or in part. These include the laws of West Gothia (*Västergötland*), East Gothia (*Östgötalagen*), Småland (*Smålandslagen*), Gotland (*Gutalagen*), Uppland (*Upplandslagen*), Hälsingland (*Hälsingelagen*), Södermanland (*Södermannalagen*), Dalarna (*Dalalagen*) and Västmanland (*Västmannalagen*). Scholars often distinguish between the Göta laws (after Götaland) in Southern Sweden — West and East Gothia, and Småland — while Uppland, Hälsingland, Södermanland, Dalarna and Västmanland belong to the Svea laws (Svealand) of Central Sweden. The oldest existing manuscripts of Swedish provincial laws date roughly to 1280–1350. Some of the provincial laws were private compilations (*rättsböcker*), while two of the Swedish provincial laws had received royal confirmation: the Law of Uppland (1296) and the Law of Södermanland (1327) (*lagböcker*).[14]

---

11 See S Gagnér, *Studien zur Ideengeschichte der Gesetzgebung*, Stockholm: Almquist & Wiksell, 1960.

12 S Bagge, *From Viking Stronghold to Christian Kingdom*, Copenhagen: Museum Tusculanum Press, 2010, 180; D Strauch, *Mittelalterliches nordisches Rechts bis ca 1500: Eine Quellenkunde*, Berlin: De Gruyter, 2016, 111–112; J Ø Sunde, "Above the Law: Norwegian Constitutionalism and the Code of 1274" in J Ø Sunde (ed), *Constitutionalism before 1789: Constitutional Arrangements from the High Middle Ages to the French Revolution*, Oslo: Pax Forlag, 2014, 172–173; M Korpiola, "High and Late Medieval Scandinavia: Codified Vernacular Law and Learned Legal Influences", in H Pihlajamäki, M D Dubber, M Godfrey (eds), *The Oxford Handbook of European Legal History*, Oxford: Oxford University Press, 2018, 378–429, 380–385.

13 Strauch, *Mittelalterliches nordisches Rechts*, 269–270.

14 Ibid, 618–619; Korpiola, "High and Late Medieval Scandinavia", 384–385.

The provincial laws were strongly based on customary law, albeit not exclusively. For a long time, therefore, we may assume that the law practised in courts derived its legitimacy and authority from long-standing practice and not from written law. It is difficult to say just when written statutes began to gain authority. It is worth highlighting, however, that written law distanced itself a further step from the local or provincial customs around the mid-fourteenth century, when King Magnus Eriksson issued two important laws: the laws for the town and the laws for the countryside. These laws were based heavily on the provincial laws of the most important Swedish provinces (e.g. the Uppsala province). The continuation between Magnus Eriksson's Land Law and King Christopher's Land Law (of 1442) was also remarkable: it has been estimated that almost 80 per cent of the normative material is the same.[15]

The culmination of statutory development was the Swedish Law of 1734, which replaced all previous compilations and set the course for the eighteenth century. The effect of the Law on Swedish legal scholarship was much the same as that of Napoleon's *Code Civil* of 1804 on French nineteenth-century legal scholarship: there was little to add. Swedish statutory law consisted not only of large-scale compilation, but also of piece-meal legislation (*stadga*). Important statues include the Statute of Alsnö (1280), which created Swedish nobility through tax exemptions, as well as several of Magnus Eriksson's statutes of the 1330s and 1340s, which made the punishments system harsher. Previous royal statutes also influenced the Land Law of Magnus Eriksson.[16] An important subspecies of statute were the police ordinances, which, as everywhere in Europe, began to flow out of the royal chancery in the sixteenth and seventeenth centuries.[17]

From the sixteenth century and, in particular, the seventeenth century onwards, at least three arguments speak for an increased authority of statutory law. First, presiding judges of the lower courts now began to be able to read and write – although the same can hardly be said of the jury members.[18] This was the case in most of the lower courts from the sixteenth century

15 M Ulkuniemi, *Kuningas Kristoferin maanlaki 1442*, Helsinki: Suomalaisen Kirjallisuuden Seura, 1978, 18.
16 Å Holmbäck and E Wessén (eds), *Magnus Erikssons landslag*, Stockholm: Insitutet för rättshistorisk forskning, 1902, XXIV–XXVII.
17 See T Kotkas, *Royal Police Ordinances in Early Modern Sweden: The Emergence of Voluntaristic Understanding of Law*, Brill: Leiden, 2014.
18 The composition of the Swedish lower court remained the same from the Middle Ages until the second half of the twentieth century (in both Finland and Sweden). A panel of lay members was presided over by a judge, who, from the sixteenth century onwards, could usually read and, from the seventeenth century onwards, usually had at least some legal training.

onwards. Lower-court judges often also held other high posts and hired substitutes (a "law reader", *lagläsare*) to take care of the assizes. These substitutes had sometimes studied at least some law. Second, the surviving court protocols from the late Middle Ages to the seventeenth century include some references to written laws, but to hardly any other legal sources. Let us look at some examples. Mia Korpiola has examined the cases of the Upper Civil Court of Uppsala (*lagmansrätt*) 1400–1494. The court's record book includes about 200 cases, twenty-three of which mention a statutory source. The *ratio decidendi* mention no other legal sources.[19] My own studies of lower-court protocols of the Finnish country demonstrate an even usage of legal sources, until use of statutory source becomes slightly more frequent. Throughout the seventeenth century, decisions on homicide cases were frequently backed up with statutory references. Again, lower-court records fail to mention any other legal sources.[20] Third, the frequency with which central legal texts appeared in print says something of their significance. In 1608, King Charles IX confirmed King Christopher's Law of Land, originally of 1442. Between 1608 and 1726, the Law went through at least eleven widespread editions until the next major statutory work, the Law of the Realm (*Sveriges rikes lag*) was given in 1734.[21] Both printed books in small format and manuscript collections were also prepared specifically for travelling judges. Such a collection could typically include the Land Law of King Christopher, the Town Law of Magnus Eriksson and the *Instructions for the Judge*.[22] In addition to the above arguments, we can assume the significance of statutory law from the context in which it operated. As we will soon see, there was little competition from legal sources. This was because, since the Reformation, Sweden was politically, by comparison with other European

19 M Korpiola, *"Ratio decidendi* in Seventeenth-Century Sweden: The Practice of the Svea Court of Appeal in a Comparative Perspective" (unpublished presentation at the British Legal History Conference, Cambridge, 16 July 2011).

20 H Pihlajamäki, "Legality before the Legality Principle: Royal Statutes and Early Modern Swedish Criminal Law", in G Martyn, A Musson and H Pihlajamäki (eds), *From the Judge's Arbitrium to the Legality Principle: Legislation as a Source of Law in Criminal Trials*, Berlin: Duncker & Humblot, 2013, 169–188, at 184–187.

21 Of the different printed versions, see H S Collin and C J Schlyter (eds), *Corpus iuris sueogothorum antiqui: Samling af Sweriges gamla lagar*, vol XII, Stockholm: Berlingska boktryckeriet, 1869, xciii–ci.

22 The *Instructions* were a variant of a *brocardica*, compiled and written by Sweden's main Lutheran reformer, Olaus Petri, in the 1540s. The *Instructions* acquired a status equivalent to written and have enjoyed high prestige as moral norms until this day. See H Pihlajamäki, "Gründer, Bewahrer oder Vermittler? Die nationalen und internationalen Elemente im Rechtsdenken des Olaus Petri", in J Eckert and K Å Modéer (eds), *Juristische Fakultäten und Juristenausbildung im Ostseeraum*, Stockholm: Institutet för rättshistorisk forskning, 2004, 29–38.

powers, a centralised monarchy. This was necessarily reflected in the law and resulted in the heightened importance of statutory law. However, statutory law came only gradually on top of the base of customary law, which continued to influence legal decision making long into the eighteenth century. Cases were decided as they had always been, and in many cases not much judicial reasoning or *ratio decidendi* of any sort was needed. It is important to note that the kind of customary law that we are dealing with here is "wild", in other words, not controlled and defined by learned lawyers in the way that it was in the Europe of learned lawyers.[23]

Thus far, we have focused on how legal authority, mainly in the form of statutory law, operated at the level of the lower courts. This changes slightly when high courts enter the picture. The first of these was the Svea High Court, officially founded in 1614.[24] During the the seventeenth century, a string of high courts were established in different parts of the Swedish realm: Turku (1623), Dorpat (1629), Jönköping (1634) and Vaasa (1779). These courts, like the European high courts after which they were modelled, had learned jurists as judges, making it possible for new kinds of source to gain authority in Swedish law.

C. LEGAL LITERATURE AS LEGAL AUTHORITY IN SWEDEN

Scandinavian contacts to the heartlands of Europe have existed since the Middle Ages, and *ius commune* has influenced legislation. From the sixteenth century onwards, the influence grew more significant, although no wholesale "reception of Roman law" ever occurred. Influence spread to Scandinavia through two principle channels. Royal power in both Denmark and Sweden needed learned legal experts to deal with foreign policy and diplomatic affairs. The Scandinavian royal chanceries hired German, sometimes Dutch, legal professionals to counsel the chanceries and to represent them in diplomatic negotiations.[25] The number of Scandinavians studying

---

23 On customary law within the system of *ius commune*, see R Garré, *Consuetudo: Das Gewohnheitsrecht in der Rechtsquellen- und Methodenlehre des späten ius commune in Italien (16–18 Jahrhundert)*, Frankfurt am Main: Vittorio Klostermann, 2005.

24 On the founding history of the Svea High Court, see M Korpiola, "A Safe Haven in the Shadow of War? The Founding and the Raison d etre of the New Court, Based on its Early Activity", in M Korpiola (ed), *The Svea Court of Appeal in the Early Modern Period: Historical Reinterpretations and New Perspectives*, Stockholm: Institutet för rättshistorisk forskning, 2014, 55–108.

25 M Korpiola, "Desperately Seeking Lawyers: Contacts in the Baltic Sea Region and the Rise of Diplomacy in Reformation Sweden" in O Zcaika and H Holze (eds), *Migration und Kulturtransfer im Ostseeraum während der frühen Neuzeit*, Stockholm: Kungliga Biblioteket, 2012, 1–120.

law in foreign universities also increased. After the Reformation, Protestant (or neutral) universities in Germany or the Netherlands were the logical choice. Most law students returned and spread their knowledge of *ius commune* as high-court judges or civil servants. Domestic universities with law faculties were founded. The establishment of the high courts in the sixteenth and seventeenth centuries increased the influence of common-European legal scholarship.[26]

A review of foreign legal literature used and read in Sweden is neither necessary nor possible here. The emphasis, however, was on German and Dutch authors. Together with the founding of Swedish universities from the beginning of the seventeenth century onwards, domestic Swedish legal literature began to establish itself. Important scholars were few and far between, but domestic legal order was nevertheless presented, for the first time, as a coherent order in the works of such authors as Johannes Loccenius (1598–1677), Claes Rålamb (1622–1698), Claudius Kloot (c 1622–1690) and David Nehrman Ehrenstråhle (1695–1769). Their scholarship can be best described as following the prevailing German style of the period, *usus modernus pandectarum*. The Swedish writers presented the Swedish statutory material in the format of *ius commune*, adopting its institutions here and there.[27] However, the influence of learned law remained necessarily limited, because the high courts had to communicate effectively with non-learned lower courts, in which educated lawyers were a rare sight. It would be somewhat optimistic to assume that lower-court judges, not to mention lay members, could understand citations of learned law. The teaching of legal literature, therefore, needed to be simplified and worked into statute law.

Swedes who had studied law abroad naturally brought their learning back home with them. I will take two examples from different fields of law. The first comes from the field of legal procedure. As I have explained in more detail elsewhere, the Roman-canon law of evidence was introduced in Sweden around the sixteenth and seventeenth centuries. The new legal transplant gradually replaced the archaic system of proof based on oaths and compurgators. The new theory of proof was not, however, adopted with all the detail and finesse that was discussed in the learned European courts. Rather, the statutory theory was taken for use in a rudimentary

26 On the law studies of Finns and Swedes in Dutch and German universities, see M Vasara-Aaltonen, *Learning for the Legal Profession: Swedish Jurists' Study Journeys ca 1630–1800*, unpublished Doctoral dissertation, University of Helsinki, 2017.

27 See the account of L Björne, *Patrioter och institutionalister: Den nordiska rättsvetenskapens historia*, pt I, Lund: Institutet för rättshistorisk forskning, 1992.

form, simple enough to explain to the unlearned jurymen sitting at the rural courts. The simplified form consisted of the basic rule of two eyewitnesses or confession, required for a verdict in criminal cases. Attempts to introduce judicial torture also emerged, but torture was never legalised.[28] Another example of the diffusion of *ius commune* comes from the field of wills and testament, which – as Elsa Trolle Önnerfors has demonstrated – appeared in Swedish high-court practice during the seventeenth century.[29] Having been adopted, both statutory theory of proof and testaments made their way into statutory law – the Law of the Realm of 1734. As these examples show, the authority of the high courts reached its zenith during the seventeenth century, when statutory law was already becoming outdated as a result of the great social changes experienced in the country, which was rapidly turning into a multicultural European empire.

Even though a hierarchical court structure gradually took shape, all through the early modern period the high courts remained much more in charge of correcting wrongful decisions of the lower courts than of actively directing their course through precedents. The whole idea of a precedent, of course, was rather alien to early modern legal thought. Instead of deciding like cases in a like manner, the courts emphasised the need to decide right-fully, considering the individual circumstances of a case.

D. LEGAL PRACTICE AS LEGAL AUTHORITY IN SWEDEN

How did legal practice influence itself? If influence through appeal is not considered, legal practice gained legal authority in two ways. First, the deci-sions of the high courts – especially those of the Svea High Court, the oldest and the most prestigious – were collected and sometimes cited in the high-court decisions. Second, the Crown wielded its legal authority through the practice of *référé legislatif*. The practice, widely spread in Europe, left dif-ficult questions of legal interpretation to the lawmaker to decide.[30]

It took time until the Swedish high courts could establish themselves as the leading courts in the realm. For some decades, it remained unclear

---

28 See H Pihlajamäki, "The Painful Question: The Fate of Judicial Torture in Early Modern Sweden" (2007) 25(3) *Law and History Review*, 557–592.

29 See E Trolle Önnerfors, *Justitia et prudential: rättsbildning genom rättstillämpning – Svea hov-rätt och testamentsmålen 1640–1690*, Stockholm: Institutet för rättshistorisk forskning, 2010.

30 On the roots of *référé législatif*, see P Alvazzi del Frate, "Aux origines du référé législatif: inter-prétation et jurisprudence dans les cahiers de doléances de 1789" (2008) 86(2) *Revue historique de droit français et étranger*, 253–262.

whether the Svea Court (founded in 1614) was the last instance or whether its decisions could still be appealed to the Crown. During the initial decades, the Svea Court was also clearly seen as the *primus inter pares* among the high courts, and it sometimes even decided appeal cases from other high courts. Towards the end of the seventeenth century, the position of the high courts stabilised into a clear hierarchical order, in which high courts formed an appeals instance for lower-court decisions.

Decisions of the high courts now began to be published. The most important of these collections, the so-called "Becchius-Palmcrantz collection", was compiled around 1700 by Magnus Becchius Palmcrantz (1653–1703), a learned jurist and the first secretary of the commission in charge of preparing a new Swedish law of the realm. The large collection of high-court cases was systematically organised according to branches of law but was never printed.[31]

Cases were also published in statute collection. I will take the 1702 printed version of the Land Law of 1442 as an example of how legal practice was used in conjunction with statutory law. The 1702 version was special, because it included a large footnote apparatus of Petter Abrahamsson, one of the brightest Swedish legal minds of the time. Abrahamsson had also made other editions of Swedish laws and was a member of the Law Commission, which had been established in 1686 to reform Swedish law (and which finally, in 1734, resulted in the Swedish Law). Abrahamsson therefore had a keen interest in following the development of statute law. The apparatus was essentially an update of the old text. The update concentrates on statutory law, a large amount of which had been issued in the intervening hundred years. The notes, however, also refer to legal practice. Primarily, Abrahamsson also refers to royal decisions given in the process of *référé legislative*, and addressed to the courts and central administrative agencies. The examples are numerous. For instance, under Chapter III of the Marriage Title ("If a bride takes a man against father's and mother's wish"), a Royal Letters to Göta High Court (12 February 1699) is mentioned. In this letter, the king states that the rule applies both to noble and non-noble people. The notes also refer to many passages of Mosaic law, which was customarily referred to as law.

---

31 Riksarkivet (The Swedish National Archive, RA): Riksarkivets ämnesamlingar Juridika I: Becchius-Palmcrantz samlingar.

E. LEGAL AUTHORITY IN SWEDEN'S OVERSEAS POSSESSIONS

As a result of the Thirty Years War, Sweden acquired territories within the German Empire. In the Duchies of Bremen-Verden and Vorpommern, the Principality of Rügen, the town and the Barony of Wismar, and the Cathedral Chapter of Hamburg, the Swedish kings became the emperor's vassals. In the newly acquired territories, judiciary needed to be organised. The emperor had granted Sweden full appeals privilege (*privilegium de non appellando illimitatum*), which meant that almost all appeals to the imperial courts were forbidden. In exchange for the privilege, the Crown had to organise a territorial high court which provided the possibility of appeals.[32]

A high appellate court (*Oberappellationsgericht für die schwedischen Lehen im Heiligen Römischen Reich deutscher Nation*, or the Higher Appeals Court for the Swedish Fiefs in the Holy Roman Empire of the German Nation) was founded and, after long preparations, began functioning in Wismar in 1653. In addition to the Wismar court, the Swedish Crown established new high courts in the provinces. Town courts and middle-instance courts – such as the appellate courts and the consistory for the ecclesiastical affairs – became courts of the Swedish Crown, whereas lower courts often remained patrimonial. The judicial structure was designed from the point of view of making sure that the most important cases could, if necessary, be followed all the way up to Wismar and even to Stockholm.

Little is known on the substantive legal norms that the courts followed in Pommern, Bremen-Verden and Wismar, but we can draw conclusions based on the development of Swedish judiciary in the conquered German territories.[33] It certainly would have been unrealistic to "Swedify" the entire legal system in the German provinces. The Swedes were, quite simply, lacking legally qualified personnel to staff the new courts. It is therefore unlikely that the few Swedish judges taking positions in the new courts in Germany would have been able to exert much Swedish influence on them. Instead, the new courts continued the old tradition of German *gemeines Recht*. This tradition was carried by jurists such as David Mevius, one of the leading

---

32 H Mohnhaupt, "Organisation und Tätigkeit des 'Hohen Königlichen Tribunals zu Wismar'", in N Jörn, B Diestelkamp and K Å Modéer (eds), *Integration durch Recht: Das Wismarer Tribunal (1653–1806)* (Köln: Böhlau, 2003), 215–237, at 217–225.

33 See K Å Modéer, *Gerichtsbarkeiten der schwedischen Krone im deutschen Reichsterritorium*, vol I: *Voraussetzungen und Aufbau 1630–1657*, Stockholm: Institutet för rättshistorisk forskning, 1975.

German legal scholars of the time.[34] He served as the vice president of the Wismar Court (from 1653 until his death in 1670). Mevius also started the collection of the court's decisions, which ran until 1794, and published a codification of Mecklenburg land law.

Since flooding the new courts with Swedish law was unthinkable, other means of influencing legal development in the German territories became necessary. The *privilegium de appellando illimitatum* still did not settle the question as to whether the Swedish Crown could exercise judicial control over the Wismar tribunal. The Swedes certainly thought so, but according to the German interpretation no regular appeals to Stockholm were possible. In any case, the extraordinary claims, such as the nullity claims or cases concerning denial of justice, went to the highest courts of the empire.

Disputes between the individual provincial governments (*Landesregierungen*) and the estates of those provinces posed another problem of legal authority. In the Empire, these disputes normally pertained to the jurisdiction of the highest imperial courts, the *Reichskammergericht* and the *Reichshofrat*. Because of the appeals privilege, the Wismar tribunal now claimed the exclusive jurisdiction on these cases. The Swedish Crown was against this, claiming that the Crown should have jurisdiction on the disputes between estates and provincial governments. A visitation commission sent to Wismar in 1688 ruled according to the Crown's opinion. The third major jurisdictional dispute concerned another extraordinary legal remedy, the so-called "revision" (*beneficium revisionis*). The Swedish Crown naturally assumed that the revisions would go to the Svea High Court, as did similar cases from the Baltic provinces, but the estates of the German provinces were against this. Instead, the estates thought that the visitation commission – which included representatives from the estates, the provincial governments and the local University of Greifswald – would be a suitable organ to deal with revision cases. The commission then in fact decided some petitions in 1688. After that, however, no further visitations were organised, and the revision as a legal remedy lost its significance in Sweden's German territories.[35]

If imposing judicial authority thus proved difficult, what about statutory reforms? The Swedes realised no wholesale legislative reforms. A Government Ordinance (*Regierungsordnung*) for Bremen-Verden was passed in 1652, and drafts of Consistorial and Church Ordinances were pre-

---

34 Modéer, *Gerichtsbarkeiten*, 258, 419–420.
35 Jörn, "Integration durch Recht?" 395–396.

pared but never approved. A Church Ordinance for Wismar was issued in 1665, and it came to be used in Bremen-Verden as well. In 1672, Pommern also got a new Church Ordinance.[36] For the general governance of the territories, church laws were, of course, fundamental. The social and political situation in the new German territories thus unavoidably influenced their legal development. Similar factors also played a role in Livonia. The Swedish attempts to establish effective judicial controls over the German territories failed. The strong German legal culture was capable of resisting most Swedish attempts. Where, then, did legal authority reside? Certainly not in written statutory law, at least not the Swedish one. Nor did it reside in the judiciary, in the sense that the Swedes would have gained effective control over it. As far as legal authority is concerned, the German territories belonging to the Swedish Crown thus remained a land of *gemeines Recht* and the legal authority in the hands of legal scholars and local courts.

In Livonia, the Swedish Crown encountered considerable difficulties when attempting to establish judicial control. Although, until the founding of the University of Dorpat in 1630, Livonia had no universities or legal literature of its own, the linguistic and cultural ties of Livonia's German-speaking elite united the province to *gemeines Recht*. In addition came the political ties: until the dissolution of the Order State in 1561, Livonia remained part of the Holy Roman Empire of the German Nation.[37] As for legal culture, the difference between Livonia and Sweden was vast. At the time of the Swedish conquest, Livonians had been on their way to a reception of *ius commune*. In Sweden, the reception had gained much less ground and consisted largely of simplified *ius commune* norms.[38]

The tension between the "unlearned", archaic law of the Swedish conqueror and the learned law of Livonia is evident. What happened to Livonian law when the Swedes conquered the province? Even more so than in the German territories, the introduction of Swedish rule in Livonia produced a need to organise the province's judicial system, which was in ruins after many wars. The ordinances that the conquerors issued in the early 1630s made it quite clear that they intended to bring the Livonian legal procedures

---

36 Modéer, *Gerichtsbarkeiten*, 422.

37 J Lavory, *Germany's Northern Challenge: The Holy Roman Empire and the Scandinavian Struggle for the Baltic (1563–1576)*, Leiden: Brill, 2002, 16; J Whaley, *Germany and the Holy Roman Empire*, vol I: *Maximilian I to the Peace of Westphalia, 1493–1648*, Oxford: Oxford University Press, 2011, 373; see also E Pitz, *Papstreskript und Kaiserreskript im Mittelalter*, Tübingen: Bibliothek des Deutschen Historishcen Instituts in Rom, 1971, 198.

38 See H Pihlajamäki, *Conquest and the Law in Swedish Livonia (ca 1630–1710): A Case of Legal Pluralism in Early Modern Europe*, Leiden, Brill, 2016.

as close to the Swedish model as possible, despite the fact that the Livonian legal tradition was much closer to the learned European models than to the Swedish tradition. The Livonian *Landgerichte* were seen as counterparts of the Swedish *häradsrätter* and the newly founded Dorpat High Court was part of the chain of high courts established in Sweden since 1614, when the Svea High Court starting operating.

Due to fundamental social differences between Sweden proper and Livonia, the Livonian lower courts could not become identical with those in Sweden proper. In Sweden, free peasants contributed decisively to the working of countryside courts, the *häradsrätter*. In Livonia, free peasants were few, and serfs could not be made to sit in general law courts. Therefore, the line-up of Livonian countryside courts (*Landgerichte*) consisted of noble judges with legal training. Manorial courts continued functioning, handling the bulk of cases in which peasants were involved, such as disciplinary cases, petty criminal cases and civil cases. The urban courts followed the Riga model. When imposing their legal authority on conquered Livonia, Swedes faced social circumstances which limited their options. Swedes could not transplant their judicial system as such, and neither could they transfer their laws. Only exceptionally does one encounter any legal sources in the Livonian seventeenth-century court records. However, enough citations of Roman law, *gemeines Recht*, natural law and divine law appear to conclude that Livonia's judges followed a variant of *ius commune*, paying little attention to Swedish statutory sources.

Legal practice thus shows that Swedish statutory law gained little influence in Livonia. Some exceptions, however, prove the rule. The Swedish duel ordinances of the 1680s were effectively applied in Livonia, and towards the end of the seventeenth century, the Swedes managed to root out judicial torture from Livonia, which was never part of Swedish procedure. And how about direct interference of the Swedish Crown or its representatives in the workings of the Livonian judiciary? We have no information regarding any such meddling. By the seventeenth century the "judicial revolution" was as advanced in Sweden as it was elsewhere in Europe.[39] In other words, the division of labour had developed to the point in which the Crown and its officials rarely bothered to venture into the judicial area. If needed, commissarial (*ad hoc*) courts could be set up to handle flexibly all kinds of case which

---

39 On the concept of judicial revolution, see B Lenman and G Parker, "The State, the Community and Criminal Law in Early Modern Europe", in V A C Gatrell, B Lenman and G Parker (eds), *Crime and the Law: The Social History of Crime in Western Europe since 1500*, London: Verso, 1980, 11–48.

needed swift attention and for which, for one reason or another, ordinary courts were insufficient. This possibility was also used in Livonia.

Regarding Sweden's German territories, *beneficium revisionis* was available as an extraordinary remedy for those dissatisfied with decisions of the Dorpat High Court. Revision petitions, however, remained few, mostly because the procedures cost substantial amounts of money and time. Imposing legal authority on Livonia was therefore difficult for the Swedish conqueror. Livonian learned culture proved resistant to the influence of its considerably less-learned Swedish counterpart. As in Germany, the Swedes attempted to affect Livonian law mostly through reforming the province's judicial structure, but even this proved tough. Because of considerable social differences between Sweden proper and Livonia, the Swedish judicial system simply could not be copied directly.

F. COMPARATIVE CONCLUSIONS

I hope to have demonstrated how legal authority construed itself in early modern Sweden. Compared to the parts of Europe dominated by different versions of *ius commune*, decisive differences emerge. From early on, legal authority was exercised largely with the help of written statutes. Domestic legal scholarship emerged late and never acquired dominant authority in practical legal life, and much the same can be said about legal practice. Both legal scholarship and legal practice of the high courts grew in importance over the course of the seventeenth century, but their role remained less important than elsewhere in Europe. The reason why legal authority constituted itself differently in Sweden, when compared to countries more clearly dominated by *ius commune*, is the important role that peasants continued to exercise there long after legal professionals had taken over legal life elsewhere. Statutory law was something that peasants in courts could understand, especially since it was based on medieval legal customs. In order to flourish and function as effective channels of legal authority, scholarship and case law need trained jurists to manage them. In Swedish overseas provinces, the legal-cultural background was different. The most effective channel of legal authority that the Swedes had – statute law – could not compete with other sources in either Livonia or the German territories. The professional jurists in the overseas provinces – used as they were to *ius commune* legal culture – proved difficult, if not impossible, to convert into humble servants of Swedish statute law.

10 The Parliament of Paris and the Making of the Law at the Beginning of the Eighteenth Century

Isabelle Storez-Brancourt

A. INTRODUCTION

There is no more difficult challenge than to investigate the law making of the French Old Regime. And yet, thanks to the efforts of very active and effective teams of researchers,[1] investigations have recently been greatly increased, not only through new and complementary approaches, but also through a renewal of the problem of linking together judicial practices and ideological developments during Absolutism. Some years ago, research on French parliaments received the important help of British historiography and, more generally, of foreign researchers. Thanks to the Internet, research is now conducted on a global scale. European and, especially, French history of legal courts and institutions is one of the most dynamic research areas;

---

1 First and foremost, I would like to thank all *Centre d'Etude d'Histoire Juridique* (CEHJ) members who have been working with me in the archives of the Parliament of Paris in the French National Archives (the X and U series in particular) over the past twenty years – its various directors (Professor J-M Carbasse, G Leyte and O Descamps); Professor Louis de Carbonnières, a great expert and a kind specialist in parliament jurisdiction; and every one of its highly professional engineers, archivists and French National Archives curators who have accompanied me on such an amazing adventure.

Unless stated otherwise, translations are my own.

and so bibliographic production continues in steady evolution.[2] The largely unpublished papers and records of the General Public Royal Prosecutor have proved to be a particularly interesting source. Drawing attention to little-known sources written by magistrates and clerks of the seventeenth and eighteenth-century Parliament court service, it is possible to reach a better understanding of royal legislation during the final century of Absolutism in France.

B. THE PARIS PARLIAMENT: FIRST OF ALL, FIRST IN ALL

Here lies the main difficulty. In the institutional building of the royal French State, the royal Parliament occupies a very special place. Among all other advisory councils or deliberative assemblies which had surrounded kings and princes since the Middle Ages, the Parliament of Paris held a unique position. As a judicial court, it has fascinated hosts of historians and its archives continue to amaze researchers. By the middle of the fourteenth century it had reached a rare degree of procedural sophistication. Its legal and moral authority stretched to the geographic boundaries of the Ancient World. As the heart of the monarchical institutions, the French royal Parliament was a political body. Indeed, especially during the past thirty years, it has remained at the centre of Old France general histories, as a part of the fascinating investigations on the genesis, development and nature of the State in France. As is well known, the Paris Parliament was not a representative institution, rather the oldest and most eminent "sovereign" court of the kingdom, stemming from the medieval *Curia regis*. This was emphasised by an eighteenth-century magistrate of the court, copying a famous manuscript with pride:

> Paris is the capital of the whole Kingdom and the most famous in the world, both for the splendour of its Parliament which is an illustrious company of 130 judges followed by 300 lawyers and more, whose reputation spreads across all the Christian peoples as the best expert about human Law and Justice . . . In such a way that the other cities of France and all the magistrates and subjects have their eyes turned to it as the model of their judgments and political administrations, which is a great motive of preserving the State and Religion through the whole Kingdom.[3]

2 Only the most recent summary book is highlighted, of which publication is subsequent to this present research work: F Hildesheimer and M Morgat-Bonnet, *Le Parlement de Paris. Histoire d'un grand corps de l'État monarchique. XIIIe–XVIIIe siècle*, Paris: Librairie Honoré Champion, 2018.

3 J Le Boindre, *Débats du Parlement pendant la Minorité de Louis XIV*, Paris: Honoré Champion, 1997, vol I, 25.

More than in any other topic, we must emphasise the particular, perhaps even exceptional, character of the Parliament of Paris: its early foundation (in the middle of the thirteenth century); its longevity (until the
French Revolution); the variety and multiplicity of its competences, judicial (civil and criminal jurisdiction – mainly as appellate court, but also as
court of first instance – court of peers and court for high-ranking subjects),
as well as administrative and political; and the sheer size of its jurisdiction
(encompassing between a third and half of the whole kingdom, even in
eighteenth-century France). Its central role in royal French history makes
it a difficult subject which can give rise to discussion and controversy.
Conscious of their limits, the researcher can only move forward from
one hypothesis to another, marking their route with confirmed pieces of
information. The Parliament of Paris is undoubtedly the first, most important and most influential Court of Law of the Kingdom of France, from
the triple viewpoint of politics, judicial action and legal evolution. The
creation of provincial courts from the second half of the fifteenth century
confirmed its primacy during the whole early modern period, while at the
same time providing some relief for the enormous task of a court whose
jurisdiction was as extensive as the royal domain, and as sovereign as the
King's justice.

Among the manifold tasks of the Parliament, its involvement in law making
is one of the most sensitive topics. Scholarship has often steered towards the
political relation between monarchy and parliament on the issues of ruling,
edicts and royal Letters registration. Especially with regard to the *Parlement*
of Paris, the study of legal archives was often inspired by the intention to
analyse and understand the political relationship between parliament and
monarchy, first and foremost for the last two centuries of the Old Regime.
For instance, the trial of the Duke de la Force in 1721, was studied only as
a "scandal" in relation to the analysis of the Regency's economic and financial history following John Law's bankruptcy.[4] As for the Duke d'Aiguillon,

---

4 For gaining access to the sources, see Jean Gilbert's collection of *Conseil secret du Parlement*,
  Arch Nat, U 364 (12 July 1721). Léon Lecestre has listed all the sources and their location: "Le
  Procès du duc de la Force en 1721", (1925) 103 *Revue des questions historiques*, 330 ff. Henri
  Jacques Nompar de Caumont (1675–1726), 5th Duke de La Force, was accused of specula-
  tion and an attempt to create unlawful monopolies. Yet, in this trial, Parliament's impartiality was truly dubious, as this excerpt taken from Jean Gilbert's personal diary demonstrates:
  "*Concernant M le Duc et M le duc de La Force. Décembre 1720 et janvier 1721. Nᵃ qu'il est très
  à remarquer que depuis que Law a été disgracié et sorti de cette ville de Paris, M le Duc et M le
  duc de La Force, ses grands soutiens et ses bons amis, ont eu plusieurs mortifications à son sujet
  et pour tout le mal qu'ils ont fait avec lui qui cause aujourd'hui la perte de tout le royaume par les
  millions qu'ils ont amassés, ainsi qu'un grand nombre de Mississipiens, en prenant tout l'argent*

his momentous lawsuit (1769–1770) was analysed only from its political angle, as predicting the famous Chancelier Maupeou's "*coup*" against the Parliaments (1771).[5] The criminal trials of well-known groups of outlaws, such as Cartouche (between 1721 and 1723) and Nivet (1728–1730), were studied only to depict an anecdotal, romantic history of the 1720s, but are of poor interest – which I deplore – in terms of the understanding of the evolution of the criminal law and proceedings of the time.[6]

The parliamentary place in the French royal government had greatly advanced from its original role. As highlighted by Jean Hilaire,[7] the Parliament of Paris was a powerful means of strengthening Capetian royal power, precisely because of its jurisdictional role. It certainly was the most accomplished royal agent dealing with all forms of independent or self-governing seignories (feudal or ecclesiastic lords, cities, and so on) which progressively came under the king's jurisdiction – a king, who had been supposed to "concede" rights and benefits depending only on his will, his "pleasure". Throughout the fourteenth century, the powerful sovereign found in his Parliament the all-important "representative of his person".[8] From Charles V onwards, however, the king's power had detached itself from the *Parlement*, as well as from any other power, calling on Aristotle to help assist in building the "empire of the king".[9]

The Parliament of Paris played an important part, perhaps even the main role, in the construction of what came to be known as "French Law" between the time of the writing down of the customs[10] and the Great "*Ordonnances*" of the time of Louis XIV and Louis XV. During the medieval period of its activity, this royal institution played a crucial role in mastering the customs that early modern parliament members had not yet forgotten: as Jean Le Nain (1603–1698) highlighted it in his famous *Table*, the court

---

et laissant du papier. Surtout M le duc de La Force, qui était comme premier commis de Law et dressait des arrêts qu'ils projetaient ensemble." (U 364).

5 J Swann, *Politics and the parlement of Paris, 1754–1774*, Cambridge: Cambridge University Press, 1995.

6 Historical and sociological, but not legal, research works are currently ongoing, under the direction of Professor Pascal Bastien, UQAM (Montréal).

7 J Hilaire, *La construction de l'État de droit dans les archives judiciaires de la Cour de France au XIIIe siècle*, Paris: Dalloz, 2011.

8 J Krynen, "*Qu'est-ce qu'un Parlement qui représente le roi'''*, in B Durand and L Mayali (eds), *Excerptiones iuris: Studies in Honor of André Gouron*, Berkeley: Robbins Collection, 2000 [Studies in comparative legal history, vol XV], 353–366.

9 See J Krynen, *L'Empire du roi. Idées et croyances politiques en France XIIIe–XVe siècle*, Paris: Gallimard, 1993.

10 Ordonnance of Montils-lès-Tours, 1454, 125. Cf J-M Carbasse and G Leyte, *L'État royal XIIe–XVIIIe siècle. Une anthologie*, Paris: PUF, 2004, 206–208.

soon supported the king's role as a "guardian of the customs", separating the good and the bad customs. The same Le Nain continued, on the basis of the *Olim* registers:[11] "1261. Customs of Melun removed by the King as bad. It was to prove the violence" (*"Coutumes de Melun ôtée par le Roy comme mauvaise. C'étoit pour prouver les* violences");[12] "1263. A bad custom in Verneuil, favourable to the culprit, removed" (*"Une coutume mauvaise à Verneuil, favorable au coupable, ôtée"*),[13] and so on. This "filtering" process of the customs was the specific mark of the king's legislative power and it was effective through Parliament's action, sealing the king's power in the judicial proceedings. Later on, in the early sixteenth century, despite the multiplication of provincial parliaments since 1443, the Parisian court again played the main role in the writing down (1506–1539) and the speedy reform of customs (in the second half of the sixteenth century), addressing questions and issuing replies to guide the three "Estates" in the local assemblies, and keeping in its "sacred warehouse" of Law – that is, its registers – the definitive an permanent version of customs, which in fact amounted to converting them into Royal and "national" – diverse as it was – French Law. The influence of President Christophe de Thou (1508–1582) in promoting the reformation of the custom of Paris (and others) is all too well known.[14] Even in the subsequent period, as we are about to see, the Parisian judicial authorities retained the chief place in modern law making. Finally, we shall highlight the outstanding work of an enthusiast (a true "fan"), of the Parliament, namely Jean Papon (1505–1590): traditionally, he ranked among the least beloved French jurists of his time, but he has been recently acquitted from such a bad reputation[15] and has regained his true and well-deserved place within the rich panorama of French jurists of the sixteenth century. Despite the criticisms raised in his time by his Collection of Notable Judgments,[16]

---

11 *Olim* is the designation of the first five registers of the court, from the first word of the first one. Cf F Hildesheimer and M Morgat-Bonnet, *Le Parlement de Paris. Histoire d'un grand corps de l'État monarchique. XIIIe–XVIIIe siècle*, Paris: Librairie Honoré Champion, 2018, 74.

12 Archives nationales de France [AN], U 579, fol 694r.

13 Ibid, "A bad custom in Verneuil, favourable to the culprit, removed".

14 F Olivier-Martin, *Histoire de la coutume de la prévôté et vicomté de Paris*, Fontenay-aux-Roses: Presses universitaires de France; Paris: E Leroux, 1922–1930, 3 vols. See also the excellent work of Marie Bassano, *Introduction historique au droit*, Université numérique juridique francophone, available at: https://cours.unjf.fr/repository/coursefilearea/file.php/154/Cours/06_item/support06.pdf (last accessed 25 January 2020).

15 M Delmas-Marty, A Jeammaud and O Clerc (eds), *Droit et humanisme. Autour de Jean Papon, juriste forézien*, Paris: Classiques Garnier, 2015 [Esprit des Lois, esprit des Lettres, vol VI].

16 *Recueil d'arrestz notables des courts souveraines de France, ordonnez par tiltres en vingt-quatre livres*, par M Jehan Papon, Lyon: J de Tournes, 1556.

recent studies have done justice not only to the true legal culture of this unknown "legal writer",[17] but also to his true dedication to the administration of justice. His hard work to educate himself and to "make sure to enter the service of the Commonwealth"[18] led him to overcome particularisms in order to reach a truly comparative and therefore novel vision of the law of his day, paving the way for the Napoleonic codification that would take more than two centuries to happen. Papon undoubtedly wanted to limit himself to what was possible then, and to promote only the goal of "judging similarly in similar cases". Beyond the picturesque and enticing style of Papon's language, the way that he considers the Parliament of Paris as the main source of case law is quite paradigmatic. When he seeks "the agreement of some" (*"l'accordance d'aucuns"*) decisions, without questioning the reason why the different courts of Parliament decide thus, he assigns for himself the role of a "modest collector" (*"simple recollecteur"*), to "proclaim the greatness of the parliament of Paris in all things among all others", a supremacy of the Paris court on which he entertains little doubt and on which he frequently insists. On the philosophical founding principles of neo-Stoicism, taking the Justinian Code as a "reading grid" or frame of reference, Papon has wished for "systematisation" – which the chronology of his work clearly demonstrates – while assuring, especially through his *Three Notaries*,[19] a "historical overview of the Law". His humanism is profoundly Christian, yet on the surface it is a pessimistic vision: with the original sin, man, once the master of all creation, was stripped of all his power and is now "rude in all, *contumax [sic]*[20] and rebellious", "without justice and therefore without faith,[21] without peace, without honour and without being able to enjoy the commodities and the fruit of this human life". This gave rise to systemic inequality and thus the need to submit to the authority of another in a position of more power.

But Christ's salvation being absolute certainty – the source of Papon's profound optimism – there are men who are "prudent, virtuous, wise,

---

17 Cf B Méniel (ed), *Écrivains juristes et juristes écrivains du Moyen âge au siècle des Lumières*, Paris: Classiques Garnier, 2015, 960–963.
18 This and the next quotations are from G Cazals, *La mise en ordre du droit et les enjeux du renouvellement de la pensée juridique moderne*, in M Delmas-Marty, A Jeammaud and O Clerc (eds), *Droit et humanisme. Autour de Jean Papon, juriste forézien*, Paris: Classiques Garnier, 2015, 19, 21–22, 27 and 33, respectively.
19 J Papon, *Les Trois Notaires*, Lyon, 3 vols, 1575–1578.
20 Verbatim, "contumacy". In old French language, synonymous of *"réfractaire"* (i.e. defiant, resistant) (J Nicot, *Thresor de la langue françoyse*, Paris: David Douceur, 1606, available at: https://portail.atilf.fr/dictionnaires/).
21 That is, "unreliable".

courageous, strong, magnanimous": faithfully, those who are kings are established first as legislators with the stated goal of "maintenance of justice and
impediment of ambition".[22] Although not always steady, law and justice as
a whole has somehow improved human laws. In this context, "Roman Law"
seemed to Papon very significant progress. Actually, far from claiming to
"relegate" it, Papon set himself the goal of putting a "French scarf" (une
écharpe Françoise) on Roman Law to complete the law inherited from
Rome by parliamentary "jurisprudence" and royal laws. Such formal discourse places the Parliament in the primary role of a partner in the lawmaking process.

C. ACCESSING THE *PARLEMENT*

When entering the *Parlement de Paris* – that is, its archives – the researcher
opens up both a labyrinthine and an encrypted world, and is dumbstruck:
that is the problem with "parliamentary" studies – although it is neither
the last nor the least problem. It is not the last problem, because the main
sources are the handwritten registers and legal records, papers and manuscripts of the institution and of its "staff", judges, lawyers and court clerks.
Naturally, many of them published books with the aim of handing over the
practice, customs and *forma mentis*, a better locution than "ideology" on
issues concerning the *Ancien Régime* of France, even in the eighteenth
century.[23] That particular library grew during the modern times and has
been used by the first French legal historians since the nineteenth century.
Among the most useful and helpful of these books, mention should be made
of, for instance, the Denisart's "Collection of new decisions";[24] Ferrière's
"New introduction to the Practique"[25] or, from 1740, his "Dictionary of Law
and Practice"; and of course the monumental "*Répertoire*" of Guyot.[26]

---

22 In the original text: *"pour la conservation d'equalité et empeschement de l'ambition"*. *"Equalité"* is
    not a typo for *"égalité"*, but rather the deliberate attempt to combine equality and equity together.
23 F Di Donato, *L'ideologia dei robins nella Francia dei Lumi. Costituzionalismo e assolutismo
    nell'esprienza politico-istituzionale della magistratura di antico regime (1715–1788)*, Roma-
    Napoli: Edizioni Scientifiche Italiane, 2003.
24 J-B Denisart, *Collection de décisions nouvelles et de notions relatives à la jurisprudence présente*,
    6 vols, Paris: Savoye, Leclerc, 1754–1757.
25 Cl-J Ferrière, *Nouvelle introduction à la Pratique, contenant les principaux Termes de Pratique
    & de coutume* (Paris: Chez la Veuve Jean Cochart, 1718, 2 vols, also available at: https://gallica.
    bnf.fr/ark:/12148/bpt6k9685121j).
26 J-N Guyot et al (including P-A Merlin, known as "de Douai"), *Répertoire universel et raisonné
    de jurisprudence civile, criminelle, canonique et bénéficiale*, Paris: J Dorez (-Panckoucke), 1775–
    1783, 64 vols in 8°, soon republished in 17 vols in 4°.

However, as early as the 1860s, it became clear that a serious and reliable story of the judicial system of the ancient French Parliament could not be restricted to exclusively reading the printed sources. It therefore became necessary to deal with the handwritten sources, and in order to do that one would first have to explore the many thousands of registers, parchments, papers and notebooks, among others, sequestered after the end of the sovereign courts of the Old Regime in 1790. Today, this material amounts to around 30,000 registers and cardboard files lying in the Parisian French National Archives site – and this is just for the official records of the *Parlement de Paris*. Faced with a challenge of such proportions, scholars on the history of the Parliament have started with the medieval stocks.[27] From as early as the 1960s, several very good books and theses have come from of this approach. In order to utilise these sources, a new approach was necessary: first, it was the case of Elizabeth Brown and Alfred Soman, then of Sylvie Daubresse and Marie Houllemare (among others) for the sixteenth century. The amount of records grew exponentially since Du Tillet's time (about 1560), yet this has not discouraged a number of brave scholars. However, this has not been the case for the subsequent centuries: as late as 1995, Yves-Marie Bercé sadly lamented the almost total absence of progress on the study of the case law of the Parliament of Paris for the seventeenth and eighteenth centuries. Research for this later period has traditionally focused on the political history of the Parliament of Paris, as its opposition to the last Absolute Kings was suspected to be one of the main causes of the French Revolution.[28]

There were many difficulties to overcome: unreadable handwriting in most of the documents and the time required to study them, coupled with the poor knowledge and mastery of the bygone proceedings in legal proceedings and storing previous decisions, as well as the evolution of both. During the first half of the eighteenth century, the records of the Parliament's annual session amounts to more than fifty series per year, including thousands upon

---

27 Behind the great historians and archivists of the nineteenth century (e.g. F Aubert, H Bastard d'Estang, A-A Beugnot, E Boutaric, E Fayard, and so on), the most important work about *Parlement de Paris*, based on official records, has been set going about medieval period (cf *Centre d'Etude d'Histoire Juridique* members' bibliography, http://bibliparl.huma-num.fr: Auzary-Schmaltz, Bloch, Carbasse, Carbonnières, Hilaire, Metman, Paschel, Pillet and, the CEHJ founder (1953–1954), Pierre-Clément Timbal). The list is hardly exhaustive.

28 A common thread of most of French historical literature since Jules Flammermont and Esnest Glasson, up to Jean Egret, this point of view has obtained a very positive, hard impetus from the English historical school (see W Doyle, A Moote, A Hamscher, J Hardman, J Hardy, J Rogister, J H Shennan, B Stone and J Swann, among others).

thousands of deeds in many different side collections. In 1998 I suggested clearing a path through this maze, beginning with the "little" set of registers and papers[29] of the General Prosecutor of the King, because most of the proceedings had to pass through the public prosecution. I also argued that it was better to tackle the *Parliament* archival problems by relying on contemporary duplicates, memories and recollections, which were one of the first priorities of the Parliament officers. Not only magistrates, but also many ministers, secretaries of state and king's councillors got into the habit of expecting such copy-work from clerks of the Parliament. This proved particularly to be the case of a humble man – who remained almost anonymous even up to our own time – known as the clerk "Delisle", and who was in fact the "main secretary" of the chief civil clerk Nicolas Dongois, and then of his successor and grandson Roger François Gilbert de Voisins. Luckily, in 2010–2011, I was able to identify him as Jean Gilbert, a wine-grower's son, of the surname Delisle, not to be confused with his boss's surname. The impressive collection of his "registers of the *Parlement*" that his last will and testament (1744) mention as a legacy in favour of Roger François Gilbert de Voisins, has remained almost entirely unused for more than two centuries.

D. CASE LAW AND LEGAL PRECEDENT AS FACTORS OF LEGAL DEVELOPMENT

This subject goes to the core of the legislative functions of the Parliament of Paris. In the French kingdom, what were the legal sources of verdict, sentence and ruling? The French legal system was not based on the strength of judicial precedents. French law courts did not make decisions based on a *stare decisis* principle, but precisely according to their "interpretation" of the customs.

It is not possible here to give a full-scale account of all the multifaceted and complex legal sources of pre-Revolutionary France. However, mention should at least be made of customary law (the successor of the mixture of Roman law and the Germanic traditions of the Merovingian and Carolingian legal melting pots), oral customs, canon law, royal ruling, and so on. During the period from the thirteenth to fifteenth century, French law displayed all its intricacies – the royal government's precocious leadership in the law

---

29 A collection of conclusions, that is, 184 registers (Arch Nat, X^{1A} 8856, November 2011–November 1612, to X^{1A} 9041, from 17 December 1787–22 June 1790) and six boxes of official record papers; a stock of ten boxes of requests, always on paper.

making, first leaning on clerics and legists of the king's council, and soon on *Parlement* itself. After the strengthening of the monarchy under King François I and his son, and, even further, after the "establishment of the State"[30] under Henry IV and his successors, little doubt was left regarding the increase of the king's powers in the setting up (or, at least, the standardisation) of what, since 1679, has been termed "French Law". Jean Bodin had clearly described the legislative power of the king, but the primary application of that power is to be found in legal procedure, both civil and criminal. All legal courts, including parliaments and sovereign courts, had to apply the royal law and to resort to the king's council in case of doubt regarding its meaning and interpretation – they were not to refer to their own previous cases. This, at least, was the express requirement of one of the most important articles of the Civil Order of 1667. Yet it proved insufficient to end what has since been named "the quarrel of the interpretation",[31] especially among parliaments. Even removed from the royal legislative work during Colbert's years (1664–1683), the Parliament of Paris kept its discreet but traditional role in law making, if only by pronouncing its *"arrêts de règlement"* ("judgments of regulation"), which were a minimalist form of legislative activity.[32] Here, the main role of the General Prosecutor's department becomes evident, as well as the influence of its major leading figures: first, the king's General Prosecutor, a position kept by Jean et Jacques de La Guesle (1570–1614), Mathieu Molé (1614–1641), Achille II and III de Harlay (1661–1689); later, Henri François d'Aguesseau (1700–1717), and then famously, Joly de Fleurys, father, son and nephews (from 1717 to the end of the Parliament). As *"avocat général du roi"* (Assistant Public Prosecutor) mention should be made of the Talons, father and son (Omer and Denis), at the end of the seventeenth century, as well as of the Gilberts (de Voisins) during the reign of Louis XV. Finally, collaborating with the *"Parquet"*, as did the First President or presidents *à mortier* of the court, besides Molé or Harlay, it is

---

30 According to the proper terms of Henry IV: "Ce que j'en ai fait est pour le bien de la paix. Je l'ai faite au dehors, je la veux au-dedans. Vous me devez obéir, quand il n'y aurait autre considération que de ma qualité et de l'obligation que m'ont tous mes sujets . . . Si l'obéissance était due à mes prédécesseurs, il m'est dû autant ou plus de dévotion, *d'autant que j'ai établi l'État*, Dieu m'ayant choisi pour me mettre au royaume qui est mien par héritage et par acquisition." (7 January 1599). On the creation of the concept of French State, see J B Collins, *The State in Early Modern France*, revised edn, Cambridge: Cambridge University Press, 2009; in French, *La Monarchie républicaine. Etat et société dans la France modern*, Paris: Odile Jacob, 2016.
31 Cf J Krynen, *L'idéologie de la magistrature ancienne*, Paris: Gallimard, 2009, 139–190.
32 Cf Ph Payen, *Les arrêts de règlement du Parlement de Paris au XVIIIe siècle. Dimension et doctrine*, Paris: PUF, 1997; and *La physiologie de l'arrêt de règlement du Parlement de Paris au XVIIIe siècle*, Paris: PUF, 1999.

important to highlight the top role of Bellièvre and Lamoignon under Louis XIII and Louis XIV, and of Portail under Louis XV. While analysing requests and submissions (or *"conclusions"*) of the Public Prosecutor's department (French National Archives) with the amazing collection of documents of Joly de Fleurys' family (*Bibliothèque nationale de France*), I discovered that the General Prosecutor was the true engine of law making between the royal government (especially the royal council) and the sovereign court of the king's justice.[33] The role of the Public Prosecutor, although it did not appear in the decisions themselves, helped to promote legal development just as the Crown had wished.

As for the different chambers of the *Parlement* themselves, they had full knowledge of the parliamentary rights: on 5 April 1690, in the *Mercuriales* session,[34] a checklist of the necessary measures concerning the making of the law was deliberated on and voted for, with the clear purpose fighting the "variety" of (i.e. inconsistencies within) case law:

> As to the second [article] containing that, when there are questions established by judgments of the Great Chamber, *Tournelle* and *Enquêtes*, *which may serve as law in the future*, the Chairmen and Rapporteurs will be invited to write *le fait et les moyens* in accordance with questions of law or of custom, and the real circumstances of the fact that brought the trial about, and then to make the effort to hand over the statements that they will have drawn up, together with the judgment, in the hands of the Proctor-General of the King, so that by his ministry and his care such judgments can be printed and given to the public with the clarity of the [legal] maxims that they are establishing. It was found good.[35]

Nevertheless, most of the legal activity of *arrêts de règlement* does not concern the substantive law, but only what we call *"droit processual"*; namely, procedural rules, also judiciary administration, civil service and urban polic-

---

33 Ibid. See also, I Storez-Brancourt, "Dans l'ombre de Messieurs les gens du Roi: le monde des substituts", in J-M Carbasse (ed), *Histoire du parquet*, Paris: PUF, 2000, 157–204; D Feutry, *Plumes de fer et robes de papier. Logiques institutionnelles et pratiques politiquesdu parlement de Parisau XVIIIe siècle (1515–1790)*, Institut universitaire Varenne, 2013.

34 *Mercuriales* were sessions which took place on the first Wednesday after Saint Martin's Day and after Easter, when the First President and one of the Prosecutor Department's magistracy reminded the officers to do their job well, and read again the main edicts about judiciary ethics.

35 Arch nat U 338, fols 60r–61r: Prosecutor *"Sur le second (article) contenant que lorsqu'il y aura des questions jugées par des arrêts de la Grand Chambre, de la tournelle et des chambres des Enquêtes qui peuvent servir de loi à l'avenir, Mrs les présidents et les rapporteurs seront invités de faire rédiger par écrit le fait et les moyens suivant les questions de droit ou de coutume et les véritables circonstances du fait qui ont donné lieu au procès, et de prendre ensuite la peine de remettre les mémoires qu'ils en auront dressé, avec l'arrêt, entre les mains du procureur général du Roi afin que par son ministère et ses soins lesdits arrêts puissent être imprimés et donnés au public dans la pureté des maximes qui y sont établies. Il a été trouvé bon".* (emphasis added).

ing. For instance, one of the extracts copied by Jean Gilbert de L'Isle[36] consisted of the prohibition to inferior judges to give execution to sentences apart from the cases established by law. When Denis Talon had the floor, he denounced the frequent violation of this prohibition, saying:

> that, even though the old and modern ruling, and especially that of [1667], determined in which case [this should happen], many inferior and subordinate[37] judges, abusing the power entrusted to them, very often order that their final sentences shall be carried out although they are neither summary matters, nor on the title of the edict of the *"présidiaux"*[38] or in police matters, and they do not pronounce the execution of a contract or a judgment, the effect of which is not suspended by an appeal.

The Court of *Parlement* agreed with Talon's advice, settling on "when it will be pronounced provisional execution of a verdict, cause and motivation might be inserted into the judgment", including interlocutory judgments.

In our current understanding of case law in French courts, we must declare ourselves at a loss. If the highest magistrates – the chancellors themselves – still, in the eighteenth century, felt sorry about the *"contrariétés"* of jurisprudence, how then, three centuries on, can we unravel what is obviously an inextricable skein? Until the end of the *Ancien Régime*, the ministry had no other resources but to try to discover, through repeated inquiries, a reality that escaped it.[39] One of the most exemplary studies recently carried out concerns the officers' law and the civil jurisprudence of the intrafamilial transmission of the offices of justice: by crossing, in a virtuous way, the notaries' sources and the judgments of the Parliament of Paris, Robert Descimon and Simone Geoffroy-Poisson sketched out "the legal construction of a patrimonial system of the office" after 1604.[40]

These authors reveal several important things for our topic. First, as

---

36 Arch nat U 338, fols 55r–56r, 7 December 1689: ["*Deffenses aux juges du ressort de prononcer l'execution de leurs jugemens non obstant l'appel aux cas qui ne sont pas de l'ordonnance*"].

37 The complicated judicial organisation distinguished, under sovereign courts, royal justices (*inférieures*) and conceded justices (*subalternes*), mainly seigniorial ones.

38 The *"présidiales"* courts had been set up by Henry II, between 1552 and 1557, in the aim of discharging parliaments about appeal of minor cases. Cf C Blanquie, *Les présidiaux de Richelieu. Justice et vénalité (1630–1642)*, Paris: Editions Christian, 2000; Id *Les présidiaux de Daguesseau*, Paris: Publisud, 2004.

39 Cf F Leromain, *Monarchie administrative et justice criminelle au XVIIIe siècle. Les "états des crimes dignes de mort ou de peines afflictives" (1733–1790)*, unpublished doctoral dissertation, University of Strasbourg, 2017.

40 Cf R Descimon and S Geoffroy-Poisson, "La construction juridique d'un système patrimonial de l'office. Une affaire de patrilignagne et de genre", in R Descimon and É Haddad (eds), *Épreuves de noblesse. Les expériences nobiliaires de la haute robe parisienne (XVIe–XVIIIe siècle)*, Paris: Les Belles Lettres, 2010, 47–59.

the venal office did not exist in 1610 during the time of the writing of the *Coutume de Paris*, the case law established by a judgment of the Parliament in 1557 served as the only basis for drafting the unique article that concerns offices (article 95) in the Reformed Custom of 1580.[41] Then, given the difficulty of the doctrine in defining the office in its reality of "goods" possibly entering the trade, "the case law fills, by successive '*bricolages*' ('kludges'), the legal vacuum of the royal legislation and the custom".[42] There are several opportunities for doubt and of wavering, and therfore of inconsistencies, discrepancies and wrongs. Growing within the French and Cartesian classic mind was an aspiration to rationalise justice and law, in which these many "*contrariétés*", in all sectors of private law, were no longer tolerated.

Year after year, *Mercuriales*' reports highlighted the primary goal of the administration of justice: the decrease in number and length of lawsuits, speedier criminal trials and, in particular, reducing the inconsistencies in legal precedents so as to promote "*une jurisprudence uniforme*".[43] It is here that we find the origin of d'Aguesseau's projects. From his handwritten papers as a General Prosecutor (1700–1717) to his great work of legislation as a Chancellor (1717–1750), Henri François d'Aguesseau is exemplary of back-and-forth collaboration between the *Parlement* and the Chancery. His great, albeit incomplete, attempts at reforming judicial administration[44] are well known: this is the part of his enormous work that built, if not his reputation in his own time, but his fame among future generations. Two of the main dissertations of d'Aguesseau's are available to us today: a *Mémoire sur les Vues générales que l'on peut avoir pour la Réformation de la Justice* (1727), often called "the report of Fresnes", which d'Aguesseau wrote during his exile in his castle of Fresnes (near Meaux); and "*Idée Générale ou Plan abrégé de l'usage que l'on pourroit faire des Estats envoyés par les Intendans pour former un nouvel arrangement des Sièges ordinaires de Judicature*" (1742–1743).[45] The first gives a clear idea of the whole of d'Aguesseau's plan, which was no less than "to reform the old laws, to make new ones, and to bring together the one and the other in a single body of law".[46] If he did

41 Ibid, 50.
42 Ibid.
43 Arch nat U 338, fol 104r, 27 April 1691.
44 It was partial because he was cautious, but it was also incomplete because of a lack of time: "the word 'unfinishable' ('*inachevable*') is a turn of phrase which is so mine ('*si propre*') and that I so usually need", he wrote, in a saddened state, in a letter to a friend.
45 Cf C Blanquie, *Les présidiaux de Daguesseau*, 88–89.
46 Cf I Storez, *Le chancelier Henri François d'Aguesseau (1668–1751). Monarchiste et liberal*, Paris: Publisud, 1996, 295.

not achieve his ambitious goal – did he really want it? He was eminently a conservative![47] – d'Aguesseau did his best to convince the whole community of judges of his intentions:

> The essential thing is that the purity of the principles and the true sense of the whole new law is preserved in such a law . . . Each *Parlement* needs to give up its own opinions for the sake of the great good of legal unity and uniformity of case law.[48]

What part did d'Aguesseau envisage for case law in his – quite prophetic – project? Beginning in 1728, and continuing until his resignation in 1750, his approach clarified the role that he envisaged for the parliaments of the whole kingdom: first and foremost was collaboration between the courts and the government in his plan of reformation of the whole law, which he subdivided into coherent parts (including donations; testaments; forgery; registers of births, marriages and deaths; and handover of possession by "*substitution*") on the basis of the solutions devised by the parliaments in their long judicial experience regarding many difficult issues. The administrative correspondence of d'Aguesseau sheds light on his steady attention to promote normative solutions and, in so doing, leaning towards the custom of Paris as an instrument of legal harmonisation.

In the absence of legal unity – which could have been achieved only with codification – Chancellor d'Aguesseau made an energetic attempt at the harmonisation of case law itself, follwoing the example of others such as President Brisson[49] or First President de Lamoignon.[50] Even though he did not hesitate to bring about important reforms within the private law (regarding donations in 1731 and testaments in 1735, among others), he knew that he had to limit his plans to discrete parts of the law, and that he could not

---

47 As D'Aguesseau wrote: "tout changement est dangereux et c'est une grande présomption que celle de ceux qui ne craignent jamais d'innover" (BnF, MS fr 6821, fol 100r), which may be translated as: "any change is dangerous and it is a great presumption that of those who never fear to innovate".

48 "*L'essentiel est que la pureté des principes et le véritable esprit du droit nouveau soient bien conservés dans une pareille loi . . . Il faut que chaque parlement sacrifie ses opinions particulières au grand bien de l'unité de la loi et de l'uniformité de la jurisprudence.*" (D'Aguesseau, *Correspondance officielle*, in Id, *Œuvres complètes*, ed J-M Pardessus, Paris: Fantin et Compagnie Paris, 1819, vol XII, p 374.

49 Barnabé Brisson (1511–1591) – first barrister, then *avocat général*, then President *à mortier* at the Parliament of Paris, one of the most learned jurists of his time – is known as the author of the *Code du Roy Henry III, roy de France et de Pologne*, Lyon: pour les frères de Gabiano, 1593, that is a compilation whose headlines demonstrate that it is a question of justice order, not of an attempt to codify private law.

50 Guillaume 1er de Lamoignon (1617–1677). Cf J-L Thireau, "Les Arrêtés de Guillaume de Lamoignon: une œuvre de codification du droit français?" (2004) 39(1) *Droits*, 53–68.

reach his aim without a large consultation process with each parliament, starting with that of Paris – keen as he was to maintain the "unbeatable" superiority of its custom.[51] In so doing, he based his work both on his own experience and on the strength of the whole *Parlement* in promoting, on a case-by-case basis, a coherent interpretation of the custom in the case law.

Despite all this, it is important not to over-emphasise the actual role of case law in the making of law. Indeed, the best example regarding the influence of case law in law making under d'Aguesseau works *a contrario*. The late Henri Regnault, one of the main (if not *the* main) scholars of d'Aguesseau, related the following facts at the beginning of the second volume of his doctoral thesis:[52] on 3 April 1699, while d'Aguesseau was still Assistant Public Prosecutor, taking the floor in an important civil lawsuit in front of the Parliament of Paris, he argued that the formalities required by article 422 of the Custom of Normandy should not be applied on the basis of the place where the property was (the *lex rei sitae*), but rather according to one's personal status. As is well known, local customs applied to every person born within the territory where the custom applied, wherever this person could live and own a property. Thus, his opinion was followed by the court. The case focused on the validity of a legacy of some land in Normandy, but performed by the Marquess of Fervacques, who was personally under the Custom of Paris. In summary, Fervacques was allowed to bequeath some land in Normandy to his heir without complying with the formalities of article 422 of the Custom of Normandy, as he was under Paris custom. D'Aguesseau then confirmed this legacy in accordance with the Custom of Paris. But, in contrast to that, when drafting article 74 of the 1735 law on wills and testaments, he ultimately decided for the *lex rei sitae*. There, d'Aguesseau clearly expressed the pre-eminence of royal orthodoxy in the interpretation of the courts' case law, even of that of a parliament: "*Si veut le Roy, si veut la Loy*" ("what the King wants, the law also wants"). At a time in which legislative and judiciary powers were barely distinguished, for d'Aguesseau the king's will had to prevail over the Parliament – and this despite his personal sympathies for the Parliament.

The special case of forgery, which came to the fore at the beginning of the eighteenth century (about 1710), is also important in highlighting the

51 See the last research of C Jallamion, "D'Aguesseau et l'unification du droit privé. La réception de ses ordonnances en Languedoc", *D'Aguesseau, un illustre inconnu?* (Conference "Les Entretiens d'Aguesseau", 6 December 2018, University of Limoges, PULIM), forthcoming.

52 H Regnault, *Les Ordonnances civiles du Chancelier d'Aguesseau. Les testaments et l'Ordonnance de 1735*, Paris: PUF, 1965 (first edn Liège, 1938), 13–16.

contribution of the Parliament of Paris to the reformation of the applicable rules in 1737 (*Ordonnance sur le faux*) – the handwritten requests box of 1740 still contains the most important (and longest) document of that kind, precisely devoted to forgery.[53] This document demonstrates that the Office of the Public Prosecutor still favoured the authority of the Crown and of the Chancellor in the making of the law.

The importance of the role played by parliaments in the evolution of the law can be appreciated by using Jean Gilbert's journal as a guide through the archives of the Parliament. Let us look at one of the many examples that can be given: on 22 February 1743,[54] Gilbert, after transcribing some judges and officers' receipting records or royal Letters recordings, wrote that the First President Louis III Le Peletier, marquis of Rosambo, told the company that the *Messieurs* (the judges) of the Fifth Chamber of *Enquêtes* had come to his home, into the house of the *Bailliage*, to discuss two lawsuits that were ready for judgment:

> And, since it was a question of setting a shared legal precedent in all the Chambers, he proposed to the Gentlemen that they should be good enough to send some deputies from each Chamber to his house, in the usual way, on the first Monday of Lent, so as to reconcile between them what could be done on this occasion, to be then deliberated by all the Chambers together, as is customarily done to reach to a decision establishing a same rule for all the Chambers. With the Gentlemen's approval, the court was adjourned.[55]

So, with the aim of deciding the same case by widespread consent in the general assembly of the Parliament, the judges organised a "conference" with delegations of each chamber of the court. In clumsy writing, the next leaf (also dated 22 February 1743) explains that this case concerned a question of *"franc aleu"*[56] according to the Custom of Vitry.[57]

What has been said so far demonstrates that the lawyers referred to the case law of the courts, and that the judges, when faced with conflicting legal precedents, saw the need for uniform conduct. This need was clearly perceived by the vast majority of the judiciary, which expressed a clear

---

53 Arch nat X^{2B} 1322 (17 June 1740).
54 Arch Nat, U 394 (without pagination).
55 Ibid: *"Et comme il s'agissoit d'établir une mesme jurisprudence dans toutes les chambres, il a proposé à Messieurs à ce sujet de vouloir bien se rendre chez luy par députéz de chacune des chambres en la manière ordinaire, le premier lundy de caresme, pour concilier entre eux ce qui peut estre fait en cette occasion pour ensuite en estre délibéré toutes les chambres assemblées, ainsi qu'il est accoutumé faire pour parvenir à un règlement qui établisse une mesme jurisprudence dans toutes les chambres. Ce que Messieurs ayant approuvé, la cour s'est levée."*
56 A *"franc aleu"* was a property free of all sorts of domination.
57 See appendix for transcript of the De L'Isle's copy of the legal official record.

consensus for a cautious but unavoidable progress towards the codification of the French private law.

APPENDIX

Archives nationales de France, U 394
Concernant la Coutume de Vitry
Du vendredy 22 février 1743. Du matin
Ce jour, toutes les chambres assemblées, après l'enregistrement des Lettres de dispense d'âge et de service obtenües par Me Jean François Jolly de Fleury, conseiller en la cour, pour estre receû en l'état et office de conseiller du Roy, Maître des requêtes; des Lettres de dispense d'âge obtenues par Me Philippe Bellanger, conseiller en la cour, et par Me Estienne Berthelot aussi conseiller en la cour, pour avoir voix délibérative, et d'autres Lettres de dispense d'âge obtenües par Me Jean-Baptiste Claude de Bragelongne, advocat en la cour, pour estre receû en l'état et office de conseiller lay en lad cour, dont arrests particuliers se trouveront au registre de ce jour; M le PP a dit que Mr Couturier, président en la 5e chambre des enquestes, estant venû avec Mr de Chavannes, conseiller en la mesme chambre, luy communiquer la peine où se trouvoient Messieurs de la mesme chambre au sujet d'un procès prest à juger et dans lequel les parties se fondoient de part et d'autre sur l'allodialité ou non allodialité de la Coutume de Vitry; qu'elles raportoient chacune en leur faveur des arrests qu'elles prétendoient avoir jugé la question d'une manière toute opposée; que toute la chambre souhaiteroit ardemment que la compagnie eût pris avant le jugement de cette affaire un sentiment uniforme et qu'il pût estre décidé si la Coutume de Vitry doit estre considérée comme une coutume de franc aleu, ou rangée au nombre de celles dans lesquelles la maxime "nulle terre sans seigneur" est généralement reconnue. Que ces Messieurs l'avoient invité à en parler à la première assemblée des chambres pour scavoir de la compagnie les mesures qu'elle jugeoit à propos de prendre pour fixer la jurisprudence d'une manière certaine sur un objet si important. Mr le PP a adjouté qu'il profitoit de celle assemblée pour rendre compte à la compagnie des veües de Messieurs de la 5e chambre et luy proposer les voyes usitées en semblable occasions, dont les registres fournissent plusieurs exemples. Que si Messieurs jugeoient à propos, on pourroit députer de toutes les chambres pour s'assembler en l'hostel du Baillage, et y agiter avec les Gens du Roy qui y seroient appelez, les différens partis que l'on pourroit prendre à ce sujet, pour ensuite ces différens avis raportéz par Mrs les députéz, chacuns en leurs chambres, estre pris par les chambres

assemblées un party définitif. Messieurs ont approuvé la proposition faite par M le PP et il a esté arresté qu'il seroit convoqué deux députéz de chacune chambre des enquestes et requestes pour, avec Mrs les députéz de la Grand chambre et Mrs ces présidens de la cour, estre examiné qu'elles seroient les voyes les plus convenables pour parvenir à réunir toute la compagnie à une mesme façon de penser, et éviter à l'avenir toute diversité d'arrests au sujet de l'allodialité ou non allodialité de la Coutume de Vitry. Et que les Gens du Roy se trouveroient à cette assemblée en la manière accoutumée. Veu.
[signed] *Le Peletier*

11 Legal Fragmentation in the Dutch Republic During the Seventeenth and Eighteenth Centuries

Philip Thomas

A. INTRODUCTION

In order to discuss the forensic practice of the Dutch Republic, it is necessary to describe the birth and particular character of this state,[1] which origi-

---

1 For an excellent and detailed exposition of the history of the Low Countries during the sixteenth century, see Jane de Iongh's trilogy *Regentessen der Nederlanden: De Hertogin, Margaretha van*

nated as a result of the Dutch rebellion and became the second republic in Western Europe. Moreover, this wealthy little corner of the continent developed into a world power during the seventeenth century.[2] However, the confederate character of the Dutch state and the concomitant particularism, explain the rather limited jurisdiction of the "highest" court. Furthermore, there are few collections of decisions as the result of the practice of not motivating decisions and the secrecy of *in camera* deliberations.

In this chapter the composition of and appointment to the *Hoge Raad* will be examined. Thereafter, the birth and development of Dutch law will be illustrated by referring to Grotius as a precursor to a new paradigm and Voet as a representative of the legal tradition. On the basis of the notes of the acerbic president van Bijnkershoek, a puzzling case decided in the *Hoge Raad* will be analysed. The lectures of van der Keessel on the *Introduction* of Grotius will be mentioned as representing the end of an era.

In conclusion it will be submitted that analysis of the sparse Dutch decisions and multitude of opinions provide no indication of the advent of modern legal science, but shows that the decentralised structure of the Dutch republic was counter-productive to legal harmonisation. This confirms the conservative character of legal practice and the role of topical legal argumentation in non-codified legal systems and accusatorial procedure.

B. THE DUTCH STATE

The Low Countries were a small but prosperous corner of the Habsburg empire. Rich farmland alternated with towns, in which industry and trade were active, and fishing and maritime transport and trade both on sea and rivers provided another source of income. During the late Middle Ages, the towns acquired a degree of autonomy, particularly in jurisdiction, against one-off tax levies. Attempts at centralisation by the Hasburg rulers – increasing taxation and religious problems[3] – fermented into armed rebellion, which

---

Oostenrijk, Hertogin van Savooie 1480–1530; De Koninging, Maria van Hongarije, landvoogdes der Nederlanden 1505 1558; Madama, Margarethu van Oostenrijk, Hertogin van Parma en Piacenza 1522–1586, 3 vols, reprint, Amsterdam: Querido, 1981.

2 P J Thomas, "Colonial policy of the Dutch republic" (2015) 2 *Iura and Legal systems*, B(7), 92–102. Available at: www.rivistagiuridica.unisa.it.

3 Hugo Grotius, *De Jure Praedae Commentarius*, Hagae Comitum: apud Martinum Nijhoff, 1868, cap 11 and 13; G Parker, *The Dutch Revolt*, London: Penguin, 1979, 68–90; J and A Romein, *De lage landen bij de zee*, Amsterdam; E M Querido's Uitgeverij B V, 1979, 223–224.

led in turn to the Act of Abjuration in 1581[4] and was followed by the declaration of the Dutch Republic in 1588.

This republic was aptly described as the United States of the Netherlands. It was a confederate state in which each "province" had its own legal system; and within the individual provinces, towns and countryside had their own statutes and customs,[5] Roman law came to be accepted as a subsidiary system in varying degrees as the socio-economic development of the provinces differed. The maritime and commercial province of Holland was the wealthiest; its legal system the most developed and its higher courts – the *Hof van Holland* and the *Hoge Raad* – manned by qualified jurists. In consequence, this chapter discusses the law of Holland and not the other provinces. Within this jurisdiction, four jurists representing the different faces and phases of Dutch law – Grotius, Voet, van Bijnkershoek and van der Keessel – will be discussed.

C. ESTABLISHMENT AND FUNCTIONING OF THE *HOGE RAAD*, THE SUPREME COURT OF HOLLAND, ZEELAND AND WEST-FRIESLAND

Established in 1582 when the Great Council of Mechelen[6] fell away as the court of appeal after the abjuration of Philip II, the province of Holland created the *Hoge Raad* as a court of appeal and revision. In 1587, Zeeland accepted the jurisdiction of this court and eventually became entitled to appoint three of its ten judges.[7] The *"Instructie"* of 1582[8] delineated the

---

4 For a contemporary justification, see Grotius, *De Jure Praedae*, cap 11 and 13; further, H M Punt, *Het vennootschapsrecht van Holland, Zeeland en West-Friesland. Het vennootschapsrecht van Holland, Zeeland en West-Friesland in de rechtspraak van den Hoge Raad van Holland, Zeeland en West-Friesland*, Deventer: Kluwer, 2010, 4. Available at https://openaccess.leidenuniv.nl/handle/1887/16178 (last accessed 27 January 2020).

5 Ibid, 3–4.

6 For this court, see L Th Maes, "Rol en betekenis van de Grote Raad van Mechelen voor de Nederlanden", (1974) 78 *Neerlandia*, 4–48; Punt, *Het vennootschapsrecht van Holland*, 6.

7 L van Poelgeest, "De raadsheren van de Hoge Raad van Holland, Zeeland en West-Friesland in de achttiende eeuw", (1988) 103 *Bijdragen en Mededelingen betreffende de Geschiedenis der Nederlanden/Low Countries Historical Review Review*, 20–51, at 22. In terms of the agreement of 1587, Zeeland appointed two judges. However, a "Nader Tractaet" of 1596 raised this number to three.

8 *Groot Placaet-boeck vervattende de Placaten, Ordonnantien ende Edicten van de Staten Generael der Vereenigdhe Nederlanden ende Heeren Staten van Hollandt ende West-Vriesland mitsgaders van de Heeren Staten van Zeelandt*, (hereinafter, GPB), 9 vols and index, C Cau, S van Leeuwen, Scheltus (J, P and I), D Lulius and J van der Linden, Amsterdam: Johannes Allart, 1658–1796, vol II, 790–838, Ordonnantie en Instructie vanden Hooge Raadt van Appel (hereinafter, *"Instructie"*); J Ph de Mónte ver Loren, J E Spruit, *Hoofdlijnen uit de ontwik-*

jurisdiction of this court of appeal, which also acted as court of first instance
for maritime matters, as they did not fall within the jurisdiction of the five
colleges of admiralty.[9] The possibility of appeal was an important safeguard
for the inhabitants of the countryside, where the quality of the courts of first
instance, the colleges of bailiffs (*dijkgraven*) and the councils of *heemraden*,
was limited.[10] However, the fact that there were two courts of appeal –
namely, the *Hof van Holland* and the *Hoge Raad* – made the legal process
costly and slow. Moreover, citizens of municipalities faced a number of hur-
dles to reach the *Hoge Raad*. A resolution of 1591 by the States of Holland
made appeal in criminal cases virtually impossible.[11] The courts also had to
send complaints against cities to the municipal council first.[12] Finally, a resolution of 1674 excluded jurisdiction in political affairs.[13] All these confines on
when the *Hoge Raad* could be utilised, limited the number of cases heard.

In Holland the judges were appointed by the provincial states[14] from a list
of the candidates nominated by the court itself. In Zeeland a rotating system
applied[15] and Goes, Tholen or Vlissingen appointed the vacancies in the
Hoge Raad. In practice, this resulted in the selling of the Zeeland positions,
where for example van Bijnkershoek paid 21,000 florins to the city Tholen.[16]
His son-in-law, Willem Pauw, who was born in Holland, paid 28,000 florins

keling der rechterlijke organisatie in de Noordelijke Nederlanden tot de Bataafse omwenteling,
Deventer: Kluwer, 2000, 244, mention that this "Instructie" was based on the instruction of the
Council of Mechelen of 1559.

9 GPB, II, 792–793 (ss 18–23); Punt, *Het vennootschapsrecht van Holland*, 7; H R Hahlo
and E Kahn, *The South African Legal System and its Background*, Cape Town-Wynberg-
Johannesburg: Juta, 1973, 532, 542–543. The five "collegien van admiraliteit" were De Maze
(Rotterdam), Amsterdam, Friesland (Dokkum from 1645 Harlingen), Zeeland (Middelburg),
Noorderkwartier (Hoorn en Enkhuizen).

10 Van Bijnkershoek compared the aptitude for jurisdiction of the members of these courts to that
of the *asinus ad lyram*; L van Poelgeest, "De raadsheren van de Hoge Raad", 47. For further
detail see, Punt, *Het vennootschapsrecht van Holland*, 5.

11 GPB II, 1061, Resolutie bij welcken die vanden Hoven verboden wort, geen provisie te ver-
leenen tegen Crimineele Sententien der Steden (19 September 1691); van Poelgeest, "De
raadsheren van de Hoge Raad van Holland", 47.

12 Ibid.

13 GPB III, 495, n 29, *Resolutie van de Staten van Holland ende West-Vriesland houdende dat de
Hoven van Justitie haar geen saacken sullen aenmatigen de Policie betreffende*; and 669, n 45
(idem); van Poelgeest, "De raadsheren van de Hoge Raad van Holland", ibid.

14 This body consists of the eighteen voting cities and the body representing the nobility. Punt, *Het
vennootschapsrecht van Holland*, 16–20.

15 A Resolution of the State of Zeeland of 1708, the *instrumentum pacis*, delegated the appointment to the six cities of Zeeland. The states made the formal appointments, but in practice the
judgeships were sold to the highest bidder. In reality Middelburg, Veere and Zierikzee chose the
judges for the Hof van Holland and Zeeland. Van Poelgeest, "De raadsheren van de Hoge Raad
van Holland", 29.

16 Ibid, 31.

for the position of *pensionaris* of Vlissingen to qualify for the Zeeland seat.[17] The judges received 2,550 florins and the president 4,200 florins per year. Various emoluments connected with the office of course helped, but most judges had additional income from private means. All judges had studied law and nearly two thirds held doctorates from Leiden. All judges had previously practised as advocates, held office in municipalities or been members of a city council. It is remarkable that no member of the *Hoge Raad*, with the exception of Ockers,[18] had been a judge in the *Hof van Holland* or a law professor.[19] The majority of the judges came from the upper classes and amongst the few *homines novi*, van Bijnkershoek[20] and his son-in-law Pauw,[21] deserve special mention.

The *Instructie* of 1582 imposed secrecy on the decision-making process.[22] The underlying principle was collegial decision making, in other words, to the outside world the fiction was propagated that the court was unanimous; to consolidate this illusion the decisions were not motivated, which made contestation difficult.[23] In consequence, few collections of decisions that were published, the *Observationes* of Neostadius,[24] Coren[25] and

17 Ibid.
18 Punt, *Het vennootschapsrecht van Holland*, 28.
19 Van Poelgeest, "De raadsheren van de Hoge Raad van Holland", 26 gives as reason that most professors were born outside the two provinces as well as the distance between academia and legal practice.
20 Son of a sailmaker, see https://encyclopedievanzeeland.nl/Cornelis_Van_Bijnkershoek (last accessed 31 January 2020).
21 Son of a journalist, van Poelgeest, "De raadsheren van de Hoge Raad van Holland", 24.
22 GPB II, 791 and 797 (ss 12 and 48).
23 A J B Sirks, "Sed verum est, sententias numerari, non ponderari (Cornelius van Bijnkershoek, *Observationes Tumultuariae* 2628 and 2678)", in R van den Bergh et al (eds), *Ex iusta causa traditum. Essays in honour of Eric H Pool*, (2005) *Fundamina* (editio specialis), 285–303, at 295, text and note 37; J E de Mónte ver Loren and J E Spruit, *Hoofdlijnen uit de ontwikkeling der rechterlijke organisatie in de Noordelijke Nederlanden tot de Bataafse omwenteling*, Deventer: Kluwer 1982, 310; Punt, *Het vennootschapsrecht van Holland*, 10.
24 Cornelius Neostadius (Cornelis Mathiasz van Nieustad, 1549–1606) was the first professor of law at Leiden and member of the *Hoge Raad* from 1584–1606. He is incorrectly considered to have authored the *Curiae Hollandiae, Zelandiae et West-Frisiae Dicisiones* 1617; cf A A Roberts, *A South African legal bibliography*, Pretoria: Dept of Justice, 1942, sv "Nieustad", 224–225; L J van Apeldoorn, *Uit de practijk van het Hof van Holland in de tweede helft van de zestiende eeuw: een handschrift*, Utrecht: Broekhoff N V, 1938, 3–19. The same van Apeldoorn, *Observationes processuum in jure consistentium in curia Hollandiae controversorum* (1938) 2 *Tydskrif vir Hedendaagse Romeins-Hollandse Reg/Journal of Contemporary Roman-Dutch Law*, 248–257, convincingly argued that this collection was not written by Neostadius. Cf F J Bosman and P van Warmelo (tr), *De pactis antenuptialibus rerum judicatarum observationes* (c1605), *Observations on decided cases concerning antenuptial contracts*, *Archivalia* (prepared by J Th de Smidt and H W van Soest), Pretoria: The Government Printer, 1986, 1 n 3.
25 Jacob Coren (?–1631) was member of the *Hoge Raad* from 1621–1631. His observations were published after his death; *Observationes XLI rerum in Senatu Hollandiae,*

Loenius[26] were, all but the first, published posthumously and the *Curiae Hollandiae, Zelandiae et West-Frisiae Dicisiones*, as well as the *Sententien en Gewezen Zaken vanden Hoogen en Provincialen Raad in Holland, Zeeland en West-Vriesland*[27] were anonymous. However, several judges kept notes of the decisions in diaries or files, but these collections rarely gave permission to be published as it was a record of *in camera* discussions,[28] which explains the obscurity of the notes of van Bleiswijk and Ockers[29] and the privacy of the *Observationes Tumultuariae (Novae)*,[30] kept by van Bijnkershoek and Pauw.[31] In his notes van Bijnkershoek was critical of his fellow judges who, according to him, complained about irrelevant arguments, followed blindly the *rapporteur* and the order of voting, were reluctant to change opinion and, thus, the resulting majority opinion.[32]

The procedure in the *Hoge Raad*[33] was that an *in camera* meeting opened with the opinion of the *rapporteur*, whose opinion carried weight and was often followed. After the *rapporteur*, the other judges delivered their opinions in order of seniority and the president had the final word[34] but not the

Zelandiae, Frisiae judicatarum; item consilia XXX quaedam, The Hague: apud Arnoldum Meris, 1633.

26 Johannes Loenius (from 1621–1641 member of the *Hoge Raad*), *Decisien en Observatien: met byvoeginge van aanteekeningen, mitsgaders resolutien, placaaten, advysen van regtsgeleerden, gewysdens, enz door Tobias Boel*, Amsterdam: Jan Boom en Gerard onder de Linden, 1712.

27 Published by Nearanus in 1662.

28 Van Poelgeest, "De raadsheren van de Hoge Raad van Holland", 42, refers to the papers of de Hinojosa, Judge-President of the Hof van Holland, whose publication was blocked by the court and the States of Holland.

29 Sirks, "Sed verum est, sententias numerari, non ponderari", 293 and 293 n 30, mentions the *Observationes tumultuariae rerum a Supremo in Hollandia senatu judicatarum quibus ut senator interfui, et quas quatenus notanda putavi*, which were notes on 153 decisions from 1723–1741 kept by Van Bleiswijk, member of the *Hoge Raad*. See also van Poelgeest, "Mr Johan van Bleiswijk en zijn 'Observationes Tumultuariae'", (1987) 55 *Tijdschrift voor Rechtsgeschiedenis*, 117–122; H C Gall, *Regtsgeleerde decision: aan de raadsheer Ockers toegeschreven aantekeningen betreffende uitspraken van het Hof (1656–1669) en de Hoge Raad (1669–1678) van Holland, Zeeland en West-Friesland*, Amsterdam: Cabeljauwpers, 2002.

30 Kept private until 1926; van Bijnkershoek, *Observationes Tumultuariae*, eds E M Meyers et al, 4 vols, Zwolle: Tjeenk Willink, 1926–1962; Pauw, *Observationes Tumultuariae Novae*, eds H F W D Fischer et al, 3 vols, Zwolle: Tjeenk Willink, 1964–1972.

31 Van Bijnkershoek was a member of the *Hoge Raad* from 1704 and president from 1723 until his death in 1743; he kept notes of the cases and the deliberations in camera, which practice was continued by his son-in-law Pauw after his death until 1787. Punt, *Het vennootschapsrecht van Holland*, 28–31; Roberto, *A South African legal bibliography*, 68–71; P van Warmelo, *Registers op die Observationes Tumultuariae van van Bijnkershoek en Pauw* (sd).

32 Van Poelgeest, "De raadsheren van de Hoge Raad van Holland", 40; Sirks, "Sed verum est, sententias numerari, non ponderari", 285, 295.

33 For the full and different procedures, see Punt, *Het vennootschapsrecht van Holland*, 8–13.

34 See Bosman and Warmelo, *Archivalia*, 23–24, 51–52, 67–68, 78, 87, 101–102, 113–114, 131–132, 153, 162–163, 180–181, 203–204, 216–217, 230–231.

casting vote. The majority decision was followed and the *rapporteur* and registrar drafted and published the decision, which could be consulted in the archives.

D. SOURCES OF LAW

The *dicta* of the *Hoge Raad* were entered in the archives, but neither the facts nor motivation were given. However, in a different section of the archives the "geextendeerde sententien" where the facts and procedural history of the case were noted could be found. Finally, the *Resolutieboek* of the *Hoge Raad* was archived, in which book the report of the *rapporteur* and the opinions of the judges were collected. It is unclear who had access to the different parts of the archives. Today the *Resolutieboek* can be consulted for authorities that the court relied upon for the decision.[35] One such authority was Hugo Grotius, the founder of Dutch jurisprudence.

Hugo Grotius is internationally recognised as one of the fathers of both natural law and international law,[36] but in a national context he may be considered to be the founder of Roman-Dutch law or rather, as he called it himself, the "jurisprudence of Holland". During his busy and eventful life, he was, among other things, the *raadpensionaris* of Rotterdam from 1613 until his arrest in 1618, in which capacity he acted as secretary and legal adviser to the city council, and prepared and executed the decisions of this body of which he was the president. The *raadpensionaris* also represented the city in the States of Holland and Zeeland.[37]

His *Introduction to the Jurisprudence of Holland*[38] was the foundation stone of Dutch law. Written in Dutch and following the institutional model of Gaius, Grotius systematised and established Dutch law. In contrast to the practice current in his day of writing extensive commentaries on the *usus*

---

35 See www.gahetna.nl/collectie/archief/ead/index/eadid/3.03.02/open/c01:10.#c01.10 (last accessed 25 January 2020) n 631–680 Resoluties tot de sententies, 1582–1779 50 delen. Sirks, "Sed verum est, sententias numerari, non ponderari", 285, mentions that these resolutions contain the literature referred to, but warns that only the final conclusions are noted, not the full decision-making process.

36 Hahlo and Kahn, *The South African Legal System*, 551–552; D H van Zyl, *Geskiedenis van die Romeins-Hollandse Reg*, Durban: Butterworth, 1979, 191–194, 349–352; R Zimmermann, "Römisch-holländisches Recht. Ein Überblick", in R Feenstra and R Zimmermann (eds), *Das römisch-holländisches Recht Fortschritte des Zivilrechts im 17 und 18 Jahrhundert*, Berlin: Duncker & Humblot, 1992, 26–32.

37 Van Zyl, *Geskiedenis van die Romeins-Hollandse Reg*, 347; de Monte Verloren and Spruit, *Hoofdlijnen uit de ontwikkeling der rechterlijke organisatie*, 223.

38 *Inleydinge tot de Hollandse Regstgeleertheyt*, first published in 1631.

modernus of Roman law with, where necessary, a short reference to contemporary local law, Grotius incorporated local law, Roman law and natural law into one institutional system. The numerous subsequent editions of this textbook show it to have been a standby for every legal practitioner and the book became in time part of the academic curriculum.

E. THE USE OF LEGAL AUTHORITIES IN LEGAL PRACTICE: ROMAN LAW *VERSUS* CUSTOM

In order to illustrate the relationship between Roman law and customary law, an opinion of Grotius in the *Hollandsche Consultatien*[39] will be referred to. In 1631, Grotius had returned to the Netherlands and practised in Amsterdam as an advocate until he was forced to flee again. In the reported case, Grotius had to deal with a rule of customary law as defined by legal practice in conflict with received Roman law. The way that he dealt with the situation not only illustrates the character of Roman-Dutch law at this developmental stage, but the essence of contemporary legal practice as well. The legal question was whether the legal hypothec of the wards included the movable property of the former guardian.[40]

In 1631 a *turbe* had appeared before the aldermen of Amsterdam. A *turbe* was a judicial hearing by (preferably old) inhabitants, or experienced lawyers, on a rule of customary law.[41] Twenty-three experts, advocates, doctors of law, attorneys and notaries, all practitioners of long standing, had attested under oath that it was a rule of customary law in Amsterdam that a general mortgage bond over movable property was terminated if the movable property was alienated against consideration and delivered by the debtor to a third party, even if the movable property was transferred by way of *constitutum possessorium* and thus remained temporarily (*precario*) in possession of the transferor.[42] Confronted with customary law and legal practice, Grotius

---

39 *Consultatien, advysen en advertissementen gegeven ende geschreven by verscheyden treffelijcke rechts-geleerden in Hollandt en elders* (henceforth, *"Hollandsche Consultatien"*), Amsterdam: Jan Boom, vol III, 174.

40 For a discussion of the case, see P J Thomas, "Roman-Dutch opinion practice as a source of law" (2006) 69(4) *Tydskrif vir Hedendaagse Romeins-Hollandse Reg*, 613–621.

41 P Gerbenzon and N E Algra, *Voortgangh des rechtes. Voortgangh des rechtes: de ontwikkeling van het Nederlandse recht tegen de achtergrond van de Westeuropese cultuur*, Zwolle: Tjeenk Willink, 1972, 72, 98–101.

42 They held that this rule applied also in respect of special hypothecs over movable property in possession of the debtor, which meant that a *bona fide* acquisition under onerous title for all practical purposes extinguished the real security right over movable things. The same rule applied when such property was delivered to a third party *in securitatem debiti* before a notary and witnesses.

argued that the deposition by the *turbe* "partially" confirmed the custom, but because it represented an important deviation from the common written law – (i.e. Roman law), it had to be strictly interpreted, lest the interests of wards with hypothecs on the property of their guardians would be prejudiced. In other words, Grotius followed the medieval theory of sources and interpretation developed by Bartolus de Saxoferrato and adapted the relative positions of Dutch and Roman law to suit his case by placing the written *ius commune* first and imposing a strict interpretation on proven custom.[43]

F. *USUS MODERNUS*: JOHANNES VOET AND HIS *COMMENTARIUS AD PANDECTAS*

Johannes Voet was a luminary of Dutch law, born and educated in the province of Utrecht, but called to Leiden in 1680, where he taught Roman law.[44] Voet also became the first professor to teach contemporary law, namely the course on the *Introduction* of Grotius,[45] albeit in Latin. His main work, the *Commentarius ad Pandectas*, was published at the turn of the century and soon thereafter published in other West European countries. As the title indicates, Voet followed the "system" of the Pandects, which since the late Middle Ages had dominated the teaching of law, legal science and legal practice in Western Europe. However, Voet's *Commentarius* was not just another commentary on the Digest, as the author made ample mention of modern law, in particular of forensic questions. Voet was primarily interested in the positive law of his time and his commentary belonged to the tradition of *usus modernus Pandectarum*. Voet's main sources were the European authors from the sixteenth century onwards, more practice-oriented than humanist. Dutch legal literature from his own period, national, regional and local legislation, legal opinions and decisions of the courts, were also included. Which brings us to the authority of Voet in the *Hoge Raad* as told by van Bijnkershoek in his secret notes published 200 years after his death.

43 W J Zwalve, *Hoofdstukken uit de geschiedenis van het Europese privaatrecht*, Deventer: Kluwer, 2003, 28–30, 62–64. Grotius refers to D.1.1.9; *Libri Feudorum* 2.1; D.1.3.32.1; C.8.52.2; Decr D. 8, c 3 and 5; D.1.3.14.15 and 16 as sustaining Bartolus' restrictive interpretation of customary law; D.1.3.12 and 13 provided for an extensive interpretation of Roman law. See, however, Grotius, *Introduction*, 1.2.22.

44 P J Thomas, "Johannes Voet Commentarius ad Pandectas", in S Dauchy, G Martyn, A Musson, H T Philjamäki and A Wijffels (eds), *The formation and transmission of western legal culture. 150 books that made the law in the age of printing*, Cham: Springer, 2016, 239–242.

45 His lecture notes have been published, edited and translated into Afrikaans by P van Warmelo and C J Visser, *Johannes Voet Observationes ad Hugonis Grotii Manuductionem*, Pretoria: Staatsdrukker, 1987.

Consequently, Van Bijnkershoek proved to be *ex post facto* the primordial source for the study of the *Hoge Raad*.

G. "APPLICATION" OF *USUS MODERNUS*: VAN BIJNKERSHOEK AND THE CASE OF THE CLUMSY NOTARY

Cornelius van Bijnkershoek[46] was a native from Zeeland, who studied in Franeker and crowned his career as judge[47] and (from 1724 onwards) president of the *Hoge Raad*. He was a versatile and erudite jurist who published widely and acquired international acclaim for his contributions to international public law[48] and as a Roman lawyer.[49] His *Observationes tumultuariae* – notes on his days as a judge of the *Hoge Raad* – show us a critical jurist, whose mastery of Roman law empowered him with a scope of knowledge and a clarity of reasoning which was unsurpassed by his fellow judges.

In two of his notes,[50] Van Bijnkershoek discussed how a clumsy clause in a will ended up in the highest court on three occasions, each time with different results.[51] A childless widow had made three consecutive wills during November 1723, August 1724 and March 1725. In the last will, a clause revoking wills, which extended to the will of November 1723, was inserted.[52] The legal question was whether this insertion had revoked the will of November 1723 or only the wills before that date. In consequence, the legatees under the 1723 will instituted action against the executor for payment of the legacies. He refused, arguing that the clause in question had revoked the earlier will and therefore the legacies. The aldermen's court in Amsterdam

---

46 19 August 1673 in Middelburg, Zeeland to 16 April 1743; Zimmermann, "Römisch-holländisches Recht", 32–36; Punt, *Het vennootschapsrecht van Holland*, 20–24.

47 In 1704. The six towns of Zeeland represented in the States of Zeeland elected the candidate for the vacancy of one of the three seats reserved for this province.

48 Van Bijnkershoek's treatises *Quaestionum juris publici libri duo, De foro legatorum, De dominio maris*, are included and translated into English in the series *The Classics of International Law*, publications of the Carnegie Endowment for International Peace.

49 *De lege Rhodia de jactu liber singularis* (1703), *Observationum juris Romani libri quatuor* (1710), *Curae secundae de jure occidendi et exponendi liberos apud veteres Romanos* (1723), *Observationum juris Romani. Quatuor prioribus additi* (1733); for further reference to his publications, see van Zyl, *Geskiedenis van die Romeins-Hollandse Reg*, 370 n 378.

50 *Observationes Tumulturiae*, III, notes 2628 and 2678.

51 The notes of van Bijnkershoek and the relevant resolutions have been analysed in depth by Sirks, "Sed verum est, sententias numerari, non ponderari", 285–292, but deserve further critique in this context.

52 "[E]n verklarende sij vrouwe testatrice alhier voor geinsereert te houden de herroepinge van testamenten en actens van uyterste wille, sodanige deselve is geëxtendeert in den testament van 7 Nov 1723" (and testatrix declaring here to hold as inserted the revocations of wills and acts of last will, such as the same are extended in the will of 7 November 1723); ibid, 286.

and the *Hof van Holland* granted the claim and the executor appealed to the *Hoge Raad*. His arguments were that a later will always revoked an earlier one, even if the revocation was not made expressly. This was the position of Roman law and and traditionally followed by the courts.[53] Moreover, there had been an express revocation, and each will instituted a different heir, so they could not co-exist.

The legatees argued that in modern law it was possible to leave several valid wills, for which argument they relied on Voet.[54] Their other argument was that the legacies remained valid even if there had been a change of heir, and that they would remain valid even if they had been made by codicil, as the last will contained a codicillary clause.[55]

In the discussions the *rapporteur* held that the revocation clause had revoked the 1723 will as well. Four other judges, including president van Bijnkershoek, argued on the same basis, namely that in Roman law a later will always revoked an earlier will (except for soldiers), and found no reason why Roman law would have been abolished on this point. However, the other five judges interpreted the clause in question and the law on this point differently. Reference was made to the intention of the testatrix, and in particular the view that it had become possible to leave more than one will was followed. In consequence the appeal was denied.[56]

The case did not end here, as two other legatees followed suit and were successful in Amsterdam and in the *Hof van Holland*, whereupon the executor appealed once again. The judges kept true to their previous opinions, although several additional sources (Grotius,[57] Vinnius[58] and Sande[59]) were included. One of the judges, however, had been ill for some time and could not attend. This made the score 5:4 in favour of Roman law and the appeal succeeded.

The surviving legatee demanded revision.[60] In such event another seven

---

53 Bijnkershoek relied on *Consilia*, Book II, 166, which Sirks, loc cit, 267, note 10, interprets to have meant *Nederlands Advysboek* II, 166.

54 *Commentarius ad Pandectas*, 28.3.8.

55 Sirks, "Sed verum est, sententias numerari, non ponderari", 287.

56 Ibid, 288–289.

57 *Introduction*, II.25.9. Sirks, loc cit, 290 n 20.

58 *In quatuor libros Institutionum imperialium commentarius academicus et forensis*, II.25, para 14. Sirks, loc cit, 290 n 19 mentions that this paragraph does not exist, but assumes that the learned judge (de Grande) meant *Textus: Numerus & Solemnitas*.

59 Sirks, loc cit, 290, n 17, identifies this reference as to J and A a Sande, *Decisionum Frisicarum*, I.IV.10.

60 The special remedy of revision was taken over from the Council of Mechelen. A Wijffels, "Revisie en rechtsdwaling" (2014) 20(2) *Fundamina*, 1042–1050 explains how a litigant could challenge a

members were added to the court[61] – five *pensionarisse* from Holland and two judges from the *Hof van Holland*. The revision was based on the argument that the court had committed an error in not confirming the decision of the *Hof van Holland*. Of the additional judges from the *Hof van Holland*, one followed the rules of Roman law, while the other opined that it had become possible for two wills to co-exist. The *pensionarisse* all but one held the view that an error had been committed and the decision was overturned.[62]

Consequently, it appears that a shift away from Roman law in favour of "imaginary" customary law had taken place at the local level. Or that the authority of Voet[63] (i.e. a contemporary law professor) trumped the *Corpus Juris Civilis*. The cases in question show a sorry picture of legal argumentation or legal reasoning in the highest court. It is of interest to note that recently Boudewijn Sirks has convincingly argued that Voet's theory regarding two co-existing wills was built on quicksand, delved from a vague proposition by his father, Paulus Voet, and moreover, unsupported by the sources cited by him.[64] Nonetheless, half the judges of the *Hoge Raad* and all but one of the *pensionarisse* followed Voet blindly – bearing testimony to the authority of this professor – which absolved his followers from reading his sources. This brings us to the sources of legal practitioners.

H. THE DECREASING AUTHORITY OF ROMAN LAW AND THE INCREASING IMPORTANCE OF LEGISLATION: VAN DER KEESSEL AND HIS LECTURES

The last Dutch jurist that deserves a mention in this context is Dionysius van der Keessel, whose long career as a professor of law at Leiden made his lecture notes on the *Introduction* of Grotius the final compilation of Dutch

---

final decision of the Great Council before the same court to which additional judges were added on the argument that the judges had erred, *proposition d'erreur*. Although the alleged error had to relate to the facts, Wijffels states that the records show that in practice revision submissions often addressed both factual and legal questions. As stated above, the Instruction of the *Hoge Raad* was derived from the Instruction of the Great Council of Mechlin and ss 279–289 provided for "Van Propositien van Erreuren".

61 *Instructie*, s 282, GPB II, 4, 835.
62 Sirks, "Sed verum est, sententias numerari, non ponderari", 291–292.
63 Joannes Voet, *Commentarius ad Pandectas, in quo, praetor Romani iuris principia ac controversias illustriores, ius etiam hodiernum et praecipuae fori quaestiones excutiuntur*, 7 vols, Halle: Joan Jac Curtii, 1776–1780, 28.3.8.
64 Sirks, "Sed verum est, sententias numerari, non ponderari", 287 n 11, 293–294. Cf *Hollandsche Consultatien*, II 24 and V 42.

law during the Republic. Van der Keessel's lectures on the *Inleidinge*[65] of Grotius provide clear insight into the hybrid character of Dutch law and the differences of opinion between authors and courts.[66] The diminishing authority of Roman law and the increasing importance and volume of local, provincial and national legislation and customs, forms the essence of van der Keessel's lectures. For example, the learned professor referred to the *Hollandsche Consultatien* more than 400 times. In volume 5 of his lectures, the bibliography can be consulted, while the footnotes at the end of each volume exemplify the particularism of Dutch cities and countryside. The Dutch collections of decisions, opinions and the lectures of Voet and van der Keessel clearly show the absence of what we would think of today as a "system". Thus, the *usus modernus pandectarum* relied on traditional legal reasoning, in other words *Topik Jurisprudenz*.[67]

I. PRACTICAL LEGAL LITERATURE

For the practising lawyer, the most important source of law is contemporary legislation, be it national, provincial, municipal or otherwise – for example, for the members of a guild or polder. In view of the confederate character of the Dutch State, the main legal sources within the provinces were the states (as legislators) and the various charters, privileges, ordinances, edicts, resolutions, instructions and other legislative measures (*Ordonnantien, Plakkaten, Resolutien, Privilegien, Oorkonden, Instructien, Handvesten, Keuren*) for Holland and Zeeland, collected in the *Groot Placaetboek* van Cau[68] and the

---

65 D G van der Keessel, *Praelectiones Iuris Hodierni ad Hugonis Grotii Introductionem ad Iurisprudentiam Hollandicam*, eds P van Warmelo et al, 6 vols, Rotterdam/Kaapstad: A A Balkema, 1961–1975.

66 Cf P J Thomas, "Contributory fault in maritime collisions in the law of Holland", (2001) 48 *Revue Internationale des Droits de l'Antiquité*, 345–360. This paper showed how van der Keessel wavered on contributory negligence between the view of van Bijnkershoek (*Theses* 815 ad Grotius III 38 16 and 821 ad III 38 18) and a decision of the Hoge Raad reported by Neostadius; see also his lecture on *Inleidinge* III 38 16 (S v *Schuld van de eene*).

67 P J Thomas, "Mietmaule or thinking like a lawyer" (2013) 4 *Studia Universitatis Babes-Bolyai Iurisprudentia*, 67–84 (available at: http://studia.law.ubbcluj.ro); Id, "Ars aequi et boni, legal argumentation and the correct legal solution" (2014) 131 *Zeitschrift der Savigny-Stiftung fuer Rechtsgeschichte* (Romanistische Abteilung), 41–59; Id, "A Barzunesque View of Cicero: From Giant to Dwarf and Back", in P J du Plessis (ed), *Cicero's law. Rethinking Roman Law of the Late Republic*, Edinburgh: Edinburgh University Press, 2016, 11–25.

68 *Groot Placaet-boeck vervattende de Placaten, Ordonnantien ende Edicten van de Staten Generael der Vereenigdhe Nederlanden ende Heeren Staten van Hollandt ende West-Vriesland mitsgaders van de Heeren Staten van Zeelandt*, 9 vols and index, C Cau, S van Leeuwen, Scheltus (J, P and I), D Lulius and J van der Linden, Amsterdam: Johannes Allart, 1658–1796; Roberts, *A South African legal bibliography*, 240 and 340, refers to the *Nederlandsch Placaat en Rechtskundig*

Hollandts Placcaet boek.[69] Equally important were the statutes of the cities, the water boards, the districts and other bodies with legislative powers. In his *Overzicht van Oud-Nederlandsche Rechtsbronnen*, Fockema Andreae has sixty-four pages with sources for Holland and Zeeland, from general to special, the latter divided per district; in their turn, these last ones were divided into general and special (divided between town and countryside).[70]

The most abundant sources of forensic practice are the opinions of the Dutch jurists:[71] the *Hollandsche consultatien,*[72] the *Nieuwe Hollandsche consultatien*, the *Vervolg op de Hollandsche consultatien*, the *Advyzen* collected by van den Berg,[73] De Haas,[74] Barels[75] and others.[76]

Woordenboek (1791–1797), but it is obvious from the date that the practical use thereof was for a limited period.

69 *Hollandts Placcaet-boeck: begrijpende meest alle de voornaemste placcaten, ordonnantien ende octroyen/Uytgegeeven by de Edd. Groot-mogende Heeren Staten van Hollandt ende West-Vrieslandt*, Amsterdam: Jan Janssen, 1645.

70 S J Fockema Andreae, *Overzicht van Oud-Nederlandsche Rechtsbronnen*, Haarlem: F Bohn, 1923; see also Gerbenzon and Algra, *Voortgangh des rechtes* 122–123, who refer to the collections of Noordkerk (Amsterdam), van de Wall (Dordrecht) and van Leeuwen (Rijnland); Grotius, *Inleiding*, I 2 15ff.

71 Thomas, "Roman-Dutch opinion practice as a source of law", (2006) 69(4) *Tydskrif vir Hedendaagse Romeins-Hollandse Reg*, 613–621.

72 The full title is *Consultatien, advysen en advertissementen, gegeven en geschreven by verscheide treffelyke rechts-geleerden in Holland en elders*. The first edition was published in six volumes by Naeranus in Rotterdam between 1645 and 1666. This was the first collection of legal opinions in Holland and stands, as it were, at the cradle of Roman-Dutch law. The last edition was published in Amsterdam in 1768. The publication of a summary in 1696, *Kort begryp van de consultatien en advysen, inhoudende alle de voortreffelijke materien en voorvallen van de ses deelen der Hollandsche consultatie boeken* (Amsterdam: Hendrik Wetstein en Soonen, 1696), and the annotations by De Pape around 1700 and Van Hasselt during the 1780s, attest to enduring popularity. Roberts, *A South African legal bibliography*, 157; J C De Wet, *Die ou skrywers in perspektief*, Durban: Butterworth, 1988, 186–190. For information on the *Amsterdamsche derde deel*, see De Wet and Roberts, loc cit.

73 I Van den Berg, *Nederlandsch advys-boek, inhoudende verscheide consultatien en advysen van voorname regtsgeleerden in Nederland*, 4 vols, Amsterdam: J A de Chalmot, 1693–1698; Roberts, *A South African legal bibliography*, 50–51; De Wet, *Die ou skrywers in perspektief*, 187–188. Van den Berg practiced as an advocate in Amsterdam during the second half of the seventeenth century. His collection contains 1,120 opinions.

74 G De Haas, *Nieuwe Hollandsche consultatien, advertissementen van regten, memorien en andere schrifturen van voorname regtsgeleerden*, 's Gravenhage: Mattheus Gaillard, 1741. The work consists of 40 opinions. Roberts, *A South African legal bibliography*, 144–145; De Wet, *Die ou skrywers in perspektief*, 188.

75 J M Barels, *Advysen over den koophandel en zeevaert: mitsgaders memorien, resolutien, missives enz daer toe behoorende; meerendeels van A van den Ende, J Ardinois, D Helmans en andere*, 2 vols, Amsterdam: Hendrik Gartman, 1780–1781; Roberts, *A South African legal bibliography*, 45; De Wet, *Die ou skrywers in perspektief*, 188. Barels practised as an advocate in Amsterdam during the eighteenth century and included 174 opinions, 110 of which by Abraham van den Ende from between 1694 and 1722.

76 For example, Van der Kop, *Nieuw Nederlands Advys-boek, dienende tot een vervolg op het Nederlands Advysboek van Mr Isaac van der Berg*, 2 vols, 's Gravenhage: Hendrik Backhuysen,

Between 1778 and 1789, Nassau la Leck published a four-fold collection –
the register of Nassau la Leck[77] – so as to facilitate access to the practical aspects
of old Dutch law. In his legal bibliography Roberts[78] mentions that a total of
forty-three collections were entered in this compilation, which added up to a
total of 10,991 opinions and decisions. It is again necessary to emphasise the
fact that the judges as a body observed collegiate secrecy. As a consequence, the
twenty-three observations of Neostadius, forty-one cases of Coren, the anonymous collections of *Curiae Hollandiae, Zelandiae et West-Frisiae Dicisiones*[79]
and the *Sententien en Gewezen Zaken vanden Hoogen en Provincialen Raad
in Holland, Zeeland en West-Vriesland* constitute an extremely sparse body of
precedents. In other words, virtually all published collections contained legal
opinions by advocates, of which the majority dealt with matters concerning the
law of persons and succession, criminal law, procedure, administrative law and
other matters of pure historical interest. Although it may be argued that these
cases could give indications of different paradigms and/or methods of legal
argumentation, in the context of this contribution they fail to show any influence of forensic practice on early modern legal sources.

In some of the *Hollandsche Consultatien*, the "relevant" legal points are
listed at the beginning of the opinion, which creates the impression that
these points state positive law. However, on closer inspection the listed rules

1769 and 1782, contained 154 opinions; Roberts, *A South African legal bibliography*, 178,
180–181; De Wet, *Die ou skrywers in perspektief*, 188. In the other provinces similar collections
were published: *Utrechtsche consultatien, dat is decisoire ende andere advisen, instructien ende
advertissementen van rechten, gegeven ende gemaeckt by de vermaerste rechtsgeleerden der
stadt Utrecht*, 3 vols, Utrecht: Anthony Schouten, 1676, 1684, 1700, reported 462 opinions; De
Wet, loc cit, 188–189. *Geldersche consultatien, advysen ende advertissementen van rechten*, 3
vols, Arnhem: Wouter Troost 1776–1822, had 118 opinions; H Schrassert, *Consultatien, advysen
ende advertissementen*, 5 vols, Harderwyck: Jan Moojen, 1740–1745, had 100 opinions (including about fifty by his brother Henrick in volume IV; the fifth and last volume, more descriptive
than the others, dealt with feudal law and was not included); J Schomaker, *Selecta consilia et
responsa juris . . . coram illustribus Ducatus Gelriae et Comitatus Zutphaniae tribunalibus
ventilatarum pertinentia . . .*, 6 vols, Nymegen/Amsterdam: Hendrik Heymans/Hendril Vieroot,
1738–1782, had 431 opinions; finally, *Overijsselsch advysboek, behelzende merkwaardige zo consultatoire als decisoire advysen en sententien van veele voornaame rechtsgeleerden in Overijssel
bij een verzamelt en met nodige registers*, voorzien door L C H Strubberg, 4 vols, Te Campen:
J A de Chalmot, Jacques Alexandre de Kampen, 1784-1794, had 112 opinions.
77 Nassau La Leck, *Algemeen bereneerd register op alle de voornaamste rechtsgeleerde advysen, consultatien, decisien, observatien, sententien, in eene alphabetische order geschikt en
zamengesteld*, Utrecht: Gisbert Timon van Paddenburg, 1778–1789; Roberts, *A South African
legal bibliography*, 85–88; De Wet, *Die ou skrywers in perspektief*, 190. Nassau La Leck was a
patriot and left Holland in 1787. The third (1788) and fourth parts (1789) were compiled by an
anonymous jurist.
78 Roberts, *A South African legal bibliography*, 45.
79 Sixty decisions of the *Hof van Holland*, two of the Council of Mechelen and seventeen of the
Hoge Raad.

and principles turn out to be points raised by the counsel to bolster the case of his client. The outcome of the disputes is not stated, which entails that the validity of the arguments remains uncertain. It may be assumed that the editors and publishers selected opinions deemed of interest, but it is difficult to argue on the basis of these collections that forensic practice did more than follow legal tradition. The continued popularity of *repertoria* – for example, van Brederode[80] or van Zurck's *Codex Batavus*[81] and *concordantia iuris*, such as those of Hermannus[82] – supports this submission. However, the most influential work within forensic practice proved to be the institutes written for the sons of Grotius. The success of this work – five editions in 1631,[83] followed by the 1644 edition, which was annotated by Groenewegen[84] with references to the *Corpus Iuris Civilis*, as well as Dutch statutory and customary law, decisions of the courts and references to literature – showed the lack of books for legal practitioners, which was filled by Grotius. The 1667 edition was issued with blank pages so that practitioners could keep their copies up to date with new legislation and decisions.[85]

The manuscripts of Voet's lectures on the *Introduction* made use of the 1667 edition and contained over and above Voet's lecture notes, which referred mainly to his *Commentarius*, new decisions and legislation. The notes in Latin on the *Introduction* by Schorer[86] were translated in a further edition by Austen.[87] The most abundant commentary is found in the lectures of van der Keessel.

---

80 P C van Brederode (1559–1637), *Repertorium sententiarum et regularum*, Frankfurt: Paulus Frellon, 1587. Cf S Groenewegen van der Made, *Alphabet der Hollandsche regten ofte bladwyzer en korten inhoud van de Inleyding tot de Hollandsche Regtsgeleerdheid en de Aantekeningen van S van Groenewegen van der Made*, Amsterdam: Jan Boom, 1729; A Barbosa, *Repertorium civilis et canonici*, Lugduni: M Goy, 1675.

81 E van Zurck, *Codex Batavus, waer in het algemeen Kerk- publyk en Burgerlyk Recht van Hollant, Zeelant, en het resort der Generaliteit kortelyk is begrepen*, Delft: Adriaan Beman, 1727; F L Kersteman, *Hollandsch rechtsgeleert Woordenboek*, Amsterdam: Steven van Esveldt, 1768, Aanhangzel, 1772–1773.

82 I H Hermannus, *Concordantia Iuris*, Jenae, 1745; D G van der Keessel, *Theses Selectae juris Hollandici et Zelandici ad supplendam Hugonis Grotii Introductionem ad Jurisprudentiam Hollandicam*, Lugduni Batavorum: S et J Luchtmans, 1800.

83 Roberts, *A South African legal bibliography*, 141.

84 S van Groenewegen van der Made (1613–1652); van Zyl, *Geskiedenis van die Romeins-Hollandse Reg*, 356–357.

85 P van Warmelo, "Roman-Dutch law in practice during the seventeenth and eighteenth century", in J M Koster-van Dijk and A Wijffels (eds), *Miscellanea Forensia Historica*, Amsterdam: Werkgroep Grote Raad van Mechelen, 1988, 345–356.

86 *Inleydinge Nu met Latynsche aanteekeningen uitgebreidt door W Schorer*, Middelburg: Pieter Gillissen, 1767.

87 *Aanteekeningen van Mr Willem Schorer over de Inleiding tot de Hollandsche Rechts-geleerdheid van Mr Hugo de Groot*, Middelburg: Pieter Gilissen en Zoon, 1784.

J. EARLY MODERN LEGAL REASONING

Legal reasoning or legal argumentation is a topic which is hardly ever mentioned by legal authors. It should be noted that in the Latin school, the grammar school of the fourteenth to the nineteenth centuries, rhetoric was part of the *trivium* (grammar, logic and rhetoric), which meant that law students were familiar with the basics. Furthermore, it may be argued that the case study method of the *Digesta* taught legal reasoning by implication. Moreover, for both students and practitioners in the Low Countries, an authoritative textbook was available in the *Topica*[88] of Everardus.

Everardus was professor at Leuven and became President of the *Hof van Holland* and subsequently the *Grote Raad van Mechelen*.[89] His book was an introduction to the methods of legal argumentation, written for students and practitioners. Its twenty-seven editions indicate that the book fulfilled a need.[90] The author discussed over a hundred types of argument, which varied from those derived from general logic to specific legal subtleties.[91]

Alain Wijffels admonishes that the book of Everardus reflected the doctrinal tradition of the late Middle Ages, which prevailed both in academia and in the law courts, and showed no signs of the critical approach of the emerging legal humanism.[92] Although this comment is certainly true, it should be noted that Cicero's *Topica* is usually subjected to the same disparaging criticism, namely that it constituted a list of arguments. It should, however, be kept in mind that forensic practice has a single-minded objective – namely, to win the case, meaning to persuade court or jury. As such, find-

---

88 *Topicorum seu de locis legalibus liber*, Lugduni: in aedibus Theodorici Martini Alustensis impensis cum Henrico Eckert ab Humburch, 1516; O M D F Vervaart, *Studies over Nicolaas Everaerts (1462–1532) en zijn Topica*, Gouda: Quint, 1994.

89 G van Dievoet, D van den Auweele, F Stevens, M Oosterbosch, C Coppens, *Lovanium Docet. Geschiedenis van de Leuvense Rechtsfaculteit 1425–1914*, Leuven: Katholieke Universiteit Leuven, 1988, 60–63; A Watson, *The Making of the Civil Law*, Cambridge, MA: Harvard University Press, 1981, 53.

90 The Basel publisher advertised the book in 1543 as a work on developing arguments, illustrating method, how to judge and select, going back to Aristotle, Cicero, Baldus and other authorities.

91 The various topics from *auctoritas, a simili, a contrario, a fortiori*, and analogies such as *a servo ad monachum* were illustrated by examples and set out to teach legal reasoning and quickly find an argument.

92 Watson, *The Making of the Civil Law*, 54, considers the *Loci argumentorum legales* an innovation as the first full and systematic explanation of the various types of legal argument. He finds the *loci* based on analogy such as from slave to monk, of significant importance, since Roman law provides the analogy and so the system of Roman law is extended. See also N Benke, "In sola prudentium interpretatione. Zu Methodik und Methodologie römischer Juristen", in B Feldner and N Forgó (eds), *Norm und Entscheidung. Prolegomena zu einer Theorie des Falls*, Vienna: Springer, 2000, 1–85.

ing authoritative arguments – and thus practising the rawest form of positivism – has been the bread and butter of practitioners throughout the ages. Academia has usually been above the realities of life and taught accordingly. This explains the lasting success of Everardus' *Topica* well into the seventeenth century, and the application of rhetoric theory to legal argumentation, as elaborated by Everardus, was an updating of the Ciceronian analysis of legal reasoning in Roman law, which prescripts had been practised by lawyers and courts under the flag of *mos italicus*.

In his *On the Study Methods of Our Time*,[93] Vico distinguished the ancient method with emphasis on rhetoric from the rational Cartesian method, and drew attention to the influence of the latter on legal argumentation. Thus, the belief in a neutral legal science, consisting of a coherent legal system, took root in the footsteps of the scientific revolution within the natural sciences.

This rationalisation of the law into a science was emblematically done for the Dutch law by Grotius[94] and van Bijnkershoek, who, as founding fathers of international law, found their authority in natural law or naturalised Roman law.[95]

K. CONCLUSION

Several conclusions may be drawn. First, the origin and consequent character of the United States of the Netherlands were in opposition to the modern centralisation of the state and harmonisation of the legal system. This explains the limited jurisdiction of the *Hoge Raad* and the minimal influence of this court.

Within forensic practice two directions were noticeable: first, the conservative tradition of forensic practice which relied on rhetorical topical argumentation. Within this tradition a gradual shift took place as the authority

93 Giovanni Battista Vico (1668–1744), *De Nostri temporis studiorum ratione*, Neapoli: Felix Mosca, 1709.
94 Hugo Grotius, *De Iure Praedae Commentarius*. The young advocate developed his own system on the basis of thirteen laws and nine rules of natural law, from which he deduced the justness of war, the seizure of spoils and the acquisition of ownership thereof. P Thomas, "Piracy, privateering and the United States of the Netherlands", (2003) 50 *Revue Internationale des Droits de l'Antiquité*, 361–382, at 366–367. The rules deal with the sources of law, except rule 9 which deals with jurisdiction; the laws represent substantive law. Cf Id, *De Jure Belli ac Pacis*, III.1.5.
95 However, it should be noted that in order to construct the premises of natural law, Grotius and van Bijnkershoek delved deep into the past, drawing on Biblical, philosophical, patristic and legal authority, not ignoring the criticised late medieval Roman law, canon law and Spanish legal science.

of Roman law, Justinian and late medieval interpretation was gradually supplanted by modern authors who referred to custom and modern legislation, the subtext of which was the increasing importance of commerce and capitalism.[96]

However, the belief on the possibility of developing a legal system which, moving from the true premises by way of deductive logic, should lead to the correct legal solution (i.e. the truth) attracted the rationalist of the Enlightenment, the naturalists, the French revolutionaries with the goddess of reason anointed by Robespierre, and inspired the French, Austrian and German codifications.[97] As a consequence, it comes as no surprise that this paradigm took root in many European and European-based codified jurisdictions and had academia as her standard bearer. Thus, the great Roman lawyer Max Kaser adhered to his belief in a hidden, internal system of Roman law,[98] and Franz Wieacker never lost his faith in the correct legal solution.[99]

However, the relativists have older antecedents and persuasion will always be the approach of legal practitioners in non-codified accusatorial systems. The Roman textbook for lawyers was written by Cicero and elaborated by Quintilian, who remarked pointedly that advocates would be superfluous if logical deduction could provide the decision to legal problems.[100]

The *Observationes tumultuariae* of the critically minded van Bijnkershoek show him as a *System Denker*, but do not dispel the impression that the *Hoge Raad* reached its decisions by counting the heads of its members as well as counting authorities. Few practitioners would consult the archives to unearth the motivation of the decisions. Counting heads of authorities

---

96 See for example Coren's *observatio* 40 (decision of 21 December 1629), in his *Observationes XLI rerum in Senatu Hollandiae, Zelandiae, Frisiae judicatarum; item consilia XXX quaedam*, The Hague: apud Arnoldum Meris, 1633, where Roman law, custom and modern legislation competed. The new, and for Dutch maritime commerce more advantageous, solution was accepted; Cf P J Thomas, "Limited liability for maritime collisions in old Dutch law" (2004) 67 *Tydskrif vir Hedendaagse Romeins-Hollandse Reg*, 229–243, where Voet's inconsistency, van Bijnkershoek's dogmatic analysis of Roman law and van der Keessel's reliance on municipal ordinances are analysed.

97 *Das System* of von Savigny, and its development by the Pandectists.

98 M Kaser, *Zur Methode der römischen Rechtsfindung*, Göttingen: Vandenhoeck & Ruprecht 1962, 49–78; Thomas, "Ars aequi et boni", 41–59.

99 F Wieacker, "The *causa Curiana* and contemporary Roman jurisprudence" (1967) 2(1) *The Irish Jurist*, 151–164; P Thomas. "The intention of the testator: from the *causa Curiana* to modern South African law", in J Hallebeek, M Schermaier, R Fiori, E Metzger and J-P Coriat (eds), *Inter cives necnon peregrinos: essays in honour of Boudewijn Sirks*, Goettingen: V&R Unipress, 2014, 727–739; Id, "Ars aequi et boni", 41–59.

100 *Institutio Oratoria*, V.xiv, 14–35.

and *in camera* judges remained the methodology of choice in consulting, pleading and deciding outside codified jurisdictions. The lectures of van der Keessel on the *Introduction* by Hugo Grotius show the paradigm shift from Roman law to Dutch particularism and the regression that the Dutch State, its society and its scientific pre-eminence underwent during the eighteenth century.

Finally, it should be emphasised that an important source of information about *in camera* deliberations is found in the diaries of van Bijnkershoek and Pauw. At the same time, however, it is important to be aware that these works were not available to their contemporaries, who had few law reports to consult and an abundance of legal opinions, the authority of which did not benefit from the *ius respondendi* or the *lex citationis*.

12 Law Reports as Legal Authorities in Early Modern Belgian Legal Practice

Alain Wijffels

A. JURISDICTIONAL DIVERSITY IN THE EARLY MODERN SOUTHERN NETHERLANDS

The early modern legal landscape in the Southern Netherlands was rooted in particular interests. These interests could be local or regional, but the legal diversity was also the result of vested interest groups which were not always organised along specific territorial lines, such as the Church, merchant or feudal interests, or any other social groups enjoying privileges. In general, the particular law of a territorial or non-territorial community was backed up by a particular forum. Members of the university in Leuven, for example, enjoyed to some extent a special status which was supported by the jurisdictional privilege of their own university court. Within a given territory, land could be governed depending on its status by feudal law, law applicable on *allodia*, law applicable on tenures – and in each case, litigation would be pursued before a specific court, whether feudal, allodial or *censale*.[1] By the end of the Middle Ages, most of the Low Countries' territories (parts of which would eventually come or return under the sovereignty of the French Crown) were included in a personal union, first of the Burgundian dukes, then of the Habsburgs. Each principality of that union had by then also developed a superior court which acted as an appellate court within that principality (and, for some types of case, as a first-instance court), sometimes referred to as a "provincial court". Moreover, the Burgundian dukes developed an overarching appellate court, commonly known as the Great Council of Mechlin[2] (which also heard some first-instance cases), and, under the Habsburg rule, the Privy Council[3] exercised adjudicating powers on a regular basis. However, the main role of the Privy Council was to assist the sovereign or his representative in the Netherlands in preparing legislative acts and to act as the central executive body in domestic policies and their implementation. The Privy Council's judicial role was never fully acknowledged, it was simply a feature of the *Ancien Régime's police et justice* without separation of powers. The Great Council, on the other hand, lost over time its appellate jurisdiction for most territories, whether they came to be permanently governed by a foreign power (the United Provinces or France), or remained under Habsburg rule.[4] Neither the Privy Council nor the Great Council were therefore to play a decisive role in developing a common Belgian law. Particular laws by and large prevailed and were supported and developed by particular courts.

In spite of several common features with legal developments in both the

---

1 P Godding, *Le droit privé dans les Pays-Bas méridionaux du 12e au 18e siècle*, Bruxelles: Palais des Académies, 1987.

2 A Wijffels, "Grand Conseil des Pays-Bas à Malines – vers 1445–1797", in E Aerts et al (eds), *Les institutions du gouvernement central des Pays-Bas habsbourgeois (1482–1795)*, Bruxelles: Archives Générales du Royaume, 1995, vol I, 448–462.

3 H de Schepper, "Conseil Privé (1504–1794)", in E Aerts et al (eds), *Les institutions du gouvernement central des Pays-Bas habsbourgeois (1482–1795)*, Bruxelles: Archives Générales du Royaume, 1995, vol I, 287–317.

4 A Verscuren, *The Great Council of Malines in the 18th century. An Aging Court in a Changing World?*, Cham: Springer, 2015, 101–104.

adjacent Northern French *pays de coutume* and the Northern Netherlands, even after the latter's secession at the end of the sixteenth century, the Habsburg Netherlands presented a different picture in a number of ways. In contrast to France, there was no strong current similar to the formation of a *droit coutumier commun*, supported by the monarchy, royal courts and a significant legal literature. Nor did the Habsburgs' central government in Brussels, notwithstanding intermittent exceptions, endeavour to build any extensive common statutory framework for their Netherlandish dominions. In contrast to the situation in Holland, no systematic or sustained jurisprudential effort was made in order to achieve anything similar to the creation of the Dutch-Roman law in any of the Southern provinces. In any event, comparatively few works by early modern authors in the Habsburg Netherlands used the phrase "Belgian law".[5] Most of the academic production by Leuven law scholars was focused on Roman or canon law.[6]

B. EVIDENCE OF "FORENSIC REASONING"

Due to a persistent misunderstanding, Belgian (and more generally, European) historiography fails to acknowledge appropriately the relationship between the development of legal science and the development of legal reasoning in forensic practice. To begin with, standard historiography of the so-called *"ius commune"* underrates the successive changes in legal methods which, from the late Middle Ages until the codification era starting towards the late eighteenth century, affected the very structure of legal thinking.[7] In that sense, in spite of the progress made in *ius commune* studies during

---

5 The first legal monograph in the Southern Netherlands credited with referring in its title to "Belgian law" is: F[ranciscus] Zypaeus, *Notitia iuris belgici*, Antverpiae: Apud Hieronymum Verdussium (ed pr), 1635; a few years earlier, the phrase "Belgian" (which, at the time, could refer to the whole of the Low Countries, the political secession of the Northern provinces notwithstanding) occurred in Paul van Christijnen's law reports: P Christinaeus, *Practicarum quaestionum rerumque in supremis Belgarum curijs actarum et obseruatarum decisiones*, Antverpiae: ex officina Hieronymi Verdussii (ed pr), 1626ss. These titles were not, as regards the use of "Belgium" and "Belgian", trendsetters. A Anselmo published in the seventeenth century a compilation of statutes under the title *Codex Belgicus* (and, more originally, a *Tribonianus Belgicus*, a commentary on statute law), while in the eighteenth century, G de Ghewiet published in the Flemish regions annexed by the French Crown his *Institutions du droit belgique*.

6 See Chapters 1–4 by L Waelkens in the *History of Leuven's Faculty of Law*, Bruges: Die Keure and KULeuven, 2014.

7 As there is little point in departing here from the standard historiography, the author may *brevitatis gratia* refer to his own general understanding of the successive remoulding of Roman law texts from the Middle Ages until the nineteenth century in his textbook: A Wijffels, *Introduction historique au droit. France, Allemagne, Angleterre*, Paris: PUF 2020 (revised edition, 3rd edn).

the second half of the twentieth century, there is no *communis opinio* on the essential features of that *ius commune*. *Ius commune* historiography remains shackled by national biases and a post-codification attachment to both Enlightenment classifications and a nineteenth-century positivistic approach to the hierarchy of legal authorities. To make things worse, some legal historians tend to emphasise systematically the opportunistic traits of advocates' and other practitioners' arguments in written opinions: arguably, a rather callous way to write off the underlying methodology which even the least jurisprudentially talented advocate must comply with in order to remain functional in the interaction of litigation between legal professionals (counsel, magistrates and judges). No one would argue that advocates' memoranda (then or nowadays) are intended to reflect consistently the same standards of legal scholarship. Provided they have read law at a law faculty, however, few practitioners escape in their arguments and reasoning the general patterns and the mould of legal thinking which prevailed during their legal education and which continued to direct them through the books of authority, especially those written by legal scholars, which were commonly used or at least referred to in legal practice. In their wake, these patterns and books gradually brought up more recent literature, which in turn reinforced the changing general mould of legal reasoning. These were long-term developments, and apart from the enduring prestige of a few late Medieval authors and the occasional reliance on legal-humanistic scholarship, during the last two centuries of the *Ancien Régime*, practitioners fell back mostly on early modern literature which offered a subject-based, systematic treatment of particular topics or areas of the law, and which took into account the substantive law combining civil law and the particular laws of their jurisdiction. In the Southern Netherlands at least, there appears to be little *prima facie* evidence of any marked impact of the more theoretical literature of the Law of Reason in legal practice.

Legal reasoning in early modern practice can be traced through different sources.[8] The main ones are court records; practice-related manuscript sources; printed *consilia*; printed reports; and other printed sources.

---

8 For the Great Council of Mechlin, which takes central place in the present brief chapter, see D Leyder, *Les archives du Grand Conseil des Pays-Bas à Malines (vers 1445–1797)*, Bruxelles: Archives Générales du Royaume, 2010.

(1) Court records

Court records may vary according to the "style" of each court. For a superior court (such as the Great Council), the main records of judicial decisions ("extended sentences" and their abridged version, the "*dicta*") do not provide on the whole any relevant information with regard to the use of legal authorities. The extended sentences provide a survey of the proceedings and the mainly factual arguments of the litigants.[9] Discussions on particular laws are occasionally included (e.g. on a controversial customary or statutory rule), but references to civil law occur only exceptionally, and even then practically never with any technical references to the scholarly authorities.

The case files, which often form the bulk of an ancient court's archives, were not, strictly speaking, part of the court's records, as they contained documents submitted (in linen case bags) by the litigants' proctors during the proceedings, and then apparently left at the registrar's office after the case had been decided or when the proceedings were indefinitely discontinued. In such case files, the main evidence for legal reasoning and arguments are the written submissions, usually drafted at different stages of the proceedings by advocates in the superior courts. These submissions contain both factual and legal arguments. The latter may refer to particular laws and *ius commune* authorities. By the late sixteenth century, an increasing number of references were made to legal literature relating to particular laws (e.g. commentaries on customs or statutes), which was often at least partly buttressed by civil law scholarship. A second type of document which informs us about legal reasoning in practice occurs less frequently: these are legal opinions (for which different names are used, e.g. *motifs de droit*) sought by a litigant and submitted (in addition to the counsel's memoranda) to reinforce the legal case in favour of that litigant. Those opinions could be drafted by a senior advocate, occasionally by a judge, but typically they were requested (for consideration) from one or more members of the law faculties (in the Habsburg Netherlands, mostly from the university in Leuven). By and large, these opinions followed the patterns used in the *consilia* literature. In some cases, as was also common practice in other jurisdictions, the collected *consilia* of a law professor were published in print.

---

9 A Wijffels, "Grand Conseil de Malines: La rédaction des sentences étendues et le recueil de jurisprudence de Guillaume de Grysperre", in A Wijffels (ed), *Case Law in the Making. The Techniques and Methods of Judicial Records and Law Reports*, vol I: *Essays*, Berlin: Duncker & Humblot, 1997, 299–316.

(2) Practice-related manuscript sources

A still largely unchartered area of legal literature, at the level of both local courts and superior courts, consists of a wide and heterogenous range of manuscripts, usually written by practitioners, which deal with topics that were relevant for legal practice: procedure, customs, evidence, decisions and rulings by courts. Some fit well in more or less established genres of legal literature (e.g. procedural treatises, running commentaries on customs, reports of cases), but more often than not they are hybrid genres.[10] During the Middle Ages, the first works on customary law were usually drafted by practitioners who relied on decided cases to find out what a specific customary rule entailed, or how a disputed rule was regarded by the local forum. Customary law continued for centuries (even after customs had been more or less extensively written down) to be evidenced through judicial decisions which reflected in that respect some form of case law.

Those practice-related manuscripts which come closest to the genre of (continental-style) law reports are the most relevant for ascertaining legal reasoning methods and their use of authorities in the practice of the (higher) courts.[11] Reports were often written by judges, some of whom, in collegiate courts, had taken part in the hearings and the discussions leading to the decision. In smaller jurisdictions, or jurisdictions where the legal profession represented only a limited social group, but also in larger and more important jurisdictions, many law reports remained unpublished, although in certain cases, the evidence of surviving manuscripts indicates that they may have more widely circulated among practitioners, sometimes over several generations. For many early modern practice-related works, the distinction between printed and unpublished works is not all that important, although printed works were more likely to reach a readership beyond its jurisdiction of origin.

---

10 For an example (again, related to the Great Council), see the description of such a manuscript by J Th de Smidt, "Quelques remarques sur le MS BPL 54 de la Bibliothèque de l'Université de Leyde, le manuscrit PRAXIS", in J A Ankum et al (eds), *Saturnalia Roberto Feenstra. Sexagesimum Quintum Annum Aetatis Complenti ab alumnis collegis amicis oblata*, Fribourg: Éditions Universitaires, 1985, 533–544

11 P Godding, "L'origine et l'autorité des recueils de jurisprudence dans les Pays-Bas méridionaux (XIIIe–XVIIIe siècles)", in *Rapports belges au VIIIe Congrès international de droit comparé (Pescara, 29 août–5 septembre 1970)*, Bruxelles: Centre interuniversitaire de droit comparé, 1970, 1–37 ; Id, *La jurisprudence*, Turnhout: Brepols, 1973; Id, "Jurisprudence et motivation des sentences", in C Perelman and P Foriers (eds), *Motivation des décisions de justice*, Bruxelles: Bruylant, 1978, 37–67.

(3) Printed *consilia*

An indigenous production of *consilia* developed soon after the creation of the University of Leuven in 1425.[12] The first printed collection only appeared around the mid-sixteenth century, when opinions by Nicolaus Everardus (d 1532, in his lifetime a judge and president of the Court of Holland and of the Great Council), often written half a century earlier, were published.[13] Although the courts' archives show that in important cases it was not unusual to seek an opinion from one or more law professors in Leuven, only the *consilia* of a few have been collected and published. Elbertus de Leeuw's (Leoninus) opinions were first published during his lifetime, but Johannes Wamèse's (Wamesius), who died in 1590, were only published during the second quarter of the following century. Although *consilia* could arguably better withstand for a while the changing models of legal reasoning between the mid-sixteenth and mid-seventeenth century, these examples illustrate that even during the second half of the seventeenth century and later, such *consilia* could still prove useful as authorities on specific points. However, their patterns of reasoning were then no longer in step with the early modern more positivistic and systematic approach. As a genre, printed *consilia* in the Southern Netherlands faded by the end of the seventeenth century, without being replaced by any obvious substitute.[14]

(4) Printed reports

By comparison, the Low Countries were late in publishing law reports. Notwithstanding evidence of unpublished reports from the end of the Middle Ages onwards, and some intensification of reporting, at least in superior courts, during the second half of the sixteenth century, the first published report – and with respect to volume, the most important of the whole early modern period – was not published before the second quarter

---

12 U Wagner, "Niederlande", in H Coing (ed) *Handbuch der Quellen und Literatur der neueren europäischen Privatrechtsgeschichte*, Bd II, *Neuere Zeit (1500–1800), Das Zeitalter des gemeinen Rechts*, II/2, *Gesetzgebung und Rechtsprechung*, Munich: C H Beck'sche Verlagsbuchhandlung, 1976, 1399–1430, at 1417–1430.

13 O M D F Vervaart, *Studies over Nicolaas Everaerts (1462–1532) en zijn Topica*, Arnhem: Gouda Quint, Rotterdam: Sanders Instituut, 1994.

14 For a topic-related analysis of a very broad range of *consilia* from the (both Southern and Northern) Netherlands, see W Druwé, *Transregional Normativity in Learned Legal Practice. Loans and Credit in* Consilia *and* Decisiones *in the Northern and Southern Low Countries (c 1500–1680)*, Leiden: Brill, 2019.

of the seventeenth century: Paul van Christijnen's (Christinaeus) *Decisiones* of cases decided by the Great Council, the Council of Brabant and a few other courts in the same area where the author had practised for nearly half a century as an advocate and legal officer of the city of Mechlin. In terms of legal methods, Christinaeus' *Decisiones* appear to illustrate the late *mos italicus*, although the general arrangement of subject matter following the rubrics of Justinian's Code, supplemented by a volume on feudal law, may be regarded as a modest nudge towards the demands of the early modern systematic approach. Paul van Christijnen (and in later editions, his son Sebastian) extensively used legal authorities in their reports, referring to both the traditional late-medieval civil-law authorities and the growing body of more recent legal literature which, on the whole, remained steeped in the traditional method.[15]

In contrast to what has been observed for *consilia*, the genre of law reports continued to be developed during the eighteenth century, although not on the same scale as in other jurisdictions. Legal particularism may in that regard also have been an inhibiting factor.

(5) Other printed sources

During the eighteenth century, factums were occasionally printed,[16] but did not develop to a genre of published collections as in France. Many works by professional advocates and judges were written with a scholarly ambition and do not reflect forensic arguments. Even procedural treatises or handbooks, such as those by Filips Wielant and Joost de Damhouder, follow a descriptive and analytical mode of presentation.[17]

C. LEGAL AUTHORITIES AND JURISPRUDENTIAL CHANGES

As in most jurisdictions, the effects of sixteenth-century legal humanism on legal practice were limited and much delayed. Until the beginning of the seventeenth century, late-medieval methods prevailed, and were then only

---

15 A Wijffels, "Christinaeus, *Decisions*", in S Dauchy, G Martyn, A Musson, H Pihlajamäki, A Wijffels (eds), *The Formation and Transmission of Western Legal Culture. 150 Books that Made the Law in the Age of Printing*, Cham: Springer, 2016, 177–180.

16 For an example, see the case study discussed *infra* (argument printed as a "*motif de droit*").

17 F Wielant wrote a *Practycke civile* and a *Practycke criminele*, which were translated, edited and reworked by J de Damhouder, whose Latin version of both the treatise on civil procedure and that on criminal procedure subsequently (in the Latin version or other translations) widely circulated throughout Europe.

progressively replaced by characteristic early modern models of legal argumentation, merging particular laws and civil law in a systematic approach focused on topics defined by positive law categories.[18] A degree of *ius commune* was maintained through the extensive use, even in practice-related legal literature, of foreign legal scholarship, which was itself increasingly focused on its own *iura propria*. That may partly explain why in the Habsburg Netherlands, references to foreign authorities were increasingly sought in French and Dutch works, while references to authorities from other continental jurisdictions were apparently less common. Perhaps more so than in contemporary early modern scholarly literature, practice-related literature continued to refer explicitly, in addition to the more recent literature, to works which belonged to the older layers of legal scholarship, including the late-medieval *mos italicus* authors.

D. FORENSIC AUTHORITIES IN FORENSIC REASONING

A rough impression of legal authorities referred to by legal practitioners in the early modern Southern Netherlands may be gained from an old study on the late-fifteenth and sixteenth-century practice at the Great Council of Mechlin (Wijffels 1985),[19] and from two recent doctoral dissertations dealing with, respectively, the law reports by Charles de Méan (Lagasse 2017)[20] and eighteenth-century practice at the Great Council of Mechlin (Ronvaux 2018).[21] Those three studies do not all deal with the same types of source and the vantage-point of each researcher was different. They cannot therefore offer a homogenous view on the topic. Wijffels considered references to legal authorities in advocates' memoranda and other legal opinions in legal proceedings from c 1470 until 1580, brought before the Great Council in

---

18 J Schröder, *Recht als Wissenschaft. Geschichte der juristischen Methode vom Humanismus bis zur historischen Schule*, Munich: C H Beck (2nd edn), 2012.

19 A Wijffels, *Qui millies allegatur, Les allégations du droit savant dans les dossiers du Grand Conseil de Malines (causes septentrionales, ca 1460–1580)*, [*Rechtshistorische Studies*, XI], Leiden: Brill, 1985 [necnon in: *Verzamelen en bewerken van de jurisprudentie van de Grote Raad*, Nieuwe Reeks, X, Amsterdam: Werkgroep Grote Raad].

20 B Lagasse, *Charles de Méan, le Papinien liégeois. Travail réalisé en vue de l'obtention du grade de Doctor in law de l'Universiteit Gent et de Docteur en sciences juridiques de l'Université de Liège*, 2 vols (sd = 2017; the publication of the dissertation is forthcoming).

21 M Ronvaux, *Le Grand Conseil de Malines et le droit namurois au XVIIIe siècle. Thèse présentée en vue de l'obtention du grade de docteur en sciences juridiques, Faculté de droit et de criminologie, Université catholique de Louvain*, 3 vols (sd = 2018). Since the writing of this chapter, the dissertation has been published as: M Ronvaux, *L'ancien droit privé namurois et sa pratique au XVIIIe siècle*, 2 vols [*Annales de la Société Archéologique de Namur*, 2019 [=2020], Tome 93, Fascicules 1 & 2]. Further references to Ronvaux's dissertation are to the published version.

first-instance and appeal cases originating from the Northern Netherlands (mainly Holland, Zeeland and Utrecht); Lagasse offers a general survey of legal authors found in the printed reports of de Méan (1604–1674), a member of the higher council in the ecclesiastical principality of Liège; whereas Ronvaux gives a general survey of legal authors referred to by counsel in eighteenth-century proceedings before the Great Council originating from the county of Namur. Although the three surveys are certainly not *eiusdem generis* (neither by their object, nor by their methods), they provide at least some rough indication of general trends in the use of legal literature during, respectively, the sixteenth, the seventeenth and the eighteenth century.

(1) The sixteenth century

Wijffels' research on late fifteenth and sixteenth-century references in memoranda and opinions submitted in the course of litigation originating in the Northern Netherlands before the Great Council of Mechlin was primarily focused on civil and canon law authorities. His main finding was that throughout the period of his research, late-medieval authorities prevailed. Legal humanistic learning hardly played any role in forensic argumentation, even though several practitioners were aware of the humanistic literature and had legal-humanistic works in their library.[22] The use of those late-medieval authorities was also reflected in the prevalence of the *mos italicus* method in the practitioners' reasoning. From the case files, it was possible to establish that the same general pattern appeared both in the submissions originally presented before the Court of Holland in The Hague and (in appeal) before the Great Council of Mechlin. The research also highlighted that explicit references to *ius commune* authorities were largely based on the most conventional doctrinal authorities, both in civil law and canon law. Nicolaus Everardus' *Loci legales* (the author of which held prominent judicial offices both in The Hague and Mechlin) encapsulate and illustrate accurately some of the main features of the argumentation patterns followed by practitioners in their submissions.[23]

---

22 See, for example, A Wijffels, "Loys de Lucenne, avocat au Grand Conseil de Malines. La quiétude privée d'une bibliothèque, l'embarras public d'une liaison dangereuse" (2000) 40 *Publication du Centre Européen d'Etudes Bourguignonnes*, 129–141.

23 A Wijffels, "Everardus, *A Book on Topics*", in S Dauchy, G Martyn, A Musson, H Pihlajamäki and A Wijffels (eds), *The Formation and Transmission of Western Legal Culture. 150 Books that Made the Law in the Age of Printing*, Cham: Springer, 2016, 65–67.

For the period 1460–1580, the memoranda also show a progressive diversification of the legal literature referred to. Until the mid-sixteenth century, a growing number of civil law references were based on doctrinal writings; a similar tendency can be found for canon law references. In civil law, a handful of authors held a quasi-monopoly in the advocates' references during the first decades of the period under investigation; their predominance was gradually eroded in the course of the sixteenth century, but only to a limited extent: even by the second half of the sixteenth century, the Accursian Gloss, the commentaries by Bartolus, Baldus, Angelus de Ubaldis, Alexander Tartagnus, Paulus de Castro and Jason de Mayno represented more than 80 per cent of the references to writings on the Digest (and a similar figure may be mentioned for writings on the Code, with Cynus and Bartholomaeus de Saliceto replacing Alexander and Angelus). Canon law doctrinal authorities are somewhat more diversified, although here again, advocates in The Hague and Mechlin followed conventional patterns: for example, in both courts, the same commentaries on the *Liber Extra* represent more than 80 per cent of all the references to commentaries on that collection (viz by Nicolaus de Tudeschis, Innocent IV and, to a lesser extent, Felinus Sandeus, Antonius de Butrio, Johannes Andreae and Johannes de Imola). Those canon lawyers were the contemporaries of the civil law commentators mostly quoted by the same practitioners in the Low Countries and reflected essentially the same legal method.

Beyond the commentaries which continued to prevail, other genres of legal literature played a minor, but nonetheless increasing, part in the practitioners' references: from about 5 per cent of all references to doctrinal writings in 1461–1480 to nearly 20 per cent a century later. The growth and diversification become more obvious from the 1520s onwards, when new techniques and formats of legal imprints came on the market. Even then, a survey of the literature recurrently quoted confirms the traditional outlook of the practitioners' references: a third of the references to works other than commentaries are references to Guilelmus Durantis' *Speculum* and Alexander Tartagnus' *consilia*. They are followed by monographic works (including *consilia*) by Guido Papa, Ludovicus Romanus, Baldus, Bartolus, B de Chasseneuz and N Everardus – except for Zasius, no other author associated with legal humanism appears in the list of recurrently quoted legal writers.

(2) The seventeenth century

His political and judicial commitments notwithstanding, Charles de Méan also had scholarly interests. His *Observationes et res judicatae ad jus civile Leodiensium, Romanorum, aliarumque gentium, canonicum et feudale*,[24] was also a work of filial *pietas*, as it was intended to enhance the authority of his father's attempt to draft the Liège customs, a project which, however, failed to be officially sanctioned. The *editio princeps* of the first five parts of the 725 *Observationes* (supplemented by a sixth part of 106 *Definitiones* published posthumously by Charles' son Pierre in 1678) date from 1652–1669. Lagasse's survey of authors referred to in de Méan's work mentions 420 authorities, of which 396 from the Second Middle Ages until de Méan's own lifetime. In a chronological overview (for which Lagasse decided to allocate the same author to two different centuries if the author is deemed to have been active in both centuries, hence a total hereafter of more than 100 per cent), it appears that about a quarter of the doctrinal authorities were authors from the Second Middle Ages (eleventh to fifteenth centuries, of which more than half from the last century), two thirds from the sixteenth century, and some 40 per cent from the seventeenth century. To some extent, these figures are inevitably distorted, because second-hand references tend to increase the part of older authorities, whereas near-contemporary or contemporary authorities are less likely to appear as second-hand references. In any case, the figures clearly show that for a scholarly-minded Liège jurist of the mid-seventeenth century, late-medieval civil and canon law authors were on the wane. Lagasse also provides an overview of the authors by country of origin. A third of the authors are identified as Italians, slightly more than a fifth as French. The Low Countries (without differentiating between North and South), except Liège, represent about a tenth of the references, authors from Liège 4 per cent. Authors from the German nation represent a little more than 10 per cent; from Spain nearly 7 per cent; from Portugal nearly 1.5 per cent. Lagasse notes that the most quoted authorities are Jacques Cujas and Antoine Favre. Other frequently quoted authors are Bartolus, Baldus, André Tiraqueau, Charles Dumoulin, Diego de Covarrubias, Andreas Gail, François de Barry, Jacobus Menocchio and Jaime Cáncer. These surveys do not entirely support Lagasse's claim that de

---

24 I have used the edition, Ch de Méan, *Observationes et res judicatae ad jus civile Leodiensium, Romanorum, aliarumque gentium, canonicum et feudale*, Liège: Typis Everardi KInts (Editio tertia), in eight parts including the additions and index, 1740–1741.

Méan's work reflects a "predominant" influence of legal humanism, which the author mixes up with the so-called "practical" legal doctrine emerging in the sixteenth century.[25] In spite of de Méan's obvious interest for Roman law and its ancient historical developments, the bulk of the legal literature he cited reflects an interest for early modern scholarship which contributed to develop a more systematic and subject-related approach to legal methods, and which focused on, or integrated, developments of particular laws. Legal-humanistic expertise appears more as an ancillary genre, in particular for updating Roman law scholarship. What the survey most obviously expresses, is that in the Southern Netherlands, by the mid-seventeenth century, indigenous legal literature played a relatively minor role, whereas the civil law's scholarly tradition (especially when written in Latin or French) was still, by continental Western European standards, fairly cosmopolitan.

(3) The eighteenth century

Ronvaux's overview of doctrinal authorities in memoranda of eighteenth-century litigation from Namur before the Great Council is based on 1,027 references occurring in 276 case files.[26] Ronvaux identified 209 legal authors.[27] About half of those authors appear in one case only, whereas the five most often quoted authors represent half the total of all references found in the case files; the ten most often quoted authors represent three-quarters of all references. The top five identified by Ronvaux are: Joannes Voet (eighty-two references); Pierre Stockmans (forty-four references); Charles de Méan (thirty-nine references); Antoine Favre (thirty-seven references); and Andreas Gail (thirty-five references). A chronological overview (following somewhat different criteria than those applied by Lagasse for de Méan) shows that less than 10 per cent of the references are to medieval authors; about 30 per cent to sixteenth-century jurists; somewhat more than 50 per cent to seventeenth-century jurists; and just a little more than 10 per cent to eighteenth-century jurists.[28] Here, too, one may suppose that older references will tend to be over-represented, but it is clear that late-medieval authorities had become marginal: even so, they still occur in significant numbers, which means that as the ancient layer of *ius commune* literature, they were still part of the legal landscape at the end

25 Lagasse, *Charles de Méan, le Papinien liégeois*, vol I, 168.
26 Ronvaux, *L'ancien droit privé namurois*, op cit, vol I, 107–124.
27 See the full list, ibid, 108–114.
28 See the diagrams, ibid, 117.

of the *Ancien Régime*. Conversely, one would expect the contemporary eighteenth-century legal literature to be underrepresented, all the more so because the source material includes case files from the early decades of the century. Their low occurrence nonetheless suggests that (Namur) practitioners were not exceedingly keen to keep up with the latest legal works being produced. Ronvaux also looked at the national origins of the legal writers referred to.[29] French authors come first with 35 per cent, followed by Italians with 25 per cent. Jurists from the Habsburg Netherlands and Liège represent 13 per cent; German authors 12 per cent; Dutch authors 9 per cent; and Spanish jurists 6 per cent. However, a breakdown based on the number of references shows that the Southern and Northern Netherlands provide relatively substantially more authorities: 25 per cent for the Southern Netherlands and 17 per cent for the United Provinces. (The corresponding figures for the other countries are: France 31 per cent; Italy 14 per cent; Germany 10 per cent; and Spain 3 per cent.) The share of home-produced legal literature took a substantial part, but the general picture, even for regions such as Namur and the other Habsburg provinces in the Netherlands which had become a backwater in European legal science, remained fairly cosmopolitan. Ronvaux also observed that legal writings focusing specifically on the county of Namur (mostly circulating in handwritten collections) were rarely quoted, even though they were often far more relevant for dealing with issues of customary or statutory law.[30] The printed format of a legal work may have strengthened its status as a "book of authority".

(4) Law reports as authorities

During the sixteenth century, in the practice of the Great Council, the share of legal literature other than commentaries on the *corpora iuris* in the whole of the references to legal literature grew from approximately 5 per cent to 20 per cent or more. Half of those are references to *consilia*. By contrast, law reports represent only 8.5 per cent of the legal literature other than commentaries. Before the 1580s, most of the latter are to the reports by Guy Pape, the rest is scattered over the *Decisiones* of the Roman Rota, the *Decisiones Capellae Tholosanae*, and reports by Matteo d'Afflitto, Nicolas Bohier, Octavianus Cacheranus and Jean Papon. Although home-grown

---

29 See the diagrams, ibid, 115–116.
30 Ibid, 120–121.

manuscripts of reports circulated, the advocates' memoranda contain only exceptionally references to unpublished judicial precedents.[31]

By the early seventeenth century, when Paul van Christijnen (Christinaeus) wrote his reports, the genre of reports, in so far as one can rely on his own *Decisiones*, appears to have been a well-established authority. It provided even most of the "foreign" authorities in those reports, if one discounts the *ius commune* literature.[32] The distinction is, however, rather artificial; because, especially during the sixteenth century, collections of *Decisiones* were still very much part of *ius commune* scholarship, notwithstanding their association to a particular reporter discussing the practice of a particular court.

Lagasse's survey of authors[33] referred to in de Méan's *Observationes* does not identify their works, but the index by Mathias Gordinne[34] on which the survey is based, does specify different works by author. Although the latter's list may not be entirely reliable, it does provide some general indication to what extent de Méan used *consilia* and *decisiones* as authorities in his own work. Several of the approximately 400 authors cited as authorities (including some authors of non-legal works) have written different types of work used by de Méan, but out of those 400, at least more than fifty are authors of *consilia* mentioned by de Méan, and at least more than sixty authors of reports. More than a quarter of de Méan's authorities are therefore jurists who had written a collection of one of the two most closely practice-related genres of legal literature in the civil law tradition. The list of authors of *consilia* includes most of the late-medieval authors of such works. Late-medieval reports were much scarcer, which means that in that genre, comparatively more (late-)sixteenth and contemporary seventeenth-century authors appear in de Méan's work, from a large array of continental European jurisdictions. As in the case of van Christijnen's reports, de Méan as a legal professional was willing to draw a large variety of Belgian and foreign law reports to his pool of authorities.

---

31 A Wijffels, "References to Judicial Precedents in the Practice of the Great Council of Malines (c 1460–1580)", in A Wijffels (ed), *Miscellanea Consilii Magni III* [*Verzamelen en bewerken van de jurisprudentie van de Grote Raad*, Nieuwe Reeks, XII], Amsterdam: Werkgroep Grote Raad, 1988, 165–186.

32 A Wijffels, "*Orbis exiguus*. Foreign authorities in Paulus Christinaeus's Law Reports", in W H Bryson, S Dauchy, M Mirow (eds), *Ratio decidendi. Guiding Principles of Judicial Decisions*, vol II, *Foreign Law*, Berlin: Duncker und Humblot, 2010, 37–62.

33 Lagasse, *Charles de Méan, le Papinien liégeois*, vol II, Appendix 3 on 527–628.

34 M Gordinne, "Index omnium autorum, Qui in Operibus D Caroli de Mean citantur per ordinem Alphabeticum", in *Additamenta ad Opera Nob. D. Caroli de Mean*, Tomus Septimus sive Pars septima . . ., Liège: Typis Everardi Kints, 1741, 84–97.

Similar to Lagasse's overview, Ronvaux identifies the authors quoted by practitioners in eighteenth-century legal opinions, but not the works referred to. Perhaps the list of authors may suggest a broader range of new literary genres being used, but several of the names in Ronvaux's list of 210 authors are mainly known as *arrêtistes*, including four of the five authors who provide 50 per cent of all the quotes in Ronvaux's corpus (viz Stockmans, de Méan, Favre and Gail).[35]

E. CASE STUDY: FAMILY PROPERTY LAW IN A MILITARY HOUSEHOLD

A military officer challenged the validity of his deceased wife's will, who, while living in Namur with her mother, had left her chattels (movables) to her sister. The case was decided in revision by the Great Council of Mechlin in favour of the officer. It is reported in Coloma's law reports,[36] and a case file in the court's records contains a printed *motif de droit* on behalf of the officer's opponent, which can be dated between 1713 and 1716.[37] The decision of the Great Council (at the end of revision proceedings) is dated 27 January 1717 in the report.[38]

The officer relied on the custom of Namur, which stated:

> 52. Item, si la femme survit à son mary, elle aura pour douaire coustumier en propriété tous les biens meubles délaissés par sondit mary, restans après les debtes payées, et l'usufruict de tous les biens réels allodiaux ou cottiers apportez en mariage par sondit mary, et aussi des acquests faits ensemble, et ce quand il ne sera convenu d'autre douaire par le traicté de marriage.[39]

It was common ground that the customary provision also operated in favour of the husband. The officer's opponent argued that the Namur custom was not applicable in this case, because of the military status of the husband. In such a case, a statute issued in 1587 by Alexander Farnese, Captain-General

---

35 Ronvaux, *L'ancien droit privé namurois*, op cit, vol I, 107.

36 Jean-Alphonse, comte de Coloma, *Arrêts du Grand Conseil de S M I et R séant en la ville de Malines . . .*, Mechlin: Chez P J Hanicq, 1781, vol I, 268–279.

37 Brussels, Archives Générales du Royaume, Fonds Grand Conseil de Malines, Appels de Namur, N 352.

38 The case is discussed briefly in M Ronvaux, *L'ancien droit privé namurois*, op cit, vol I, 203.

39 "If the wife survives after her husband's death, her customary dowry will consist of all the chattels left by her husband, after debts have been paid, and of the usufruct of the real [immovable] property, whether allodial goods or tenures, brought by the husband into the marriage, and also of the property jointly acquired after the marriage, in so far as no other form of dowry will have been agreed in their ante-nuptial contract." (J Grandgagnage (ed), *Coutumes de Namur et coutume de Philippeville*, vol I, Bruxelles: Fr Gobbaerts, 1869, 11).

of the Army of Flanders and Governor-General of the Spanish Netherlands, would prevail.[40] The statute, it was submitted, referred to the civil law with regard to a soldier's estate as far as the chattels were concerned.[41]

Jean-Alphonse de Coloma's (1677–1739)[42] report of the case first concentrates on the issue whether such laws as the custom's rule are to be seen as pertaining to the person or to property, an issue for which Coloma adduces contrasting scholarly opinions, and the proposition that such laws ought to be viewed as "mixed statutes" (i.e. both personal and real), an opinion Coloma himself rejects.[43] He then considers how the action ought to be identified with regard to a usufruct, the object of which will be either movable or immovable. That issue, in turn, brings him to state that the custom of the officer's domicile should apply. The following issue is then how to determine a military officer's domicile. In this case, Coloma opts for a voluntary domicile where the officer's wife resided (Namur). The issue of the domicile and its relevance for determining the applicable custom is crucial in Coloma's reasoning for excluding the application of the 1587 statute issued by Farnese. According to that statute, the issue would have been governed by the "written" (i.e. civil) law, but Coloma argues that the statute does not apply to military staff who have a domicile. He thus bypasses the question whether that statute was in general applicable or not in the county of Namur. Apparently, the court heard several practitioners who testified that the statute was not applicable in Namur, either because it had not been published in the county at the time, or because it had never been in use, while the practice had been to apply the Namur custom to military officers who had their

---

40 The (Spanish) text is printed in *Tweeden Deel vanden Placcaert-Boeck inhoudende diverse ordonnantien, edicten ende placcaerten vande Koninicklycke Maiesteyten ende Haere Deurluchtighe Hoogheden Graven van Vlaendren, Mitsgaeders van heurlieden Provincialen Raede aldaer, Gepubliceert inden voornoemden lande van Vlaendren t' Zedert den Iaere Vijfthien-hondert t' Zestisch tot ende met den Iaere Zesthien hondert Negen-en-twintich*, Antwerp: By Hendrick Aertssens, 1667, 663–671.

41 The passage mostly focused on in this case appears to be the provision (loc cit, 664): "De manera que un Soldado no podra ser convenido, ny llamado en justiciar por ningun delicto, ny deuda, ny por otra cosa ninguna, sino es por ante los Auditores, y juezes militares, y ninguno otro, Excepto en causas de actiones reales, hypothecarias, y de succession de bienes raizes, y patrimoniales, porque en tel caso, cada uno podra proseguir y pedir su justicia segun las costumbres, y ante los juezes del lugar, donde estuuieren situados dichos bienes, ques conforme la leyes comunes, y los placartes del Emperador mi Señor, de gloriosa memoria [viz *Charles V*], sin querer derogar fuera desto en cosa chica ny grande, a los privilegios militares, losquales queremos, y es nuestra voluntad, que sean inviolablemente guardados."

42 A Wijffels, "Van Paul van Christijnen (†1631) tot Jean-Alphonse de Coloma (†1739): rechters en advocaten bij de Grote Raad van Mechelen tegen de achtergrond van de zeventiende-eeuwse Europese rechtsontwikkeling" (1993) 9(1) *De zeventiende eeuw*, 3–14.

43 Coloma, *Arrêts du Grand Conseil de S M I et R séant en la ville de Malines*, vol I, 271.

domicile in the county. Coloma adds yet another argument for disapplying the 1587 statute: the latter, he submits, because it had been enacted by the Governor General, would not have departed from the emperor's Edict of 1547, which declared that with regard to soldiers, the local custom (sc where the property was situated) would apply to real actions and actions relating to inheritance.[44] The report states that the officer had won his case in first instance before the Council of Namur, a judgment confirmed in appeal by the Council of Luxemburg, and again in revision by the Great Council of Mechlin.

Not every part of Coloma's report is reasoned along the same lines. Coloma's main purpose, in this particular report, is the justification of the court's decision to apply the customary rule of Namur in favour of the officer, which entailed precluding the 1587 statute that would have imposed the application of civil law. For the general issue, whether the particular rule is dealing with the personal status, (real) property, or is "mixed", Coloma mentions as main authorities for the opposing views Charles Dumoulin and Bertrand d'Argentré,[45] two major sixteenth-century French authors known largely for their commentaries on customary law, still strongly supported by civil law scholarship. Each opinion is further discussed with references to (more recent) early modern authors from the Low Countries, both North and South: N Burgundus, C Rodenburg, A van Wesel and P Stockmans for the Dumoulin opinion; A Matthaeus (II), J A van der Muelen, with further references to P and J Voet, and to ao S van Leeuwen on the issue of mixed statutes. (In this report, Coloma does not refer to late-medieval authorities. In a reasoning which was intended to justify the application of a customary rule, it may have seemed more political not to rely on late-medieval schol-arship, which, although it acknowledged the primacy of particular laws, restricted the latter's province through rules of construction and evidence.) Coloma's own reservations are argued with references to Roman law texts, and also to the works of some of the Dutch authors already mentioned. On the usufruct issue, the general principles are buttressed with refer-ences to early modern French and Netherlandish authors: N Burgundus, Jean Grivel, N van Tulden, Ch Loyseau, A Wesel, P Stockmans, J A van der Meulen, as well as R Bachovius. On the issue of domicile, he refers to H Kinschot, P W Clerin (compiler of a *Code militaire des Pays-Bas*, ed pr

---

44 Ibid, 278.
45 Both references also occur in the *Motif de droit*, cf *infra*.

1704, including a commentary on the 1587 statute),[46] and more generally to L Le Grand, W van Radelant, J Voet, P Stockmans, J Pollet and R A du Laury. Occasionally, Coloma also refers to more particular municipal law, such as a decree ("Acte") of the Privy Council.[47]

It is not possible to retrace the origins of every part of the reasoning and of the references: some may reflect the memoranda and arguments of counsel (at different stages of the proceedings), some may reflect the *rapporteur*'s or other councillors' opinions, while in the discussion on the mixed statutes, Coloma gives the impression of developing his own reasoning. Within the limits of this specific report, some of the general findings on the use of authorities in contemporary Belgian legal practice appear nevertheless borne out: a strong reliance on various genres of mainly early modern civil law scholarship, whether specifically focused on Roman law, customary law or statute law; a regular use of foreign scholarly authorities, although borrowed mainly from France and the United Provinces, and obviously other provinces of the Habsburg Netherlands as well.

The only evidence in the calendared records of the court which gives a fragmentary impression of the argument on behalf of one of the litigants (viz the beneficiary of the deceased wife's will) is a printed *motif de droict*, probably from the last round of proceedings (in review before the Great Council). The text (forty-one pages) is signed J O'Donnnoghue [sic] de Niele, possibly Jean O' Donnoghue (1678–1742), who became a member of the Great Council.[48]

The *motif de droict* is structured around two main issues. The first is the counsel's thesis arguing that the case should be governed by civil law (*"droit commun"*, i.e. *ius commune*) and military laws, excluding any local custom, such as the one of Namur. The second main argument is that the 1587 statute was in force and applicable with respect to movable property in Namur. Compared to the fragmentary information that the present state of the art offers with regard to the use of authorities in eighteenth-century legal prac-

---

46 Edition used: *Code militaire des Païs-Bas contenant Les Edits, Ordonnances, Decrets, le Stile de l'Audience Generale tant Civil que Criminel, & les Privileges de Gens de Guerre. Ensemble Les Arrêts, Declarations, & autres Preuves de leur usage, avec un Commentaire très-exact sur le Placard du Prince de Parme du 15. Mai 1587 . . .*, Maastricht: Chez Lambert Bertus, 1721.

47 Coloma, *Arrêts du Grand Conseil de S M I et R séant en la ville de Malines*, 278 ("Voyez aussi l'Acte du Conseil Privé du 9 Octobre 1641, imprimé derriere la Coutume de Gand").

48 J O'Donnoghue (sd), *Motif de droit pour Dame Agnes Badot veuve de feu Messire Philipe Emanuel de Franquen, Chevalier Conseiller & Commis des Domaines & Finances de Sa Majesté Impetrante de Lettres de Revision contre Le Sieur Jean François Joseph Du Menil, Lieutenant Colonel d'Infanterie Adjourné*. Mechlin: Chez Iean François Jaye.

tice in Belgium, the *motif* offers few surprises. In addition to some direct references to Roman law texts and a somewhat jocular obiter reference to Baldus de Ubaldis,[49] the range of legal literature referred to looks familiar, and to some extent matches the range in the report on the same case in Coloma's work. But for a couple of exceptions (N Burgundus, P Peckius), most of the authors quoted are "foreign", but as already noted previously, the cosmopolitan outlook remains limited; in this case comprising almost exclusively authors from the Northern Netherlands (Grotius's Hollandish consultations, C Rodenburgh, J van Someren, J Voet, here also quoted with some insistence, and A van Wesel) and France (B d'Argentré, C de Ferrière and C Dumoulin). On issues of evidence, the counsel's memorandum also refers to G Mascardo and J Menocchio. All the Dutch and French authors mentioned no doubt belong to the *ius commune* literature in a broader sense, but most of them, because of the subject of their work or their method, would be strongly associated with their particular legal tradition. The predominance of Dutch and (Northern) French authors may therefore reflect a more restricted perception of a degree of common legal culture in adjacent territories.

One rather unusual use of authorities in the *motif* is linked to the "law of nations" (in the text: *droit des gens, ius gentium*).[50] The reference occurs in a passage which rejects the idea that joint property of spouses would be part of the "general customs in the world" which can be equated with the law of nations (i.e. a fairly traditional concept of *ius gentium*). The memorandum's author refers to several countries where, he submits, such a joint property does not apply. For each country adduced in support of that counter-argument, he mentions a legal authority borrowed from legal literature: for parts of France, De Ferrière's commentary on the custom of Paris;[51] for Sicily, M Giurba on the laws of Messina;[52] for Germany,

---

49 Ibid, 31, challenging a *turbe* detrimental to his client's interest: "Ces Messieurs doivent être ravis qu'ils ne sont pas tombés entre les mains de [f]eu Maître Balde. *Testis*, dit-il, *deponens absque alia ratione dictitur non ut homo sed ut pecus deponere*." The reference may seem unsubstantial, but the Namur *turbae* had, according to Coloma (*Arrêts du Grand Conseil de S M I*, 277), made a deep impression on the judges in Mechlin.

50 *Motif de droit*, loc cit, 16–17.

51 In the edition I have used C[laude] de Ferrière, *Nouveau commentaire sur la coutume de la prevosté et vicomté de Paris*, vol II, Paris: Chez la Veuve de Jean Cochart, 1703, Tit X (*De communauté de biens*), inc 3.

52 In the Dutch edition I have used M[arius] Giurba, *Lucubrationum pars prima, in omne ius municipale, quod statutum appellant, S P G. Messanensis, suique districtus, & totius fere Siciliae*, Amsterdam: Ex Typographejo Ioannis Blaeu, 1651, cap 1, inc, 9.

A Matthaeus (II) *Paræmia*;[53] for England and Ireland, J Cowell's *Institutes*;[54] and even in Holland, where such joint property had been introduced, C Neostadius provides exceptions.[55] The selection of legal systems (and thus of authors supposed to document those legal systems) may at first glance seem arbitrary (and the extension of Cowell's English Institutes to Ireland may raise eyebrows), but it is at least partly explained by the counsel's remark that the Habsburg sovereign's armies included Germans, Englishmen and Irishmen, in some cases even organised as distinct national army corps.[56] Again, literature which is part of the civil law tradition in a wider sense is used each time in order to focus on a rule of substantive *ius proprium*. The link with the national provenance of soldiers deployed in the Habsburg Netherlands is a further argument for justifying the need to apply civil and military laws as uniform rules in multinational armed forces.[57]

Some of the references which occur in the *motif* reappear in Coloma's report, but not necessarily in exactly the same light or to deal with the same issue. An example is Dumoulin's *consilium* 53, which Coloma mainly mentions as the leading opinion according to which a statute on joint matrimonial property is of a personal nature.[58] The *motif* does briefly refer to the

53   In the Brussels edition I have used (note the extension to other regions in the sub-title, including provinces of the Habsburg Netherlands) A[ntonius II] Matthaeus, *Paroemiae Belgarum Jurisconsultis usitatissimae: Editio altera, cui accesserunt Additiones post quamlibet Paroemiam, continentes Jus et praxim, Tam in Bonis Allodialibus quam Feudalibus, Circa easdem, non tantum in Foederato Belgio, sed & in Hispania, Gallia, Saxonia, Bavaria, Hannonia, Flandria, Brabantia, Aliisque Provincis observatum*, Brussels: Apud Petrum de Dobbeleer, 1694, on the rule 'Man ende wijf hebben geen verscheyden goet', 18, n 6 *in fine*.

54   In the edition I have used J[ohn] Cowell, *Institutiones juris anglicani, ad methodum et seriem Institutionum imperialium compositae & digestae* . . ., Oxford: W Hall pro Ed Forrest, 1664, Book I, *De nuptiis*, n 18, 25.

55   In the edition I have used C[ornelius] Neostadius, *De pactis antenuptialibus rerum judicatarum observationes*, Arnhem: Typis Jacobi Biesii, 1657, Obs 9, notae, 25a *supra*.

56   *Motif de droit*, loc cit, 16: "Or il est notoir que dans les Armées de Sa Majesté il y a toujours eu Allemands & des Anglois & Irlandois, même des Corps de ces Nations." The reference to Giurba therefore remains in that sense unaccounted, unless the *motif*'s author was anticipating that it would be mentioned in the editor's present volume.

57   *Motif de droit*, loc cit, 23, the insistence on a uniform legal regime for the whole army echoes a provision in the 1587 statute: "En el juzgar se conoramran con las leyes, y derecho commun, y las ordines, bandos, costumbres, previlegios, y constituciones de Guerra, sin atarie a ningunas leyes municipales, costumbres, ny constitutiones particulares de ningunas provincias y lugares, a losquales los Soldados non estan subjectos, Porque los soldados qu'estan debaxo de sus vanderas a qualquiera parte que vayan, han de tener siempre las mismas leyes, costumbres, y privilegios, quo non es razon, que por andar de una provincia, o tierra a otra, ayan de mudar a caso paso de leyes, ny costumbres : ny tan poco conviene a la autoridad de la disciplina militar, que los soldados esten subjectos a las leyes, y costumbres de la provincia en que hazen la guerra." (loc cit, 667–668).

58   I have used the edition C[arolus] Molinaeus, *Omnia quae extant opera*, Tomus Secundus, Paris:

Dumoulin-d'Argentré[59] controversy on the nature of particular law rules governing the matrimonial joint property,[60] but it discusses the case of Dumoulin's *consilium* 53 more at length[61] in order to argue *a contrario* that in that case, the military judge would have applied the civil law rule excluding joint property if the particulars of that case had not established that the spouses had mixed up their chattels and intended to create a community of ownership, conditions which were not met (counsel submitted) in the present case.

The author of the *motif* also refers more or less in detail to several other (unreported) cases, some older, some more recent, but not in the sense of modern case law.[62] The cases are not primarily mentioned because a judicial decision would have explicitly established a particular principle, but for the twofold argument on behalf of his client (i.e. the application by default of civil law to military persons and the validity (and hence justiciability) of the 1587 statute), the counsel presents a rationale from which he infers that the courts in those other cases (in the Habsburg Netherlands) must have followed the same reasoning.

F. CONCLUSION. THE BELGIAN *USUS MODERNUS*: A WEAK FORM OF *IUS COMMUNE*

From the second half of the seventeenth century onwards, early modern legal scholarship in the Southern Netherlands developed only to a comparatively limited extent a Belgian *usus modernus* (i.e. a mainstream doctrinal model combining civil law scholarship with the territories' particular laws by subject matter). Several factors may contribute to explain why Belgian legal scholarship remained in that respect a backwater of continental European legal developments. Unlike the political situation in France, or in some

---

Sumptibus Joannis Cochart, 1681, Cons 53, 963–966, which deals with a matrimonial community of goods established explicitly or implicity, and which may extend to property wherever it is located.

59 I have used the edition B[ertrand] d'Argentré, *Commentarii in patrias Britonum leges, seu Consuetudines generales antiquissimi Ducatus Britanniae*, Paris: Sumptibus Nicolai Buon, 1628, ad art 218, with references to the controversy with Dumoulin at Nos 33–34, col 684–690.

60 *Motif de droit*, loc cit, 10.

61 *Motif de droit*, loc cit, 13s.

62 *Motif de droit*, loc cit, 13–15 (the case of *Don Pedro de Tosse and children* sd), 17 (case of the countess *d'Annapes*, 1698), 17–18 (case of *Baroness de Courreres*, 1703; see also 20), 18–19 (case of the *pléban* of St Rombouts ao v the widow of Desmarets, a medic, 1678). The case of de Courieres (different spelling) is also mentioned by Coloma, *Arrêts du Grand Conseil de S M I et R séant en la ville de Malines*, 276.

German principalities, there was from the second half of the sixteenth century onwards no longer a ruler who sought to reinforce central government and consolidate political unity through a greater degree of legal uniformity. As a result, scholars were less keen to develop, through civil law or particular laws, a common Belgian legal tradition. Institutional and legal particularisms in the Habsburg Netherlands were rife and resisted either a *gemeines Recht* culture such as in the Holy Roman Empire or a *droit coutumier commun* momentum such as in France. The most convincing attempts at developing an inchoative Belgian *usus modernus*, as for example some of the works by Antoon Anselmo, were characteristically focused primarily on particular law authorities, such as the Perpetual Edict of 1611.

All that did not preclude a general *ius commune* culture, especially since Belgian jurists' scholarly contribution to civil law had been relatively strong until the second half of the seventeenth century. The training in civil and canon law at the University of Leuven continued to ensure that at different levels of executive governance and legal practice, law graduates maintained and extended at least a basic civil law culture. Legal practice of the era, however, shows the limitations of that acculturation in general. During the last century of the *Ancien Régime*, the Belgian legal landscape was not unlike that of the Northern French *pays de coutume*, but with far fewer unifying tendencies in statutory law, customary doctrine and legal literature. The lack of such unifying factors was not compensated by a strong Roman-law-based tradition comparable to the *Rooms-Hollands recht*. Early modern Belgian law was primarily an archipelago of particular laws surrounded by a sea of *ius commune*, but most Belgian legal practitioners increasingly remained landlubbers, only resorting to what the sea could offer in order to supplement the structural deficiencies of resources available on land.

That development seems confirmed through the, on the whole, rather modest output of practice-oriented legal literature such as consultations and law reports after the mid-seventeenth century. Law in the early modern Belgian territories certainly belonged to the civil law tradition, but it was a weak form of *ius commune* which, during the last centuries of the *Ancien Régime*, hardly contributed to major or innovative European legal developments. In that respect, Belgium had, as in international politics, become a peripheral area at the heart of North-Western Europe.

Bibliography

SOURCES PUBLISHED BEFORE 1800

Álvarez de Posadilla, Juan, *Comentario a las Leyes de Toro*, Madrid: imprenta de la Viuda de Ibarra, 1796.

Antonio, Nicolás, *Biblioteca Hispana Nova*, 2 vols, Madrid: apud Joachinum de Ibarra, 1783–1788.

Aragão, António Barnabé de Elescano Barreto e, *Demétrio Moderno, ou o bibliografo jurídico portuguez*, Lisboa: officina de Lina da Silva Godinho, 1781.

Aristotle, *Topics*.

Arredondo Carmona, Manuel, *Senatus Consulta Hispaniae illustrata*, 2 vols, Madrid: ex typographia Ildephonsi à Riego, 1729–1732.

Asinio, Giovanni Battista, *De executionibus tractatus*, Venice: apud J. B. Natolinum, 1589.

Austen, Jacobus Egmondt, *Aanteekeningen van Mr Willem Schorer over de Inleidinge tot de Hollandsche rechts-geleerdheid van Hugo de Groot: door den aanteekenaar aanmerkelijk vermeerderd en uit het Latijn vertaald*, Middelburg: Pieter Gilissen en Zoon, 1784–1786.

Azevedo, Alfonso de, *Commentariorum juris civils in Hispaniae Regias Constitutiones*, 4 vols, Lyon: apud fratres Deville, 1737.

—*Consilia sive responsa, post obitum autoris. . . congesta*, Valladolid: excudebat Ioannes a Bostillo, 1604.

Azpilcueta, Martín de, "Consiliorum seu responsorum", in Id, *Opera omnia in sex tomos distincta*, Venice: apud Juntas, 1602.

Bachovius, Reinhardus, *Commentarii in primam partem Pandectarum*, Speyer: Ioannes Bernerus, 1630.

Bacmeister, Johann Christian, *Abhandlung von dem Recht der vollen und halben Geburt nach denen natürlichen, römischen, deutschen und besonders lübischen Rechten zu einer Prüfung des zu Lübeck herausgekommenen Versuchs, die Lehre von dem Vorrechte der vollen Geburt vor der halben in Erbschafts-Fällen ... in Richtigkeit zu bringen*, Hannover: Förster 1748.

Barbosa, Agostinho, *Repertorium civilis et canonici*, Lyon: M. Goy, 1675.

Barels, Jeronimo Mattheus, Advysen over den koophandel en zeevaert: mitsgaders memorien, resolutien, missives, enz daer toe behoorende; meerendeels van A van den Ende, J Ardinois, D Helmans, en andere gerenommeerde Amsterdamsche Advocaten, 2 vols, Amsterdam: Hendrik Gartman, 1780–1781.

Berg, Isaak, van den, *Nederlandsch advys-boek, inhoudende verscheidene consultatien en advysen van voorname regtsgeleerden in Nederland*, 4 vols, Amsterdam: J. A. de Chalmot, 1693–1698.

Bermúdez de Pedraza, Francisco, *Arte legal para estvdiar la iurisprudencia*, Salamanca: en la Emprenta de Antonía Ramirez, 1612.

Berní y Catalá, José, *Disertación sobre la Llave de la Jurisprudencia Española que escrive a sus pasantes*, Valencia: Josef Estevan y Cervera, 1774.

Blye, Jean-Baptiste de, *Résolutions du conseil souverain de Tournai ...*, et *Arrêtés du conseil souverain de Tournai sur différents articles de l'ordonnance criminelle du mois d'août 1670 ...*, in *Recueil d'arrêts du parlement de Flandres*, Lille: J.-B. Henry, 1773, vol II, 369–414.

Brederode, Petrus Cornelius van, *Repertorium sententiarum et regularum itemque definitionum, divisionum*, Frankfurt: Paulus Frellon, 1587.

Brito, Diogo de, *Consilium in causa maioratus regiae coronae Regni Lusitaniae*, Lisbon: ex officina Petri Crasbeeck, 1612.

Buridan, Jean-Baptiste de, *Coustumes de la cite et ville de Rheims ville et villages regis selon icelles, avec le commentaire . . . Par M. Iean Baptiste de Buridan . . .*, Paris: Louis Billaine, 1665.

Cabedo, Jorge de, *Practicarum observationum, sive decisionum Supremi Senatus Regni Lusitaniae*, Antwerp: apud viduam et filium Joannis Baptistae Verdussen, 1699.

Caldas Pereira, Francisco de, *Commentarivs analyticvs, de renovatione emphyteutica*, Lisbon: Emmanuel de Lyra Typo., 1585.

Calvino, Giulio Cesare, *De aequitate tractatus novus usque receptissimus*, Milan: ex typ. F. Vigoni, 1676.

Cambolas, Jean de, *Decisions notables sur diverses questions du droit, jugées par plusieurs arrests de la Cour de Parlement de Toulouse. Divisées en six livres*, Toulouse: Guillaume-Louis Colomiez & Ierosme Posvel, 1682.

Cantiuncula, Claudius, *. . . Claudii Cantivncvlae . . . Topica Legalia . . .*, Basel: Apvd Hieronymnm Cvrionem . . ., 1545.

Carpzov, Benedict, *Practicae novae Imperialis Saxonicae rerum criminalium pars prima*, Leipzig: apud Johannem Fridericum Gleditschium, 1739.

—*Practicae novae Imperialis Saxonicae rerum criminalium*, pars II, Wittenberg: typis excusa Mathæi Henkelii, 1670.

—*Practicae novae imperialis Saxonicae rerum criminalium*, pars III, Wittenberg: typis excusa Matthæi Henckelii, 1665.

Castejón, Aegidio, *Alphabetum Juridicum, Canonicum, Civile, Theoricum, Practicum, Morale atque Politicum*, 2 vols, Madrid: ex Typographia Regia Joannen García Infançon, 1678.

Castillo de Bovadilla, Jerónimo, *Política para corregidores y señores de vasallos en tiempo de paz y guerra. . .expurgada según el expurgatorio de MDCXL*, 2 vols, Madrid: en la Imprenta de la Gazeta, 1775.

Castillo de Sotomayor, Juan, *Quotidianarum Controversiarum Iuris*, 8 vols, 1603–1634; Lyon: sumptibus Lavr. Anisson et Io. Bapt. Devenet, 1658.

Castro, Juan Francisco de, *Discursos críticos sobre las Leyes y sus intérpretes en que se demuestra la incertidumbre de éstos y la necesidad de un nuevo y metódico cuerpo de Derecho para la recta administración de Justicia*, 2 vols, Madrid: Joachim Ibarra, 1765.

Cavalcani, Ortensio, *Tractatus de brachio regio*, Venice: apud B. Iuntam, 1608.

Cevallos, Jerónimo, *Speculum practicarum et variarum quaestionum communium contra communes*, 2 vols, Toledo: apud Thomas Guzmanium Typographum, 1599.

Choppin, René, *Commentaire sur les coustumes de la prevosté et vicomté de Paris, divisé en trois livres, Composé par M. René Choppin . . .*, vol III, Paris: Louis Billaine, 1662.

Christinaeus, Paulus, *In leges municipales civium Mechliniensium ... notae seu commentationes*, Antwerp: apud Martinum Nutium, 1625.

Cicero, *Topica*.

Claro, Gulio, *Iulii Clari patritii Alexandrini, iurisconsulti longe clarissimi, et serenissimi Philippi Hispaniarum regis Catholici in Prouincia Mediolanensi supremi consilliarii, ac regentis dignissimi. Receptarum Sententiarum Opera Omnia: quae quidem hactenus per auctorem in lucem edita sunt. . .*, Frankfurt: ex officina typographia Nicolai Bassaci, 1596.

—*Volumen, alias liber Quintus*, Venice: expensis I. A. de Antonijs, 1570.

Coello, Pedro, "Al Doctor Don Ivan Bautista de Larrea", in Francisco de la Pradilla (ed), *Suma de las leyes penales*, Madrid: en la imprenta del Reyno, 1639.

Conring, Hermann, *De origine iuris Germanici Commentarius Historicus. Obiter de Justinianei Juris in scholas et fora reductione disseritur, ac Nihusiani Triumphi exploduntur*, Helmstedt: Henning Müller 1643.

Constitutiones mediolanensis Dominii jam primum illustratae decisionibus et annotationibus ab egregio jurisconsulto et advocato Pio Antonio Mogno Fossato, Milan: ex typ. J. Marelli, 1764.

Consultatien, advysen en advertissementen gegeven ende geschreven by verscheyden treffelijcke rechts-geleerden in Hollandt en elders ... merkelyk verbetert. Daar en boven is het geheele "Amsterdamse derde deel" hier nu ook ingevoegd, Leiden: Pieter van der Aa, 1716.

Consultatien, advysen en advertissementen gegeven ende geschreven by verscheyden treffelijcke rechts-geleerden in Hollandt en elders, Amsterdam: Jan Boom et al, 1728–1739.

Consultatien, advysen en advertissementen gegeven ende geschreven by verscheyden treffelijcke rechts-geleerden in Hollandt en elders, Amsterdam-Utrecht: Gerrit de Groot en Zoon, Gysbert Tieme van Paddenburg, en De Wed: Mattheus Visch, 1768.

Consultatien, advysen en advertissementen, gegeven ende geschreven by verscheyden treffelijcke rechts-geleerden in Holland ten elders, 6 vols, Rotterdam: Joannes & Isaak Naeranus, 1645–1686.

Coren, Jakob, *Observationes XLI rerum in Senatu Hollandiae, Zelandiae, Frisiae judicatarum; item consilia XXX quaedam,* The Hague: apud Arnoldum Meris, 1633.

Costumen der stede, casselrye ende vassalryen van Berghen S. Winocx, Ghent: Maximiliaen Graet, 1664; Petrus de Goesin, 1777.

Covarrubias y Leyva, Diego de *"Variarum resolutionum",* in Id, *Omnium Operum tomus secundus,* Frankfurt: apud Ioan. Feuerab., 1583.

—*Practicarum quaestionum,* Salamanca: Andreas à Portonarijs, 1556.

Cramer, Johann Ulrich von, *Wetzlarische Nebenstunden, worinnen auserlesene, beym Höchstpreißlichen Cammergericht entschiedene Rechts-Händel zur Erweiter- und Erläuterung der Deutschen in Gerichten üblichen Rechts-Gelehrsamkeit angewendet werden,* 28 vols, Ulm: Johann Conrad Wohler, 1755–72.

Dalrymple of Stair, James, *The Decisions of the Lords of Council and Session,* 2 vols, Edinburgh: printed by the heir of Andrew Anderson, 1683–87.

—*The Institutions of the Law of Scotland,* Edinburgh: printed by the heir of Andrew Anderson, 1681.

—*The Institutions of the Law of Scotland,* Edinburgh: printed by the heir of Andrew Anderson, 1693.

Damhouder, Joos de, *Praxis rerum criminalium,* Antwerp: apud Ioannem Bellerum sub Aquila aurea, 1570.

De Haas, Gerard, *Nieuwe Hollandsche consultatien, advertissementen van regten, memorien en andere schrifturen van voorname regtsgeleerden*, 's Gravenhage: Mattheus Gaillard, 1741.

De Pape, Abraham, *Observationes ad Consilia Iuris Consultorum Batavicorum*, 2 vols, Leiden: apud Henricum Teering, 1702–1703.

Denisart, Jean-Baptiste, *Collection de décisions nouvelles et de notions relatives à la jurisprudence présente*, 6 vols, Paris: Savoye and Leclerc, 1754–1757.

Dodderidge, John, *The English Lawyer. Describing a Method for the Managing of the Lawes of this Land*, London: Printed by the Assignees of I. More Esq., 1631.

Dreyer, Johann Henrich, *Einleitung zur Kenntniß der ... von E Hochw. Rath der Reichsstadt Lübeck von Zeit zu Zeit ergangenen allgemeinen Verordnungen*, Lübeck: Christian Gottfried Donatius, 1769.

Dubois d'Hermaville, Antoine-Augustin, "Recueil d'arrêts", in *Recueil d'arrêts du parlement de Flandres*, vol I, Lille: J.-B. Henry, 1773.

Dumoulin, Charles, *Le coustumier du pays de Bourbonnois. Avec le Proces Verbal. Corrigé et annoté de plusieurs Decisions et Arrests, par M Charles du Molin* ..., Lyon: pour Georges Vernoy Libraire de Molins, 1599.

Dyer, James, *Cy ensuont ascuns nouel cases, collectes per le iades tresreuerend iudge, Mounsieur Iasques Dyer*, London: Richard Tottel, 1585.

Excelentissimae allegationes et consilia, Vallisoleti: excudebat Didacus Fernández a Córdoba Bibliopolae, 1588.

Everardus, Nicolaus, *Topicorum seu de locis legalibus liber*, Louvain: in aedibus Theodorici Martini Alustensis impensis cum Henrico Eckert ab Humburch, 1516.

Fahnenberg, Egid Joseph Karl von, *Litteratur des Kaiserlichen Reichskammergerichts*, Wetzlar: Phil. Jac. Winkler, 1792.

Falconer of Newton, David, *The Decisions of the Lords of Council and Session*, Edinburgh: James Watson, 1701.

Febo, Belchior, *Decisionum Senatus Regni Lusitaniae*, Lisbon: Petrum Craesbeeck, 1625.

Ferrière, Claude-Joseph, *Nouvelle introduction à la Pratique, contenant les principaux Termes de Pratique & de coutume*, 2 vols, Paris: Chez la Veuve Jean Cochart, 1718.

Flines, Séraphin de, "Recueil d'arrêts", in *Recueil d'arrêts du parlement de Flandres*, vol II, Lille: J.-B. Henry, 1773, 263–368.

Fulbecke, William, *A Direction, or Preparative to the study of the lawe*, London: Thomas Wight, 1600.

Gama, Antonio da, *Decisiones Supremi Senatus Regni Lusitaniae*, Barcelona: Lelij Marini, 1597.

—*Decisionum Supremi Senatus Lusitaniae Centuriae IV*, Antwerp: Apud Viduam et filium Joannis Baptistae, 1699.

García de Saavedra, Juan, *De hispanorum nobilitate et exemptionen sive ad Pragmaticam Cordubensem quae est l. 8 tit. 12 lib. 2 Recopilationis Commentarij*, Valladolid: apud Haeredes Bernardi de Sancto Domingo, 1588.

Garoni, Angelo Stefano, *Commentaria in tit de Senatoribus Novarum Constitutionum Status Mediolani*, Milan: apud Ph. Ghisulphium, 1643.

—*Observationes in Constitutiones Dominii Mediolanensis*, Milan: apud I. B. Bidellium, 1627.

Gentili, Alberico, *Lectionum et Epistolarum quae ad Ius Civile Pertinent, Liber I [-IV]*, London: Wolfius, 1584.

Ghewiet, Georges de, *Institutions du droit belgique par raport tant aux XVII. provinces qu'au Pays de Liège. Avec une Métode pour étudier la Profession d'Avocat*, Lille: Charles-Maurice Cramé, 1736.

Gibson of Durie, Alexander, *The Decisions of the Lords of Council and Session*, Edinburgh, 1690.

Gilmour of Craigmillar, John, *The Decisions of the Lords of Council and Session*, Edinburgh: James Watson, 1701.

Giussani, Giulio Cesare, *Commentarius in decretum novarum Constitutionum Mediolani. Liber secundus, de bonis in solutum dandis, aut ad hastam vendendis*, in O Carpani (ed), *In quatuor insigniores novarum Mediolani Constitutionum §§ ... doctissimi commentarii*, Milan: ex typ. B. Somaschi, 1609.

—*Tractatus de precio et aestimatione*, Milan: apud H. Bordonum, 1615.

Gousset, Jean, *Les loix municipales, et coustumes generales du balliage de Chaulmont en Bassigny et ancien ressort d'iceluy, corrigées, interpretées et annotées fidellement de plusieurs decisions, sentences, arrests, et autres raisons y convenables: et concordées à plusieurs autres coustumes de ce Royaume de France: Par M. Iean Gousset . . .*, Espinal: Pierre Hovion, 1623.

Grenet, "Préface", in Jacques Pollet, *Arrests du parlement de Flandre sur diverses questions de droit, de coutume, et de pratique ...*, Lille: Liévin Danel, 1716.

Grivel de Perrigny, Jean, *Decisiones celeberrimi sequanorum senatus Dolanus*, Antwerp, 1619.

Grociki, Bartłomiej, *Ten Postępek wybran iest z Praw Cesarskich. . .*, Cracow: Lazarus Andreae, 1562.

Groenewegen van der Made, Simon van, *Alphabet der Hollandsche regten ofte bladwyzer en korten inhoud van de Inleyding tot de Hollandsche Regtsgeleerdheid en de Aantekeningen van S van Groenewegen van der Made*, Amsterdam: Jan Boom, 1729.

Groot Placaet-boeck vervattende de Placaten, Ordonnantien ende Edicten van de Staten Generael der Vereenigdhe Nederlanden ende Heeren Staten van Hollandt ende West-Vriesland mitsgaders van de Heeren Staten van Zeelandt, 9 vols and index, C Cau, S van Leeuwen, Scheltus (J, P and I), D Lulius and J van der Linden, Amsterdam: Johannes Allart, 1658–1796.

Grotius, Hugo, *Inleijdinge tot de Hollandse Regstgeleertheyt*, 's Gravenhage: Weduwe van Hillebrant, 1631.

Guerreiro Camacho de Aboim, Diogo, *Decisiones, seu quaestiones forenses ad amplissimo, integerrimoque Portuensi Senatu*. Lisbon: ex officina Bernardi Antonii de Oliveira, 1759.

Gutiérrez, Juan, *Consilia varia*, Salamanca: excudebat Petrus Lasus, 1595.

—*Operum, Tomus octavus, seu repetitiones VI. Allegationes XIV: et consilia sive responsa LII*, Louvain: apud Ant Servant et socios, 1730.

Guyot, Joseph-Nicolas, et al, *Répertoire universel et raisonné de jurisprudence civile, criminelle, canonique et bénéficiale*, 64 vols, Paris: J. Dorez (-Panckoucke), 1775–1783.

Gylmann, Adrian, *Symphorematis Supplicationum, pro processibus, super omnibus ac singulis imperii romani constitutionibus, in supremo Camerae Imperiolis Auditorio impetrandis*, 6 vols, Frankfurt: Wolfgang Richter, 1601–1608.

Hasselt, J J van, *Aanteekeningen en Bijvoegzelen op de consultation, advijzen en advertissementen van verscheidene treffelijke rechtsgeleerden in Holland bekent onder de naam van de Hollandsche Advijzen*, Nijmegen: A. van Goor, 1782.

Hermann, Johann Hieronymus, *Concordantia Iuris*, Jena: Franciscus Buch, 1745.

Hog of Harcarse, Roger, *Decisions of the Court of Session*, Edinburgh: printed for G. Hamilton and J. Balfour, 1757.

Hollandts Placcaet-boeck: begrijpende meest alle de voornaemste placcaten, ordonnantien ende octroyon, Uytgegeeven by de Edd Groot-mogende Heeren Staten van Hollandt ende West-Vrieslandt, Amsterdam: Jan Janssen, 1645.

Iaskierus, Nicolaus, *Iuris Municipalis Maideburgensis Liber vulgo Weichbild nuncupatur. . .*, Cracow: Hiernonymys Vietor, 1535.

Jiménez, Sebastián, *Concordantiae utriusque iuris ciuilis et canonici cum legibus Partitarum*, Toledo: Typis Petri Roderici: expensis Michaelis de Vililla, 1596.

Jurisprudence de Flandres ..., 6 vols, Lille: C. F. Lehoucq, 1777.

Kersteman, Franciscus L, *Hollandsch rechtsgeleert Woordenboek*, Amsterdam: Steven van Esveldt, 1768, Aanhangzel, 1772–1773.

Kop, Cornelis, van der, *Nieuw Nederlands Advys-boek, dienende tot een vervolg op het Nederlands Advysboek van Mr. Isaac van der Berg*, 2 vols, 's Gravenhage: Hendrik Backhuysen, 1769–1782.

Kort begryp van de "Consultatien en Advysen", inhoudende alle de voortreffelyke materien en voorvallen van de ses delen der Hollandse consultatieboeken, in ordre gecolligeert, en by een gestelt door den letter A. B. C., tot dienst van die gene welke deselve consultatien en advysen gebruiken, Amsterdam: Abraham van Someren, 1696.

Kort begryp van de "Hollandse Consultatien en Advysen", inhoudende alle de voortreffelyke materien en voorvallen daar in begrepen in ordre van het A. B. C. geschikt tot gerief der naazoekers. Den laatsten druk van zoo veele zwaare fouten gezuivert en zoo merkelyk verbeetert dat het by naa voor een nieuw werk passeeren kan, Amsterdam: Jacob Graal, 1740.

Kort begryp van de "Hollandse Consultatien en Advysen", inhoudende alle de voortreffelyke materien en voorvallen daar in begrepen in ordre van het A. B. C. geschikt tot gerief der naazoekers. 3. druk van zoo veele zwaare fouten gezuivert en zoo merkelyk verbeetert dat het by naa voor een nieuw werk passeeren kan, Amsterdam: Henrik Wetstein, 1709.

Krohn, Hermann Georg, *Abhandlung von dem Vorrechte der vollen Geburth vor der halben in Erbschafts-Fällen mit den dabey gemachten Einwürfen*, Lübeck-Leipzig: Jonas Schmidt, 1748.

—*Versuch die Lehre von dem Vorrechte der vollen Geburth vor der halben in Erbschafts-Fällen nach den in Teutschland üblichen Rechten und Statuten aus zulänglichen Gründen in Richtigkeit zu bringen*, Lübeck: Jonas Schmidt, 1746.

—*Weitere Ausführung des Versuchs die Lehre von dem Vorrechte der vollen Geburth vor der halben in Erbschafts-Fällen nach den in Teutschland üblichen Rechten und Statuten aus zulänglichen Gründen in Richtigkeit zu bringen; Samt dessen Bestärckung wieder die vermeyntliche Widerlegung desselben, in idem, Abhandlung von dem Vorrechte der vollen Geburth vor der halben in Erbschafts-Fällen mit den dabey gemachten Einwürfen*, Lübeck-Leipzig: Jonas Schmidt, 1748.

Ladislas de Baralle, Antoine-Augustine, "Recueil d'arrêts", in *Recueil d'arrêts du parlement de Flandres*, Lille: J.-B. Henry, 1773, vol II, 1–261.

Lamzweerde, Maarten Alexander van, *Geldersche consultatien, advysen ende advertissementen van rechten*, 3 vols, Arnhem: Wouter Troost 1776–1822.

Lanckeren, Laurens van, *Utrechtsche consultatien, dat is decisoire ende andere advisen, instructien ende advertissementen van rechten, gegeven ende gemaeckt by de vermaerste rechtsgeleerden der stadt Utrecht*, 3 vols, Utrecht: Anthony Schouten, 1676, 1684, 1700.

Larrea, Juan Bautista de, *Allegationum fiscalium*, Lyon: sumptibus Petri Borde, Joannis et Petri Arnaud, 1699.

—*Novae decisiones Sacri Regii Senatus Granatensis*, Lyon: Iacobi et Petri Prost, 1636.

—*Novarum decisiones Sacri Regii Senatus Granatensis Regni Castellae*, Lyon: Jacobi et Petri Prost, 1639; then printed as *Novarum Decisionum Granatensium. Pars secunda, editio postrema*, Lyon: sumptibus Deville Fratrum et Ludov Chalmette, 1736.

Le Grand, Louis, *Coustume du bailliage de Troyes, avec les commentaires de Me Louis Le Grand* ..., Nouvelle Edition, Paris: Jean Guignard, 1681.

León, Gómez de, *Informationum decisionum et responsorum juris Centuria*, Seville: excudebat Petri Martínez, 1564.

Les coustumes et loix des villes et des chastellenies du comté de Flandre traduites en François ..., vol II, Cambrai: Nicolas-Joseph Douillez, 1719.

Lipski, Andrzej, *Practicarum Observationum ex Iure Civili et Saxonico. . ., centuria prima*, Riga: Nikolaus Mollyn, 1602.

Littleton, Thomas, *Tenures*, London: John Lettou and William de Machlinia, c 1481.

Loenius, Joannes, *Decisien en Observatien: met byvoeginge van aanteekeningen, mitsgaders resolutien, placaaten, advysen van regstsgeleerden, gewysdens, enz door Tobias Boel*, Amsterdam: Jan Boom en Gerard onder de Linden, 1712.

Louet, Georges, *Recueil d'aucuns notables arrests, donnez en la cour de Parlement de Paris* . . ., Nouvelle et dernière edition, *Reveuë, corrigée, et augmentée de plusieurs Arrests intervenues depuis les Impressions precedents, et d'autres notables Decisions, Par Me Iulion Brodeau, Advocat au Parlement*, Paris: P. Rocolet & Iean Guignard, 1650.

Ludolff, Georg Melchior von, *Collectio quorundam statutorum provinciarum et urbium Germanicae cum praefatione*, Wetzlar: Nicolaus Ludwig Winckler, 1734.

Mackenzie of Rosehaugh, George, *Observations on the Acts of Parliament*, Edinburgh: printed by the Heir of Andrew Anderson, 1686.

—*The Institutions of the Law of Scotland*, Edinburgh: John Reid, 1684.

Martínez de Olano, Juan, *Concordia et novum reductio antinomiarum iuris communis ac Regi Hispaniarum*, Burgos: apud Philippum Iunctam, 1575.

Matheu y Sanz, Lorenzo, *Tractatus de re criminali sive controversiarum usufrequentium in causis criminalibus cum earum decisionibus . . .*, Lyon: sumptibus Petri Anisso, 1672.

Meichsner, Johann, *Decisionum diversarum in camera imperiali judicatarum, adjunctis votis et relationibus* ... 4 vols, Frankfurt: Wolfgang Richter, 1603–1606.

Menochio, Jacopo, *Consiliorum sive responsorum liber duodecimus*, Frankfurt: sumptibus C. Marnij, 1609.

—*Consiliorum sive responsorum liber quintus*, Frankfurt: sumptibus haeredum A. Wecheli et I. Gymnici, 1594.

—*Consiliorum sive responsorum liber septimus*, Frankfurt: sumptibus haeredum A. Wecheli et I. Gymnici, 1604.

—*Consiliorum sive responsorum liber tertius*, Frankfurt: sumptibus haeredum A. Wecheli et I. Gymnici, 1594.

—*De arbitraris Ivdicvm Qvaestionibvs et cavsis*, Frankfurt: apud Petrum Fabricium, impensis Sigismundi Feyrabend et Petri Longi, 1576.

—*De praesumptionibus, coniecturis, signis, et indiciis commentaria*, Venice: apud haeredes F. Ziletti, 1597.

Molina, Ludovico de, *De hispanorum primogeniorum origine ac natura libri quatuor*, Köln: Ioannis Baptistae Ciotti Senensis, 1588.

Montemayor, Juan Francisco de, *Excubationes semicentum ex decisionibus Regiae Chancellariae Sancti Dominici insulae, vulgo dictae Española, totius Novi Orbis primates compaginatas*, Méjico: apud Franciscum Rodriguez Lupercio, 1667.

Mornac, Antoine, *Observationes In viginti quatuor priores Libros Digestorum. Ad usum Fori Gallici.* Nova editio locupletior et auctior, vol I, Paris: Franc Montalant, 1721.

Muratori, Ludovico Antonio, *Dei difetti della giurisprudenza*, Venice: Giambattista Pasquali, 1742; in Spanish, *Defectos de la jurisprudencia. Tratado utilísimo para todos los que se dedican al estudio de esta Facultad, y llegan al honor de actuar como Abogados, ó decidir como Jueces en los Tribunales. Escrito en idioma italiano por Luis Antonio Muratori. . . . y traducido al castellano con varias ilustraciones y Notas segun el Derecho real de España por el Lic D Vicente Maria de Tercilla*, Madrid: En la Imprenta de la Viuda de D. Joachim Ibarra, 1793.

Nassau La Leck, Lodewijk Theodorus van, *Algemeen bereneerd register op alle de voornaamste regtsgeleerde advijsen, consultatien, decisien, observatien, sententien, in eene alphabetische order geschikt en zamengesteld*, Utrecht: Gisbert Timon van Paddenburg, 1778–1789.

Nederlandsch Placaat en Rechtskundig Woordenboek, Amsterdam: Johanness Allart, 1791–1797.

Nicot, Jean, *Thresor de la langue françoyse*, Paris: David Douceur, 1606.

Nisbet of Dirleton, John, *Some Doubts and Questions in the Law, Especially of Scotland*, Edinburgh: printed by George Mosman, 1698.

—*The Decisions of the Lords of Council and Session*, Edinburgh: printed by George Mosman, 1698.

Nolasco de Llano, Pedro, *Compendio de los comentarios extendidos por el Maestro Antonio Gómez a las ochenta y tres Leyes de Toro*, Madrid: en la Imprenta de D. Joseph Doblado, 1785.

Novario, Giovanni Maria, *Tractatus de insolutum bonorum datione*, Naples: apud I. Gaffarum, 1636.

Nuñez de Avendaño, Pedro, "Dictionarium Hispanum", in Id, *Quadraginta responsa, qvibus qvam plurimae leges regiae explicantur*, Madrid: apud Petrum Madrigal, 1593.

Oldradi, Giuseppe, *De litteris et mandatis principum et praesertim excellentissimi sacrique regii Senatus Mediolanensis ac aliorum supremorum totius orbis Senatuum commentaria in tres partes digesta, in quibus Caesareae Provinciae Mediolanensis Constitutiones in tit De rescriptis ... explicantur ... Pars prima*, Milan: ex typ. I. B. Bidellij, 1630.

Olive, Simon de, *Questions notables du droit decidées par divers arrests de la Cour de Parlement de Toulouse. ... Nouvelle édition*, Toulouse: Jean-Dominique Camusat, 1682.

Ordines excellentissimi Senatus Mediolani, Milan: in Curia Regia, 1743.

Overijsselsch advysboek, behelzende merkwaardige zo consultatoire als decisoire advysen en sententien van veele voornaame rechtsgeleerden in Overijssel bij een verzamelt en met nodige registers, voorzien door L. C. H. Strubberg, 4 vols, Te Campen. J. A. de Chalmot, Jacques Alexandre de Kampen, 1784–1794.

Papon, Jean, *Les Trois Notaires*, 3 vols, Lyon: 1575–1578.

—*Recueil d'arrests notables des cours souveraines de France*, Paris: Jean Houzé, 1584.

—*Recueil d'arrestz notables des courts souveraines de France, ordonnez par tiltres en vingt-quatre livres*, Lyon: J. de Tournes, 1556.

Peckius, Petrus, *Commentaria in omnes pene iuris civilis titulos ad rem nauticam pertinentes*, Louvain: Petrus Colonaeus, 1556.

—*Tractatus de testamentis conjugum, in quinque libros distinctus*, in *Opera Omnia*, Antwerp: apud Hieronymum Verdussen, 1679.

—*V. Cl. Petri Peckii in titt. Dig. et Cod. ad rem nauticam pertinentes commentarii, quibus nunc accedunt notae cum ampla dote variorum circa rem navalem observationum, beneficio Arnoldi Vinnii*, Leiden: A. Wyngaerden, 1647.

Pegas, Manuel Álvares, *Allegaçoens de Direito*, Lisbon: Officina de Antonio Isidoro da Fonseca, 1738.

—*Resolutiones Forenses practicabiles in quibus multa, quae in utroque foro controversa*, Lisbon: typographia Michaelis Deslandes, 1682.

—*Tractatus de exclusione, inclusione, successione, & erectione maioratus. Pars prima*, Lisbon: typographia Michaelis Deslandes, 1685.

Pereira de Castro, Gabriel, *Decisiones Supremi eminentissimique Senatus Portugalliae ex gravissimorum patrum responsis collectae*, Lisbon: Petrum Craesbeeck, 1621.

Perez, Antonius, *Praelectiones in duodecim libros Codicis Justiniani imp.*, Amsterdam: apud Ludovicum & Danielem Elzevirios, 1661.

Perkins, William, *Perutilis Tractatus*, London: Redman, 1528.

Petrus Gregorius Tholosanus, *Syntagma iuris universi, atque legum pene omnium gentium et rerum publicarum praecipuarum*, Orléans: Philippus Albert, 1611.

Pinault, Mathieu, *Recueil d'arrêts notables du parlement de Tournay ...*, Valenciennes: Gabriel-François Henry, 1702.

Pinault, Matthieu, *Suite des arrests notables du Parlement de Flandres*, vol III, Douai: Michel Mairesse, 1715.

—*Histoire du Parlement de Tournay. Contenant l'Etablissement et les Progrès de ce Tribunal avec un detail des Édits, Ordonnances et Reglements concernants la Justice y envoyez*, Valenciennes: Gabriel François Henry, 1701.

Plowden, Edmund, *Commentaries*, 2 vols, London: Richard Tottell, 1571–1578.

Pollet, Jacques, *Arrests du parlement de Flandre sur diverses questions de droit, de coutume, et de pratique ...*, Lille: Liévin Danel, 1716.

Pufendorf, Friedrich Esajas, *Observationes iuris universi* (2nd edn), vol II, Hannover: Förster, 1779.

Pütter, Johann Stephan, *Litteratur des Teutschen Staatsrechts*, vol I, Göttingen: Vandenhoek, 1776.

Quintilian, *Institutio Oratoria Recueil d'arrêts du parlement de Flandres ...*, 2 vols, Lille: J.-B. Henry, 1773.

Recueil des édits, déclarations, arrests, et règlemens, Qui sont propres et particuliers aux Provinces du Ressort du Parlement de Flandres, Douai: Jacq. Fr. Willerval, 1730.

Redenaschi, Francesco, *Consilia sive responsa*, Pavia: apud I. A. Magrium, 1652.

Ricard, Jean-Marie, *Traité des donations entre-vifs et testamentaires*, vol II, Paris: Rollin, 1754.

Rodenburgius, Christianus, *Tractatus de jure conjugum. In quo de viri in uxorem potestate, eorumque obligationibus, judiciis, mutuis gratificationibus, bonorum communionem, pactisque dotalibus, illustriores controversiae, ad usum fori patrii, vicinarumque regionum expenduntur, cum tractatione praeliminari de jure, quod oritur ex statutorum, vel consuetudinum discrepantium conflictu*, Utrecht: Apud Gisbertum Zylium, et Theodorum ab Ackerdijck, 1653.

Rugginelli, Giulio Cesare, *Practicarum quaestionum rerumque iudicatarum liber singularis*, Venice: Apud B. Baretium, 1610.

—*Tractatus de Senateribus sive Commentaria ad Novas Constitutiones Mediolani hoc titulo*, Milan: ex typ. C. I. Quinti, 1697.

Sadarini, Francesco, *Responsorum rerumque a Senatu iudicatarum liber primus*, Milan: apud F. Agnellum et C. I. Quintum, 1671.

Salón de Paz, Marcos, *Ad leges Taurinas insignes commentario*, Valladolid: apud Franciscum Ferdinan à Corduba Regal Typogra, 1568.

—*Consilia seu iuris responsa decisiva*, Medina del Campo: excudebat Franciscus à Canto, 1576.

Sanchez, Thomas, *De Sancto matrimonii sacramento ...*, Venice: Apud Nicolaum Pezzana, 1754.

Sande, Joan van den, *Theatrum Practicantium hoc est, Decisiones aureae sive Rerum in Suprema Frisiorum Curia judicatarum libri quinque*, Leeuwarden: Joannis Jansonius, 1635.

Sanz y Costanzo, Agustín Fernando, *Glosa expedita ó inllce general de la Nueva Recopilación en la qual se demuestran por el orden y método de la glosa puesta en las ediciones de 1745, 1772 y 1775 las leyes y autos acordados. . .* Madrid: Joachim Ibarra, 1779.

Schmauß, Johann J, Senckenberg, Heinrich C von (eds), *Neue und vollstän-*

digere Sammlung der Reichs-Abschiede, 4 vols, Frankfurt: Ernst August Koch, 1747; reprint, Osnabrück: Otto Zeller 1967.

Schneidewinus, Johannes, *In quatuor Institutionum imperialium D Iustiniani libros commentarii*, Strasbourg: Casparus Dietzelius, 1632.

Schomaker, Joost, *Selecta consilia et responsa juris . . . coram illustribus Ducatus Gelriae et Comitatus Zutphaniae tribunalibus ventilatarum pertinentia . . .*, 6 vols, Nymegen/Amsterdam: Hendrik Heymans/Hendril Vieroot, 1738–1782.

Schorer, Willem, *Aanteekeningen van Mr. Willem Schorer over de Inleidinge tot de Hollandsche Rechts-geleerdheid van Mr. Hugo de Groot*, Middelburg: Pieter Gilissen en Zoon, 1784.

—*Inleydinge Nu met Latynsche aanteekeningen uitgebreidt door W Schorer*, Middelburg: by Pieter Gillissen, 1767.

Schrassert, Henrick, *Consultatien, advysen ende advertissementen*, 5 vols, Harderwyck: Jan Moojen, 1740–1745.

Seyfart, Johann Friedrich, *Teutscher Reichs-Proceß, wie er bey dem Kayserlichen Reichs-Hof-Rathe, dem Kayserlichen Cammer-Gerichte zu Wetzlar, in denen Königl. Preußl. Churfürstl. Sächsischen, Chrfürstl. Hannöverischen und allen übrigen Provintzien von Teutschland gebäuchlich ist*, Halle: Fritschische Buchhandlung, 1738.

Seyler, Raphael; Barth, Christian, *Urtheil Und Beschaydt Am Hochlöblichen Kayserlichen Cammergericht*, 5 vols, Speyer: Melchior Hartmann, 1604–1605.

Skene of Curriehill, John, *Regiam maiestatem: Scotiae veteres leges et constitutions*, Edinburgh: Thomas Finlason, 1609.

Statuta Mediolani cum appostillis clarissimi viri iureconsulti mediolanensis Domini Catelliani Cottae, Milan: apud I. A. Castilionaeum, 1552.

Stein, Joachim Lucas, *Gründliche Abhandlung des lübischen Rechts*, 5 vols, Leipzig, Rostock: J. Schmidt, 1738–1746.

Stewart of Goodtrees, James, *Dirleton's Doubts and Questions in the Law of Scotland, Resolved and Answered*, Edinburgh: J. Watson, 1715.

Stryk, Samuel, *Tractatus de dissensu sponsalitio, cum materiis quibusdam affinibus, de nullitate matrimonii et desertione malitiosa, variis praeiudiciis ac collegiorum responsis confirmatus, accessit index rerum locupletisimus*, Wittenberg: Johann Wilhelm Meyer & Gottfried Zimmermann, 1699.

Suárez de Paz, Gonzalo, *Praxis ecclesiastica et saecularis*, Lyon: apud Fratres Deville, 1739.

Suárez, Rodrigo, *Excelentissimae allegationes et consilia*, Valladolid: excudebat Didacus Fernández a Córdoba Bibliopolae, 1588.

The Actis and Constitutiounis of the Realm of Scotland, ed Edward Henryson, Edinburgh, 1566.

The Acts of Sederunt of the Lords of Council and Session, 1553–1790, Edinburgh, 1790.

The Decisions of the Lords of Council and Session, 2 vols, Edinburgh: printed for G Hamilton and J Balfour, 1759–1761.

Valenzuela Velázquez, Juan, *Consilia sive juris responsa*, Geneva: sumptibus Marci-Michaelis Bousquet et Sociorum, 1727.

Vela de Oreña, José, *Dissertationum juris controversi in Hispalensi Senatu*: Granada: apud Vicentium Aluarez à Mariz, 1638.

—*Dissertationum juris controversi tam in Hispalensi quad Granatensi Senatu secundus tomus. . .*, Granada: apud Baltasarem de Bolibar, 1653.

Vico, Giambattista, *De Nostri temporis studiorum ratione dissertatio*, Napoli: Felix Mosca, 1709.

Villalobos, Juan Bautista de, *Antinomia juris Regni Hispaniarum ac ciuilis*, Salamanca: excudebat Alexander à Canoua, 1569.

Vinnius, Arnoldus, *In quatuor libros Institutionum imperialium Commentarius Academicus et Forensis*, Lyon: Anisson & Joan. Pasuel, 1700.

Voet, Johannes, *Commentarius ad Pandectas, in quo, praetor Romani iuris principia ac controversias illustriores, ius etiam hodiernum et praecipuae fori quaestiones excutiuntur*, 7 vols, Halle: Joan. Jac. Curtii, 1776–1780.

Vulteius, Hermannus (ed), *Consilia sive responsa doctorum et professorum facultatis iuridicae in Academia Marpurgensi*, 4 vols, Marburg: Paulus Egenolphus, 1604–1614.

Wamesius, Johannes, *Responsorum sive consiliorum ad ius forumque civile pertinentium Centuria quinta*, Antwerp: apud Henricum Aertssens, 1641.

—*Responsorum sive consiliorum de iure pontificio*, tomus II, Louvain: typis Iacobi Zegers, 1643.

Welwod, William, *The Sea-Law of Scotland, Shortly Gathered and Plainly Dressit for the Reddy Use of All Seafairingmen*, Edinburgh: Robert Waldergrave, 1590.

Wesel, Abraham van, "De connubiali bonorum societate", in Id, *Opera omnia*, Amsterdam: apud Henricum, & Viduam Theodori Boom, 1701.

Zavattari, Giovanni Antonio, *De Fori Mediolanensis praxi, et nonnullis depravationibus ex eo tollendi dialogus*, Venice: apud H. Polum, 1584.

Zurck, Eduard van, *Codex Batavus, waer in het algemeen Kerk- publyk en Burgerlyk Recht van Hollant, Zeelant, en het resort der Generaliteit kortelyk is begrepen*, Delft: Adriaan Beman, 1727.

SOURCES PUBLISHED FROM 1800

Abbott, Lewis W, *Law Reporting in England 1485–1585*, London: Athlone, 1973.

Aguesseau, Henri François de, *Œuvres complètes*, ed J-M Pardessus, 16 vols, Paris: Fantin et Compagnie, 1819.

Alexander King's Treatise on Maritime Law, ed J D Ford, Edinburgh: The Stair Society, 2018.

Alonso Romero, María Paz, "Catedráticos salmantinos de Leyes y Cánones en las Chancillerías y Audiencias regias durante el siglo XVII", in M P Alonso Romero (ed), *Salamanca, escuela de juristas. Estudios sobre la enseñanza del Derecho en el Antiguo Régimen*, Madrid: Universidad Carlos III, 2012, 375–398.

—"El proceso penal en la Castilla moderna" (1996) 22 *Estudis. Revista de Historia Moderna*, 199–216.

—"Lectura de Juan Gutiérrez (c 1535/40–1618), un jurista formado en Salamanca", in Id, *Salamanca, escuela de juristas. Estudios sobre la enseñanza del Derecho en el Antiguo Régimen*, Madrid: Universidad Carlos III, 2012, 119–164.

Álvarez Cora, Enrique, *La teoría de los contrato en Castilla (siglos XIII–XVIII)*, Madrid: Colegio de Registradores de la Propiedad, 2005.

Álvarez-Ossorio Alvariño, Antonio, *Milán y el legado de Felipe II. Gobernadores y corte provincial en la Lombardia de los Austrias*, Madrid: Sociedad Estatal para la Conmemoración de los Centenarios de Felipe II y Carlos V, 2001.

Alvazzi del Frate, Paolo, "Aux origines du référé législatif: interprétation et jurisprudence dans les cahiers de doléances de 1789" (2008) 86(2) *Revue historique de droit français et étranger*, 253–262.

Amend-Traut, Anja, *Die Spruchpraxis der höchsten Reichsgerichte im römisch-deutschen Reich und ihre Bedeutung für die Privatrechtsgeschichte*, Wetzlar: Gesellschaft für Reichskammergerichtsforschung, 2008.

Ascheri, Mario, "Between Statutory Law and Learned Law: Delay in the Early History of the Medieval Italian Communes (and Beyond)", in C H van Rhee (ed), *Within a Reasonable Time: The History of Due and Undue Delay in Civil Litigation*, Berlin: Duncker & Humblot, 2010, 37–56.

—"Italy from Medieval Times to 1800", in A Wijffels and C H van Rhee (eds), *The European supreme courts. A portrait through history*, London: Third Millennium Publishing, 2013, 46–48.

—*Tribunali, giuristi e istituzioni dal medioevo all'età moderna*, Bologna, Il Mulino, 1989; 1995.

Astuti, Guido, sv "Dazione in pagamento (storia)", in *Enciclopedia del diritto*, vol XI, Milano: Giuffrè, 1962, 732–733.

Babusiaux, Ulrike, *Wege zur Rechtsgeschichte: Römisches Erbrecht*, Cologne-Weimar-Vienna: Böhlau Verlag, 2015.

Bagge, Sverre, *From Viking Stronghold to Christian Kingdom*, Copenhagen: Museum Tusculanum Press, 2010.

Baker, John H, *Baker & Milsom Sources of English Legal History* (2nd edn), Oxford: Oxford University Press, 2010.

—"English Law Books and Legal Publishing, 1557–1695", in J Barnard and D F McKenzie (eds), *The Cambridge History of the Book in Britain*, vol IV (1557–1695), Cambridge: Cambridge University Press, 2002, 474–503, and now in J H Baker, *Collected Papers on English Legal History*, Cambridge: Cambridge University Press, 2013, 637–669.

—*Introduction to English Legal History* (5th edn), Oxford: Oxford University Press, 2019.

—"New Light on Slade's Case" (1971) 29 *Cambridge Law Journal*, 51–67 and 213–236, and now in J H Baker, *Collected Papers on English Legal History*, Cambridge: Cambridge University Press, 2013, 1129–1175.

—"Preface", in J H Baker (ed), *Judicial records, Law reports and the growth of case law*. Berlin: Duncker & Humblot, 1989.

—"The Books of the Common Law", in L Hellinga and J B Trapp (eds), *The Book in Britain: Volume III, 1400–1557*, Cambridge: Cambridge University Press, 1999, 411–432, and now in J H Baker, *Collected Papers on English Legal History*, Cambridge: Cambridge University Press, 2013, 611–636.

—*The Law's Two Bodies: Some Evidential Problems in English Legal History*, Oxford: Oxford University Press, 2001.

—*The Oxford History of the Laws of England, Volume VI: 1483–1558*, Oxford: Oxford University Press, 2003.

—"The Third University of England" (2002) 55 *Current Legal Problems*, 123–150, and now in J H Baker, *Collected Papers on English Legal History*, Cambridge: Cambridge University Press, 2013, 143–167.

Barbot, Michaela, "Between Market and Architecture: The Role of the College of Engineers, Architects and Land Surveyors in Real Estate Pricing in 16th–18th Century Milan", in R Carvais, A Guillerme, V Negre and J Sakarovitch (eds), *Nuts and Bolts of Construction History. Culture, Technology and Society*, vol II, Paris: Picard, 2012, 237–244.

Barrero, Ana María, sv "Decisionistas", in M Artola (ed), *Enciclopedia de Historia de España*, vol VII, Madrid, Espasa Calpe, 1988, 389–390.

Barrientos Grandón, Javier, "Derecho común y derecho indiano en el reino de Chile" *Memoria X Congreso del Instituto Internacional de Historia del Derecho Indiano*, México: UNAM, 1995, vol I, 133–159.

Bassano, Marie, *Introduction historique au droit*, Université numérique juridique francophone, 2013, available at: https://cours.unjf.fr/repository/coursefilearea/file.php/154/Cours/06_item/indexI0.htm.

Baumann, Anette, "The Holy Roman Empire: The Reichskammergericht", in A Wijffels and C H van Rhee (eds), *European Supreme Courts. A portrait through History*, London: Third Millennium Publishing, 2013, 96–103.

Beale, Joseph, *Bibliography of Early English Law Books*, Cambridge MA: Harvard University Press, 1925; supplement by Robert Anderson, Cambridge MA: Ames Foundation, 1943.

Bellomo, Manlio, sv "Dote (diritto intermedio)", in *Enciclopedia del diritto*, vol XIV, Milan: Giuffrè, 1965, 8–32.

Benke, Nikolaus, "In sola prudentium interpretatione. Zu Methodik und Methodologie römischer Juristen", in B Feldner and N Forgó (eds), *Norm und Entscheidung. Prolegomena zu einer Theorie des Falls*, Vienna: Springer, 2000, 1–85.

Bergh, Govaert C J J, van den, *The Life and Work of Gerard Noodt*, Oxford: Oxford University Press, 1988.

Bijnkershoek, Cornelis van, *Observationes Tumultuariae*, eds E M Meyers et al, 4 vols, Zwolle: Tjeenk Willink, 1926–1962.

Bily, Inge; Wieland, Carls; Gönczi, Katalin, *Sächsisch-magdeburgisches Recht in Polen. Untersuchungen zur Geschichte des Rechts und seiner Sprache*, De Gruyter: Berlin/Boston, 2011 [Ivs Saxonico-Maidebvrgense in Oriente, vol II].

Birocchi, Italo, *Alla ricerca dell'ordine. Fonti e cultura giuridica nell'età moderna*, Torino: Giappichelli, 2002.

Björne, Lars, *Patrioter och institutionalister: Den nordiska rättsvetenskapens historia*, part I, Lund: Institutet för rättshistorisk forskning, 1992.

Blanquie, Christophe, *Les présidiaux de Daguesseau*, Paris: Publisud, 2004.

—*Les présidiaux de Richelieu. Justice et vénalité (1630–1642)*, Paris: Editions Christian, 2000.

Boersma, Frederick, *Introduction to Fitzherbert's Abridgement*, Abingdon: Professional Books, 1981.

Bosman, F J and P van Warmelo, *De pactis antenuptialibus rerum judi-*

*catarum observationes (c 1605), Observations on decided cases concern-
ing antenuptial contracts, Archivalia* (prepared by J Th de Smidt and H
W van Soest), Pretoria: The Government Printer, 1986.

Brancourt [Storez], Isabelle, "Au plus près des sources du Parlement criminel: jalons sur l'inceste au début du XVIIIe siècle" (2014) 92(3) *Revue
historique de droit français et étranger*, 437–451.

—"Dans l'ombre de Messieurs les gens du Roi: le monde des substituts", in
J-M Carbasse (ed), *Histoire du parquet*, Paris: Presses Universitaires de
France, 2000, 157–204.

—"De la biographie d'un chancelier à l'histoire d'un commis, plongée dans
un océan archivistique et historiographique", in B Augé (ed), *Essais
en hommage à John Rogister: Regards nouveaux sur les institutions
représentatives de l'ancien régime, la Cour, la diplomatie, la guerre et la
littérature*, Paris: Éditions A Pedone, 2017, 63–84.

—"Du parquet à la chancellerie: D'Aguesseau et le contrôle des juges dans
la première moitié du XVIIIème siècle", in A Follain (ed), *Contrôler
et punir les agents du Pouvoir (XVIe–XVIIIe siècle)*, Dijon: Éditions
Universitaires de Dijon, 2015, 49–62.

—"Les conclusions du procureur général au parlement de Paris. Analyse
du fonds des Archives Nationales" (1999) 6(2) *Histoire et Archives*,
5–24.

—"Petit guide d'une recherche à propos de la rédaction des coutumes", in
*Parlement(s) de Paris et d'ailleurs. XIIIème–XVIIIème siècle. Chronique
des recherches dans des archives hors norme*, 12 November 2009, available at: http://parlementdeparis.hypotheses.org/190.

—"Vers la 'punition'", in S Daubresse, M Morgat-Bonnet and I Storez-
Brancourt (eds), *Le Parlement en exil ou Histoire politique et judici-
aire des translations du parlement de Paris (XVe–XVIIIe siècle)*, Paris:
Librairie Honoré Champion, 2007, 537–731.

—*Le Régent, la Robe et le commis greffier*, introduction au *Journal du
Parlement de Pontoise* de Jean Gilbert de L'Isle, Saint-Agnan: Association
des Amis de Guy Augé, 2013.

—*Un Gilbert méconnu. Magistrature et quotidien du Parlement de Paris
dans le premier XVIIIe siècle*, Paris: SFEDS, 2016.

Brand, Paul; Gotzler, Joshua (eds), *Judges and Judging in the History of
the Common Law and the Civil Law*, Cambridge: Cambridge University
Press, 2012.

Brand, Paul, "The Origins of English Law Reporting", in C Stebbings (ed),
Law Reporting in Britain, London: Hambledon, 1995, 1–14.

Brisson, Barnabé, *Code du Roy Henry III, roy de France et de Pologne*, Lyon: pour les frères de Gabiano, 1593.

Burbank, Jane, and Cooper, Frederick, *Empires in World History: Power and the Politics of Difference*, Princeton: Princeton University Press, 2010.

Buridan, John, *Summulae de Dialectica*, ed G Klima, New Haven: Yale University Press, 2001.

Cairns, John W, Fergus, T David, and MacQueen, Hector L, "Legal humanism and the history of Scots law: John Skene and Thomas Craig", in J MacQueen (ed), *Humanism in Renaissance Scotland*, Edinburgh: Edinburgh University Press, 1990, 48–74.

Cairns, John W, "Advocates' hats, Roman law and admission to the Scots bar, 1580–1812" (1999) 20 *Journal of Legal History*, 24–61.

—"Importing our lawyers from Holland: Netherlands influences on Scots law and lawyers in the eighteenth century", in G G Simpson (ed), *Scotland and the Low Countries, 1124–1994*, East Linton: Tuckwell Press, 1996, 136–53.

Carbasse, Jean-Marie, and Guillaume Leyte, *L'État royal XIIe–XVIIIe siècle. Une anthologie*, Paris: Presses Universitaires de France, 2004.

Cardim, Pedro, *Cortes e cultura política no Portugal do Antigo Regime*. Lisboa: Cosmos, 1998.

Cavanna, Adriano, "La conscience du juge dans le stylus iudicandi du Sénat de Milan", in J-M Carbasse and L Depambour-Tarride (eds), *La conscience du juge dans la tradition juridique européenne*, Paris: Presses Universitaires de France, 1999, 229–262.

—*La codificazione penale in Italia. Le origini lombarde*, Milano: Giuffrè, 1975.

Cazals, Géraldine, "La mise en ordre du droit et les enjeux du renouvellement de la pensée juridique moderne", in M Delmas-Marty, A Jeammaud and O Clerc (eds), *Droit et humanisme. Autour de Jean Papon, juriste forézien*, Paris: Classiques Garnier, 2015, 15–39.

—"Les arrêts notables et la pensée juridique de la Renaissance", in G Cazals and S Geonget (eds), *Des arrests parlans. Les arrêts notables à la Renaissance*, Genève: Droz, 2014.

—*L'arrestographie flamande. Jurisprudence et littérature juridique à la fin de l'Ancien Régime (1668–1789)*, Genève: Droz, 2018.

Clavero, Bartolomé, *Mayorazgo. Propiedad feudal en Castilla*, Madrid: Siglo XXI, 1989.

Coing, Helmut, *Europäisches Privatrecht*, 2 vols, Munich: C H Beck, 1985–

1989; in Spanish, *Derecho privado europeo*, 2 vols, Madrid: Fundación Cultural del Notariado, 1996.

Collin, Hans S, and Schlyter, Carl J (eds), *Corpus iuris sueo-gothorum antiqui: Samling af Sweriges gamla lagar*, vol XII, Stockholm: Berlingska boktryckeriet, 1869.

Collins, James B, *The State in Early Modern France* (revised edn), Cambridge: Cambridge University Press, 2009; in French, *La Monarchie républicaine. Etat et société dans la France modern*, Paris: Odile Jacob, 2016.

Conring, Hermann, *Der Ursprung des deutschen Rechts*, tr Ilse Hoffmann-Meckenstock, ed Michael Stolleis, Frankfurt-Leipzig: Insel Verlag, 1994.

Cortes de los Antiguos reinos de León y de Castilla, vols IV–V, Madrid: Establecimiento tipográfico de los Sucesores de Rivadeneyra, 1882–1906.

Covini, Maria N, "La trattazione delle suppliche nella cancelleria sforzesca: da Francesco Sforza a Ludovico il Moro", in C Nubola and A Würgler (eds), *Suppliche e "gravamina". Politica, amministrazione, giustizia in Europa (secoli XIV–XVIII)*, Bologna: Il Mulino, 2002, 107–146.

Czapliński, Władysław, sv "Lipski Andrzej", in *Polski słownik biograficzny*, vol XVII, Wrocław: Zakład Narodowy im Ossolińskich – Wydawnictwo Polskiej Akademii Nauk, 1972, 415–417.

Czeguhn, Ignacio, *Die kastilische Höchstgerichtsbarkeit*, Berlin: Dunker & Humblot, 2002.

Dargun, Lotar, "O źródłach prawa miast polskich w wieku szesnastym. I O źródłach przepisów karnych w dziełach Groickiego" (1888) 22 *Rozprawy Akademii Umiejętności. Wydział Historyczno-Filozoficzny*, 11–16.

Dauchy, Serge, "L'arrestographie genre littéraire" (2011) 31 *Revue d'histoire des facultés de droit*, 41–53.

—"L'arrestographie science fort douteuse?" (2010) 23 *Sartoniana*, 87–99.

—sv "Georges de Ghewiet", in P Arabeyre, J-L Halpérin, J Krynen, avec la collaboration de G Cazals (eds), *Dictionnaire historique des juristes français*, Paris: Presses universitaires de France, 2007, 235–236.

Dauchy, Serge; Bryson, William H, and (for the second volume) Mirow, Matthew C (eds), *Ratio decidendi. Guiding Principles of Judicial Decisions*, 2 vols, Berlin: Duncker & Humblot, 2006–2010.

Dauchy, Serge; Demars-Sion, Véronique, "A propos d'un 'recueil d'arrêts' inédit: la *Jurisprudence du parlement de Flandre* de Georges de Ghewiet» (2009) 77 *Tijdschrift voor Rechtsgeschiedenis*, 157–189.

—"La bibliothèque du juriste flamand Georges de Ghewiet" (2007) 48

Bulletin de la Commission royale pour la publication des anciennes lois et ordonnances de Belgique, 277–320.

—"Introduction", in G de Ghewiet, *Jurisprudence du parlement de Flandre*, Bruxelles: Service public fédéral Justice, Recueil de l'ancienne jurisprudence de la Belgique, 2008.

— (eds), *Les recueils d'arrêts et dictionnaires de jurisprudence (xvie–xviiie siècles)*, Paris: La mémoire du droit, 2005.

De Iongh, Jane, *De Hertogin, Margaretha van Oostenrijk, Hertogin van Savooie 1480–1530 (Regentessen der Nederlanden, vol I)*, Amsterdam: EM Querido's Uitgeverij B V, 1981.

—*De Koningin, Maria van Hongarije, landvoogdes der Nederlanden 1505–1558 Regentessen der Nederlanden, vol II)*, Amsterdam; EM Querido's Uitgeverij B V, 1981.

—*Madama, Margaretha van Oostenrijk, Hertogin van Parma en Piacenze 1522–1586 (Regentessen der Nederlanden, vol III)*, Amsterdam: EM Querido's Uitgeverij B V, 1981.

De Monte Verloren, Johan P; Spruit, Johannes E, *Hoofdlijnen uit de ontwikkeling der rechterlijke organisatie in de Noordelijke Nederlanden tot de Bataafse omwenteling*, Deventer: Kluwer 1982.

De Wet, Johannes C, *Die ou skrywers in perspektief*, Durban: Butterworth, 1988.

Dedieu, Jean-Pierre, "La muerte del letrado", in F J Aranda Pérez (ed), *Letrados, juristas y burócratas en la España moderna*, Toledo: Universidad de Castilla-La Mancha, 2005, 479–512.

Dekkers, René, *Bibliotheca Belgica Juridica. Een bio-bibliographisch overzicht der rechtsgeleerdheid in de Nederlanden van de vroegste tijden af tot 1800*, Brussels: Koninklijke Vlaamse Academie voor Wetenschappen, Letteren en Schone Kunsten van België, 1951.

Delmas-Marty, Mireille, Antoine Jeammaud and Olivier Clerc (eds), *Droit et humanisme. Autour de Jean Papon, juriste forézien*, Paris: Classiques Garnier, 2015 [*Esprit des Lois, esprit des Lettres*, vol VI].

Demars-Sion, Véronique, "Le Parlement de Flandre: une institution originale dans le paysage judiciaire français de l'Ancien Régime" (2009) 91/382 *Revue du Nord. Histoire Nord de la France, Belgique, Pays-Bas*, 698–725.

Demir, Ipek, "Incommensurabilities in the work of Thomas Kuhn" (2009) 39 *Studies in the History and Philosophy of Science*, 133–42.

Denzler, Alexander, Über den Schriftalltag im 18. Jahrhundert. Die Visitation des Reichskammergerichts von 1767 bis 1776, Cologne-Weimar-Vienna: Böhlau Verlag, 2016.

Derasse, Nicolas, sv "Pollet, Jacques", in P Arabeyre, J-L Halpérin, J Krynen, *avec la collaboration de* G Cazals (eds), *Dictionnaire historique des juristes français*, Paris: Presses universitaires de France, 2007, 632.

Descimon, Robert, Geoffroy-Poisson, Simone, "La construction juridique d'un système patrimonial de l'office. Une affaire de patrilignage et de genre", in R Descimon and É Haddad (eds), *Épreuves de noblesse. Les expériences nobiliaires de la haute robe parisienne (XVIe–XVIIIe siècle)*, Paris: Les Belles Lettres, 2010, 47–59.

Di Donato, Francesco, *L'ideologia dei robins nella Francia dei Lumi. Costituzionalismo e assolutismo nell'esprienza politico-istituzionale della magistratura di antico regime (1715–1788)*, Roma-Napoli: Edizioni Scientifiche Italiane, 2003.

Diestelkamp, Bernhard, "Das Reichskammergericht im Rechtsleben des 16. Jahrhunderts", in Id, *Recht und Gericht im Heiligen Römischen Reich*, Frankfurt: Vittorio Klostermann 1999, 213–262 (*necnon* in H-J Becker et al (eds), *Rechtsgeschichte als Kulturgeschichte. Festschrift für Adalbert Erler zum 70. Geburtstag*, Aalen: Scientia, 1976, 435–480).

Dievoet, Guido van, "Ghewiet, Georges de", in *Nationaal biografisch woordenboek*, vol VI, Brussels: Paleis der Academiën, 1974, col 340–347.

—van den Auweele, D, Stevens, F, Oosterbosch, M, Coppens, C, *Lovanium Docet. Geschiedenis van de Leuvense Rechtsfaculteit* 1425–1914, Leuven: Katholieke Universiteit Leuven, 1988.

Dios, Salustiano, "La doctrina regalista en el doctor Juan del Castillo Sotomayor", in *Facultades y Grados. X Congreso Internacional de Historia de las Universidades hispánicas*, Valencia: Universidad de Valencia, 2010, 303–350.

—*Fuentes para el estudio del Consejo Real de Castilla*, Salamanca: Universidad de Salamanca, 1986.

—"Tendencias doctrinales en la época de la jurisprudencia clásica salmantina" (2002) 47 *Salamanca. Revista de Estudios*, 285–311.

Dolezalek, Gero, "The Court of Session as a *ius commune* court: Witnessed by 'Sinclair's Practicks', 1540–49", in H L MacQueen (ed), *Stair Society Miscellany IV*, Edinburgh: Stair Society, 2002, 51–84.

Doms, Matthias, *Rechtsanwendung im Usus modernus. Eine Fallstudie zum Erbrecht der halben Geburt*, Doctoral dissertation, University of Münster, 2010, available at https://d-nb.info/1010264680/34.

Drønen, Tomas S, "Scientific revolution and religious conversion: a closer look at Thomas Kuhn's theory of paradigm-shift" (2006) 18 *Method and Theory in the Study of Religion*, 232–53.

Druwé, Wouter, *Transregional Normativity in Learned Legal Practice. Loans and Credit in Consilia and Decisiones in the Northern and Southern Low Countries (c 1500–1680)*, Leiden: Brill, 2019.

Du Plessis, Paul J, "Innkeeper's liability for loss suffered by guests: *Drake v Gow*" (2007) 11 *Edinburgh Law Review*, 89–94.

—and Cairns, John W (eds), *Reassessing Legal Humanism and its Claims: Petere Fontes?*, Edinburgh: Edinburgh University Press, 2016.

Duve, Thomas, "Mit der Autorität gegen die Autoritäten? Überlegungen zur heuristischen Kraft des Autoritätsbegriffs für die Neuere Privatrechtsgeschichte", in W Oesterreicher, G Regn and W Schulze (eds), *Autorität der Form — Autorisierung — Institutionelle Autorität*, Münster: Lit Verlag, 2003, 239–256.

Duxbury, Neil, *The Nature and Authority of Precedent*, Cambridge: Cambridge University Press, 2008.

Eisenhardt, Ulrich, *Die kaiserlichen privilegia de non appellando*, Cologne-Vienna: Böhlau Verlag, 1980.

Estreicher, Karol, *Bibliografia polska*, vol XVII, Kraków: Drukarnia Uniwersytetu Jagiellońskiego pod zarządem Józefa Filipowskiego, 1899.

—*Bibliografia polska*, vol XX, Kraków: Drukarnia Uniwersytetu Jagiellońskiego pod zarządem Józefa Filipowskiego, 1906.

Extracts from the Records of the Burgh of Edinburgh, 2nd ser, 9 vols, ed M Wood and H Armet, Edinburgh: Scottish Burgh Record Society, 1927–1967.

Falk, Ulrich, *Consilia. Studien zur Praxis der Rechtsgutachten in der frühen Neuzeit*. Frankfurt am Main: Klostermann, 2006.

Feutry, David, *Plumes de fer et robes de papier. Logiques institutionnelles et pratiques politiques du parlement de Paris au XVIIIe siècle (1515–1790)*, Paris: Institut universitaire Varenne, diff. LGDJ, 2013.

Finlay, John, "*Ratio decidendi* in Scotland, 1650 to 1800", in W H Bryson and S Dauchy (eds), *Ratio decidendi: Guiding Principles of Judicial decisions*, Berlin: Duncker & Humblot, 2006, 117–35.

—*The Community of the College of Justice: Edinburgh and the Court of Session, 1687–1808*, Edinburgh: Edinburgh University Press, 2012.

Fischer, Herman F W D, "De publicatie van fideicommissen" [pt 1] (1953) 16 *Tydskrif vir Hedendaagse Romeins-Hollandse Reg*, 159–239.

—"De publicatie van fideicommissen" [pt 2] (1954) 17 *Tydskrif vir Hedendaagse Romeins-Hollandse Reg*, 45–81.

Fockema Andreae, Sybrandus J, de Blécourt, Anne S, *Overzicht van Oud-Nederlandsche Rechtsbronnen*, Haarlem: F Bohn, 1923.

Fontaine, Clotilde, *Histoire du parquet du parlement de Flandre. Ladislas de Baralle, Procureur général (1691–1714)*, unpublished Doctoral dissertation, Université de Lille 2, 2019.

—*Le ministère public au parlement de Flandre: étude sur l'activité de Ladislas de Baralle au cours de l'année 1691*, unpublished Master's thesis in legal history (Master 2), Université de Lille 2, 2013.

Fontaine, Laurence, *The moral economy. Poverty, credit, and trust in early modern Europe*, Cambridge: Cambridge University Press, 2014

Ford, John D, "Conciliar authority and equitable jurisdiction in early-modern Scotland", in A M Godfrey (ed), *Law and Authority in British Legal History, 1200–1900*, Cambridge: Cambridge University Press, 2016, 140–169.

—*Law and Opinion in Scotland during the Seventeenth Century*, Oxford: Hart Publishing, 2007.

—"The legal provisions in the acts of union" (2007) 66 *Cambridge Law Journal*, 106–41.

—"William Welwod's treatises on maritime law" (2013) 34 *Journal of Legal History*, 171–210.

Fortescue, John, *De Laudibus Legum Anglie*, ed S B Chrimes, Cambridge: Cambridge University Press, 1949.

Frankenau, Gerardo Ernesto [*sed* Lucas Cortés, Juan], *Sagrados Misterios de la Justicia hispana* [*Sacra Themidis Hispaniae Arcana*, 1703], Madrid: Centro de Estudios Constitucionales, 1993.

Freda, Dolores, "Law Reporting in Europe in the Early-Modern Period: Two Experiences in Comparison" (2009) 20 *Journal of Legal History*, 263–278.

Frost, Robert, *The Oxford History of Poland-Lithuania*, vol I: *The Making of the Polish-Lithuanian Union, 1385–1569*, Oxford: Oxford University Press, 2018.

Gagnér, Sten, *Studien zur Ideengeschichte der Gesetzgebung*, Stockholm: Almquist & Wiksell, 1960.

Gall, Heleen C, *Regtsgeleerde decisien: aan de raadsheer Pieter Ockers toegeschreven aantekeningen betreffende uitspraken van het Hof (1656–1669) en de Hoge Raad (1669–1678) van Holland, Zeeland en West-Friesland*, Amsterdam: Cabeljauwpers, 2002.

Gamberini, Andrea (ed), *A Companion to Late Medieval and Early Modern Milan. The distinctive features of an Italian State*, Leiden: Brill, 2015.

García Martín, Javier, *Costumbre y fiscalidad de la dote: Las Leyes de Toro, entre derecho común germánico y ius commune*, Madrid: Universidad Complutense, 2004.

—"El Fuero de Vizcaya en la doctrina y la práctica judicial castellanas", in J Arrieta, X Gil, and J Morales (eds), *La Diadema del Rey. Vizcaya, Navarra, Aragón y Cerdeña en la Monarquía de España (siglos XVI–XVIII)*, Bilbao: Universidad del País Vasco, 2017, 53–168.

—"En los orígenes del derecho comparado. Pierre Rebuffi (1487?–1557) y la creación de una tradición jurisprudencial salmantina en el comentario del Derecho regio", in S de Dios, J Infante, and E Torijano (eds), *Juristas de Salamanca, siglos XV–XX*, Salamanca: Universidad de Salamanca, 2009, 13–79.

—"Las bibliotecas y las alegaciones jurídicas impresas de los abogados en Castilla (siglos XVII y XVIII). El problema de la *communis opinio*", in S Muñoz Machado (ed), *Historia de la abogacía española*, Pamplona: Aranzadi, 2015, vol I, 717–765.

—"*Leges de Toro*. Construcciones interpretativas e historiográficas" (2006) 1 *e-Legal History Review*, 1–70.

Garnett, George, "'The Ould Fields': Law and History in the Prefaces to Sir Edward Coke's Reports" (2013) 34 *Journal of Legal History*, 245–284.

Garré, Roy, *Consuetudo: Das Gewohnheitsrecht in der Rechtsquellen und Methodenlehre des späten ius commune in Italien (16.–18. Jahrhundert)*, Frankfurt am Main: Vittorio Klostermann, 2005.

Garriga Acosta, Carlos, "Estudio preliminar", in *Recopilación de las Ordenanzas de la Real Chancillería de Valladolid (1566)*, Madrid: Consejo General del Poder Judicial-Tribunal Supremo, 2007, 7–125.

—"*Iudex perfectus*. Ordre traditionel et justice de juges dans l'Europa del *ius commune* (Couronne de Castilla, XVe–XVIIIe siècles", in *Histoires des justices en Europe*, vol I: *Valeurs, representation, symboles*, Toulouse: Université Capitole, 2014–15, 79–99.

—"La consolidación de la jurisdicción suprema en Castilla", in I Czeguhn, S Lopez Nevot, A Aranda, and J Weizen (eds), *Die Höchstgerichtsbarkeit im Zeitalter Karls V Eine vergleichende Betrachtung*, Baden-Baden: Nomos Verlagsgesellschaft, 2011, 133–176

—"La Real Audiencia y Chancillería de Valladolid", in R Payo Hernán and R Sánchez Domingo (eds), *El Régimen de Justicia en Castilla y León: de Real Chancillería a Tribunal Superior. XXV Aniversario de Tribunal Superior de Justicia de Castilla y León*, Burgos: TSJCL-Junta de Castilla y León, 2014, 13–96.

—"La trama jurídica castellana a comienzos del siglo XVI (Notas y materiales)", in B González Alonso (ed), *Las Cortes y las Leyes de Toro de 1505*, Salamanca: Junta de Castilla y León, 2006, 299–379.

Garriga, Carlos and Lorente, Marta, "El juez y la ley: la motivación de las sentencias (Castilla, 1489–España, 1855)" (1997) 1 *Anuario de la Facultad de Derecho de la Universidad Autónoma de Madrid*, 97–144.

Gehrke, Heinrich, "Deutsches Reich", in H Coing (ed), *Handbuch der Quellen und Literatur der neueren europäischen Privatrechtsgeschichte*, vol II: *Neuere Zeit (1500–1800)*, part 2: *Gesetzgebung und Rechtsprechung*, Munich: C H: Beck'sche Verlagsbuchhandlung, 1976, 1343–1398.

—*Die privatrechtliche Entscheidungsliteratur Deutschlands: Charakteristik und Bibliografie der Rechtsprechungs- und Konsiliensammlungen vom 16. bis zum Beginn des 19. Jahrhunderts*, Frankfurt am Main: Vittorio Klostermann, 1974.

Gerbenzon, Pieter, Algra, Nikolaas E, *Voortgangh des rechtes: de ontwikkeling van het Nederlandse recht tegen de achtergrond van de Westeuropese cultuur*, Zwolle: Tjeenk Willink, 1972.

Ghewiet, Georges de, *Jurisprudence du Parlement de Flandre*, ed S Dauchy and V Demars-Sion [Recueil de l'ancienne jurisprudence de la Belgique, Deuxième série], Brussels: Service public fédéral Justice, 2008.

Gilli, Patrick, "Les *consilia* juridiques de la fin de Moyen Âge en Italie: sources et problèmes" (2000) *Reti medievali*, available at: http://www.rmoa.unina.it/2102/1/RM-Gilli-Consilia.pdf.

Glozier, Matthew, *Scottish Soldiers in France in the Reign of the Sun King: Nursery for Men of Honour*, Leiden: Brill, 2004.

Godding, Philippe, "Jurisprudence et motivation des sentences", in C Perelman and P Foriers (eds), *Motivation des décisions de justice*, Bruxelles: Bruylant, 1978, 37–67.

—*La jurisprudence*, Turnhout: Brepols, 1973.

—*Le droit privé dans les Pays-Bas méridionaux du 12e au 18e siècle*, Brussels: Palais des Académies, 1987.

—"L'origine et l'autorité des recueils de jurisprudence dans les Pays-Bas méridionaux (xiiic–xviiie siècles)", in *Rapports belges au VIIIe Congrès international de droit comparé (Pescara, 29 août–5 septembre 1970)*, Bruxelles: Centre interuniversitaire de droit comparé, 1970, 1–37.

Godfrey, A Mark, *Civil Justice in Renaissance Scotland: The Origins of a Central Court*, Leiden: Brill, 2009.

Gómez Gonzáles, Inés, *La justicia, el gobierno y sus hacedores. La Real Chancillería de Granada en el Antiguo Régimen*, Granada: Comares, 2003.

Gönczi, Katalin; Carls, Wieland, *Sächsisch-magdeburgisches Recht in Ungarn und Rumänien. Autonomie und Rechtstransfer im Donau- und Katpatenraum*, Berlin/Boston: De Gruyter, 2013 [Ivs Saxonico-Maidebvrgense in Oriente, vol III].

Gorla, Gino, "Civilian Judicial Decisions — An Historical Account of Italian Style" (1970) 44 *Tulane Law Review*, 740–749.

—"Die Bedeutung der Prazedentenscheidungen der Senate von Piemont und Savoyen im 18. Jahrhundert", in E Von Caemmerer, S Mentschikoff, K Zweigert, M Rheinstein (eds), *Ius Privatum Gentium: Festschrift Fur Max Rheinstein Zum 70. Geburtstag*, Tübingen: Mohr Siebeck, 1969, 103–125.

—*I 'grandi tribunali' italiani fra i secoli XVI e XIX: un capitolo incompiuto della storia politico-giuridica d'Italia*, Rome: Quaderni del Foro Italiano, 1969.

—"I tribunali supremi degli stati italiani fra i secoli XVI e XIX quali fattori della unificazione del diritto nello stato e della sua uniformazione fra stati", in G Gorla, *Diritto comparato e diritto comune europeo*, Milan: Giuffrè, 1981, 543–617.

—"La giurisprudenza come fattore del diritto", in G Gorla, *Diritto Comparato e diritto Comune Europeo*, Milan: Giuffrè, 1981, 263–301.

—"L'origine e l'autorità delle raccolte di giurisprudenza" (1970) 44 *Annuario di diritto comparato e di studi legislativi*, 4–23.

Gouron, André, "Coutumes et commentateurs, essai d'analyse quantitative", in *Droit privé et institutions régionales: études historiques offertes à Jean Yver*, Paris: Presses universitaires de France, 1976.

Gouron, André, and Terrin, Odile, *Bibliographie des coutumes de France. Editions antérieures à la Révolution*, Geneva: Droz, 1975.

Graes, Isabel, *Contributo para um estudo histórico-jurídico das cortes portuguesas entre 1481–1641*. Coimbra: Almedina, 2005.

Graham, Howar J, and Heckel, John W, "The Book that 'made' the Common law: The First Printing of Fitzherbert's 'La Graunde Abridgement', 1514–1516" (1958) 51 *Law Library Journal*, 100–116.

Grant, Francis J, *The Faculty of Advocates in Scotland, 1532–1943*, Edinburgh: Scottish Record Society, 1944.

Grant, Michael, *From Imperium to Auctoritas*, Cambridge: Cambridge University Press, 1946.

Groicki, Bartłomiej, "Porządek sądów i spraw miejskich prawa majdeburskiego w Koronie Polskiej", in K Koranyi (ed), *Biblioteka Dawnych*

Polskich Pisarzy-Prawników, vol I, Warszawa: Wydawnictwo Prawnicze, 1953.

Grotius, Hugo, *Commentary on the law of Prize and Booty*; a translation of the original manuscript of 1604 by Gwladys L Williams with the collaboration of Walter H Zeydel, New York-London: Oceana Publications; Wildy & Sons reprint, 1964.

—*De Jure Praedae Commentarius*, Hagae Comitum: apud Martinum Nijhoff, 1868.

Günzl, Clara, "*Germany's Case Law Revolution. Dealing with previous decisions in the 19th Century*", in W Eves, J Hudson, I Ivarsen and S White (eds), *Common Law, Civil Law, and Colonial Law: Essays in Comparative Legal History, Twelfth to Twentieth Centuries*, Cambridge: Cambridge University Press, 2021, forthcoming.

—*Auf dem Weg zur modernen Entscheidungsbegründung*, Doctoral dissertation: University of Münster, 2019.

Gustafsson, Harald, "The Conglomerate State: A Perspective on State Formation in Early Modern Europe" (1998) 23 *Scandinavian Journal of History*, 189–213.

Hacking, Ian, "Paradigms", in R J Richards and L Daston (eds), *Kuhn's Structure of Scientific Revolutions at Fifty: Reflections on a Science Classic*, Chicago: University of Chicago Press, 2016, 96–110.

Hahlo, Halle R and Kahn, Ellison, *The South African Legal System and its Background*, Cape Town-Wynberg-Johannesburg: Juta, 1973.

Harris, Tim, *Revolution: The Great Crisis of the British Monarchy, 1685–1720*, London: Penguin, 2006.

Hausmann, Jost, *Repertorien des Hessischen Hauptstaatsarchivs Wiesbaden*, sect 1: *Reichskammergericht*, vol III: *Prozeßakten des preußischen Kreises und der Stadt Wetzlar*, parts 1–3, Wiesbaden: Hauptstaatsarchiv, 1984–86.

Hespanha, Antonio Manuel, "Form and content in early modern legal books" (2008) 12 *Rechtsgeschichte*, 12–39.

—*As vésperas do Leviathan. Instituições e poder político, Portugal - século XVII*, Coimbra: Almedina, 1994.

—*Como os juristas viam o mundo. Direitos, estados, pessoas, coisas, contratos, ações e crimes*, Lisboa: Creative Space Independent Publishing, 2015.

—*História das Instituições. Épocas medieval e moderna*, Coimbra: Almedina, 1982.

Hilaire, Jean, *La construction de l'État de droit dans les archives judiciaires de la Cour de France au XIIIe siècle*, Paris: Dalloz, 2011.

Hildesheimer, Françoise, and Morgat-Bonnet, Monique, *Le Parlement de Paris. Histoire d'un grand corps de l'État monarchique. XIIIe–XVIIIe siècle*, Paris: Librairie Honoré Champion, 2018.

Hocks, Stephan, *Gerichtsgeheimnis und Begründungszwang: zur Publizität der Entscheidunsgründe im Ancien Régime und im frühen 19. Jahrhundert*. Frankfurt am Main: Vittorio Klostermann, 2002.

—*Gerichtsgeheimnis und Begründungszwang. Zur Publizität der Entscheidungsgründe im Ancien Régime und im frühen 19. Jahrhundert*, Frankfurt: Vittorio Klostermann, 2002.

Hollinger, David A, "T S Kuhn's theory of science and its implications for history" (1973) 78 *American Historical Review*, 370–93.

Holmbäck, Åke, and Wessén, Elias (eds), *Magnus Erikssons landslag*, Stockholm: Insitutet för rättshistorisk forskning, 1962.

Homem Barbas, António Pedro, *Judex Perfectus: função jurisdicional e estatuto judicial em Portugal, 1640–1820*, Coimbra: Almedina, 2003.

Hope's Major Practicks, 2 vols, ed J A Clyde, Edinburgh: The Stair Society, 1937–1938.

Houston, Rab, "Custom in context: Medieval and early modern Scotland and England", (2011) 211 *Past & Present*, 35–76.

Humbert, S, sv "Séraphin de Flines", in P Arabeyre, J-L Halpérin, J Krynen, *avec la collaboration de* G Cazals (eds), *Dictionnaire historique des juristes français*, Paris: Presses universitaires de France, 2007, 335.

Ibbetson, David J and Wijffels, Alain, "Case law in the Making: The Techniques and Methods of Judicial Records and Law Reports", in A Wijffels (ed), *Case Law in the Making*, vol I: *Essays*, Berlin, Duncker & Humblot, 1997, 13–35.

Ibbetson, David J, "Authority and Precedent", in M Godfrey (ed), *Law and Authority in British Legal History, 1200–1900* (Cambridge 2016), 60–84.

—"Coventry's Reports" (1995) 16 *Journal of Legal History*, 281–303.

—"Edward Coke, Roman Law, and the Law of Libel", in L Hutson (ed), *Oxford Handbook of English Law and Literature, 1500–1700*, Oxford: Oxford University Press, 2017, 487–506.

—"Errores in Camera Scaccarii", in D Ibbetson, N Jones, N Ramsay (eds), *Legal History and its Sources: Essays in Honour of Sir John Baker*, Cambridge: Cambridge University Press, 2019, 23–43.

—"Law Reporting in the 1590s", in C Stebbings (ed), *Law Reporting in Britain*, 73–88.

—"Report and Record in Early-Modern Common Law", in A Wijffels (ed), *Case Law in the Making. The Techniques and Methods of Judicial Records and Law Reports*, vol I: *Essays*, Berlin: Duncker & Humblot, 1997, 55–69.

Isambert, François-André, Decrusy, A, Jourdan, Athanase J L (eds), *Recueil général des anciennes lois françaises, depuis l'an 420, jusqu'à la Révolution de 1789*, 29 vols, Paris: Belin-Leprieur, 1821–1833.

Ives, Eric, *The Common Lawyers of Pre-Reformation England. Thomas Kebell: a case study*, Cambridge: Cambridge University Press, 1983.

—"The Purpose and Making of the Later Year Books" (1973) 89 *Law Quarterly Review*, 64–86.

Jahns, Sigrid, *Das Reichskammergericht und seine Richter. Verfassung und Sozialstruktur eines höchsten Gerichts im Alten Reich*, 2 vols in 3 parts, Cologne-Weimar-Vienna: Böhlau Verlag, 2003–11.

Jallamion, Carine, "D'Aguesseau et l'unification du droit privé. La réception de ses ordonnances en Languedoc", in *D'Aguesseau, un illustre inconnu?*, Limoges: PULIM, forthcoming.

Janicka, Danuta, *Prawo karne w trzech rewizjach prawa chełmińskiego z XVI wieku*, Toruń: Towarzystwo Naukowe w Toruniu, 1992 [Studia Iuridica, vol XIX/1].

Jansen, Nils, *The Making of Legal Authority. Non-legislative Codifications in Historical and Comparative Perspective*, Oxford: Oxford University Press, 2010.

Jessen, Peter, *Der Einfluß von Reichshofrat und Reichskammergericht auf die Entstehung und Entwicklung des Oberappellationsgerichts Celle unter besonderer Berücksichtigung des Kampfes um das kurhannoversche Privilegium De Non Appellando*, Aalen: Scientia Verlag, 1986.

Jori, Alberto, *Hermann Conring (1606–1681): Der Begründer der deutschen Rechtsgeschichte, mit Anhang ‚In Aristotelis laudem oratio prima' (Originalfassung) und ‚De origine juris germanici' (Auszüge)*, Tübingen: MVK Medien Verlag Köhler, 2006.

Jörn, Nils (ed), *David Mevius (1609–1670). Leben und Werk eines pommerschen Juristen von europäischem Rang*, Hamburg: Verlag Dr Kovač, 2007.

Kagan, Richard I., *Lawsuits and litigants in Castile 1500–1700*, Chapel Hill: North Carolina University Press, 1981.

Kannowski, Bernd, *Die Umgestaltung des Sachsenspiegelrechts durch die Buch'sche Glosse*, Hannover: Hahn 2007 [Schriften der Monumenta Germaniae Historica, vol LVI].

Keessel, Dionysius Godefridus, van der, *Praelectiones Iuris Hodierni ad Hugonis Grotii Introductionem ad Iurisprudentiam Hollandicam*, eds P van Warmelo et al, 6 vols, Rotterdam/Kaapstad: A A Balkema, 1961–1975.

—*Theses Selectae juris Hollandici et Zelandici ad supplendam Hugonis Grotii Introductionem ad Jurisprudentiam Hollandicam*, Leiden: S et J Luchtmans, 1800.

Kempis, Karl von, *Andreas Gaill (1526–1587). Zum Leben und Werk eines Juristen in der frühen Neuzeit*, Frankfurt-Bern-New York-Paris: Peter Lang, 1988.

Kaser, Max, *Zur Methode der römischen Rechtsfindung*, Göttingen: Vandenhoeck & Ruprecht, 1962.

Kern, Bernd-Rüdiger, *Die Gerichtsordnungen des Kurpfälzer Landrechts von 1583*, Cologne-Vienna: Böhlau Verlag, 1991.

Kitowski, Piotr, *Sukcesja spadkowa w mniejszych miastach województwa pomorskiego w II połowie XVII i XVIII wieku: studium prawno-historyczne*, Warszawa: Neriton, 2015.

Kleinheyer, Gerd, and Schröder, Jan (eds), *Deutsche und Europäische Juristen aus neun Jahrhunderten* (6th edn), Tübingen: Mohr Siebeck, 2017.

Koenigsberger, Helmut G, "Monarchies and Parliaments in Early Modern Europe: *dominium regale* or *dominium politicum et regale*" (1978) 5 *Theory and Society*, 191–217, and now also in Id, *Politicians and Virtuosi: Essays in Early Modern History*, London: The Hambledon Press, 1986, 1–26.

Koranyi, Karol, and Patkaniowski, Michał, sv "Groicki Bartłomiej", in *Polski słownik biograficzny*, vol VIII, Wrocław: Zakład Narodowy im Ossolińskich – Wydawawnictwo Polskiej Akademii Nauk, 1959–1960, 628–629.

Korpiola, Mia, "A Safe Haven in the Shadow of War? The Founding and the Raison d'être of the New Court, Based on its Early Activity", in M Korpiola (ed), *The Svea Court of Appeal in the Early Modern Period: Historical Reinterpretations and New Perspectives*, Stockholm: Institutet för rättshistorisk forskning, 2014, 55–108.

—"High and Late Medieval Scandinavia: Codified Vernacular Law and Learned Legal Influences", in H Pihlajamäki, M D Dubber, M Godfrey (eds), *The Oxford Handbook of European Legal History*, Oxford: Oxford University Press, 2018, 378–429.

Kort begryp van de consultatien en advysen, inhoudende alle de voortreffelijke materien en voorvallen van de ses deelen der Hollandsche consultatie boeken, Amsterdam: Hendrik Wetstein en Soonen, 1696.

Kotkas, Toomas, *Royal Police Ordinances in Early Modern Sweden: The Emergence of Voluntaristic Understanding of Law*, Brill: Leiden, 2014.

Kowalski, Grzegorz M, *Bartłomiej Groicki. Prawnik polskiego Odrodzenia. Wystawa w 400-setną rocznicę śmierci. Biblioteka Jagiellońska 5–29 kwietnia 2005*, Kraków: Księgarnia Akademicka, 2005.

Kowalski, Grzegorz M, *Zwyczaj i prawo zwyczajowe w doktrynie prawa i praktyce sądów miejskich karnych w Polsce XVI–XVIII w.*, Kraków: Jagiellonian University Press, 2013.

—sv "Szczerbic Paweł", in *Polski słownik biograficzny*, vol XLVII, Wydawnictwo Towarzystwa Naukowego Societas Vistulana: Kraków–Wrocław, 2010–2011, 397–401.

—and Pietrzyk, Zdzisław, "Testament Bartłomieja Groickiego (1603)" (2005) 55 *Biuletyn Biblioteki Jagiellońskiej*, 219–226.

Kriele, Martin, "Il precedente nell'ambito giuridico europeo-continentale e angloamericano", in *La sentenza in Europa. Metodo, tecnica e stile*, Padova: CEDAM, 1988, 515–528.

Krynen, Jacques, "Droit romain et état monarchique. A propos du cas français", in J Blanchard (ed), *Représentation, pouvoir et royauté à la fin du moyen âge*, Paris: Picard, 1995, 13–23.

—*L'empire du roi. Idées et croyances politiques en France – XIIIe–XVe siècle*, Paris: Gallimard, 1993.

—*L'idéologie de la magistrature ancienne* (vol I of *L'État de justice. France, XIIIe–XXe siècle*), Paris: Gallimard, 2009.

—"*Qu'est-ce qu'un Parlement qui 'représente le roi'*", in B Durand and L Mayali (eds), *Excerptiones iuris: Studies in Honor of André Gouron*, Berkeley: Robbins Collection, 2000 [Studies in comparative legal history, vol XV], 353–366.

Kuhn, Thomas S, *The Structure of Scientific Revolutions* (3rd edn), Chicago: University of Chicago Press, 1996.

Kunkel, Wolfgang, review of A Magdelain "Auctoritas principis" (1953) 70 *Zeitschrift der Savigny-Stiftung für Rechtsgeschichte* (Romanistische Abteilung), 437–445.

Kutrzeba, Stanisław, *Historia źródeł dawnego prawa polskiego*, vol II, Lwów: Zakład Narodowy im Ossolińskich, 1926.

Lanaro, Paola, "La restituzione della dote. Il gioco ambiguo della stima tra beni mobili e beni immobili (Venezia tra Cinque e Settecento)" (2010) 135 *Quaderni storici*, 753–778.

Landsberg, Ernst, *Geschichte der Deutschen Rechtswissenschaft*, sect 3, pt 1, Munich-Leipzig: R Oldenbourg, 1898.

Langbein, John H (ed), *Prosecuting Crime in the Renaissance: England, Germany, France*, Cambridge MA: Harvard University Press, 1974.

Lario, Dámaso, and García Martín, Javier, "La *impermeabilización ideológica* de Felipe II: cronología de una coyuntura (1558–1571)" (2014) 40 *Estudis*, 31–69.

Lario, Dámaso de, *Escuelas de imperio. La formación de una elite en los colegios mayores*, Madrid: Dykinson, 2019.

Lattes, Alessandro, *Studi di diritto statutario*, vol I: *Il procedimento sommario o planario negli statuti*, Milano: Hoepli, 1886.

Lauder of Fountainhall, John, *Historical Notices of Scotish Affairs*, 2 vols, Edinburgh: T Constable, 1848.

Laufs, Adolf (ed), *Die Reichskammergerichtsordnung von 1555*, Cologne-Vienna: Böhlau Verlag, 1976.

Lavery, Jason, *Germany's Northern Challenge: The Holy Roman Empire and the Scandinavian Struggle for the Baltic (1563–1576)*, Leiden: Brill, 2002.

Le Boindre, Jean, *Débats du Parlement pendant la Minorité de Louis XIV*, R Descimon, O Ranum, and P M Ranum (eds), vol I, Paris: Honoré Champion, 1997.

Le Boindre, Jean, *Débats du Parlement pendant la Minorité de Louis XIV*, vol II, I Storez-Brancourt (ed), Paris: Honoré Champion, 2002.

Le Bras, Gabriel, Lefebvre, Charles, and Rambaud, Jacqueline D, *L'âge classique, 1140–1378. Sources et théorie du droit*, Paris: Sirey, 1965 [G Le Bras and J Gaudemet, series eds, *Histoire du droit et des institutions de l'Eglise en Occident*, vol VII].

Le Marc'Hadour, Tanguy, sv "Antoine-Augustin Dubois d'Hermaville", in P Arabeyre, J-L Halpérin, J Krynen, *avec la collaboration de* G Cazals (eds), *Dictionnaire historique des juristes français*, Paris: Presses universitaires de France, 2007, 262–263.

Lebküchler, Florian, *Die Grafschaft Tecklenburg und die Justizreform von 1613*, Münster: Aschendorff Verlag, 2019.

Lecestre, Léon, "Le Procès du duc de la Force en 1721" (1925) 103 *Revue des questions historiques*, 322–360.

Lefebvre, Charles, "Les origines romaines de la procédure sommaire aux XIIe et XIIIe s." (1956) 12 *Ephemerides iuris canonici*, 149–197.

—*Le pouvoirs du juge en droit canonique*, Paris: Recueil Sirey, 1938.

Lenman, Bruce, Parker, Geoffrey, "The State, the Community and Criminal Law in Early Modern Europe", in V A C Gatrell, B Lenman, and Parker G (eds), *Crime and the Law: The Social History of Crime in Western Europe since 1500*, London: Verso 1980, 11–48.

Leromain, Emilie, "Monarchie administrative et justice criminelle au

XVIIIe siècle. Les états des crimes dignes de mort ou de peines afflictives (1733–1790)", 2 vols, unpublished Doctoral dissertation, University of Strasbourg, 2017.

Lieberwirth, Rolf, "Einführung oder Rezeption? Mittelalterlich deutsches Recht in slawischen Herrschaftsgebieten. Das Beispiel: Polen", in E Eichler, H Lück, W Carls (eds), *Rechts- und Sprachtransfer in Mittel- und Osteuropa. Sachsenspiegel und Magdeburger Recht. Internationale und interdisziplinäre Konferenz in Leipzig vom 31. Oktober bis 2. November 2003*, Berlin: De Gruyter, 2008 [Ivs Saxonico-Maidebvrgense in Oriente, vol I], 167–179.

Llamas Molina, Sancho, *Comentario crítico-jurídico-literal a las ochenta y tres leyes de Toro,* 2 vols, Madrid: imprenta de Repullés, 1827

Lombardi, Luigi, *Saggio sul diritto giurisprudenziale*, Milano: Giuffrè, 1975.

Lópcz Nevot, José Antonio, "The *Visitatio Generalis Magistratuum* in the *Decisiones* of Juan Bautista Larrea (1639)", in I Czeguhn, J A López Nevot, and A Sánchez Aranda (eds), *Control of Supreme Courts in Early Modern Europe*, Berlin: Duncker & Humblot, 2018, 149–173.

—"Literatura juridical y tribunales superiores en la Andalucía del Barroco", in M L López-Guadalupe and J J Iglesias Rodríguez (eds), *Realidades conflictivas. Andalucía y América en la España del Barroco*, Seville: Universidad de Sevilla, 2012, 429–456.

Lorgnier, Jacques, sv "Mathieu Pinault", in P Arabeyre, J-L Halpérin, J Krynen, *avec la collaboration de* G Cazals (eds), *Dictionnaire historique des juristes français*, Paris: Presses universitaires de France, 2007, 626.

Lück, Heiner, "Aspects of the transfer of the Saxon-Magdeburg Law to Central and Eastern Europe" (2014) 22 *Rechtsgeschichte – Legal History*, 79–89.

—"Benedict Carpzov (1595–1666) und das "römisch-sächsische Recht". Zu Seinem 350. Todestag am 31. August 2016" (2016) 4 *Zeitschrift für europäisches Privatrecht*, 888–927.

—sv "Jaskier Mikołaj", in *Handwörterbuch zur deutschen Rechtsgeschichte*, vol II (2nd edn), Berlin: Erich Schmidt Verlag, 2012, col 1355–1356.

Luig, Klaus, "*Usus modernus*", in A Erler, E Kaufmann and D Werkmüller (eds), *Handwörterbuch zur deutschen Rechtsgeschichte*, vol V, Berlin: Erich Schmidt Verlag, 1998, col 628–636.

Machadu Cabral, Gustavo César, *Direito natural e iluminismo no direito português do final do Antigo Regime*, Fortaleza: Universidade Federal do Ceará, 2011.

—*Literatura jurídica na Idade Moderna. As decisiones no Reino de Portugal* (*séculos XVI e XVII*). Rio de Janeiro: Lumen Juris, 2017.

—*Os decisionistas portugueses entre o direito comun e o direito patrio*, Doctoral dissertation, Universidade de Sâo Paulo, 2013.

—"Pegas e Pernambuco: notas sobre o direito comum e o espaço colonial" (2018) 9(2) *Direito & Práxis*, 704–706.

Maciejewski, Tadeusz, *Zbiory wilkierzy w miastach państwa zakonnego do 1454 r. i Prus Królewskich lokowanych na prawie chełmińskim*, Gdańsk: Wydawnictwo Uniwersytetu Gdańskiego, 1989.

MacQueen, Hector L, "Pleadable brieves, pleading and the development of Scots law" (1986) 4 *Law and History Review*, 403–422.

Maes, Louis Th, "Rol en betekenis van de Grote Raad van Mechelen voor de Nederlanden" (1974) 78 *Neerlandia*, 4–48.

Magdelain, André, *Auctoritas Principis*, Paris: Les Belles Lettres, 1947.

Martinat, Monica, "Chi sa quale prezzo è giusto? Moralisti a confronto sulla stima dei beni in età moderna" (2010) 135 *Quaderni Storici*, 825–856.

Martyn, Georges (ed), *Het Eeuwig Edict van 12 juli 1611. Facsimile uitgave van een originele Brusselse druk ...*, Antwerp: Berghmans Uitgevers, 1997.

—*Het Eeuwig Edict van 12 juli 1611. Zijn genese en zijn rol in de verschrift-elijking van het privaatrecht*, Brussels: Algemeen Rijksarchief, 2000.

Massetto, Gian Paolo, "Il lucro dotale nella dottrina e nella legislazione statutaria lombarda dei secoli XIV–XVI", in *Ius Mediolani. Studi di storia del diritto milanese offerti dagli allievi a Giulio Vismara*, Milano: Giuffrè, 1996, 189–364.

—"La prassi giuridica lombarda nell'opera di Giulio Claro (1525–1575)", in G P Massetto, *Saggi di storia del diritto penale lombardo (Secc XVI–XVIII)*, Milano: Led, 1994, 11–59.

—sv "Sentenza (diritto intermedio)", in *Enciclopedia del diritto*, vol XLI, Milano: Giuffrè, 1989, 1200–1245, and now in Id, *Scritti di storia giuridica*, vol II, Milano: Giuffrè, 2017, 1007–1052.

—*Un magistrato e una città nella Lombardia spagnola. Giulio Claro pretore a Cremona*, Milano: Giuffrè, 1985.

Matthew, Henry C G, and Harrison, Brian H (eds), *Oxford Dictionary of National Biography*, 61 vols, Oxford: Oxford University Press, 2004.

Matuszewski, Józef, "Prawo sądowe na wsi polskiej lokowanej na prawie niemieckim" (1995) 2 *Studia z Dziejów Państwa i Prawa Polskiego*, 54–59.

—"Rodzaje własności gruntu we wsi lokowanej na prawie niemieckim", in K Iwanicka, M Skowronek, K Stembrowicz (eds), *Parlament, prawo, ludzie. Studia ofiarowane Profesorowi Juliuszowi Bardachowi*, Warszawa: Wydawnictwo Sejmowe, 1996, 158–164.

Meccarelli, Massimo, "Dimensions of Justice and Ordering Factors in Criminal Law from the Middle Ages till Juridical Modernity", in G Martyn, A Musson and H Pihlajamäki (eds), *From the judge's arbitrium to the legality principle: legislation as a source of law in criminal trials*, Berlin: Duncker & Humblot, 2013, 49–67.

—*Arbitrium. Un aspetto sistematico degli ordinamenti giuridici in età di diritto commune*, Milano: Giuffrè 1998.

Méniel, Bruno (ed), Écrivains juristes et juristes écrivains du Moyen âge au siècle des Lumières, Paris: Classiques Garnier, 2015.

Merino, Imanol, "Larrea y Tablares, Juan Bautista", in *Notitia Vasconiae. Diccionario de historiadores, juristas y pensadores políticos de Vasconia*, Madrid: Marcial Pons, 2019, vol I, 387–389.

Merlin, Philippe Antoine (ed), *Répertoire universel et raisonné de jurisprudence* (5th edn), tom 13, Bruxelles: H Tarlier, 1828.

Mikołajczyk, Marian, "'Stosując się do prawa wyraźnego. . .'. Podstawy prawne wyroków kryminalnych grodziskiego sądu miejskiego w latach 1702–1756" (2013) 19 *Studia Iuridica Lubliniensia*, 201–216.

—*Proces kryminalny w miastach Małopolski XVI–XVIII wieku*, Katowice: Wydawnictwo Uniwersytetu Śląskiego, 2013.

Mikuła, Maciej (ed), *Księga kryminalna miasta Dobczyc 1699–1737*, Kraków: Wydawnictwo Uniwersytetu Jagiellońskiego, 2013 [Fontes Iuris Polonici. Prawo Miejskie, vol II].

—"Na marginesie edycji miejskich ksiąg kryminalnych. Prawo pisane i dzieła prawnicze w praktyce sądu krakowskiego i dobczyckiego" (2017) 20 *Studia z Dziejów Państwa i Prawa Polskiego*, 427–439.

—*Prawo miejskie magdeburskie (Ius municipale Magdeburgense) w Polsce XIV–pocz XVI w. Studium o ewolucji i adaptacji prawa* (2nd edn), Kraków: Jagiellonian University Press, 2018.

Miletti, Marco N, *Stylus Judicandi. Le raccolte di "decisiones" del Regno di Napoli in età moderna*, Napoli, Jovene editore, 1998.

Modéer, Kjell Å, *Gerichtsbarkeiten der schwedischen Krone im deutschen Reichsterritorium*, vol I: *Voraussetzungen und Aufbau 1630 – 1657*, Stockholm: Institutet för rättshistorisk forskning, 1975.

Mohnhaupt, Heinz, "La discussion sur "theoria et praxis" aux XVIIème et XVIIIème siècles en allemagne", in *Confluence des droits savants et des pratiques juridiques*, Milano: Giuffrè, 1979, 277–296.

—"Organisation und Tätigkeit des 'Hohen Königlichen Tribunals zu Wismar'", in N Jörn, B Diestelkamp and K Å Modéer (eds), *Integration durch Recht: Das Wismarer Tribunal (1653–1806)*, Köln: Böhlau, 2003, 215–237.

Monti, Annamaria, "Between Case Law and Legislation: the *Senato* of Milan, a Supreme Court during the *Ancien Régime*", in B Feldner et al (eds), *Ad Fontes. Europäisches Forum Junger Rechtshistorikerinnen und Rechtshistoriker Wien 2001*, Frankfurt am Main, Peter Lang, 2002, 303–318.

—"Constitutiones Dominii mediolanensis, 1541. Constitutions pour le Milanais (extraits relatifs à la procédure criminelle)", in J Hautebert and S Soleil (eds), *La procédure et la construction de l'État en Europe: XVIe–XIXe siècle. Recueil de textes, présentés et commentés*, Rennes: Presses Universitaires de Rennes, 2011, 423–448.

—"Fedecommessi lombardi: profili giuridici e riflessi privati delle dispense Senaterie" (2012) 124(2) *Mélanges de l'École française de Rome. Italie et Méditerranée*, 489–500.

—"*L'immunitas duodecim liberorum* nella prassi Senateria lombarda di antico regime", in A Padoa-Schioppa, G di Renzo Villata, G P Massetto (eds), *Amicitiae Pignus. Studi in ricordo di Adriano Cavanna*, vol II, Milano: Giuffrè, 2003, 1509–1563.

—"L'intervento pubblico nei rapporti contrattuali privati e la stima dei beni. La prassi lombarda della *datio in solutum* (Secoli XVI–XVII)", in M Barbot, M Cattini, M Di Tullio, L Mocarelli (eds), *Stimare il valore dei beni: una prospettiva europea*, Udine: Forum, 2018, 67–80.

—*I formulari del Senato di Milano (secoli XVI–XVIII)*, Milano: Giuffré, 2001.

—*Iudicare tamquam deus. I modi della giustizia Senateria nel Ducato di Milano tra cinque e settecento*, Milano: Giuffrè, 2003.

Moureau, François, *La plume et le plomb. Espaces de l'imprimé et du manuscrit au siècle des Lumières*, Paris: Presses de l'université Paris-Sorbonne, 2006.

Mozzarelli, Cesare, "Nella Milano dei re cattolici. Considerazioni su uomini, cultura e istituzioni tra Cinque e Seicento", in P Pissavino and G Signorotto (eds), *Lombardia borromaica Lombardia spagnola 1554–1659*, Roma: Bulzoni, 1995, vol I, 421–456.

Muldoon, James, *Empire and Order: The Concept of Empire, 800–1800*, New York: St Martin's, 1999.

Murray, Andrew L, "Sinclair's practicks", in A Harding (ed), *Law-Making and Law-Makers in British History*, London: Royal Historical Society, 1980, 90–104.

Müßig, Ulrike, "*Superior courts in early modern France, England an the Holy Roman Empire*", in P Brand and J Getzler (eds), *Judges and Judging in the History of the Common Law an Civil Law: From Antiquity to modern Times*, Cambridge: Cambridge University Press, 2012, 209–233.

Nexon, Daniel H, *The Struggle for Power in Early Modern Europe: Religious Conflict, Dynastic Empires & International Change*, Princeton: Princeton University Press, 2011.

Nickles, Thomas, "Kuhn, historical philosophy of science and case-based reasoning" (1998) 6 *Configurations*, 51–85.

Nörr, Knut W, "Rechtsgeschichtliche Apostillen zur Clementine Saepe", in C H van Rhee (ed), *The Law's delay: essays on undue delay in civil litigation*, Cambridge: Intersentia, 2004, 203–215.

—*Zur Stellung des Richters in gelehrten Prozess der Frühzeit. Iudex secundum allegata non secundum conscientiam iudicat*, München: Beck, 1967.

Nubola, Cecilia, "Supplications between Politics and Justice: The Northern and Central Italian States in the Early Modern Age", in L H van Voss (ed), *Petitions in Social History*, Cambridge: Cambridge University Press, 2002, 35–56.

—and Andreas Würgler (eds), *Bittschriften und Gravamina: Politik, Verwaltung und Justiz in Europa (14.–18. Jahrhundert)*, Berlin: Duncker & Humblot, 2005.

Nuno Espinosa Gomes da Silva, José (ed), *Livro de leis e posturas*. Lisboa: Universidade de Lisboa, 1971.

Oestmann, Peter, *Ein Zivilprozeß am Reichskammergericht. Edition einer Gerichtsakte aus dem 18. Jahrhundert*, Cologne-Weimar-Vienna: Böhlau Verlag, 2009.

—"Lotharische Legende", in F Jaeger (ed), *Enzyklopädie der Neuzeit*, Stuttgart: Verlag J B Metzler, 2008, vol VII, col 1009–1011.

—"Lübecker Rechtspraxis um 1700: Der Streit um die Entführung der Catharina Lefever" (2000) 80 *Zeitschrift des Vereins für Lübeckische Geschichte und Altertumskunde*, 259–293.

—"Observationes. Practicarum observationum, tam ad processum iudiciarium, praesertim imperialis camerae, quam causarum decisiones pertinentium, libri duo. Andreas Gail", in S Dauchy, G Martyn, A Musson, H Pihlajamäki and A Wijffels (eds), *The Formation and Transmission of Western Legal Culture. 150 Books that Made the Law in the Age of Printing*, Cham: Springer 2016, 129–132.

—*Rechtsvielfalt vor Gericht. Rechtsanwendung und Partikularrecht im Alten Reich*, Frankfurt: Vittorio Klostermann, 2002.

—"The Law of the Holy Roman Empire of the German Nation", in H Pihlajamäki, M Dubber and A M Godfrey (eds), *The Oxford Handbook of*

European Legal History, Oxford: Oxford University Press, 2018, 731–759.

—*Wege zur Rechtsgeschichte: Gerichtsbarkeit und Verfahren*, Cologne-Weimar-Vienna: Böhlau Verlag, 2015.

Olivier-Martin, François, *Histoire de la coutume de la prévôté et vicomté de Paris*, 3 vols, Fontenay-aux-Roses: Presses universitaires de France; Paris: E Leroux, 1922–1930.

Ordenanzas de la Real Chancillería de Granada (1601), Granada: Diputación, 1997.

Ortego Gil, Pedro, "El arbitrio de los jueces inferiores: su alcance y limitaciones", in J Sánchez-Arcilla (ed), *El arbitrio judicial en el Antiguo Régimen (España e Indias, siglos XVI–XVIII)*, Madrid: Dykinson, 2013, 133–220.

Ortlieb, Eva, *"The Holy Roman Empire: the Imperial Court's System an the Reichshofrat"*, in A Wijffels and C H van Rhee (eds), *European Supreme Courts. A Portrait through History*, London: Third Millennium Publishing, 2013, 86–95.

Padoa Schioppa, Antonio, "Sur la conscience du juge dans le jus commun européen", in J-M Carbasse, L Depambour-Tarride (eds), *La conscience du juge dans la tradition juridique européenne*, Paris: Presses Universitaires de France, 1999, 95–129.

Parker, Geoffrey, *The Dutch Revolt*, London: Penguin, 1979.

Payen, Philippe *La physiologie de l'arrêt de règlement du Parlement de Paris au XVIIIe siècle*, Paris: Presses Universitaires de France, 1999.

—*Les arrêts de règlement du Parlement de Paris au XVIIIe siècle. Dimension et doctrine*, Paris: Presses Universitaires de France, 1997.

Pauw, Willem, *Observationes Tumultuariae Novae*, eds H F W D Fischer et al, 3 vols, Zwolle: Tjeenk Willink, 1964–1972.

Pérez Juan, José A, "La visita de Ramírez Fariña a la Audiencia de Sevilla (1623–1632)" (2002) 29 *Historia, Instituciones, Documentos*, 357–405.

Pérez-Prendes, José M, *Historia del Derecho español*, Madrid: Universidad Complutense, 2004.

Pérez-Victoria de Benavides, Manuel M, "La teoría estatutaria como solución al conflicto entre el derecho histórico de los distintos reinos (A propósito de una sentencia de la Chancillería de Granada en el s XVII)" (2001) 6 *INITIUM*, 445–468.

Petit, Carlos, "Derecho común y derecho castellano. Notas de literatura jurídica para su estudio" (1982) 50 *Tijdschrift voor Rechtsgeschiedenis*, 157–196.

Petronio, Ugo, *Il Senato di Milano. Istituzioni giuridiche ed esercizio del potere nel Ducato di Milano da Carlo V a Giuseppe II*, Milano: Giuffrè, 1972.

—"Burocrazia e burocrati nel Ducato di Milano dal 1561 al 1706", in *Per Francesco Calasso. Studi degli allievi*, Roma: Bulzoni, 1978, 481–561.

—"I Senati giudiziari", in *Il Senato nella storia. Il Senato nel Medioevo e nella prima età moderna*, Roma: Istituto Poligrafico e Zecca dello Stato, 1997.

—"La burocrazia patrizia nel Ducato di Milano nell'età spagnola (1561–1706)", in *L'educazione giuridica*, pt 4: *Il pubblico funzionario: modelli storici e comparativi*, vol I, Perugia: Libreria universitaria, 1981, 253–328.

Pihlajamäki, Heikki, "Gründer, Bewahrer oder Vermittler? Die nationalen und internationalen Elemente im Rechtsdenken des Olaus Petri", in J Eckert and K Å Modéer (eds), *Juristische Fakultäten und Juristenausbildung im Ostseeraum*, Stockholm: Institutet för rättshistorisk forskning, 2004, 29–38.

—"Legality before the Legality Principle: Royal Statutes and Early Modern Swedish Criminal Law", in G Martyn, A Musson and H Pihlajamäki (eds), *From the Judge's* Arbitrium *to the Legality Principle: Legislation as a Source of Law in Criminal Trials*, Berlin: Duncker & Humblot, 2013, 169–188.

—"The Painful Question: The Fate of Judicial Torture in Early Modern Sweden" (2007) 25(3) *Law and History Review*, 557–592.

—*Conquest and the Law in Swedish Livonia (ca 1630–1710): A Case of Legal Pluralism in Early Modern Europe*, Leiden: Brill, 2016.

Pitz, Ernst, *Papstreskript und Kaiserreskript im Mittelalter*, Tübingen: Bibliothek des Deutschen Historishcen Instituts in Rom, 1971.

Plouvain, Pierre-Antoine, *Notes historiques relatives aux offices et aux officiers de la cour de parlement de Flandre*, Douai: Deregnaucourt, 1809.

Poelgeest, L van, "De raadsheren van de Hoge Raad van Holland, Zeeland en West-Friesland in de achttiende eeuw" (1988) 103 *Bijdragen en Mededelingen betreffende de Geschiedenis der Nederlanden/Low Countries Historical Review*, 20–51.

—"Mr Johan van Bleiswijk en zijn 'Observationes Tumultuariae" (1987) 55(1) *Tijdschrift voor Rechtsgeschiedenis*, 117–122.

Poncet, Olivier, and Storez-Brancourt, Isabelle (eds), *Une histoire de la mémoire judiciaire*, (Actes du colloque international des 12, 13 et 14 mars 2008) Paris: ENC, 2009.

Prest, Wilfred, *The Rise of the Barristers: A Social History of the English Bar, 1590–1640*, Oxford: Clarendon Press, 1988.

Punt, Hendrik M, *Het vennootschapsrecht van Holland, Zeeland en West-Friesland. Het vennootschapsrecht van Holland, Zeeland en West-Friesland in de rechtspraak van den Hoge Raad van Holland, Zeeland en West-Friesland*, Deventer: Kluwer, 2010, available at https://openaccess.leidenuniv.nl/handle/1887/16178.

Ramsay, Nigel, "The Fees they Earned: The Incomes of William Staunford and Other Tuydor Lawyers", in in D Ibbetson, N Jones, N Ramsay (eds), *Legal History and its Sources: Essays in Honour of Sir John Baker*, Cambridge: Cambridge University Press, 2019, 139–158.

Ranieri, Filippo, "Juristische Literatur aus dem Ancien Régime und historische Literatursoziologie. Einige methodologische Vorüberlegungen", in C Bergfeld (ed), *Aspekte europäischer Rechtsgeschichte: Festgabe für Helmut Coing zum 70. Geburtstag*, Frankfurt am Main: Vittorio Klostermann, 1982, 292–322.

Recopilación de las Ordenanzas de la Real Audiencia y Chancillería de su Magestad, que reside en la villa de Valladolid (1566) Madrid: Consejo General del Poder Judicial, 2007.

Regnault, Henri, *Les Ordonnances civiles du Chancelier d'Aguesseau. Les testaments et l'Ordonnance de 1735* Paris: Presses Universitaires de France, 1965 (1st edn Liège, 1938).

Renzo Villata, M Gigliola, "Tra consiglia, decisiones e tractatus. . . Le vie della conoscenza giuridica nell'età moderna" (2008) 81 *Rivista di Storia del Diritto Italiano*, 15–76.

—"Diritto comune e diritto locale nella cultura giuridica lombarda dell'età moderna", in *Diritto comune e diritti locali nella storia dell'Europa*, Milano: Giuffrè, 1980, 329–388.

—"Tra ius nostrum e ius commune. Il diritto patrio nel Ducato di Milano", in I Birocchi, A Mattone (eds), *Il diritto patrio tra diritto comune e codificazione (secoli XVI–XIX)*, Roma: Viella, 2006, 217–254.

Reske, Christoph, *Die Buchdrucker des 16. und 17. Jahrhunderts im deutschen Sprachgebiet: auf der Grundlage des gleichnamigen Werks von Josef Benzing*, Wiesbaden: Harrassowitz Verlag, 2007.

Reszczyński, Jarosław, *Sądownictwo i proces w kodyfikacji Macieja śliwnickiego z 1523 roku: o wpływach prawa rzymskiego i praw obcych na myśl prawną polskiego Odrodzenia*, Kraków: Jagiellonian University Press, 2008.

Rezábal y Ugarte, José, *Biblioteca de los escritores que han sido individuos de los seis Colegios Mayores: de San Ildefonso de la Universidad de Alcalá, de Santa Cruz de Valladolid, de San Bartolomé, de Cuenca, San Salvador de Oviedo y del Arzobispo de la de Salamanca*, Madrid: Imprenta de Sancha, 1805.

Rhee, Remco van and Wijffels, Alain (eds), *European Supreme Courts. A Portrait throughout History*, London: Third Millenium, 2013.

Riccarton of Craig, Thomas, *Ius feudale tribus libris comprehensum*, tr L Dodd, Edinburgh: The Stair Society, 2017.

Roberts, Alfred A, *A South African legal bibliography*, Pretoria; Dept of Justice, 1942.

Rodger, Alan, "The praetor's edict and carriage by land in Scots law" (1968) 3 *Irish Jurist*, 175–186.

Romano, Andrea, "Letteratura consiliare e formazione dei diritti privati europei: l'esperienza del diritto di famiglia siciliano tardomedievale", in M Ascheri, I Baumgärtner, and J Kirshner (eds), *Legal Consulting in the Civil Law Tradition*, Berkeley: The Robbins Collection, 1999, 255–291.

Romein, Jan, and Romein-Verschoor, Anna, *De lage landen bij de zee*, Amsterdam; E M Querido's Uitgeverij B V, 1979.

Savelli, Rodolfo, *Censori e giuristi. Storie di libri, di idee e di costumi (secoli XVI–XVII)*, Milano: Giuffrè, 2011.

Schäfer, Frank Ludwig, *Juristische Germanistik. Eine Geschichte der Wissenschaft vom einheimischen Privatrecht*, Frankfurt: Vittorio Klostermann, 2008.

Scheurmann, Ingrid, "'Wetzlarische Beiträge zu einer pragmatischen allgemeinen Rechtsgelehrsamkeit'. Die Geschichte der kameralen Bibliothek von der Gelehrtenstube zur Universität", in W Speitkamp (ed), *Staat, Gesellschaft, Wissenschaft. Festschrift für Hellmut Seier zum 65. Geburtstag*, Marburg: N G Elwert, 1994, 229–244.

Schmoeckel, Mathias, "Holy Roman Empire of the German Nation", in H Pihlajamäki, M D Dubber and A M Godfrey (eds), *The Oxford Handbook of European Legal History*, Oxford: Oxford University Press, 2018, 358–377.

—"Lotharische Legende", in A Cordes, H-P Haferkamp, H Lück, D Werkmüller, C Bertelsmeier-Kierst (eds), *Handwörterbuch zur deutschen Rechtsgeschichte* (2nd edn), Berlin: Erich Schmidt Verlag, 2016, vol III, col 1056–1058.

Scholz, Johannes-Michael, "Legislação e jurisprudência em Portugal nos séculos XVI a XVIII: fontes e literatura" (1976) 25 *Scientia Juridica*, 512–587.

—sv "Portugal", in H Coing (ed), *Handbuch der Quellen und Literatur der neueren europäischen Privatrechtsgeschichte.* vol II: *Neuere Zeit (1500–1800), das Zeitalter des Gemeinen Rechts,* part 2: *Gesetzgebung und Rechtsprechung.* München: C H Beck, 1977, 1319–1342

—sv "Spanien", in H Coing (ed) *Handbuch der Quellen und Literatur der neueren Europäischen Privatrechtsgeschichte,* vol II: *Neuere Zeit (1500–1800). Das Zeitalter des Gemeinen Rechts,* part 2: *Gesetzgebung und Rechtsprechung.* München: C H Beck'sche Verlagsbuchhandlung, 1976, 1299–1302.

Schröder, Jan, "Legal scholarship: the theory of sources and methods of law", in H Pihlajamäki, M D Dubber and A M Godfrey (eds), *The Oxford Handbook of European Legal History,* Oxford: Oxford University Press, 2018, 551–565.

—"Specimen Usus Moderni Pandectarum", in S Dauchy, G Martyn, A Musson, H Pihlajamäki and A Wijffels (eds), *The Formation and Transmission of Western Legal Culture. 150 Books that Made the Law in the Age of Printing,* Cham: Springer, 2016, 235–238.

Schumann, Sabine, *Joachim Mynsinger von Frundeck (1514–1588). Herzoglicher Kanzler in Wolfenbüttel — Rechtsgelehrter — Humanist. Zur Biographie eines Juristen im 16. Jahrhundert,* Wiebaden: Harrassowitz, 1983.

Sella, Domenico, and Capra, Carlo, *Il Ducato di Milano dal 1535 al 1796,* Torino: Utet, 1984.

Sellert, Wolfgang, "Mynsinger von Frundeck, Joachim (1514–1588)", in A Cordes, H-P Haferkamp, H Lück, D Werkmüller, C Bertelsmeier-Kierst (eds), 2nd edn, Berlin: Erich Schmidt Verlag, 2016, vol III, col 1731–1732.

Siber, Heinrich, *Römisches Verfassungsrecht,* Lahr: M Schauenburg, 1952.

Sirks, Adrian J Boudewijn, "Sed verum est, sententias numerari, non ponderari (Cornelis van Bijnkershoek, Observationes Tumultuariae 2628 & 2678)", in R van den Bergh et al (eds), *Ex iusta causa traditum. Essays in honour of Eric H Pool* (2005) *Fundamina* (editio specialis), 285–303.

Smend, Rudolf, *Das Reichskammergericht. Erster Teil: Geschichte und Verfassung,* Weimar: Hermann Böhlaus Nachfolger, 1911; reprint, Aalen: Scientia Verlag, 1965.

Smith, Thomas, *De Republica Anglorum,* ed L Alstone, Cambridge: Cambridge University Press, 1906.

Spagnesi, Enrico, "Iurisprudentia, stilus, au(c)toritas", in M Sbriccoli and A Bettoni (eds) *Grandi tribunali e Rote nell'Italia di Antico Regime,* Milano: Giuffrè, 1993, 574–604.

Spruyt, Hendrik, *The Sovereign State and Its Competitors: An*

Analysis of Systems Change, Princeton: Princeton University Press, 1994.

Stein, Peter G, *The Character and Influence of the Roman Civil Law: Historical Essays*, London: Hambledon Press, 1988.

Stobbe, Otto, *Geschichte der deutschen Rechtsquellen*, 2 vols, Braunschweig: C A Schwetschke und Sohn, 1860–1864.

Stodolkowitz, Stefan A, *Das Oberappellationsgericht Celle und seine Rechtsprechung im 18. Jahrhundert*, Cologne-Wiemar-Vienna: Böhlau Verlag, 2011.

Stolleis, Michael (ed), *Hermann Conring (1606–1681). Beiträge zu Leben und Werk*, Berlin: Duncker & Humblot, 1983.

Storez [Brancourt], Isabelle, *Le chancelier Henri François d'Aguesseau (1668–1751). Monarchiste et liberal*, Paris: Publisud, 1996.

Storti Storchi, Claudia, "Giudici e giuristi nelle riforme viscontee del processo civile per Milano (1330–1386)", in *Ius Mediolani. Studi di storia del diritto milanese offerti dagli allievi a Giulio Vismara*, Milano: Giuffrè, 1996, 47–187.

Strauch, Dieter, *Mittelalterliches nordisches Rechts bis ca 1500: Eine Quellenkunde*, Berlin: De Gruyter, 2016.

Sunde, Jørn Ø, "Above the Law: Norwegian Constitutionalism and the Code of 1274", in J Ø Sunde (ed), *Constitutionalism before 1789: Constitutional Arrangements from the High Middle Ages to the French Revolution*, Oslo: Pax Forlag, 2014.

Süß, Thorsten, *Partikularer Zivilprozess und territoriale Gerichtsverfassung. Das weltliche Hofgericht in Paderborn und seine Ordnungen 1587–1720*, Cologne-Weimar-Vienna: Böhlau Verlag, 2017.

Swann, Julian, *Politics and the Parlement of Paris under Louis XV, 1754–1774*, Cambridge: Cambridge University Press, 1995.

Szczerbic, Paweł, *Ius Municipale, to jest prawo miejskie majdeburskie nowo z łacińskiego i z niemieckiego na polski język z pilnością i wiernie przełożone*, ed Grzegorz Maria Kowalski, Kraków: Księgarnia Akademicka, 2011 [Bibliotheca Iagiellonica. Fontes et Studia, vol XX].

The Acts of the Parliaments of Scotland, 12 vols, ed T Thomson and C Innes, Edinburgh, 1814–1875.

The Decisions of the Court of Session, from Its First Institution to the Present Time, 22 vols, ed W M Morison, Edinburgh: Bell and Bradfute, 1801–1804.

The Digest of Justinian, 4 vols, ed A Watson, Philadelphia: University of Pennsylvania Press, 1985.

The Earl of Stirling's Register of Royal Letters Relative to the Affairs of Scotland and Nova Scotia from 1615 to 1635, 2 vols, ed C Rogers, Edinburgh (printed for private circulation), 1885.

"The Lord Chancellor Egertons Observations upon ye Lord Cookes Reportes" (1615), ed L A Knafla, *Law and Politics in Jacobean England: The Tracts of Lord Chancellor Ellesmere*, Cambridge: Cambridge University Press, 1977, 297–318.

The Register of the Privy Council of Scotland, 2nd ser, 8 vols, ed D Masson and P Hume Brown, Edinburgh: General Register House, 1899–1908.

Thireau, Jean-Louis, "Les Arrêtés de Guillaume de Lamoignon: une œuvre de codification du droit français?" (2004) 39(1) *Droits*, 53–68

Thomas, Philip J, "A Barzunesque View of Cicero: From Giant to Dwarf and Back", in P J du Plessis (ed), *Cicero's law. Rethinking Roman Law of the Late Republic*, Edinburgh: Edinburgh University Press, 2016, 11–25.

—"Ars aequi et boni, legal argumentation and the correct legal solution" (2014) 131 *Zeitschrift der Savigny-Stiftung fuer Rechtsgeschichte* (Romanistische Abteilung), 41–59.

—"Colonial policy of the Dutch republic" (2015) 2 *Iura and Legal systems*, B(7), 92–102, available at http://www.rivistagiuridica.unisa.it

—"Contributory fault in maritime collisions in the law of Holland" (2001) 48 *Revue Internationale des Droits de l'Antiquité*, 345–360.

—"Johannes Voet Commentarius ad Pandectas", in S Dauchy, G Martyn, A Musson, H T Pihlajamäki and A Wijffels (eds), *The formation and transmission of western legal culture. 150 books that made the law in the age of printing*, Cham: Springer, 2016, 239–242.

—"Limited liability for maritime collisions in old Dutch law" (2004) 67 *Tydskrif vir Hedendaagse Romeins-Hollandse Reg*, 229–243.

—"Mietmaule or thinking like a lawyer" (2013) 4 *Studia Universitatis Babes-Bolyai Iurisprudentia*, 67–84, available at http://studia.law.ubbcluj.ro.

—"Piracy, privateering and the United States of the Netherlands" (2003) 50 *Revue Internationale des Droits de l'Antiquité*, 361–382.

—"Roman-Dutch opinion practice as a source of law" (2006) 69(4) *Tydskrif vir Hedendaagse Romeins-Hollandse Reg*, 613–621.

—"The intention of the testator: from the causa Curiana to modern South African law", in J Hallebeek, M Schermaier, R Fiori, E Metzger, J-P Coriat (eds), *Inter cives necnon peregrinos: essays in honour of Boudewijn Sirks*, Goettingen: V&R Unipress, 2014, 727–739.

Tilly, Charles, *Coercion, Capital, and European States, AD 990–1992*, Cambridge MA: Blackwell, 1992.

Trolle Önnerfors, Elsa, *Justitia et prudentia: rättsbildning genom rättstillämpning – Svea hovrätt och testamentsmålen 1640–1690*, Stockholm: Institutet för rättshistorisk forskning, 2010.

Tuchtenhagen, Ralph, *Zentralstaat und Provinz im frühneuzeitlichen Nordosteuropa*, Wiesbaden: Harrassowitz 2008.

Tymieniecki, Kazimierz, "Prawo czy gospodarstwo?" (1946) 8(2) *Roczniki Dziejów Społecznych i Gospodarczych*, 275–291.

—"Prawo niemieckie w rozwoju społecznym wsi polskiej" (1923) 37 *Kwartalnik Historyczny*, 38–78.

Ulkuniemi, Martti, *Kuningas Kristoferin maanlaki 1442*, Helsinki: Suomalaisen Kirjallisuuden Seura, 1978.

Uruszczak, Wacław, *Historia państwa i prawa polskiego*. vol I (966–1795) (2nd edn), Warszawa: Wolters Kluwer business, 2013.

—"Model procesu karnego według Practica nova imperialis Saxonicae rerum criminalium Benedykta Carpzowa (†1666)", in J Czapska, A Gaberle, A Światłowski, A Zoll (eds), *Zasady procesu karnego wobec wyzwań współczesności. Księga ku czci Profesora Stanisława Waltosia*, Warszawa: Wydawnictwa Prawnicze, Państwowe Wydawnictwo Naukowe, 2000, 154–165.

—"Ustawy okołokonstytucyjne Sejmu Wielkiego z 1791 i 1792 roku" (2013) 6(3) *Krakowskie Studia z Historii Państwa i Prawa*, 247–258.

Uruszczak, Wacław; Mikuła, Maciej; Fokt, Krzysztof (eds), *Księgi kryminalne miasta Krakowa z lat 1630–1633, 1679–1690*, Kraków: Wydawnictwo Uniwersytetu Jagiellońskiego, 2016 [Fontes Iuris Polonici. Prawo Miejskie, vol IV].

Uruszczak, Wacław; Mikuła, Maciej; Fokt, Krzysztof, and Anna Karabowicz (eds), *Księga kryminalna miasta Krakowa z lat 1589–1604*, Kraków: Wydawnictwo Uniwersytetu Jagiellońskiego, 2016 [Fontes Iuris Polonici. Prawo Miejskie, vol III].

Uruszczak, Wacław; Mikuła, Maciej, and Anna Karabowicz (eds), *Księga kryminalna miasta Krakowa z lat 1554–1625*, Kraków: Wydawnictwo Uniwersytetu Jagiellońskiego, 2013 [Fontes Iuris Polonici. Prawo Miejskie, vol I].

Vallone, Giancarlo, "Le *decisiones* di Matteo d'Afflitto", in H J Baker (ed), *Judicial Records, Law Reports, and the Growth of Case Law*, Berlin: Duncker & Humblot, 1989, 143–179.

—*Le "decisiones" di Matteo d'Afflitto*, Lecce: Milella, 1988.

Valsecchi, Chiara M, "L'istituto della dote nella vita del diritto del tardo

Cinquecento: i Consilia di Jacopo Menochio" (1994) 67 *Rivista di storia del diritto italiano*, 205–282.

Vasara-Aaltonen, Marianne, *Learning for the Legal Profession: Swedish Jurists' Study Journeys ca 1630–1800*, unpublished Doctoral dissertation, University of Helsinki, 2017.

Vervaart, Otto M D F, *Studies over Nicolaas Everaerts (1462–1532) en zijn Topica*, Gouda: Quint, 1994.

Volpini, Paola, *Lo spazio politico del "letrado". Juan Bautista Larrea magistrato e giurista nella monarchia di Filippo IV*, Bologna: Il Mulino, 2004.

—"Por la autoridad de los ministros: observaciones sobre los letrados en una alegación de Juan Bautista Larrea (primera mitad del siglo XVII)" (2005) 30 *Cuadernos de Historia Moderna*, 63–84.

Warmelo, Paul van, *Registers op die Observationes Tumultuariae van Cornelis van Bijnkershoek en van Willem Pauw*, Pretoria: Staatsdrukker, 1971.

—"Roman-Dutch law in practice during the seventeenth and eighteenth century", in J M Koster-van Dijk and A Wijffels (eds), *Miscellanea Forensia Historica*, Amsterdam: Werkgroep Grote Raad van Mechelen, 1988, 345–356.

—and C J Visser, *Johannes Voet Observationes ad Hugonis Grotii Manuductionem*, Pretoria: Staatsdrukker, 1987.

Watson, Alan, "Justinian's Institutes and Some English Counterparts", in P Stein and A Lewis (eds), *Studies in Justinian's Institutes in Memory of J A C Thomas*, London: Sweet & Maxwell, 1984, 181–186.

—*Sources of Law, Legal Change and Ambiguity*, Edinburgh: T & T Clark, 1985.

Whaley, Joachim, *Germany and the Holy Roman Empire*, vol I: *Maximilian I to the Peace of Westphalia, 1493–1648*, Oxford: Oxford University Press, 2011.

—*The Making of the Civil Law*, Cambridge MA: Harvard University Press, 1981.

Wieacker, Franz, "The causa Curiana and contemporary Roman jurisprudence" (1967) 2(1) *The Irish Jurist*, 151–164.

Wijffels, Alain (ed), *Case Law in the Making*, 2 vols, Berlin: Duncker & Humblot, 1997.

—"Early-modern literature on international law and the *usus modernus*" (1995) 16 *Grotiana*, 35–54.

—"Early-modern scholarship on international law", in A Orakhelashvili (ed), *Research Handbook on the Theory and History of International Law*,

Cheltenham: Edward Elgar Publishing, 2011, 23–60.

—"La loi dans le discours judiciaire: l'article 15 de l'Édit Perpétuel de 1611 dans le ressort du Parlement de Flandre", in É Bousmar, P Desmette, N Simon (eds), *Légiférer, gouverner et juger. Mélanges d'histoire du droit et des institutions (IXe–XXIe siècle) offerts à Jean-Marie-Cauchies à l'occasion de ses 65 ans*, Brussels: Presses de l'Université Saint-Louis, 2016, 317–335.

—"*Orbis exiguus*. Foreign Legal Authorities in Paulus Christinaeus's Law Reports", in S Dauchy, W Hamilton Bryson and M C Mirow (eds), *Ratio decidendi. Guiding Principles of Judicial Decisions*, vol II, Berlin: Duncker & Humblot, 2010, 37–62.

—"Revisie en rechtsdwaling" (2014) 20(2) *Fundamina*, 1042–1050.

Williams, Ian, "Early-modern Judges and the Practice of Precedent", in P Brand and J Getzler (eds), *Judges and Judging in the History of the Common Law and the Civil Law*, Cambridge: Cambridge University Press, 2012, 51–66, at 53–54.

—"He Credited More the Printed Booke: Common Lawyers' Receptivity to Print, c1550–1640" (2010) 28 *Law and History Review*, 39–70.

Würgler, Andreas, "Voices from among the "Silent Masses": Humble Petitions and Social Conflicts in Early Modern Central Europe", in L H van Voss (ed), *Petitions in Social History*, Cambridge: Cambridge University Press, 2002, 11–34.

Zientara, Benedykt, "Das Deutsche Recht (ius teutonicum) und die Anfänge der städtischcn Autonomie", in K Fritze, E Mueller-Mertens, W Stark (eds), *Autonomie, Wirtschaft und Kultur der Hansestädte*, Weimar: H Böhlaus, 1984 [Hansische Studien vol VI; Abhandlungen zur Handels- und Sozialgeschichte, vol 23], 94–100.

Zimmermann, Reinhard and Simpson, Philip, "Strict liability", in K Reid and R Zimmermann (eds), *A History of Private Law in Scotland*, 2 vols, Oxford: Oxford University Press, 2000, vol II, 548–583.

Zimmermann, Reinhard, "Römisch-holländisches Recht Ein Überblick", in R Feenstra and R Zimmermann (eds), *Das römisch-holländisches Recht Fortschritte des Zivilrechts im 17. und 18. Jahrhundert*, Berlin: Duncker & Humblot, 1992.

—"Statuta sunt stricte interpretanda? Statutes and the Common Law: a Continental Perspective" (1997) 56 *Cambridge Law Journal*, 315–328.

Zorzoli, Maria Carla, "Una incursione nella pratica giurisprudenziale milanese del Seicento e qualche riflessione su temi che riguardano la famiglia", in *Ius Mediolani. Studi di storia del diritto milanese offerti dagli allievi a Giulio Vismara*, Milano: Giuffrè, 1996, 617–657

Zwalve, Willem J, *Hoofdstukken uit de geschiedenis van het Europese privaatrecht*, Deventer: Kluwer, 2003.

Zyl, Deon H van, *Geskiedenis van die Romeins-Hollandse Reg*, Durban: Butterworth, 1979.

ARCHIVAL SOURCES

Bergues, City Library
    MS 65
Brussels, Archives Générales du Royaume
    Fonds Grand Conseil de Malines, Appels de Namur, 352
Cambridge, Cambridge University Library
    MS Ii 5.34
Douai, City Library
    MS 662–1
    MS 664
    MS 628
    MS 1223
    MS 1224
Edinburgh, National Library of Scotland
    Adv MS 24.1.12 – practicks of Sir John Baird and Sir Peter Wedderburn
    Adv MS 24.3.4(2) – practicks of Sir Patrick Hume
    Adv MS 24.3.9 – practicks of Sir George Lockhart
    Adv MS 24.4.1 – practicks of Sir John Lauder
    Adv MS 25.6.1–2 – epitome of Thomas Craig, *Ius feudale*
Edinburgh, National Records of Scotland
    CS18 – lords of council and session, registers of acts and decreets
    CS22 – lords of council and session, registers of acts and decreets
    CS26– lords of council and session, registers of acts and decreets
    CS98 – lords of council and session, court processes
    CS167 – lords of council and session, court processes
    GD52 – Forbes papers
    PC2 – privy council, registers of decreets
    PC4 – privy council, minute books
Gniezno, Archdiocesan Archive
    MS 104

Kortrijk, Rijksarchief
  MS 288
Kraków, National Archive of Kraków, City Records (*Archiwum Narodowe w Krakowie, Akta Miasta Krakowa*)
  MS 869
  MS 870
Kraków, Jagiellonian Library, Stare Druki
  Cim 5008
  Cim 6326
  Cim 6432
Lille, Archives Départementales du Nord
  8B1/2383
  8B1/14873
  8B1/27495
  8B2/9
  8B2/2019
  8B2/560
  PF 27495
Lille, City Library
  MS 661
  MS 771–777
  MS God. 111
London, British Library
  Lansdowne MS 1076
  Sloane MS 3828
Milano, Biblioteca Ambrosiana
  MS D 118
  MS I 90
  MS I 40
Mons, UMons Library
  MS 315/262 R 2/G
Records of the Parliaments of Scotland (http://www.rps.ac.uk)

Index